THE VAMPIRE

THE

VAMPIRE

A NEW HISTORY

NICK GROOM

YALE UNIVERSITY PRESS
NEW HAVEN AND LONDON

For information about this and other Yale University Press publications, please contact:
U.S. Office: sales.press@yale.edu   yalebooks.com
Europe Office: sales@yaleup.co.uk   yalebooks.co.uk

Set in Adobe Garamond Pro by IDSUK (DataConnection) Ltd
Printed in Great Britain by Gomer Press Ltd, Llandysul, Ceredigion, Wales

Library of Congress Control Number: 2018951682

ISBN 978-0-300-23223-3

A catalogue record for this book is available from the British Library.

10 9 8 7 6 5 4 3 2 1

For my parents

For her house inclineth unto death, and her paths unto the dead.
None that go unto her return again, neither take they hold of the paths
of life.

Proverbs 12:18–19 (1611)[1]

Mortui non mordent.

Proverbial: 'dead men do not bite';
attrib. by Desiderius Erasmus to Theodotus of Chios
(first century BC)[2]

We could hardly expect anyone, even did we wish to, to accept these
[documents] as proofs of so wild a story.

Bram Stoker, *Dracula* (1897)[3]

CONTENTS

CONTENTS

ILLUSTRATIONS

Text

Plates

Kiss of Judas' (1893). © Victoria and Albert Museum, London. Purchased with Art Fund support.

23 Albert von Keller, *Im Mondschein* (1894). History and Art Collection / Alamy Stock Photo.

24 Edvard Munch, *Love and Pain* (later known as *Vampire*) (1893–95).

25 Philip Burne-Jones, *The Vampire* (1897).

26 Illustrated front cover of Bram Stoker, *Dracula* (1901). © British Library Board. All Rights Reserved / Bridgeman Images.

27 *Abattoir de la Villette: Les Buveurs de Sang* (late nineteenth century).

28 Wilhelm Röntgen, X-ray of his wife's hand (1895). Wellcome Collection CC-BY.

29 Madeleine Wallis, *Vampire* (1921). © Victoria and Albert Museum, London.

30 Theda Bara in *Sin* (1915).

31 Maila Nurmi in *Plan 9 from Outer Space* (1959). Moviestore Collection Ltd / Alamy Stock Photo.

32 Patricia Morrison of The Gun Club performing at the Peppermint Lounge in New York City (11 November 1982). Ebet Roberts / Redferns / Getty Images.

33 *Weird Tales* (vol. 27, no. 6, June 1936), cover art by Margaret Brundage.

34 David Bowie and Catherine Deneuve in *The Hunger* (1983). Photo 12 / Alamy Stock Photo.

35 Vampire-slaying kit (*c.* 1970). © The Royal Armouries (XII. 11811).

ACKNOWLEDGEMENTS

My principal debts are to my editor Julian Loose and my agent David Godwin, without whom this book would not exist. The three anonymous readers for Yale University Press provided meticulous and insightful reports, and the book has benefited greatly from their generous care and capacious expertise. I am indebted to Clive Liddiard, who scrupulously edited the text and who tactfully drew my attention to various errors and infelicities; any that remain are, of course, my own. The team at Yale have provided much assistance, notably Marika Lysandrou with the illustrations and Rachael Lonsdale with production. I would also like to thank Valerie Aldridge, Nicholas Allen, Jonathan Barry, Henry Bartholomew, Heide Crawford, Lora Fleming, Jim Frank, Sam George, Paul Grant-Costa, Jonathon Green, Kate Hext, Roger Luckhurst, Steve Matthews, David Punter, Tom Shippey, Dale Townshend, Ursula Radford, Carla Valentine, Terri Windling and my colleagues at the University of Exeter Wellcome Centre for Cultures and Environments of Health for providing points of information, discussing material and challenging my ideas. Early versions of some of this material were given at Aarhus University; the BARS Conference, University of York; Durham University; the Knowledge Spa, Royal Cornwall Hospital, Truro; Plymouth Athenaeum; the Willson Center, University of Georgia, Athens; and Yale University; and a preliminary essay was published by

Cambridge University Press in *The Cambridge Companion to Dracula*, ed. Roger Luckhurst (2018). Much of the research for this study was undertaken while I was working on a larger project funded by the Leverhulme Trust, and I am very grateful to the Trust for its support. Likewise, the final draft of the manuscript was prepared in splendid isolation in my evenings at Root House (again on another project), and I would like to thank the librarians and staff of the Lewis Walpole Library for accommodating me and my diverse interests at that time – they were extremely supportive. Various institutions have made this book possible: the Beinecke Library, the Bodleian Library, the British Library, the Codrington Library, the Lewis Walpole Library and the University of Exeter Library; I have also made use of the Cambridge online translation service, and the King's (in South Zeal) and the Academy (in Soho) have, as ever, provided their own characteristic forms of sustenance on the all-too-rare occasions when I have been able to visit. I owe my family a particular debt: to Joanne for her patience (and specifically for help with the Conclusion and graciously answering my often bizarre questions over dinner), to Matilda and Dorothy for their enthusiasm whenever vampires went on the rampage, and of course to Rowley and Pesky for keeping me warm whenever my blood chilled; also to Leonard and Rosemary Parker for their invaluable support; and finally to my parents, Michael and Elisabeth – especially my father's tireless clipping of vampire news items from the papers.

Nick Groom
Ramsley
Summer Solstice, 2018

FOREWORD

Of all that is written, I love only that which an individual writes with his
blood. Write with blood: and you will experience that blood is spirit.

Friedrich Nietzsche (1883–85)[1]

From the early eighteenth century, the figure of the vampire has
stalked through the western intellectual and cultural tradition – not
merely as a supernatural agent of Gothic fictions, but rather as a
powerful tool for making sense of the human predicament. The investigation of vampires as undead revenants is therefore profoundly shadowed by
changes in the definition of the human – changes brought about by new
thinking and developments in medicine and biosciences, Enlightenment
theology and philosophy, politics and sociology, psychosexual theory, and
environmentalism and ecology. But while most accounts of the vampire
tend to focus on Bram Stoker's supernatural thriller *Dracula* (1897) and the
horror-film sensation of the twentieth century, over a century and a half
before Dracula landed at Whitby vampires were already challenging
conventional attitudes. They were sinister renegades whose militant emer-
gence exposed the major issues and anxieties of the time – from new
medical research into life sciences to the power games of imperial politics.
And despite the saturation of vampires today in young-adult fiction and

TV and film franchises, vampires still maintain the power both to convey and to confront the most pressing contemporary issues of our times. They are, in effect, roving thought-experiments lingering on the periphery of comprehension, and even now can help us think through current anxieties from border control to epidemic contagion.

This book is a new history of the vampire. But some words of warning. First, it is not a comprehensive account of every sort of supernatural blood-sucker from time immemorial. There are plenty of trans-historical, trans-national surveys that cherry-pick demons, witches, werewolves and ghosts from world culture to propose that the vampire has been an eternal (indeed, undying) threat to humankind. That is not the premise of this book. Instead, I argue that the vampire is a recognizable thing that dates from a precise period in a certain place, and which consequently has recognizable manifest-ations and qualities – especially concerning blood, science, society and culture. Although vampires may have their origins in the opaque chronicle of assorted folklore beliefs, they only become 'vampires' *qua* vampires when they enter the European bloodstream *as vampires*, rather than as part of the general pantheon of the undead, many of whom – ghosts, ghouls, revenants – have displayed their taste for blood for centuries. But they are not vampires.

Secondly, being a 'new history', the emphasis is very much on the eight-eenth- and nineteenth-century instances of vampires that pre-date Bram Stoker's epoch-making novel. For that reason, I hope that it will appeal to readers whose interest in vampires instead begins with *Dracula*, and for whom the preceding two centuries of vampirology and the fields in which it was debated may come as a surprise. That, in a nutshell, is the ambition of this book: that fans of *True Blood*, for example, will begin to investigate vampire history – all those pre-*Dracula* vampires – to understand how and why Stoker's book is the brilliant culmination of decades of debate, and why *Dracula* was a game-changer that initiated twentieth- and twenty-first-century vampirology. In truth, I had originally intended to downplay *Dracula* simply as a representative example of late-Victorian vampire fiction; but the novel is so profoundly informed by the myriad deliberations of its time on vampires, blood, science, technology and literature that all the paths of the (un)dead lead to *Dracula*, just as they all lead away from it. Nevertheless, it is that first journey, the genealogy of *Dracula*, on which I focus in this book –

and I hope that the bloodlines to the later vampirism of our own time will be clear to contemporary readers, and also that (perhaps more importantly) the differences between current vampires and those of the past will give meaningful pause for thought.

Yet – thirdly – this is not just another cultural history of a 'rather over-worked cultural trope', as one commentator once described vampires to me.[2] The political, philosophical, theological and scientific histories of the vampire are complex enough, but I have endeavoured to link these incidences to later literary and artistic representations. And although it is only once these earlier areas become exhausted that culture can appropriate the figure of the vampire, the vampire remains indelibly stamped with questions of territory and identity, metaphysics and medicine throughout the nineteenth century and up to the present day. This is the first extended study to unite these two realms. Consequently, this book focuses primarily on the pre-*Dracula* history of the vampire, drawing together the empirical scientific encounter with 'real' Eastern European vampires and the eventual imagined representations in Gothic literature.[3] To this end, I examine evidence from theological treatises to medical reports, travelogues to political allegories, and poetry and fiction to occult tractates. Furthermore, I am not averse to speculating occasionally about the allure of vampire thinking across the centuries in figurative language (such as 'oozing') – although such digressions should be treated as incidental asides rather than *ex cathedra* statements.[4]

Vampires and vampirology are a pan-European phenomenon with distinctly Eastern European roots, and a phenomenon that in the twentieth century became a mainstay of American culture through cinema and television. But as we shall see, its main artery is England; and accordingly, a good deal of this book focuses on England in particular, as well as on Britain and Ireland more generally. There is certainly a need for a global history of the vampire, but that may be beyond the expertise of any one individual.[5] Yet if a *cloud* of vampirologists ever settle on such an enterprise, I hope they will agree that vampires are not to be confined within the comparatively limited categories of myth, science and culture, but should instead combine many fields of human inquiry within a single, weird being that can challenge us today as powerfully as it has done for nearly three centuries. Vampires are good to think with.[6]

A NOTE ON THE ETYMOLOGY OF
THE WORD *VAMPIRE*

Where does the word 'vampire' come from? It is not at all clear. One of the earliest suggestions was made by the antiquary Samuel Pegge, who ingeniously derived the word *vampire* from the French '*Avant-pere*, or Ancestor' by analogy with similar borrowings.[1] If only it were that simple.

In 1869, the Russian folklorist Aleksandr Afanasev speculated that *vampire* derives from the Lithuanian *wempti* or *vamptî* ('to drink') or *vampyti* ('barking or yammering').[2] In contrast, Jan Louis Perkowski, the leading Slavonic vampirologist, provides a detailed etymology in his study *The Darkling*, arguing that the Serbo-Croatian *vàmpīr* and Old Russian *Upirь* (a personal name) are cognate; variants of these occur in Serbo-Croatian, Ukrainian, Belorussian, Polish, Kashubian and Bulgarian. Perkowski himself speculates that the word is perhaps a part-Syriac, part-Slavonic compound. The Manichean god Bām or Bān, who 'will carve a tomb of stone to serve as the grave of Darkness', would be pronounced in Slavonic *van* (from the Greek letter β, representing v in modern Greek), and the Slavonic *pirь* means 'revelry, drinking bout': hence, *vanьpirь*, or 'Van's Festival'.[3] The Old Russian name *Upirь*, which first appears in an East Slavonic manuscript from the year 1047 describing a Novgorodian prince named Upirь Lichiy, may in turn be linked to *upiór* – Polish for sorcerer, and similar terms.[4] This etymology has, however, been disputed by Peter Mario Kreuter, who in a pungent and idiosyncratic essay finds linguistic similarities with words for steam, flame and butterfly.[5] The most detailed analysis has been by Brian Cooper, who distinguishes Slavonic superstitions surrounding terminology for the undead from the subsequent western conception of the vampire, which he describes as 'distorted'.[6] Cooper confirms the Old Russian origins in a proper name, *upirĭ*, and argues that the word is a Slavonic borrowing from the Dacian Latin *impūrus*, meaning unclean (i.e. of a corpse), borrowed back and forth among Balkan and Greek forms. The *Oxford English Dictionary* evenhandedly describes the word as being of Slavonic origin and recognizably the same form in Russian, Polish, Czech, Serbian and Bulgarian, with variants such as the Bulgarian *vapir, vepir*; the Ruthenian *vepyr, vopyr, opyr*; the Russian *upir, upyr*; and the Polish *upiór*. The north Turkish *uber* ('witch') is offered as a possible source.[7]

The tangled folklore of the Slavonian undead overlaps with other supernatural beings and creatures, from witches to Romanian *strigoi* to barn owls.[8] The most significant of these are werewolves. According to Afanasev, Serbian vampires and werewolves are both called *vukodlak* (in Bulgarian, *varkolak*); likewise the Greeks confuse (or conflate) vampires with werewolves (*vourkólakes*). In Rennell Rodd's *The Customs and Lore of Modern Greece* (1892), the author states that the 'genuine vampire is the Vourkólakas', though 'the word itself is undoubtedly of Sclavonic origin'.[9] A bizarre article by Agnes Murgoçi, 'The Vampire in Roumania', proposes that '*Vârcolaci* (*svârcolaci*) and *pricolici* are sometimes dead vampires, and sometimes animals which eat the moon' (presumably alluding to the werewolf's portentous association with full moons and eclipses).[10] It is clear, however, that in Eastern Europe and Greece, vampires and werewolves overlap, as they do more generally with buried corpses that eat grave clothes (and sometimes themselves) and the fascination with dead bodies that remain incorruptible.[11] Perkowski points out that *vukodlak* is thirteenth-century Serbian for a vampire/werewolf, meaning 'wolf pelt' or 'wolf-pelt wearer', and that although the word *vampir* had become established in South Slavic by the fifteenth century, in contemporary Balkan Slavic the two words remain synonymous.[12] The historian Gábor Klaniczay widens the frame of reference further by suggesting that, for folklorists, the vampire fuses the characteristics of revenants, night spirits (*Alp*), classical bloodsuckers (*stryx*), Slavonian witches and werewolves, all of which combined to form 'the historically unified concept of the vampire that emerged in early-modern Central and Balkan Europe'.[13] Balkan cults are described by the early-twentieth-century travel writer and anthropologist Mary Edith Durham, who identifies the *tentaz* of Montenegro, the *lampir* of Bosnia and the *kukuthi* or *lugat* of Albania as vampires, which she compares with bacterial infection.[14]

There is, however, a significant distinction to be made in the English language. In English, the werewolf was established by medieval times as a human shape-changer, with origins in Anglo-Saxon and possibly Old Norse culture, as well as in classical accounts of the disease of lycanthropy; the word *vampire*, however, was adopted in the 1730s to describe a contemporary wonder. The vampire emerged, then, at a certain moment and developed clear meanings and associations, and it is predominantly this vampire that the present book will examine.

INTRODUCTION

CREATING
THINKING WITH VAMPIRES

For the life of the flesh is in the blood: and I have given it to you upon the altar to make an atonement for your souls: for it is the blood that maketh an atonement for the soul.

Leviticus 17:11 (1611)[1]

[Diseases] crucifie the soule of man, attenuate our bodies, dry them, wither them, rivell them up like old apples, make them as so many Anatomies.

Robert Burton (1621)[2]

Let us guard against saying death is the opposite of life; the living creature is simply a kind of dead creature, and of a very rare kind.

Friedrich Nietzsche (1882)[3]

In 1685, the philosopher, mathematician, inventor and demonologist George Sinclair published *Satans Invisible World Discovered*. Among the cases of witchcraft, possession and poltergeist activity he described was an account of a murder in Dalkeith. What interested Sinclair was not the crime itself, but the uncanny aftermath. The murderer, a local man named Spalding, had immediately fled after killing his victim, exiling himself from the town. But after some years he began returning to his house in Dalkeith at night, and eventually gave himself up. He was imprisoned and sentenced to hang, inspiring him to cry out: 'Oh must I die like a Dog! Why was I not sentenced to lose my head?' On the scaffold he entreated God, 'let never this Soul of mine depart from this Body till it be reconciled with thee.' Sinclair takes up the tale:

And having said this, the Executioner *threw him off the* Ladder. *When he had hung the ordinary time sufficient to take any mans life he was cut down, and his Body put into a* Bier, and carried to the Tolbuith to be Woon [wrapped in a winding sheet]. When they had opened *the lid of the* Bier; *the man bangs up upon his* Bottom, *and his eyes staring in his head, and fomeing at the mouth, he made a noise and roared like a* Bull, *stricking about him with his* Fists, *to the great consternation of all. The* Magistrates *hearing of it, gave orders that he should be strangled better. The*

Executioner fell to work, and puting the Rope about his neck, stood upon his Breast, and strained his neck so hard, that it was no bigger about than his Wrist. And he continuing after this manner for a sufficient time, was carried to the Grave: and covered with earth. Notwithstanding of all this, he made such a rumbling and tumbling in it, that the very Earth was raised, and the Muiles were so heaved up that they could hardly keep them down. After this his house at the East end of the town (as I am informed) was frequented with a Ghost, which made it stand empty for a long time. Whether any have dwelt in it since I know not. This I have from a very creditable Person, who being a Schollar there, at that time, was an eye and ear witness, who is yet alive.[4]

The return of the dead is a primaeval fear. Myth, legend and folklore abound with tales of revenants and ghosts; stories of the restless, unavenged dead seeking retribution against the living. Black magic, demonic possession, or simply a terrifying intensity of will can drag lifeless corpses back into some macabre form of animation to wreak havoc, before they are eventually dispatched or dispelled – or ultimately exhaust their supernatural energies.

Vampires are usually numbered among this hellish crew; but vampires are in fact very different entities from spirits and the ranks of the undead. For vampires first came to the attention of European intellectuals at a particular time and under very specific circumstances. Unlike ghosts or demons, for instance, which have biblical antecedents, vampires were effectively discovered, and for that reason they have a definable history and significance. The nascent science of vampirology investigated these entities not primarily from the testimony of witnesses, as experiences of ghosts and apparitions were examined, but as physical beings that crucially had a literal 'body' of evidence consisting of the corpses of perpetrator and victims. For that reason, vampires are not returning primordial demons from ancient days, but creatures of the Enlightenment: their history is rooted in the empirical approaches of the developing investigative sciences of the eighteenth century, in European politics and in the latest thinking. They are, in other words, very much of the modern world – or rather, the ways in which they were scrutinized were strikingly modern. Vampires came into being when Enlightenment rationality encountered East

European folklore – an encounter that attempted to make sense of them through empirical reasoning and that, by treating them as credible, gave them reality.

So vampires do have a folkloric prehistory, and from the early nineteenth century, vampirologists applied themselves to tracing their origins through archetypal, ahistorical examples of monstrosity. But for all his posthumous vitality, Spalding of Dalkeith is obviously not a vampire: whatever undead activities he may have pursued, he did not return from the grave to suck the blood of the living. Nonetheless, in the manner of execution and the subsequent treatment of his body, Spalding's case does reveal the bones of post-mortem superstition immediately before the advent of vampirism proper.

Despite notorious beheading machines such as the Halifax Gibbet (last used in 1650) and the Scottish Maiden (last used in 1710), decapitation was a form of capital punishment usually reserved in Britain for the aristocracy. Following Roman law, it was considered less ignominious than hanging: historically (and politically), beheading was unmistakably associated with the machinations of Henry VIII and especially the execution of Charles I.[5] Elsewhere in Europe, decapitation was more common, especially following the adoption of the guillotine in France in 1789. It was also alarmingly prevalent in Germany.[6] Spalding, in contrast, is hanged – a felon's death – and as he is taken onto the scaffold, he effectively curses himself in the eyes of God. He is cast into space and swings a good while. Thereafter his body is put on a bier, evidently confined within a coffin, from which he then tries to escape: shockingly, '*his eyes staring in his head, and fomeing at the mouth, he made a noise and roared like a Bull, stricking about him with his* Fists, *to the great consternation of all*'. He is then strangled and his neck brutally wrung, but he continues to writhe and convulse and snarl about him as he is buried, placed in the ground where '*the very Earth was raised*'. Spalding does not, of course, rest in peace, but now becomes a ghost, literally haunting his abandoned home in the town.

The key features of this account, then, are Spalding's sentence (which defines him), his direct speech (including his last words), the apparent divine intervention that prolongs the murderer's life, the violence and yammering of the animated corpse (with particular attention paid to glaring eyes and slavering mouth), the disturbance of the grave, and the rational testimony from '*a very creditable Person . . . a Schollar . . . who is yet alive*' that verifies the incident. As the following chapters will reveal, such features would come to form the contours of vampire reports – with one very important addition: the lust for blood.

Bloody folklore

Bloodsucking demons have haunted civilized society since at least biblical times, and are described in accounts on ancient Chaldean and Assyrian tablets.[7] Lilith was a female demon, the first rebellious wife of Adam; in some translations of the Talmud, her name has – anachronistically – been translated as 'vampire'.[8] Lamia was a bisexual female monster of ancient Greece who drank the blood of children; she is sometimes treated as synonymous with the Judaeo-Christian Lilith.[9] The Romans were familiar with ghosts that sucked blood and brought nightmares, and attributed such characteristics to the marauding Goths (also known as Scythians) who sacked Rome in the fifth century: 'they thought that Thessalian witches, accompanying the barbarian armies, were darkening [the sun's] rays with their country's magic spells'.[10]

The invading Huns, too, were steeped in blood and ruin: 'Behold the wolves, not of Arabia, but of the North, were let loose upon us last year from the far-off rocks of the Caucasus, and in a little while overran great provinces', bemoaned St Jerome. 'How many monasteries were captured, how many streams were reddened with human blood!'[11] Their leader Attila (who choked on his own blood) was lamented 'not by effeminate wailings and tears but by the blood of men'.[12]

In Norse myth, which drew on Hunnish and Gothic legends, a *draugr* (also known as an *aptgangr*, or revenant) was an undead being in which 'spirit is not so much breathed into matter so much as material corporeality is retained by the restless spirit'.[13] *Draugrs* appear in the fourteenth-century *Grettir's Saga*, for example, as barrow-wights, or the living dead.[14] Sometimes they simply guarded hoards, but often actively raided the living, such as in the pagan corpus the *Eyrbyggja Saga* of the mid-thirteenth century, which is replete with the undead (and which was later studied by Sir Walter Scott – an early laureate of vampires).[15] Grendel, the founding monster of English poetry in the Anglo-Saxon epic *Beowulf*, drinks blood.[16] Indeed, a number of 'deviant burials' in Britain in this period suggest fears of the dead returning.[17] In particular, the twelfth-century *Life and Miracles of St Modwenna* by Geoffrey of Burton includes an episode in which the saint is invoked in an altercation between a local baron and the monks of Burton Abbey, resulting in two peasants being struck dead. That night, the two peasants return – 'now in the shape of men carrying wooden coffins on their shoulders, now in the likeness of bears or dogs or other animals' – and spread a fatal contagion through the village of Stapenhill. Their corpses are exhumed and the winding sheets covering their faces found to be stained with blood. The bodies are duly decapitated and the hearts removed (cardio-ectomy, or decoronation); the heads are then placed between the legs and the hearts cremated. The pyre burns for a whole day: 'When at last they had been burned up, they cracked with a great sound and everyone there saw an evil spirit in the form of a crow fly from the flames.'[18]

The twelfth-century chronicler William of Malmesbury meanwhile described the Devil reanimating his servants to continue his work from beyond the grave, and William of Newburgh and the Monk of Byland likewise recorded several stories of the dead returning – either to revisit their kin, terrorize their enemies, or simply through restlessness of spirit. One of Newburgh's revenants is only dispatched when, having been discovered in its grave engorged with blood, it is summarily exhumed, has its heart torn out and is cremated.[19] The English and Scottish ballad tradition is subsequently haunted by demon lovers, ghosts and wraiths in verses such as 'The Unquiet Grave', and the dead return to wreak bloody vengeance in revenge tragedies and, of course, in William Shakespeare's play *Macbeth*.

Witches – which also appear in *Macbeth* – were also reputed to be bloodsuckers. The fifteenth-century occultist Marsilio Ficino claimed that:

> It is an ancient and common opinion that certain crones, called witches, suck the blood of infants in order to rejuvenate themselves as best they can. Then why might not our elderly, finding themselves all but without hope of survival, suck the blood of a lad? Of a lad, I say, of stalwart forces

– healthy, cheerful, well-tempered, excellent blood that might by happy chance be excessive. Let them suck, then, like a leech – that is, a blood-sucker – from a slightly opened vein in the skinny part of the arm, an ounce or two, then immediately take the same amount of syrup or wine. This should be done precisely when they are hungry and thirsty, and at the waxing of the moon.[20]

Indeed, in 1492 Pope Innocent VIII was given the blood of three young boys to rejuvenate him; if true, he may have drunk this blood, or it could even have been a transfusion. Whatever the case, all four died.[21] And neither are bloodsuckers confined to Europe: unsurprisingly, they are a worldwide phenomenon, described in countries as far afield as China, India and the Philippines.[22]

There were other demons, too, that literally stirred the blood. Incubi and succubi were sexual predators sent to defile the innocent. They are described in witchcraft manuals such as the *Malleus Maleficarum* (attributed to Heinrich Kramer, c. 1486), and appear in Thomas Middleton's Jacobean drama *The Witch* (written 1609–16, first published in 1778). Hecate, the chief witch in the play, declares:

'Tis Almachildes: fresh blood stirrs in me –
The man that I have lusted to enjoy,
I've had him thrice in Incubus already.[23]

Elizabethan and Jacobean revenge tragedy is anyway, of course, awash with blood and bloody symbolism, littered with corpses and haunted by avenging ghosts and other supernatural beings, from hobgoblins to were-wolves. In John Webster's horrific play *The Duchess of Malfi* (first performed 1614), for instance, the lupine character Ferdinand is stricken with 'A very pestilent disease . . . They call lycanthropia.'[24] Murdered bodies were more-over believed to bleed in the presence of their killer, as noted by Shakespeare in *Richard III* (c. 1592–93):

O gentlemen, see, see! Dead Henry's wounds
Ope their congealèd mouths and bleed afresh.[25]

Likewise, in Webster's *Appius and Virginia*, Icilius enters with the body of Virginia, declaring:

> See
> her wounds still bleeding at the horrid presence
> of yon stern Murderer, till she find revenge.[26]

King James VI and I's *Daemonologie* (1597), which also recorded incubi possessing dead cadavers in order to rape their earthly lovers, gave the phenomenon of 'cruentation' legal force in the seventeenth century:

> as in a secret murder, if the dead carcass be at any time thereafter handled by the murderer it will gush out of blood, as if the blood were crying to the heaven for revenge of the murderer, God having appointed that secret supernatural sign for trial of that secret unnatural crime.[27]

Such uncanny and apparently proven properties of blood exerted a compelling fascination. It was evident that blood could testify against murderers: it could bear witness. A report of a murder committed in 1629 described how the unfortunate victim, one Jane Norkot, had been discovered with her throat cut and a knife stuck in the floor beside her. A verdict of suicide was given, but a month later the case was reopened, the body exhumed and four members of her family charged with the murder:

> the body being taken up out of the grave, 30 days after the party's death, and lying on the grass, and the four defendants being present, were required each of them to touch the dead body. Okeman's wife fell upon her knees, and prayed God to shew tokens of her innocency. The appellant did touch the dead body, whereupon the brow of the dead, which before was of a livid and carrion colour (*in terminis*, the verbal expression of the witness), began to have a dew, or gentle sweat, arise on it, which increased by degrees till the sweat ran down in drops on the face; the brow turned to a lively and fresh colour, and the deceased opened one of her eyes, and shut it again; and this opening the eye was done three several times. She likewise thrust out the ring or marriage

finger three times, and pulled it in again, and the finger dropped blood from it on the grass.

Witnesses to the event were sure it was fresh blood: one dipped his finger in it as confirmation. Circumstantial forensic evidence also depended on blood: there was no blood in Jane Norkot's bed 'saving a tincture of blood on the bolster whereon her head lay', but 'From the bed's head there was a stream of blood on the floor . . . a very great quantity . . . and there was also another stream of blood on the floor at the bed's foot.' In addition to these two separate bloodstains on the floor, 'there were clots of congealed blood in the straw of the mat underneath'. The knife was bloodstained and, most chillingly, 'There was the print of a thumb and four fingers of a left hand.'[28]

James Guthrie, a Scottish Presbyterian minister hanged in 1661 following the Restoration of the Stuart monarchy, also bled on the guilty. His corpse was decapitated and the head publicly displayed, but it would shed blood on the coach of the commissioner who had presided at his trial. These bloodstains were impossible to remove: 'all their art and diligence could not wipe it off'.[29] Likewise in 1688, the son of Sir Philip Stansfield was discovered to have murdered him when, on helping to lift the corpse into its coffin, the two-day-old cadaver 'bled afresh' on the son's hands, and on no one else's. Cruentation continued to be cited in criminal law on occasion, especially in Scotland, until the nineteenth century.[30]

Blood is essential to life.[31] It is sticky and indelible, and it is earthy. And – at least until fairly recently – it was a common sight in villages, towns and cities, in butchers' shops and shambles. Nowadays, though ubiquitous, it is invisible (the sight of menstrual blood, for instance, remains a taboo). Blood has inevitably accrued a vast lore concerning its reputed powers: Pliny recorded epileptics drinking the warm blood of dying gladiators; the medieval mystic Hildegard of Bingen recommended baths of menstrual blood (*sanguis menstruus*) to cure leprosy – a belief that lasted for centuries; and the Hungarian Countess Elizabeth Báthory (d. 1614) was reputed to bathe in the blood of young girls in order to retain her youthful beauty.[32]

The blood of Christian martyrs was particularly beneficial, and even the water used to soak the gore out of the martyr Thomas Becket's vestments acquired the capacity for sacred healing.[33] In 1815, the Brothers Grimm recorded the continuing folk belief that leprosy and blindness could be cured by bathing in or being anointed with the blood of a virgin.[34] *Sanguis menstruus* was also used in folk magic, as it was reputed to be a love potion.[35] However, according to blood historian Hermann Strack, the blood of 'executed persons' was 'even more efficacious than menstrual blood' (again finding a source in Pliny).[36] Hans Christian Andersen attended an execution in 1823, whereupon 'I saw a poor sick man, whom his superstitious parents made drink a cup of the blood of the executed person, that he might be healed of epilepsy; after which they ran with him in wild career till he sank to the ground.'[37] The blood of an executed felon was in any case considered lucky, as were gallows chains and nails; even the rope used by a hangman or suicide brought – somewhat ghoulishly – good health and fair fortune.[38] Executioners were accordingly held in some repute as healers – not least, perhaps, as they had an intimate knowledge of the human body and its inner workings.[39]

Other bodily matter, such as human fat, also had curative properties, as did body parts such as hands and fingers, and, perhaps most morbidly, the hearts of unborn children.[40] A human skull baked, pulverized and ingested was yet another cure for epilepsy.[41] Indeed, the English College of Physicians included 'mummy, human blood, and human skull' in their official pharmacopoeia of 1618, and expanded these corporeal ingredients in later editions.[42] The most outlandish example of this is the (doubtless apocryphal) claim that the Catholic order of the Brothers of Mercy (*Barmherzige Brüder*) at Graz annually prepared remedies from an entire corpse. Every Easter, a young man being treated for some minor ailment in one of their hospitals would be seized, suspended upside down and tickled to death. 'The honourable brethren thereupon boil the corpse to a paste and utilise the latter as well as the fat and the burnt bones in their drug store.'[43] Graves were frequently robbed of remains for folk medicine, especially in nineteenth-century Germany.[44]

But blood was also a bond, and there is much evidence from earliest times to the present day of the ritual drinking and co-mingling of blood between allies to create blood brotherhoods, in taking oaths and in swearing allegiance.[45] This secular sacrament was allegedly practised by the ancient Scythians in the fourth century BC, by characters in the Norse and Teutonic sagas (e.g. Sigurd the Volsung) and by Hungarian *hajduks* (guerrilla soldiers).[46]

The obsession with blood as the 'juice of life' (in Piero Camporesi's resonant phrase) is in direct contrast to the fear of death.[47]

The awakening dead

But none of these blood rites are directly vampiric; rather, they form a sanguinary backdrop to vampirism. Vampires are not demons, ghosts, wraiths, revenants or witches – although their stories are sometimes entwined.[48] Vampires occupy their own distinctive category among blood-suckers, and likewise they should not be too closely tied to a bundle of generalized fears about the dead, the undead, contagion or death. Nevertheless, they do emerge from the tangled folklore of Eastern Europe, and it is worth outlining these beliefs to establish just what it was that the Enlightenment intelligentsia encountered. Indeed, Serbian legislation on vampirism goes back to at least the first half of the fourteenth century, when Article 20 of the Emperor Stefan Dušan undertook to prohibit the unlawful exhumation of those accused of being undead: 'When it happens that, by magic means, people are taken out of their graves and cremated, the village where that was done must pay a fine, and the priest who came to the cremation must be deprived of his vocation.'[49] The practice was clearly endemic, though, and there is a rich mythology attached to the undead across the entire region.[50]

The West Slavic Kashubians (or Cassubians), for example, believe that a vampire (*vjeszczi* or *wupji*) is destined from birth, indicated by being born with a caul and two teeth and often having a red face and lips. At the moment of death, he or she will refuse the Eucharist; the body cools slowly, there is no rigor mortis, and spots of blood may appear on the face and under the fingernails. At midnight, the creature awakes and eats its own grave clothes and flesh.[51] It may wait days or months, sitting in its coffin with eyes wide open, perhaps mumbling incoherently; but eventually it will visit its kin – starting with its closest relations – to infect them. Protection against such creatures is possible by taking communion at the graveside and making the sign of the cross. The vampire's body can also be hampered in its career by placing a crucifix or coin in its mouth, wedging a brick under the chin to break its teeth, severing tendons in the legs, or laying a net in the coffin (all the knots must be undone before the coffin can be vacated); meanwhile, placing earth in the coffin from the threshold of a dwelling will protect a home. Sand or poppy seeds can act as impediments if scattered in the coffin or strewn on the path from the grave – the vampire is required to count each and every grain of sand or seed before proceeding (and by some accounts, at the rate of only one a year); poppy is also a narcotic, and the seeds are sometimes said to be eaten. Burial face-downwards is also recommended. To slay a vampire, a nail is driven through its forehead, and its head is severed and placed between its feet; infected relatives can be treated with fresh blood.[52]

Joakim Vujić, in his narrative *Travelling through Serbia* (1827), described how a vampire was caught in a village near Novi Pazar. The priest Stavra was called, who prised open the vampire's mouth with a sharpened hawthorn stick, inserted a hawthorn twig and trickled three drops of Holy Water onto the vampire's tongue; meanwhile a village elder named Petko took the hawthorn stick and impaled the vampire through the chest with a single thrust.[53] According to the Russian folklorist Aleksandr Afanasev, 'Every deceased person can become a vampire if a bird flies over him or if an animal (chicken, cat, dog) jumps over him.'[54] In Serbia, vampires are ruddy and engorged while in their coffins and will rise after 40 days in the grave, possessed by a demon. Since vampires characteristically possess a rosy (rather than a cadaverous) complexion, Serbs and Slovaks describe rubicund drinkers as 'red as a vampire'.[55]

In Slavonic folklore, vampires can enter a house through any gap. They choke their victims and drink their blood from the chest, near to the heart; those on whom they prey then also become vampires. A male vampire will often seek to sleep with his former wife. Any offspring conceived with a vampire has no skeleton. They also have elemental qualities: 'Russian peasants are convinced that vampires and werewolves can bring on a drought, send down storms, crop failures, livestock plagues, and various diseases.'[56] Consequently, graves were regularly desecrated in Russia by vigilantes searching for vampires, 'because the people believe the dead person is going about sucking their blood, or causing epidemics, or producing drought by milking the clouds'.[57] Greek Orthodox gypsies in Kosovo-Metohija believe that it is a protection against vampires to cross oneself and call on Saints

Cosmas and Damian.[58] In Bulgaria, meanwhile, it was suggested that vampires could be bottled.[59] In Macedonian folklore, the *vrykolakas* or *vompiras* (a term of abuse) is

> an animated corpse throttling people and sucking the blood of men and beasts, or damaging household utensils, ploughs, etc. He is described as being in personal appearance like a bull-skin full of blood, with a pair of eyes on one side, gleaming like live coals in the dark . . . People born on a Saturday (. . . Sabbatarians) are believed to enjoy the doubtful privilege of seeing ghosts and phantasms, and of possessing great influence over vampires.[60]

As elsewhere, the blood of the vampire was believed in Macedonian folk religion to have restorative properties: Tanas Vrazhinovski comments that after a vampire had been slain (in this case, shot), 'people took the blood of the killed vampire and rubbed their bodies with it as protection against sickness, to attain good health and to be resistant to other vampires'.[61] Likewise, in nineteenth-century Prussia it was held that a cure for those infected with vampirism was to drink blood from a vampire's severed head; such measures were still being taken in 1877.[62]

Most peculiar among the Slavic lore collected by vampirologist Jan Louis Perkowski is the Slavonic gypsy belief in vampiric agricultural tools and vampire vegetables. A rod for tethering sheaves of wheat, for example, would turn vampire if kept for more than three years, while pumpkins and watermelons took only ten days to animate into shuddering, murmuring vampires; a pumpkin kept after Christmas will also become a vampire. Fortunately, the potential for injury from an undead squash is not that great, and so, we learn, 'people are not very afraid of this kind of vampire'.[63]

As the occultist Montague Summers observes, the distinction between the bloodsucking ghosts of the classical world and the modern vampire is that 'the peculiar quality of the vampire, especially in Slavic tradition, is the re-animation of a dead body, which is endowed with certain mystic properties such as discerptibility [extension], subtility [tenuity], and temporal incorruption'.[64] And although some of this Slavonic lore is doubtless retrospective, it is nevertheless striking how common specified elements were carried into the earliest reports of true vampires, and how the accretive nature of folk beliefs fleshed out, so to speak, the body of vampire knowledge. Certain features of the vampire reverberate through later accounts: their eyes open in the coffin, eyes that glower like fire; their influence over the weather and association with epidemic contagion; their ability to pass into houses through tiny gaps; their predation on their kin, choking victims and taking blood from the chest; the protection afforded by Holy Communion, the sign of the cross and the blood of the vampire; and their extermination by staking and decapitation. Other elements remained in doubt – principally, what caused vampirism. The Hungarian orientalist Ármin Vámbéry (of whom more later) provided the entry on vampires for the eleventh edition of the *Encyclopædia Britannica* (1910–11), which began with a brief summary of Slavonic lore:

> The persons who turn vampires are generally wizards, witches, suicides and those who have come to a violent end or have been cursed by their parents or by the church. But any one may become a vampire if an animal (especially a cat) leaps over his corpse or a bird flies over it. Sometimes the vampire is thought to be the soul of a living man which leaves his body in sleep, to go in the form of a straw or fluff of down and suck the blood of other sleepers.[65]

Vámbéry's account presents vampirism as the consequence of bad magic, suicide or accident; but the Slavonic traditions are clearly much broader in scope, covering vampirism as demonic possession, the malign influence of an animal passing over a corpse and, importantly, vampirism considered as a congenital condition: being born vampire. These questions of origin haunt vampire writing, but one cause in particular stands out: infection, often as the prey of the vampire. So before examining the first scientific reports of vampirism, this element needs to be added to the witches' brew.

Black death

Many accounts of vampires associate outbreaks of vampirism with contagion, making them vectors and consequently part of the history of infectious diseases. Although the means by which illness and infection spread was not fully understood until the middle of the nineteenth century, William Harvey had, in 1628, published his theory of the circulation of blood, *Exercitatio Anatomica de Motu Cordis et Sanguinis in Animalibus*. The word 'circulation' was soon being used in England to describe the passions, and there are instances of fashionable use in seventeenth-century popular literature.[66] By at least 1701, credit in the economy was being described as 'circulating', and Johnson's *Dictionary* (1755) quotes Jonathan Swift writing on the '*circulation* of human things'.[67] From the early eighteenth century, the notion of 'circulation' was applied to a wide range of fields: from botany (the circulation of sap in trees) to maritime navigation (the tides of the sea), and also to the spread of ideas. Terms such as 'liquidity', 'fluid' and 'lubricate' were also applied to various areas of learning. And the first use of 'rejuvenate' came in 1742.[68] Circulation was then a defining and ubiquitous symbol, and so blood was, in a sense, the medium of thought, with appealingly sanguine associations of vitality and flow. Vampires thus emerged in a context in which both tangible objects and intangible concepts were imagined to ooze and seep and stir, much as bodily fluids did in the cardiovascular system. Circulatory networks are the very media of vampirism: they roam, feed and infect through the circulation of blood.[69]

Nevertheless, the idea that disease or infection could circulate independently did not develop until the end of the century.[70] Early theories of plague considered it to be an instrument of holy displeasure – the key element of the biblical pestilence being 'a divine sovereign who, in the form of a judgment and/or punishment, sends down – or better, emanates – a form of miasmatic life that is indissociable from decay, decomposition, and death', and early vampires need to be understood within this sacred context.[71] These mystical plagues were manifested through invisible forces – qualities that would come to characterize vampires – and the more radical conjectures on contagion speculated that it could be spread by immaterial means, by the words or simply the breath of an infected person:

This epidemic, according to some people, has the power to kill large numbers by air alone, simply by the breath or the conversation of the sick. They say that the air breathed out by the sick and inhaled by the healthy people round about wounds and kills them, and that this occurs particularly when the sick are on the point of death.[72]

Bengt Knutsson, a fifteenth-century Swedish bishop whose influential work on the plague was translated into English as *A Litil Boke for the Pestilence* (first published *c.* 1485), dwelt upon the dangers of 'venomous and infected air' caused by 'dead carrion or the corruption of standing waters in ditches or sloughs or other corrupt places', by thick air (i.e. dark summer days that threatened rain 'and yet it does not rain'), by dirty hands and by the breath of infected people.[73] He advocated bloodletting.

Even more alarming was the deadly eye of a victim.[74] The basilisk, a venomous reptile, was reputed to be able to kill with a look – 'a visible poisonous vapour passes from the eyes of the basilisk into the eye of the observer' – and, inspired by such thinking, in 1349 a doctor of Montpellier specifically compared plague carriers to these dreadful monsters.[75] Physicians were accordingly advised to 'take precautions against the gaze and breath of people in the throes of illness'.[76] As the plague chronicler Gabriele de' Mussis warned, 'one infected man could carry the poison to others, and infect people and places with the disease by look alone'.[77] In practical terms, this meant that doctors blindfolded their patients.[78] Looking is lethal and to be seen is fatal. Such medicalized fears of the evil eye would be embodied in the weaponized gaze of the vampire.

Plague was both supernaturally incorporeal and yet an identifiable condition.[79] And despite the awareness of contagion being rudimentary, plague was nevertheless deployed as an instrument of mass destruction. De' Mussis described the Caffa atrocity of 1346 in Crimea, when the attacking army of Tartars played God by visiting a plague on their enemies – a plague that struck from the skies:

The dying Tartars, stunned and stupefied by the immensity of the disaster brought about by the disease, and realising that they had no hope of escape, lost interest in the siege. But they ordered corpses to be placed in catapults and lobbed into the city in the hope that the intolerable stench would kill everyone inside. What seemed like mountains of dead were thrown into the city, and the Christians could not hide or flee or escape from them, although they dumped as many of the bodies as they could into the sea. And soon the rotting corpses tainted the air and poisoned the water supply, and the stench was so overwhelming that hardly one in several thousand was in a position to flee the remains of the Tartar army . . . No one knew, or could discover, a means of defence.[80]

By the end of the seventeenth century, plague theory had been refined. Gideon Harvey's *A Discourse of the Plague* (1665, no relation of William) defined the pestilence in the medical language of the time as 'Pestilential Miasms, insinuating into the humoral and consistent parts of the Body'.[81] The Earth was conceived of as an organism that could either thrive or sicken, depending on weather and natural phenomena, from mild winters to meteor storms. An ailing Earth was like an ailing body, exhaling poisonous miasma that congregated in 'close, dirty, stinking, and infected places, as Alleys, dark Lanes, Church-yards, Chandlers shops, common Alehouses, Shambles, Poultries, or any places where old houshold-stuff is kept, as musty beddings and hangings'.[82] The plague could be contracted through 'converse' with infected persons, but usually straight from the diseased air – either breathing in 'flaming Arsenical corpuscles floating in the air' or, more commonly, intra-venously by these corpuscles piercing the skin, 'penetrat[ing] into the body through the pores of the Arteries'.[83] The plague was then carried throughout the body by, of course, the cardiovascular system:

> gradually corrupting the blood, and converting its parts into bodies of their own nature. The blood being afterwards rendred so turgid with a daily access of new Pestilential atoms from without, and increase of others within, Nature finds her self incapable of resisting any longer, and yields; whereupon the concepted fiery atoms unite, and excite a Pestilential fermentation, the genuine cause of all those ensuing symptoms.[84]

The victims themselves were then transformed into pestilence, and their blood became putrid; again, bloodletting was advised.

William Harvey's understanding united conventional classical models with new post-Paracelsian thinking, investigating blood through physical observation and examination, rather than by deferring to ancient authorities.[85] Following Harvey's groundbreaking work, in 1656 the architect Christopher Wren pioneered hypodermic injections by intoxicating his dog with wine injected straight into its veins.[86] In 1665, Wren then suggested that Dr Richard Lower attempt a blood transfusion on a dog. The scientist Robert Boyle wrote to Lower on the possibility that temperament and other characteristics could be transferred by blood, wondering 'whether the blood of a mastiff, being frequently transferred into a bloodhound, or a spaniel, will not prejudice them in point of scent'.[87] The diarist Samuel Pepys discussed blood transfusion between dogs in 1666, reflecting that there may well be benefits to humans: 'As Dr. Croune says, [it] may, if it takes, be of mighty use to man's health, for the mending of bad blood by borrowing from a better body.' The Royal Society began to investigate human blood transfusion, and the next year Pepys reported on the remarkable case of Arthur Coga.[88]

Coga, a 32-year-old Divinity graduate of Cambridge University, was 'looked upon as a very freakish and extravagant man'.[89] On 23 November 1667, he was treated to become more docile by receiving a blood transfusion from a lamb. Pepys observed that the medical fraternity 'differ in the opinion they have of the effects of it: some think it may have a good effect upon him as a frantic man by cooling his blood, others that it will not have any effect at all'.[90] Coga saw the lamb as emblematic of meekness and humility, declaring in Latin, '*Sanguis ovis symbolicam quandam facultatem habet cum sanguine Christi, quia Christus est agnus Dei*' ('the blood of sheep has symbolic power like the blood of Christ, for Christ is the Lamb of God').[91] The lamb's blood was transfused using quills and silver pipes. Coga received a payment of 20 shillings, drank Canary wine and smoked a pipe in celebration, and the operation was repeated on 12 December. Coga's mood was not noticeably softened by the treatment; however, some change had apparently taken place. He wrote a begging letter to the Royal Society, complaining that he had been transformed into 'another species' and was reduced to pawning his clothes – or, as he bombastically (and in the third person) put it, he 'dearly purchases your sheep's blood with the loss of his own wool in this sheep-wrackt vessel of his, like that of Argos, he addresses himself to you for the Golden Fleece'. He signed himself 'Agnus Coga' – 'Coga the Sheep'.[92]

Coga was more fortunate than he perhaps appreciated. A few months earlier, in France, Jean-Baptiste Denys had performed cross-species transfusions into two human patients. Both subjects died and Denys was accused of murder, although he was later acquitted.[93] In January 1668, another patient (who again required a calming of the spirit) died from a similar transfusion, and by 1678 the pope had prohibited such animal-to-human treatments.[94] Attempts were made to continue this line of experimentation in Britain regardless – on inmates of the Bedlam lunatic asylum. These were prevented by the hospital's surgeon, who had a 'scruple' against vivisecting mad people. And so this line of research was halted until, in 1818, James Blundell published his accounts of experimental transfusions given to dogs.[95]

Blood oozed through eighteenth-century thought. In the period between the scientific experiments performed on Coga the Sheep and Blundell's dogs, blood was simultaneously part of everyday life, a mysterious substance of folklore and superstition, and lay at the heart of the Christian mass and the symbolism of the Church. It was both natural and supernatural, and this abundance of meaning was encapsulated in the figure of the vampire. The vampire embodied the contradictions of blood: it obscured distinctions between the living and the dead, the human and the non-human, even between psychological stability and physical metamorphosis. The vampire was also the quintessence of bad blood: of blood corrupt and virulent. And as the following chapters will show, these fears of tainted blood were heightened with the dread of contagion from musty and confined places, churchyards, rottenness and decay, foul air, infections borne in the atmosphere, fog and mist, and invisible perils. All these horrors congregate at the advent of the vampire.

PART I

CIRCULATING
THE SEVENTEENTH AND EIGHTEENTH CENTURIES

CHAPTER 1

UNEARTHING THE DEAD
Medicine and Detection, Body and Mind

The voice of thy brother's blood crieth unto me from the ground.

Genesis 4:10 (1611)[1]

Yours in the ranks of death.

William Shakespeare (1605)[2]

A corpse-like countenance, with eye
That iced me by its baleful peer –
Silent, as from a bier . . .

Thomas Hardy (1922)[3]

In the early eighteenth century, the traditional bloodsuckers of Eastern European folklore came face to face with empirical science and became vampires. They appeared between the hours of noon and midnight to suck the blood of humans and animals; once sated, blood would flow from their orifices and pores, and their coffins were often found to be swimming in gore. They were known to feast on grave clothes; continuing this fascination with grisly nutrition, a prophylactic bread could be made from their blood that afforded protection against contracting vampirism. Vampires thus became recognized as an apparently extreme natural phenomenon, and a body of evidence that could be scrutinized and analysed in new ways. They were identified less as supernatural blood-suckers and more as nocturnal asphyxiators and/or as vectors for contagious diseases, and they were a notably physical phenomenon: corporeal, tangible, of flesh and blood, and exhibiting particular dietary requirements. Detailed forensic examinations were accordingly made and records kept, including catalogues of signs and symptoms, and much learned (and pseudo-learned) work was published in professional journals, covering an increasingly broad range of possible sources and causes of the condition.

Not all were convinced, and there were some who debunked the whole thing as deluded – often risible – superstition. But even the sceptics had to agree that although vampires may not exist *per se* as prodigies of the natural world, they were nevertheless at least evidence of mass hysteria, psychological disturbance or hallucination. Consequently, investigations of vampire outbreaks and belief helped to shape not only knowledge of the body and theories of contagion, but also understanding of the brain and mental faculties. Moreover, the ways in which this state-of-the-art intellectual rationality responded to cases of vampirism, characterized as it was by material evidence and the corroboration of witnesses, profoundly affected the depiction of the condition. Vampires, then, did not exist until the emerging medical profession and natural philosophers began to try to explain them and they were thus named and categorized as vampires. This chapter will explain the earliest such cases of vampirism, and the extraordinary impact they had across Europe.[4]

Morbid corporeality

The detection of the first vampires and cases of vampirism occurred at the beginning of the eighteenth century and were investigated by medical scientists working in the field: military surgeons, physicians and apothecaries. But immediately prior to the explicit identification of vampires there had already been considerable undead activity. One celebrated early case was reported in Croatian Istria, in 1672. A dead man, one Giure (or Jure) Grando, rose from his grave as a restless corpse (*Leichnam*) and visited his neighbours; he was dealt with by a priest performing an exorcism, an attempt to stake him with hawthorn, and finally decapitation.[5] There was a further incident in Ljubljana in 1689. The French *Mercure Galant* (later *Mercure de France*) described undead activity in Poland and Russia in 1693 and 1694, and there were notices in journals such as the *Mercure Historique et Politique* and *Glaneur Historique* (or *Glaneur de Hollande*); there were also reports from Prussia in 1710 and 1721.[6] In 1718, at Lubló on the old Hungarian–Polish border, a merchant named Kaszparek rose from the dead, and further cases were reported in Késmárk (then northern Hungary, now Slovakia) and Brassó and Déva (Transylvania) in the 1720s.[7] The tangibility of these predators was evident: in Zemplén (then Hungary, now eastern Slovakia), it was understood that 'The body's return from the dead can be averted by nailing its clothes, hair, or limbs to the coffin' – a characteristic of deviant burials from earlier times.[8]

Evidence of the post-mortem behaviour of the undead when confined in their coffins had already been surveyed by Phillip Rohr in his *Dissertatio De Masticatione Mortuorum* (1679), an empirical study of 'grave-eating' or manducation (posthumous chewing).[9] Rohr gives grisly details of graves being opened to reveal that the undead had been consuming their own shrouds and winding cloths, and in some cases had even devoured their own limbs and bowels. But what is most striking about these occurrences is perhaps the sounds that accompanied infernal mastication. While the dead were in any case 'known to have grunted, gibbered, and squeaked' under the ground, the Devil makes 'curious noises' in manducation: 'he may lap like some thirsty animal, he may chaw, grunt and groan' – suggestive of the bestial slavering and mastication that accompanied later vampire feasts.[10]

But while the Devil incontrovertibly existed, his power was severely limited: he could not, for instance, raise the dead – as could God – but he might trick the unwary into believing that the dead were abroad and predating on the living. Rohr reasons that if the Devil could not restore the dead to life, but did have powers over dead bodies (being able to prevent corruption of a corpse and also inspire cruentation), then the undead must be animated corpses. Accordingly, Rohr includes remedies to prevent the dead from rising, such as clasping the hands of a corpse together, or placing earth on its lips – as well as more decisive measures, such as decapitation or exhumation followed by staking through the heart to pin the corpse to the ground. He supports his examination with examples from the fourteenth century on, but also digresses on the crimes and sins of disinterment and the posthumous violation of corpses. Rohr's demonology was therefore both empirical in proposing practical ways of dealing with the restless dead, and also institutional in his awareness of the need for formal authorization for exhumation. The necessary ecclesiastical permission and approval for excavating graves was, of course, seldom sought by small communities dealing with extreme phenomena, but official consent and certification was to become highly significant not only in reporting vampires, but in establishing the authenticity of supernatural narratives more generally, and this would come to characterize western encounters with wild folklore in the next century.[11] But notwithstanding this serious attention, as the lawyer and memoirist Roger North also reported, such beliefs could simply be a pretext for orientalist anti-Semitism and obnoxious bigotry:

> The *Turks* have an Opinion, that Men that are buried, have a sort of Life in their Graves. If any Man makes Affidavit before a Judge, that he heard a Noise in a Man's Grave, he is, by Order, dug up, and chopt all to-pieces. The Merchants, once airing on Horseback, had (as usual for Protection) a Janizary with them. Passing by the burying Place of the *Jews*, it happened that an old *Jew* sat by a Sepulchre. The Janizary rode up to him, and rated him for stinking the World a second Time, and commanded him to get into his Grave again.[12]

Contemporary thinking in science, law and politics directly confronted superstition, then, and out of this clash emerged the vampire. The new approach is typified by *Magia Posthuma* (*Post-Mortem Magic*, 1704) by the Moravian antiquarian, lawyer and economist Karl Ferdinand Schertz. Schertz roundly criticized the exhumation and mutilation of alleged undead persons not only as a woefully misguided rural practice, but, more tellingly, as criminal – arguing that disinterment was a fundamentally unlawful act, unless due legal process was observed through coroners' courts; moreover, he argued that exhumed bodies could be cremated only after examination by a medical professional.[13] Again, this was to become a critical issue in vampire hunting, as it placed post-mortem investigation under the jurisdiction of state officers. Schertz's actual work was rarely read, but his reputation rests upon defining these legal facets, and the criteria outlined in *Magia Posthuma* became a touchstone of the subsequent vampire debate, due to the frequency of exhumations and cremations of the suspected undead.[14]

A Hungarian doctor, Sámuel Köleséri, gives a similar account of activities undertaken in attempting to contain a plague epidemic in Transylvania in 1709.[15] The Transylvanians ascribed the outbreak to the Devil, who was contaminating the populace through itinerant revenants. In four villages affected, those suspected of rising from the dead and spreading the infection – including a former Orthodox priest – were exhumed and staked, sometimes face-down. In terms of halting the spread of pestilence, the results were patchy at best. Likewise, in *A Voyage into the Levant* (1718), Joseph Pitton de Tournefort, botanist to French King Louis XIV, gives what was to become a celebrated account of a Greek 'Vroucolacas' on the island of Mykonos, dated to 1 January 1701. *Vrykolakas* were defined as 'Corpses, which they [the Mykonians] fancy come to life again after their Interment', and which (in this case at least) were aggressively violent.[16] The locals attempt to destroy the *vrykolakas* by removing the heart from the original, stinking corpse and burning the offending organ; but the creature continues to roam the island until it is dosed with Holy Water and cremated. Just as Schertz dismissed post-mortem desecration not only as unlawful but also ridiculous, so Tournefort's account mocks the islanders' credulity by similarly asserting modern rational thinking over peasant superstition. But while he treats the episode as irrational and absurd, Tournefort nevertheless also proposes his own scientific explanation: the inhabitants of Mykonos must be suffering from an 'epidemical disease of the brain', similar to the bite of a mad dog.[17] In making his acerbic diagnosis, Tournefort gives a perturbing glimpse of the desperation associated with the terror of epidemic contagion among closed and peripheral communities. Such extreme anxiety in the face of the rapid, devastating and inexplicable spread of disease – and the frantic attempts to contain it – forms the background to subsequent outbreaks of vampirism. Indeed, the ancient Hippocratic treatise 'De Aere Aquis et Locis' ('On Airs, Waters and Places', *c.* 400 BC) had already 'yoked together medicine, physical geography and ethnology' in arguing why certain regions were particularly subject to specific diseases.[18] In addition, epidemics often accompanied war and famine, and the mass movements of displaced peoples. Such visitations could also be God's punishment for communal wrongs. But now vampires presented a third alternative.

By the early 1720s, the modern vampire had all but materialized. In 1721, the first natural history study of Poland was published, in which Fr Gabriel Rzączyński quotes from a manuscript written by a fellow Jesuit, Fr Gengell. Gengell's essay bears the title 'Eversio Atheismi' ('The Destruction of Atheism') and includes the first account of modern vampirism in the figure of the *upier* (linked to the Old Russian *upirъ* or *upiři*, and the Polish *upiór*):[19]

I have frequently heard from credible eyewitnesses, that human bodies have been found not only incorrupt, flexible, and ruddy for a long time, but, moreover, the head, the mouth, the tongue, the eyes sometimes move. The winding-sheet in which they are wrapped is undone and parts of the body are devoured. At times it is also noted that a body of this kind rises again from the grave, wanders past crossroads and houses showing himself now to one, now to another, and also attacks many, trying to suffocate them. If it is a male body, it is called *Upier*. If it is female, it is called *Upierzyca*, as if to say a feathered one, i.e. a body provided with down or feathers, light and agile for movement.[20]

The erroneous folk etymology aside (which confuses the word *Upierzyca* with the Polish *pierze*, meaning 'feathers'), this account is typical of what was to follow: key features being the ever-fresh corpse, the ruddiness of the skin, the grave-eating, the rising from the dead and the murderous craving to suffocate victims – and although the freshness and repletion of the corpse is not here attributed to sucking the blood from victims (the creature is rather an autophage), it is noteworthy that it can be either male or female. But Gengell is here describing folk superstition. What followed almost immediately was a series of well-documented incidents at the frontiers of the Habsburg Empire, and it is from these that both the definition of *vampire* and the word itself arose.

Genesis of the vampire

In 1725, one Frombald, a medical officer in the Imperial Army, reported to his commanding officers in Vienna that Serbian *hajduks* had exhumed and staked a corpse before cremating it. They claimed that the corpse had risen from the grave to strangle victims and infect them with a condition that caused death within 24 hours.[21] In a Latin aside in his report, Frombald called these creatures '*vampyri*'. On 21 July the same year, the Viennese newspaper *Wienerisches Diarium* carried this report, naming the vampire in question as Peter Plogojowitz, a local peasant. Once dead, Plogojowitz had allegedly been responsible for throttling nine people in the space of eight days in the village of Kisolova (or Kisilova), in Serbia. Plogojowitz may have been ithyphallic, thus posing a predatory sexual threat (as well as a paranormal vampirical threat); but most importantly, 'according to the common observation, he had sucked from the people killed by him'. Plogojowitz was one of the 'vampiri or bloodsuckers'.[22] His body was exhumed in the presence of two local officials from Gradiška District, one of whom reported:

> first of all I did not detect the slightest odor that is otherwise character-istic of the dead, and the body, except for the nose, which was some-what fallen away, was completely fresh. The hair and beard – even the nails, of which the old ones had fallen away – had grown on him; the old skin, which was somewhat whitish, had peeled away, and a new fresh one had emerged under it . . . Not without astonishment, I saw some fresh blood in his mouth . . .[23]

Plogojowitz had been dead and buried for a good ten weeks. Having been exhumed and discovered to be a vampire, he was staked – whereupon fresh blood spurted from his pierced chest, as well from as his ears and mouth – before being incinerated.

Meanwhile, a similar instance was dealt with by the Count de Cabreras, captain of the regiment of the Alandetti infantry, in 1730. The contours of the case are very similar: the dead father of a peasant appears at the house of a landlord billeting a Habsburg soldier; the peasant dies. News reaches Captain de Cabreras, who visits, accompanied by a retinue of imperial officialdom: 'several officers, a chirurgeon, and a notary'. De Cabreras orders the body to be exhumed – of course, it is fresh, 'the blood like that of a living person'. He orders it to be decapitated. He then identifies a similar 'spectre' who has sucked the blood out of his brother, his own child and a family servant. The fresh corpse has a nail driven into his head. A third bloodsucker, 16 years dead but again murdering his own children, is cremated. In his vampire-slaying career, then, de Cabreras is admirably varied in his techniques, but he is also careful to justify his activities with witnesses approved by central government. The Habsburg emperor Charles VI responded by sending out a delegation of 'officers, lawyers, physicians, chirurgeons, and some divines' to inquire further, confirming that de Cabreras's actions were legitimated by the apparatus of the state.[24]

Nonetheless, it is worth remembering that medical practitioners (at least) were held in great suspicion in this period, due to their meddling in the mechanics of the body, and their dissection and dealings with death and cadavers. Doctors embraced both the new science and the basic facts of life – whether a being was alive or dead – but in doing so threatened to rework the very nature of what it was to be human. A satirical print published in London *c.* 1730–45, probably deriving from a Dutch engraving, shows a barber-surgeon's shop hung with stuffed monsters.[25] All the figures are metamorphic hybrids: humans with the heads of animals, including a pig, an ass and an elephant. A catwoman is being bled, and blood arches across the room into a basin held by a monkeyboy; meanwhile, another catperson is having teeth removed – they lie on a table next to various implements that bear an uncanny resemblance to instruments of torture. William Hogarth's later celebrated print, *The Reward of Cruelty* (1751), displays the executed corpse of Tom Nero, still with the hangman's noose around his neck, being dissected in a crowded operating theatre. The chief anatomist is wielding a butcher's filleting knife with undisguised enthusiasm, while one colleague delicately brandishes a scalpel over Nero's Achilles tendon and another pokes about in his eye socket with a bodkin. The cadaver itself is crudely suspended by means of a block and tackle fixed to a hook bolt screwed into its forehead. Nero's entrails have been dumped into a bucket, beside which a dog is gnawing tidbits of offal. Nearby is a steaming cauldron, into which the skulls and bones of previous scientific subjects have been deposited, in order to boil off the fat and leave the bones in a suitable condition to be displayed. The whole grisly scene is a reminder of the horribly corporeal business of anatomical science, as deliciously macabre as a Jacobean revenge tragedy.

The dissecting room was a notoriously putrid place, and cadavers were already rotting and foetid by the time they came under the knife.[26] But not all corpses decomposed, and so the preservation of vampire carcasses already had a place within the history of scientific curiosities. Reiterating Rohr's research, Paul Ricaut had in 1679 provided a detailed account of the consequences of excommunication from the Orthodox Church. In Greece and Armenia, it was believed that

> the Bodies of the Excommunicated are possessed in the Grave by some evil spirit, which actuates and preserves them from Corruption . . . and that they feed in the night, walk, digest, and are nourished, and have been found ruddy in Complexion, and their Veins, after forty days Burial, extended with Blood, which, being opened with a Lancet, have yielded a gore as plentiful, fresh, and quick.[27]

Ricaut described a specific incident in which an excommunicant was buried on the Isle of Milo, following which his family and the locals were haunted by 'strange and unusual apparitions'. When the grave was opened, the corpse of the excommunicant was found to be 'uncorrupted, ruddy, and the Veins replete with Blood'. The islanders urged that the body be dismembered and boiled in wine to dissolve the remains and thereby 'dislodge the evil Spirit' – the dissolving of the body being a persistent and recurrent theme in such cases.[28] However, the friends of the deceased obtained a reprieve and the corpse was accorded a proper funeral service. Once this had been completed, 'on a sudden was heard a rumbling noise in the Coffin of the dead party, to the fear and astonishment of all persons then present; which when they had opened, they found the Body consumed and dissolved as far into its first Principles of Earth, as if it had been seven years interred.' Tellingly, 'This story I should not have judged worth relating, but that I heard it from the mouth of a grave person, who says, That his own eyes were Witnesses thereof.'[29] The testimony of one who had been present and seen and heard what had come to pass was paramount.

More germane to later vampirism, Richard Gough's *Sepulchral Monuments in Great Britain* (1786–96) offers a range of historical corporeal marvels discovered in Britain. The corpse of the Anglo-Saxon archbishop Elphege (d. 1012) was found entire and undecayed, as were those of Etheldritha, founder of Ely monastery, and her sister; at the other end of the social scale, Alice Hackney, a fishmonger's wife (d. 1321), was accidentally disinterred in 1497, and she too was comparatively fresh. More recently, Robert Braybroke, bishop of London (d. 1401), 'being dug up after the [Great] fire' had flesh 'like singed bacon'; William Parr (d. 1573), brother to Katherine Parr, had apparently been preserved by rosemary, bay and the dryness of his burial plot; and Dr Caius (d. 1573) of Gonville and Caius College, Cambridge, was exhumed in 1725, when his beard was discovered to have grown noticeably. A male child buried in St Margaret's churchyard, Westminster, in the 1670s was found a century later, 'perfect and beautiful as a waxwork'; the bodies of the drummer and trumpeter to George I were so sound that they were briefly exhibited in the later eighteenth century at St Martin-in-the-Fields (also in Westminster). Elsewhere, at Staverton, near Totnes in Devon, the coffin of Simon Worth (d. 1669) was opened in February 1750 to reveal 'the body of a man entire and uncorrupt; his flesh solid and not hard, his joints flexible as if just dead, his fibres and flesh retained their natural elasticity'. More alarmingly, there was also discovered a poor parish boy who had accidentally been shut in a vault in St Botolph's, Aldgate, in 1665 and was found in 1742 'with the fancied marks of having gnawed his shoulder'. The account goes on to comment that in the Antonian crypt of Kiev, 'There are some sculls lying in dishes, which exude a kind of oil', although Gough is sceptical of any therapeutic properties this fluid may have.[30]

Bloodsucking was itself also a feature of contemporary natural history on the continent. In *The Female Physician* (1730), John Maubray claims that monstrous conceptions were the result of 'impure and unseasonable COPULATION', causing a '*Menstruous Contagion*' of the blood that could lead to venereal disease, elephantiasis and leprosy, as well as monstrous births (most often, it transpired, in Holland):

THAT these BIRTHS in those *Parts*, are often attended and accompany'd with a *Monstrous little Animal*, the likest of any thing in Shape and Size to a MOODIWARP [mole]; having a *hooked Snout, fiery sparkling Eyes*, a long *round Neck*, and an acuminated *short Tail*, of an extraordinary *Agility of FEET*. At first *sight* of the World's Light, it commonly *Yells* and *Shrieks* fearfully; and seeking for a *lurking Hole*, runs up and down like a *little Dæmon*, which indeed I took it for, the first time I saw it, and *that* for none of the *better Sort*.[31]

The author describes delivering such a creature on a voyage to Amsterdam:

upon the *Membran*'s giving way, this forementioned ANIMAL made its wonderful *Egress*; filling my *Ears* with dismal SHRIEKS, and my *Mind* with greater CONSTERNATION . . .

AFTERWARDS I had occasion to talk with some of the most *learned Men*, of the several famous Universities in these *Provinces* upon this Head; who ingenuously told me, that it was so common a Thing, among the *Sea-faring*, and *meaner sort of People*, that scarce ONE of these *Women* in *Three* escaped this kind of strange BIRTH; which my own small *Practice* among them afterwards also confirmed . . . the *Women* in like manner, make a respective suitable *Preparation*, to receive it warmly, and throw it into the *Fire*; holding *Sheets* before the *Chimney*, that it may not get off; as it always endeavours to safe it self, by getting into some *dark Hole* or *Corner*. They properly call it *de Suyger*, which is (in our Language) the SUCKER, because, like a *Leech*, it sucks up the INFANT's *Blood* and *Aliment*.[32]

As was later pointed out in *The Athenæum* (1807) – and with direct reference to the first vampires – there is a striking confluence of cases of bloodsucking in the medical science of the 1730s.[33]

The second coming

While the Plogojowitz case simmered on in the public imagination, two more outbreaks were reported in the Serbian village of Medwegya, near Belgrade.[34] In 1727, a former soldier or *hajduk*, Arnod Paole (variously Arnond, Arnont or Arnold Paul or Paule), returned and settled to farm in

Medwegya, his native village, where he was betrothed to his neighbour's daughter Nina. Regrettably Paole died before they could wed, when a hay cart he was driving overturned; but it transpired that the reason he had left the army and fled home was that he had contracted vampirism, possibly from a Turkish-Serbian *vrykolakas*. Paole had been tormented by the creature and had tried to dispel it by eating earth from the vampire's grave and smearing himself with its blood; but some 40 days after his death (the period varies) he rose and killed four people. Although Paole appeared only at night, he could pass through locked doors and barred windows:

> they exhumed this Arnold Paole forty days after his death and found that he was whole and intact with fresh blood flowing from his eyes, nose, mouth, and ears. His shirt, shroud and coffin were blood soaked. The old nails on his hands and feet had fallen out, and new ones had grown in their place. They could now see that he was really a vampire. When they followed their custom and drove a stake through his heart, he let out a fierce shriek, and blood gushed forth from him. Then on that very day they cremated him and threw his ashes into the grave.[35]

Then the four people he had murdered were dug up and dealt with in the same way.

There things may have rested, but a second wave of attacks followed in 1731, 13 deaths again attributed by locals to 'vambyres'. Graves were once more exhumed and the corpses there were found to be fresh. The authorities sent a medical team to investigate. It was led by an epidemiologist named Glaser (the '*Contagions-Medicus*' or infectious diseases doctor); also present were Johann Flückinger (a military surgeon) and two medical officers, Isaac Siedel and Johann Friedrich Baumgartner.[36] The medical team found that corpses feared to be vampires were being summarily decapitated and cremated:

> The people also assert that all those who have been killed by vampires must in turn become the same thing. For that reason the four people mentioned above were treated in a similar manner. Add to this the fact that this Arnold Paole attacked not only people, but also livestock, and

drained their blood. Since people fed on meat from this livestock, several vampires again appeared among them. In the course of three months seven young and old people passed away, among whom several died without any previous illness in two or at most three days. Heyducke Jehovitza reports that his daughter-in-law Stanicka fifteen days earlier went to bed fresh and healthy. At midnight, however, she started from sleep with a frightful shriek, fear and trembling and complained that Milove, son of the Heyducke, who had died nine weeks earlier, had choked her, whereupon she experienced several chest pains and grew worse from hour to hour until she finally died on the third day.[37]

Vampires discovered included a number of named women (Stanacka, Stana, Miliza, Ruscha, Stanoicka), two *hajduks* (Stancha and Milloe), a servant (Rhade), two teenage boys (Milloe and Joachim), children aged eight and ten, and two women with babies.[38] Flückinger appears to have performed an autopsy on at least one of the corpses – Stana, a woman who had died in childbirth and daubed herself with vampire blood to protect herself. When her corpse was opened up, she was found to be full of fresh blood, with new nails and a new skin growing under the old. The outbreak was virulently contagious: Paole had been unable to protect himself from the initial contamination and had vampirized not only humans, but also sheep. When eaten, they had spread the pestilence further: this was a cross-species condition.

Flückinger wrote a report, in which he also investigated the earlier incidents involving Arnod Paole nearly five years previously.[39] This document was endorsed as '*visum et repertum*' ('manifestation seen and corroborated') and signed by Flückinger, his two colleagues and two officers of the Alexandrian Regiment. His account was received in Belgrade and sent to Vienna, where it was published the same year. It was then republished in *Glaneur Historique* and swept across Europe.[40]

Michael Ranft, a Lutheran pastor who had already published a treatise on grave-eating,[41] described Flückinger's investigation thus:

In the year 1731, vampires disturbed the village of Medvedja. The High Command from Belgrade immediately sent a commission of

German officers and others to the spot. They excavated the whole cemetery and found that there were really vampires there, and all those dead found to be vampires were decapitated by the Gypsies, their bodies cremated and the ashes thrown into the river Morava.[42]

Ranft confirmed that the military commission which oversaw the exhumation and disposal of Paole's corpse noted that he 'had all the marks of an arch-vampire. His body was fresh and ruddy, his hair, beard and nails were grown, and his veins were full of fluid blood.'[43] These were now the hallmarks of the vampire, and it is noteworthy, too, that gypsies (so called) are here enlisted as vampire slayers – a relationship with the undead that continued in later vampire writing, and which often proved ambivalent.[44] For Ranft, it was the psychic force of Paole that constituted his vampirism. But Flückinger also noticed a mark on the neck of Stanoicka, one of Paole's victims: the calling card of the vampire at this stage was not puncture wounds from over-developed incisor or canine teeth, but bruising from strangulation. Stanoicka had just such a contusion on the right side of her neck, under the ear: 'a bloodshot blue mark, the length of a finger'.[45]

Debate on vampires detonated across Europe. Glaser's father, also a physician, immediately wrote to a recently established weekly medical journal with the news that

[a] magical plague has been rampant [in Serbia] for some time. Perfectly normal buried dead are arising from their undisturbed graves to kill the living. These too, dead and buried in their turn, arise in the same way to kill yet more people. This occurs by the following means: the dead attack people by night, while they are asleep, and suck blood out of them, so that on the third day they all die. No cure has yet been found for this evil.[46]

Vampirism made the journal's reputation, and it published 17 articles on the subject in 1732 alone. The news was carried by journals such as the *Wienerisches Diarium*, *Vossische Zeitung*, *Leipziger Zeitung* and the *Breßlauische Sammlungen* to Vienna, Nuremberg, Leipzig, Tübingen, Berlin and other places, and translations of the Flückinger report were later published in Paris and London.[47] Twelve books and four dissertations on vampirism appeared in 1732–33; over the next three years, a further 22 learned treatises were published in European cultural and intellectual centres such as Amsterdam, Halle, Jena, Leipzig and Vienna.[48] Vampires were, in the words of anthropologist Peter Bräunlein, a 'media sensation'.[49] The appetite for sensation was also probably accelerated by early serial killers such as Stephen Hübner of Trutnov, who, in the early 1730s, strangled several victims. Pope Benedict XIV was sceptical, but the British monarch George II believed in vampires. Discussing Giuseppe Balsamo – also known as Count Alessandro di Cagliostro – a contemporary necromancer who claimed to be able to raise and converse with the spirits of the dead, the writer and connoisseur Horace Walpole noted: 'I have been told that Prince Ferdinand himself had faith in him [the imposter Balsamo]. I know that our late King, though not apt to believe more than his Neighbours, had no doubt of the existence of Vampires & their banquets on the dead.'[50]

What did all this mean? In Britain, the news was reported in the *London Journal* for 11 March 1732 as a horror story from 'Heyducken', Hungary: 'namely, of *dead Bodies* sucking, as it were, the Blood of the *Living*; for the *latter* visibly dry up, while the *former* are fill'd with Blood'.[51] This was the country that had weathered civil war and regicide, restoration and rebellion to lead the global economy through free enterprise and colonial exploitation, and so these vampire debates and depictions were conducted in a highly charged political atmosphere. In the overpowering and incendiary context of British party politics, then, it was inevitable that the vampire, too, would be politicized. In the earliest in-depth discussion in Britain of vampirism, a commentator styling himself 'Caleb D'Anvers' introduces the case of Arnod Paole to a fashionable salon. D'Anvers describes how the case provoked a spirited debate between a society lady and a doctor, the lady pointing out the authenticating devices of the piece (names, dates, testimonies) to the sardonic medic. D'Anvers is called on to adjudicate and puts the Paole report into context by pointing out that in Eastern Europe narratives are often allegorical:

> it deserves our Consideration that the States of *Hungary* are, at present, under the Subjection of the *Turks*, or the *Germans*, and govern'd by Them with a pretty hard Rein; which obliges Them to couch all their

Complaints under *Types*, *Figures* and *Parables*. I believe you will make no Doubt that this Relation of the Vampyres is a Piece of that Kind, and contains a secret Satire upon the Administration of *those Countries*, when you consider the following Particulars.

D'Anvers (in reality Nicholas Amhurst, a satirist and political writer for the opposition) goes on to argue that '*sucking out all their Blood*' is a 'common Phrase for a *ravenous Minister* . . . who preys upon human Gore, and fattens Himself upon the Vitals of his Country'; likewise, 'a *plundering Minister*' oppresses from beyond the grave through such practices as continued taxation, obliging remaining citizens to sell or mortgage their property and hence turning them into vampires too.[52]

D'Anvers thus – remarkably – recommends a figurative reading of vampirism. Even in Britain, 'In former Times, the *Gavestons*, *Spencers* and *De la Poles*, *Empson* and *Dudley*, *Wolsey*, *Buckingham* and an Hundred more were *Vampyres* of the first Magnitude, and spread their Cruelties far and wide through this Island.'[53] He sees all usurers, corrupt officials and promoters of the South-Sea Bubble as vampiric. Nor was D'Anvers alone in this: a week later, *Applebee's Journal* reported the case and firmly insisted on evidence, testimony, reason, rationality and experience to 'solve the *Credibility* of Vampyres'.[54]

An equally sceptical response appeared in the digest journal *The Political State of Great Britain*, which reproduced Flückinger's account, as endorsed by Lieutenant Battuer, Captain Gutschitz, Flückinger and three other surgeons, before the anonymous reporter declared his 'great Suspicion'. The reporter compares the Paole affair to the '*Rabbet Woman* in *England*', meaning the infamous Mary Toft. In late 1726, it was reported that she had given birth to several rabbits (as well as miscellaneous body parts of other animals). The episode was held up as a freak of nature – a monstrous birth – caused by her fixation with rabbits and by her favourite cat sleeping on her bed (which had naturally generated sympathetic embryos in her womb). The authenticity of these births – corroborated by apparently dependable witnesses – immediately split the medical world; when the affair was exposed as a hoax, it made a mockery of contemporary obstetrics.[55] Now once again, doubt was being cast on the reliability of expert testimony.

The following year, 1733, in an open letter to Prime Minister Robert Walpole, the political pamphleteer Charles Forman depicted government tax revenue as a device 'to indulge the Luxury, and gratify the Rapine of a fat-gutted *Vampire*'.[56] Forman returned to the image in another open letter to Walpole (written in the same year but not published until 1741), seeing the country being bled dry by foreign trading enterprises, primarily the Dutch East India Company:

> Our Merchants, indeed, bring Money into their Country, but, it is said, there is another Set of Men amongst us who have as great an Address in sending it out again to foreign Countries without any Returns for it, which defeats the Industry of the Merchant. These are the *Vampires* of the Publick, and Riflers of the Kingdom.[57]

Vampire imagery became common: Charles Hornby makes a passing reference to vampires in 1738 when he criticizes an error of fact committed by William Dugdale in his book *Baronage of England*: 'is it not very miraculous, that his Disappointment should make him as blood-thirsty as a *Vampire*, and that after about ten Years he should steal out of his Grave, with a malicious Design to commit Murder?'[58] Meanwhile, the poet and political satirist Alexander Pope adopts the outsider guise of the vampire in a letter of 1740, in which he sardonically claims to have died:

> Since his burial . . . he has been seen sometimes in mines and caverns and been very troublesome to those who dig marbles and minerals. If ever he has walked above ground he has been (like the Vampires in Germany) such a terror to all sober and innocent people that many wish a stake were drove thro' him to keep him quiet in his grave.[59]

Among the first to analyse outbreaks of vampirism on the borders of the Habsburg Empire, then, were political commentators who saw in these accounts allegories of imperial oppression, martial law, border control and the creation of buffer states, as well as tensions arising from the management of colonized peoples by centralized government.[60] Thus, vampires were not only to be found in politics; they also – consistent with Paole and those who investigated him – served in the military. Oliver Goldsmith included a Major Vampyre (alongside a Colonel Leech) in his orientalist satire on British society and values, *The Citizen of the World* (1762). He also placed vampires in the judiciary:

> it is said of the Hyena that naturally it is in no way ravenous, but once it has tasted human flesh, it becomes the most voracious animal of the forest, and continues to persecute mankind ever after: A corrupt magistrate may be considered as a human Hyena, he begins perhaps by a private snap, he goes on to a morsel among friends, he proceeds to a meal in public, from a meal he advances to a surfeit, and at last sucks blood like a vampire.[61]

Vampires were everywhere: in 1750 Henry Fielding irresistibly condemned literary critics as '*Vampyres, being dead and damn'd*' who '*with the Blood of living Bards are cramm'd*', while the very next year the earl of Sandwich mordantly christened a bay gelding racehorse 'Vampire'.[62] Although vampires were by now increasingly recognized as able to rise from the dead and infiltrate dwelling places, as murderous stranglers and bloodsuckers, as incorruptible corpses responsible for the spread of epidemic disease, as embodiments of fears of medicine and anatomical science, as allegories of East European politics and metaphors for the oppressive practices of commerce and the armed forces, and as impervious to most forms of physical assault except decapitation, staking and cremation, it is unlikely that Sandwich had any of these things in mind. For him, the name was contemporary, modish, edgy and alluringly dangerous. The earl was ahead of his time.

CHAPTER 2

THE LANDS OF BLOOD
Place and Race, Territory and Travel

He was eaten of worms, and gave up the ghost.

Acts 12:23 (1611)

'Tis now the very witching time of night,
When churchyards yawn, and hell itself breathes out
Contagion to this world. Now could I drink hot blood,
And do such bitter business as the day
Would quake to look on.

William Shakespeare (1600)[1]

They are drunken, but not with wine.

Isaiah 29:9 (1611)

The political vampire that emerged in Britain has famously been read as embodying a fear of the victims of colonialism biting back. This has memorably been dubbed 'reverse colonization'. It has inspired much critical debate and painstaking scholarship, which has argued that vampires – along with denizens of the criminal underworld, mad scientists, the 'Yellow Peril' of the demonized Orient, ancient Egyptian mummies and even interplanetary aliens – represent the empire (or rather, imperial subjects) striking back.[2]

However, the territorial facets of vampirism in fact reflect the ordeals of the immediate regions in which they occurred, rather than symbolizing a generalized colonial guilt that can be applied to various other political circumstances and national institutions, and so they are variously attributed to the mass trauma of occupation by a foreign power, local dietary deficiencies, grass-roots fundamentalist religious radicalization and communal hallucination. And in any case, with regard to later British literature the metaphor seems stretched. Certainly, novels such as H. Rider Haggard's *She* (1887) and even Joseph Conrad's *Heart of Darkness* (1899) so sensationalize the United Kingdom's colonial adventure as struggles with mysterious forces or malign psychologies that they may be considered examples of 'imperial Gothic'; but at least in part this is because Britain had serious territorial interests in Africa.[3] Yet the country had very few direct concerns in Eastern Europe, home of the vampire.[4] And vampires in any case already come with their own history of imperial Habsburg geopolitics and Ottoman exoticism. While it is certainly 'imperial', vampire territory can hardly be identified with Britain – as early commentators, such as Nicholas Amhurst, are careful to point out.

Moreover, territorial issues and their bearing on outbreaks of vampirism were not simply coloured by attitudes to insularity and the uncanniness of remote places; they also constituted another dimension in the advance of medical science into peripheral communities. The relationship of vampires with the land was – as for those very communities – literally disturbing: they emerged from beneath the ground to terrorize edgelands; their grave-earth was believed to be a protection against contracting vampirism (one actually had to eat the contaminated soil); and they appeared to be able to move from one world to the next. And so the prevalent image of blood in vampire reports not only encompasses notions of circulation, but could also be understood as irrigating the land – seeping into the mud. And in doing so, it bonds identity to place and heritage. It is no coincidence, then, that when Dracula voyages to Whitby, he does so with 50 coffin-sized crates of fine Transylvanian loam. But he travels not as an oppressed colonial son intent on avenging himself on the mother country, but as the dark quintessence of the horrors of modernity, cold-bloodedly extinguishing the radiance of everyday life.

The undead body politic

The language of predation and exploitation, bloodsucking and cannibalism, runs through religion and politics like a dark stain. In England especially, this marks both sides of the Reformation and Protestant debate, linking vampires to religious crisis and conflict. Abbot Thomas Marshall had, on the one hand, condemned the executioners of Bishop John Fisher and Sir Thomas More as 'wretched tyrants and bloodsuckers', and considered Fisher and More to be Catholic martyrs and saints for defending the authority of the pope. By contrast, the notorious Puritan Philip Stubbes prefaced the 1583 edition of John Foxe's *Book of Martyrs* with the Latin words '*In sanguisugas Papistas*', pillorying the 'Papist Bloodsuckers'.[5] This imagery was part of a much larger concept: the body politic. Since ancient times, the nation and its institutions had been described in terms of the human anatomy; but it was the philosopher Thomas Hobbes who influentially revived the image in 1651, by famously depicting constitutional power as the *Leviathan*, a gigantic human figure.[6] This figure of the political colossus continued well into the eighteenth century as a shorthand model for the body politic in both statutory discourse and satires on the government. As the contemporary radical philosopher Eugene Thacker points out, 'the body politic is a way of thinking about politics as a living, vital order'.[7]

Portraying politics as embodied and alive offered a profusion of connected ideas that could extend this metaphor: bodies – political bodies – could be in good health, or they could become infected and sick. As Henry Sacheverell suggested in *The Political Union* (1702), combining politics, faith and pathology, 'Heresy and Schism have such a Natural Communication with Rebellion and Usurpation, that where the *Ecclesiastical Body* is Infested with the One, the *Body Politick*, is seldom found Free from the Other Plague.'[8] The integrity of the nation could thus be menaced by pestilence and parasites – 'diseases' of the 'body politic' such as 'Civil war, strife, rebellion, dissent, factionalism, mob rule'.[9]

What is more, the understanding of the body itself gives meaning to the image of the body politic. As the natural sciences of the seventeenth and eighteenth centuries increasingly medicalized the human body by focusing on its corporeality, so the metaphor and anatomy of the body politic changed, too. This is how vampires became assimilated into political discourse. They already stood accused of posing a literal threat to a tangible body, both by bringing plague and by removing lifeblood; but now they also endangered the metaphorical political body. This mix of medicine and politics gave the vampire a contemporary resonance. What is telling about the influence of the vampire in this thinking is that, as Thacker suggests more generally, 'the lines between the supernatural and the natural, miracle and exception, theology and medicine, are not always clearly demarcated'.[10] This pathological ontology consequently means that references to, for example, epidemic contagion may be understood not only medically and biologically, but also theologically and politically, simultaneously endangering personal health, spiritual wellbeing and social stability.[11] From the outset, then, vampirology in the period exposed the entangled operations of the life sciences within power politics and institutionalized religion.

The political import of the inaugural outbreaks of vampirism was recognized both at the time and in subsequent commentary. Vampires were, in other words, perceived as both a symptom and a cause of an ailing or traumatized body politic. The 1718 Treaty of Passarowitz had transferred the Banat of Temesvár, Lesser Wallachia (Moldavia), Belgrade and the territories of northern Serbia from the Ottomans to the Habsburg Empire, whose territory now extended as far as it ever would.[12] These areas were effectively a buffer zone between the two empires. They had highly mixed populations and pluralistic cultures, and they now became pawns in the game of international relations.[13] Moreover, the imposition of a military border enforced an authoritarian and foreign imperial regime, which inevitably circumscribed local freedoms and rights. The outbreaks of vampirism were, in other words, a bizarre side-effect of the Habsburg occupation and a consequence of the establishment of martial law. Indeed, the Imperial Army was a key player in the occurrences of vampirism, being deployed both to calm (or police, or suppress) regional peoples and to gather evidence of fatalities and the precautionary measures implemented by communities. In a sense, vampires signalled that the very ground was rising in an act of weird resistance: they embodied the will of the populace against the unnatural subjugation by the Habsburg powers.[14] It was thus in these newly seized edgelands that the dead rose and preyed upon the living.[15]

Vampirarchy

After the first two waves of vampire outbreaks, attention increasingly focused on the pathology of vampirism. Symptoms were well attested:

> Shivering, enduring nausea, pain in the stomach and intestines, in the kidney region and in the back and shoulder blades as well as the back of the head, further, a clouding of the eyes, deafness and speech problems. The tongue has a whitish-yellow to brownish-red coating, and dries out to the accompaniment of unquenchable thirst. The pulse is erratic (*caprinus*) and weak (*parvus*); on the throat and in the hypochondria, that is to say, in the area of the belly (*abdomen*) beneath the chest cartilage, livid or reddish spots (*maculae rubicundae vel lividae*) are to be seen, though in part only after death. The paroxysm exhibits itself in extreme night terrors, associated with a loud cry, strong trembling, a spasmodic contraction of the muscles of the upper body (*thorax*), a constriction of the airway and hot flushes; with the additional symptom of constriction of the heart (*praecordium angusta*), that is, a sensation of anxiety in the hollow of the breast, associated with pain in the mouth of the stomach; lastly nightmares (*incubus*), which frequently evoke the image of the returning dead.[16]

Such detailed evidence led the Lutheran philosopher Johann Heinrich Zopf, director of the *Gymnasium* (Academy) of Essen, to declare his belief in the existence of vampires. He observed in his *Dissertatio de Vampyris Serviensibus* (1733) that:

> Vampires issue forth from their graves in the night, attack people sleeping quietly in their beds, suck out all their blood from their bodies

and destroy them. They beset men, women and children alike, sparing neither age nor sex. Those who are under the fatal malignity of their influence complain of suffocation and a total deficiency of spirits, after which they soon expire. Some who, when at the point of death, have been asked if they can tell what is causing their decease, reply that such and such persons, lately dead, have risen from the tomb to torment and torture them.[17]

Zopf's account, like the Flückinger report, was widely disseminated, reaching Britain in a travelogue of 1734, thus: '*Vampyres* are supposed to be the Bodies of deceased Persons, animated by evil Spirits, which come out of the Graves, in the Night-time, suck the Blood of many of the Living, and thereby destroy them.'[18]

However, in the same year that Zopf published his proofs of vampirism, Johann Christoph Harenberg linked vampire outbreaks to the effects of drugs, in particular to opium and *datura stramonium*, a New World plant that had been introduced to the Old World and which had rapidly spread through the countryside as a weed – another example of infestation.[19] Although by the next century its use in Hungary was common as a narcotic and a cure for leprosy, heavy doses of datura could bring on mind-boggling deliria.[20] Its effects on soldiers in Virginia were described by Robert Beverley in 1722:

The *James* Town Weed (which resembles the thorny Apple of *Peru*, and I take to be the Plant so call'd) is supposed to be one of the greatest Coolers in the World. This being an early Plant, was gather'd very young for a boil'd Salad, by some of the Soldiers sent thither, to quell the Rebellion of *Bacon*; and some of them eat plentifully of it, the Effect of which was a very pleasant Comedy; for they turn'd natural Fools upon it for several Days: One would blow up a Feather in the Air; another would dart Straws at it with much Fury; and another stark naked was sitting up in a Corner, like a Monkey, grinning and making Mows [grimaces] at them; a Fourth would fondly kiss, and paw his Companions, and snear in their Faces, with a Countenance more antick, than any in a *Dutch* Droll. In this frantick Condition they were confined, lest they should in their Folly destroy themselves; though it was observed, that all their Actions were full of Innocence and good Nature. Indeed they were not very cleanly; for they would have wallow'd in their own excrements, if they had not been prevented. A thousand such simple Tricks they play'd, and after eleven Days, return'd to themselves again, not remembering any thing that had pass'd.[21]

Datura is technically not a hallucinogenic, but a deliriant that produces comprehensive delusions indistinguishable from reality, in particular intense paranoia in which whispers and evil laughter are heard, and hostile shapes seen.[22]

This relationship between ingestion and the powers of the imagination was fascinating to contemporaries. Gottlob Heinrich Vogt similarly attributed vampirism to the effects of poison on the brain, while 'Putoneus' (Johann Christoph Meinig) and Johann Christian Fritsch (who published anonymously) thought that it was the result of eating meat from infected livestock – reverting to one of the key features of the Paole case. More prosaically, the Dutch paper *Glaneur Historique* proposed that the belief in vampires simply resulted from a poor diet: if people 'eat nothing but bread made of oats, roots, or the bark of trees' it will raise 'gloomy and disagreeable ideas in the imagination'.[23] Such thinking was again predicated on the inscrutable potency of blood: drug use or certain eating habits caused 'a stagnation of the Blood', which brought on nightmares ('the Incubus') – and that accounted for vampire delusions.[24]

Some theories were literally more grounded. Jean-Baptiste de Boyer, marquis d'Argens, argued that what appeared to be blood in a vampire was in fact nitrous traces in the earth reacting with decomposing bodily fluids that had been warmed by the sun, and even in the previous century there had been evidence of abnormal decomposition being noted in areas that were later associated with vampire activity.[25] Other explanations were more occult. In 1734, the Lutheran pastor Michael Ranft postulated that although many instances of grave-eating and post-mortem manducation could be put down to vermin infiltrating coffins, corpses nevertheless retained *vis vegetans*; that is, dead bodies maintained a level of consciousness, which accounted for phenomena such as crudentation.[26] This ancient esoteric notion linked vampirism to the Aristotelian hierarchy of the three souls (vegetal, animal and human), the ethereal spirit and, again, the 'power of human Phantasy'.[27] For Ranft, the human imagination could survive death and continue to exert its will over physical entities until the original body finally disappeared into dust.

There were also fresh cases to fuel speculation. The next incident (often overlooked) was in Croatia.[28] In August 1737, the island of Lastovo was struck by a severe outbreak of dysentery, and the sickness was blamed on a vampire. The case is intriguing, as it again suggests the terrors posed by debilitating diseases that could strike suddenly and rapidly lead to death. Corpses were duly exhumed, and those that were bloated with blood (and therefore proven to be vampires) were impaled, decapitated and hamstrung; in addition, two corpses were mutilated with knives, one of them being dismembered. A series of depositions was duly made to the archbishop of Dubrovnik, beginning on 14 October 1737, and on 3 December 1737 the priest Dom Marin Pavlović reported that 'Some say that illness comes when a person catches a chill, others that the air is infected with the plague, others that it is God's punishment, and others that vampires (kosci) cause it.'[29]

This scapegoating of vampires was widespread, and led to a mass desecration of graves in response to the incident. Meanwhile, several people confessed to having carried out earlier post-mortem impalements. Eventually, some 18 islanders were charged with violating the dead in their search for vampires, 'which without any basis they accuse of spreading virulent infectious diseases among the people'.[30] The archbishop gave his verdict on 30 June 1738. He was singularly unimpressed and ordered that those indicted should do penance by having a stone hung around their necks and attending mass in three churches; they were required to make this pilgrimage on the first Sunday in Lent for the next three years (or seven years in the case of the 12 worst offenders). They were also each fined 14 ducats and risked excommunication if they did not comply.[31] It was a belated attempt by the Church to reassert its authority over an endemic lawlessness that was so impious as to be almost pagan.

Meanwhile in Britain, the translation of the marquis d'Argens' work from the French returned attention to the Plogojowitz case. D'Argens described how Plogojowitz had reappeared three days after his death, upon which villagers recounted that they had dreamt he was sucking their blood from their throats; they subsequently fell ill and died. There were further tantalizing details: Plogojowitz's coffin had filled with blood when he was staked, and other corpses in the graveyard had then been protected with garlic and whitethorn – details that would be enthusiastically taken up by later writers.[32]

Neither was this a backwoods phenomenon: in Vienna, rumours abounded that Princess Eleonore von Schwarzenberg (1682–1741) had risen as a vampire following her death. At the same time, stories spread across Paris in 1750 that Louis XV had kidnapped children and stolen their blood, in order to cure either his leprosy or that of his daughter, leading to riots in which at least 20 people died.[33] Leprous princes were not uncommon in France: three centuries previously, Louis XI had allegedly drunk infants' blood for the same reason.[34] Both provincial peasantry and blue-blooded aristocracy could be vampirized.

The vampire rage had taken hold, and further outbreaks followed in Banat, Moravia and Wallachia in the years 1754–56. For instance, in Hermersdorf (a village near the Silesian–Moravian border) a vampire was believed to be attacking villagers. The body of a recently deceased woman, one Rosina Polakin, was exhumed and found to have fresh blood in its veins; her remaining family members were then obliged to drag the corpse by a hook through a hole in the wall of the churchyard, after which she was duly decapitated and cremated. The authorities again responded actively. The Holy Roman Empress Maria Theresa (last of the Habsburgs) sent two doctors, Johannes Gasser and Christian Vabst, to investigate and report back to Gerard van Swieten.[35] Van Swieten (1700–72) was 'one of the most powerful advisers to the Empress', as well as being her personal physician; he was also head surgeon of the military, had recently been made director of the Vienna teaching clinic (1753), and went on to reform Vienna university and instigate social welfare policies.[36] He was a paragon of rationality who, in 1755, guided Maria Theresa to decree that those suspected of vampirism and supernatural crimes should not be customarily executed; he also recommended that books on demonology and witchcraft should be banned.

Van Swieten's treatise on vampires followed this investigation. Written in French as *Remarques sur le Vampyrisme de Sylésie de l'an 1755, faites à S. M. I. et R.* (1755), the book was translated into German the following year and reprinted in 1768.[37] In it, van Swieten makes a vigorous attempt to categorize vampirism as a mass delusion, rather than a physical condition. He dismisses the language of superstition and proposes a core–periphery social model of internal colonialism, in which it is the role of the enlightened centre (Vienna) to tame and civilize the irrational and barbaric periphery: in other words, geopolitics was both the cause of and the solution to the problem. Van Swieten's tone in this treatise is hence one of reasonable Christian piety (acknowledging God, miracles and also the Devil's wiles), while admitting that there were natural scientific explanations for electricity and similar marvels. He describes the Polakin case and earlier incidents, and argues that there are chemical reasons for the non-decomposition of corpses and rational causes of nightmares – such as ignorant credulity and the appetite for fairy tales. Like Karl Ferdinand Schertz (author of *Magia Posthuma*) before him, van Swieten also points out that the desecration of graves is illegal and sacrilegious, adopting a legal position that left the methods of counter-vampirism outside the law.[38] Van Swieten subsequently wrote a *Mémoire* on witchcraft (1758) that examined the case of the Croatian witch Magdalene Heruczina (Lodomer), who had been tortured to obtain a confession; van Swieten had himself treated the unfortunate woman, and he again dismissed the charges.

The upshot of van Swieten's rationalist attention to magic was that the empress decreed on 1 March 1755 that vampires were figments of the imagination: official investigations had uncovered nothing supernatural. Cases of alleged vampirism were accordingly removed from the jurisdiction of both religious orders and regional government.[39] Following further decrees, the courts also began to throw out cases of supposed witchcraft. The empress outlawed practices inspired by supernatural beliefs, such as witch-hunting and customary ways of combating *magia posthuma*, and eventually witch-persecution was explicitly made illegal in 1766. Witches were effectively protected by being made to disappear in the eyes of the law; vampires, too, became imperceptible, though their ambiguous legal status would haunt later tales. Konstantin Franz von Cauz, author of *De*

Cultibus Magicus (1767), commended both the empress and van Swieten for their campaign against superstition.[40] István Weszprémi concurred a decade later, in 1778, commenting that:

> The imaginary illness, due to perverted fantasy, was at last analysed marvellously by the immortal van Swieten in his treatise on Vampires, published in Vienna in 1755. By dint of wise advice he managed to convince the queen to chase this illness from the mind of the uneducated and superstitious people, so since that time such absurdities cannot be heard about within the territories of our country.[41]

More generally, these attempts to 'medicalize and explain' the supernatural, such as the miraculous cures at Lourdes, were, according to Erik Midelfort, 'part of a doctrinaire positivist campaign to take the Catholic Church out of French politics and the spirit out of the world in general'.[42] The Church, of course, responded with more miraculous and better-documented cases – once again pitting rationalism against personal experience and testimony. According to historian of the supernatural Gábor Klaniczay, Maria Theresa's decree is 'an early manifestation of so-called enlightened absolutism'.[43] Although such thinking had clearly been developing for decades, it was not until the empress's interventions that it formally made it onto the statute books. Klaniczay attributes van Swieten's rationalist disbelief to his Dutch education (despite his Catholicism), the Netherlands having the smallest number of witch trials in Europe – the last occurring as early as 1603. Whatever the case, vampires continued to provide doctors with a 'new and exciting riddle' that could be scrutinized using the latest epistemological and forensic scientific methods focused on rates of decomposition and the fluid states of blood.[44]

Remarques sur les Vampyrisme was followed in 1756 by a work by the Hungarian doctor Georg Tallar.[45] A regimental surgeon, Tallar focused on possible alternative causes of straightforward vampirism. He noted that, critically, the condition of vampirism did not affect German settlers or the military, but was confined to Orthodox Wallachians; and so it was evidently not an epidemic disease.[46] He then examined the customary diet of the Wallachians – their winter fast, their subsistence on a broth of cabbage and pumpkin, and their proclivity to drink brandy – and concluded that their meagre diet and fasting made them prone to anaemia. This built on earlier theories linking food to nightmares. Tallar prescribed bloodletting and emetics, as well as an end to fasting; and although these were conventional Galenic therapies, Tallar was again using medical understanding as a way of consolidating and enforcing the established imperial rule. Costantino Grimaldi likewise attributed the vampire plague to nightmares brought on by 'dietary etiopathogenesis': hoppy beer, heavy bread, peas, fava beans and pork.[47] As the German vampirologist Klaus Hamberger has remarked, 'Therapy was here understood as practical Enlightenment; the disciplining of the body had its converse in the education of the imagination to a "cognizance [knowledge] of the body".'[48] In other words, vampires arose in part through rationalist medicine challenging customary physiological thinking by locating notions of identity, especially political, regional and religious identity, in the flesh and blood of the community, in regional food and drink, and in the shared convictions of provincial imagination. That is one reason why they appeared at imperial borders as an expression of resistance by subjugated native citizens.

It also appeared that the Orthodox Church had been actively fostering the vampire belief among communities as a way of enforcing their faith: exhumations, decapitation and staking had been overseen by Orthodox priests, and the Bishops' Consistory itself had been authorizing exhumation and cremation since 1731. Hence the rebuttal of vampirism was an assertion of Holy Roman Catholicism.[49] But the Protestant German response sardonically linked vampires to Catholic superstition, the Royal Prussian Academy of Sciences (*Königlich-Preußische Akademie der Wissenschaften*) declaring that 'It is certain that the Apparition of these blood-suckers, and the account of their substance, is not demonstrated [in the report], and we have no traces thereof in history, in our own, or in other Protestant lands, ever.'[50] Thus, aside from vampire thinking entailing both 'a medicalisation of colonial policy . . . [and] a militarisation of medicine', the cultural critic Erik Butler has proposed that the vampire represented 'a crisis within Christendom' involving Eastern Orthodoxy, Roman Catholicism and Protestantism in the areas of the supernatural, the afterlife and the symbolism of blood.[51] One could add that the exercise of spiritual rule was consistently conducted through legal channels, further complicating the condition of the vampire.

Red ill-being

Vampirism was indeed indelible in these lands, which were already drenched with gore. Among the more alarming regional history were tales of the fifteenth-century Wallachian warlord Vlad Țepeș, who allegedly tortured and executed tens of thousands of people. He would supposedly roast children and feed them to their mothers, and force husbands to devour their wives. Finally, he would impale all his victims.[52] Vampire legends fed on such stories and later became a staple of travel narratives describing Central and Eastern Europe; they also carried a dark echo of the ancient Scythian and Gothic races who were believed to have settled in these lands, and whose mysterious culture provided an eerie alternative to the classical civilizations of Greece and Rome. Alberto Fortis, for example, described the Morlacchi people (Morlachs) in *Travels into Dalmatia* (1774), observing that:

> They are firmly perswaded of the reality of witches, fairies, enchantments, nocturnal apparitions and sortileges, as if they had seen a thousand examples of them. Nor do they make the least doubt about the existence of Vampires; and attribute to them, as in Transylvania, the sucking of the blood of infants. Therefore when a man dies suspected of becoming a vampire, or *Vukodlak*, as they call it, they cut his hams [hamstrings], and prick his whole body with pins; pretending, that after this operation, he cannot walk about. There are even instances of Morlacchi, who imagining that they may possibly thirst for children's blood after death, intreat their heirs, and sometimes oblige them to promise to treat them as vampires when they die.[53]

Fortis's account was reprinted many times. It seems little had changed when, a generation later, Joseph Lavallée edited the travelogue of the artist and antiquary Louis-François Cassas. Equally influential, Cassas also dwelt on the Morlachs' superstitions and their belief in ghosts, witchcraft, sorcery, enchantments, talismans and amulets of protection:

The wretched people add to such torments of the imagination the folly of believing in the existence of hobgoblins; and the precautions which they take on the death of a man, whom they suspect to be under the influence of those spirits, are truly extravagant. Before the funeral, they cut the hamstrings of the corpse, and mark certain characters upon the body, with a hot iron; they then drive nails or pins into different parts of it, and the sorcerers finish the ceremony, by repeating certain mysterious words; after which, they rest confident, that the deceased cannot return to the earth, to shed the blood of the living. Some of them pretend to have the presentiment, that they shall become hobgoblins after their death, and decree, by their will, that their bodies shall be submitted to this species of purification.[54]

Likewise, Inigo Born's *Travels through the Bannat of Temeswar, Transylvania, and Hungary* (1777) described the death rites of Banat:

Their funerals are singular. The corpse is with dismal shrieks brought to the tomb, in which it is sunk down as soon as the Pope has done with his ritual. At this moment the friends and relations of the deceased raise horrid cries. They remind the deceased of his friends, parents, cattle, house and household, and ask for what reason he left them. As no answer ensues, the grave is filled up, and a wooden cross, with a large stone placed at the head, to avoid the dead of becoming a *vampyr*, or a strolling nocturnal bloodsucker. Wine is thrown upon the grave, and frankincense burnt around it, to drive away evil spirits and witches.[55]

Originally a borderline 'undead' phenomenon, the vampire becomes increasingly accommodated through the century.[56]

Vampires are an uncanny double of regional national identity and belonging: the unspeakable, indefinable other.[57] They emerge at borders, symbolically blurring national frontiers by obscuring the boundaries of life and death.[58] But rather than representing a 'reverse colonialism', vampires are better described as exemplifying a 'transverse' colonialism, seizing territory from an oblique direction. They do not come from afar, from outside imperial borders; at most they are merely from the periphery and are already European, already incorporated. Rather, vampires rose both physically and geopolitically from beneath the ground; theologically from beyond the grave; and biologically from after death. As such, they do not simply present the remote and exotic as racially different and thereby monstrous, or threaten the body politic simply as a 'figurative or literal disease'; instead, by mobilizing the idea of the other as a wild and predatory species, they imperil the state through 'multiplicity'.[59] In other words, the vampire is not a unique or singular monstrous being, but a condition that proliferates. Through circulation, oozing and passing, vampirism spreads and flows: it is a multiplicity, an *array*, a contagion.[60] This is another way of thinking about the super-mobility of vampires: vampires are manifestations of metaphobia: they personify the fear of moving beyond what is familiar – into the afterwards or the beyond; and they incarnate a fear of the unknown.[61] It is not that vampires exist on boundaries and borderlines and are therefore defined by this liminality – whether geographical, biological or supernatural; rather, their nature is to confound these limitations. Vampires are not both dead and alive; they are also undead. And so they disturb the primacy of animated life and humanity by replacing the fundamental distinction of life and death with a third state of being (or rather, *un*being). By being so bloody tangible, so to speak, they throw the whole 'biological domain' into crisis.[62]

But that is not all. Vampires also proved to be profoundly disruptive in theology and philosophy. They were a real problem, and the epistemological dilemmas they presented went far beyond the usual conflicts between new science and traditional Christianity. It is this extraordinary capacity to disrupt thinking that has guaranteed their longevity – indeed, for some, their immortality. The question of whether the human body is purely matter, or instead has some sort of indissoluble 'supernatural reality' or spectrality, has provoked intellectual and spiritual debate for centuries. The ways in which vampirism recast this thinking is assessed in the next two chapters.[63] This unnerving ubiquity of the vampire begins to explain their fascination for later writers: once they are let in, they dye – everything.

CHAPTER 3

GHOSTLY THEOLOGY
Rational Religion, Spiritual Reason

It will have blood, they say. Blood will have blood.
Stones have been known to move, and trees to speak,
Augurs and understood relations have
By maggot-pies and choughs and rooks brought forth
The secret'st man of blood.

William Shakespeare (1606)[1]

I am a little world made cunningly
Of elements, and an angelic sprite.

John Donne (1609)[2]

As a god self-slain on his own strange altar,
    Death lies dead.

Algernon Charles Swinburne (1876)[3]

The insistently scientific approaches of imperial physicians such as Johann Flückinger, Gerard van Swieten and Georg Tallar endeavoured to separate the perception of vampires from the tangled definitions of supernatural folklore and to explain the phenomenon rationally as the cause-and-effect consequences of social problems such as dietary deficiencies, collective trauma, drug use or outbreaks of infectious disease. But the Church also took a keen interest in the eighteenth-century vampire plague, drawing on both proverbial wisdom and eerie folklore, as well as the new empirical evidence. For Catholic scholars, vampires were (like ghosts) evidence of the afterlife and (like miracles) proof of the supernatural. But they were also less elusive than ghosts and clearly malevolent – suggesting that they might instead be diabolical illusions. Enlightenment thinkers such as the French *philosophes*, too, found food for thought in epistemology, the laws of nature, the reliability of evidence and the nature of the human condition, and thinkers such as Voltaire, Diderot and Rousseau all wrote on the subject. As the following chapters will show, vampires were a hot topic of debate in the mid-eighteenth century.

Others, however, were more suspicious of what they perceived to be a cocktail of Catholic and Orthodox superstitions, and while Protestant theologians from Neoplatonist mystics to Methodist preachers pondered the significance of spirits and ghosts, they were not drawn directly into the vampire debate. Ghost stories were highly popular in both the pulpit and the press, helping to inspire the 'Graveyard School' of poetry of the mid-century and eventually paving the way for what was to become known as the 'Gothic novel'. These 'apparition narratives' anchored the metaphysical in human experience and both personal and communal testimony, and thereby challenged the down-to-earth mechanistic and materialist thinking that insisted there could be no supernatural dimension to life (or, indeed, death).[4] As such, this thinking would have long-term – if indirect – effects on the reception and depiction of the vampire in the next century.

Rising dead

At the heart of vampire theology was the condition of the undead. Scripture is haunted by the risen dead: Jesus performs resurrections, is Himself resurrected and also promises the resurrection of all at the end of days – indeed the whole notion of the afterlife is predicated on death being a mysterious threshold rather than extinction. In the Old Testament, Saul beseeches the Witch of Endor to raise the ghost of the Prophet Samuel, in order to benefit from his guidance. She does so, but the posthumous Samuel coolly prophesies the imminent death of Saul, his sons and his entire army at the forthcoming battle against the Philistines; he then swiftly dematerializes.[5] In the New Testament, Jesus restores Jairus's 12-year-old daughter to life, and famously raises Lazarus of Bethany, the brother of Mary and Martha, who has lain in the grave for four days.[6] The appearance of the resurrected Lazarus is certainly striking – 'he that was dead came forth, bound hand and foot with graveclothes'[7] – though more awe-inspiring is the climax of the Revelation of St John the Divine:

> the sea gave up the dead which were in it; and death and hell delivered up the dead which were in them . . . And death and hell were cast into the lake of fire . . . And whosoever was not found written in the book of life was cast into the lake of fire.[8]

All of this mortal matter gave clergymen and philosophers much to muse on and work with.[9]

According to Catholic belief, ghosts could return to confess their sins on earth, in order to expedite their progress through Purgatory; thus there was often a moral import to sightings and hauntings, with ghosts habitually exposing injustices, announcing crimes, and revealing and punishing wrongdoers.[10] In 1585, Archbishop Sandys had confidently declared that 'the gospel hath chased away walking spirits'; but the dead – as ever – refused to remain in the grave.[11] Despite the spiritual watershed of the Reformation, all manner of witcheries and demonic possession escalated in the sixteenth and seventeenth centuries, and this ensured that ghosts in particular remained a central aspect of theological debate and a defining characteristic of sectarian faith. This contemporary hauntology covered the abstruse conjectures of Pneumatology (theories of the Holy Ghost) to prompt appraisals of contemporary sightings of itinerant apparitions.[12] Moreover, a belief in ghosts did not, as Sandys clearly hoped, distinguish Protestants from Catholics, but fractured Protestantism itself for centuries. Protestantism, less obsessed than Catholicism with the materiality of the body, gave serious credence to ghost stories, as they could be construed as part of a revelatory and natural religion. In particular, Henry More and Joseph Glanvill analysed the relevance of ghosts for empirical philosophy, and there remained a popular appetite for supernatural incidents in cheap broadside ballads and news books, and on the stage – which the clergy ignored at their peril. And if by the eighteenth century such supernatural activities as witchcraft and possession looked like decidedly old-fashioned superstitions, vampirism in effect stimulated a renaissance of these black arts and demonology in a new and empirical context.[13]

As the cultural historian Sasha Handley has argued, for Britain 'The years 1660–1700 saw ghost beliefs and ghost stories elevated to public prominence thanks to their congruence with the religious, political, intellectual and social imperatives that followed Charles II's return to the throne.'[14] Ghosts were in one sense a response to the cataclysms of recent history, from the Reformation to the Civil Wars: they embodied haunting memories of the nation's violent past that had forged the present and established modern constitutional rights – they were at the very heart of national history and remembrance that would come to typify the 'Gothic'. These ghosts, then, were deeply entangled in religious and political controversy, and in the state of the nation.

Among the first and most influential of the theologians of the seventeenth century to investigate ghosts was Henry More, the leader of the 'Cambridge Platonists', an early Cartesian, fellow of the Royal Society, and a pioneering broad-church latitudinarian. More was an early advocate of the methods and arguments of rational scientific inquiry, using hard evidence to prove the existence of the Christian God. In *An Antidote Against Atheism* (1655), he tests his methods on two cases presented by Martinus Weinrichius, a Silesian physician and philosopher, and these cases can – in retrospect – be seen as forerunners of the vampire debate, and indeed exhibit several features that were to become familiar.

Case one is that of a shoemaker of Silesia who committed suicide in 1591. The crime was hushed up and he was buried, but a '*Spectrum* in the exact shape and habit of the deceased' appeared.[15] Although this undead being could not appear in direct sunlight, it could nevertheless manhandle and stifle the living, and was reputed to have powers of shape-shifting – variously appearing as a hen, dog, cat, goat and a woman. The cobbler's corpse was exhumed eight months after being buried and was found to be still fresh. After an unsuccessful attempt to rebury it at the gallows, the body was exhumed a second time and dismembered, decoronated (had its heart removed) and cremated; the ashes were scattered in a river.

Case two is that of Johannes Cuntius, another Silesian, who was fatally trampled by horses.[16] A black cat appeared at his deathbed and a tempest raged from the moment he died until he was interred. He then rose as a '*Spiritus incubus* or *Ephialtes*' – again a violent and aggressive spectre: noisy (in manducation) and malodorous, frequently attacking citizens by breathing fire on them, biting and tearing at their throats, his unearthly presence heralded by candles burning blue.[17] Cuntius was an abductor of babies, a strangler and a rapist; he sucked cows dry and ate live chickens. He could also transmute milk into blood, and was a shape-shifter himself, although – in contrast to the shoemaker – Cuntius's metamorphoses changed him either into a malicious dwarf or an animate wooden staff. Six months after being buried, his corpse was exhumed and found to be wholly fresh, his eyelids batting. The corpse was duly cut into small pieces and, with great difficulty, cremated; his ashes were likewise cast into a river.

More provides ample testimonial of the existence of ghosts. He is resolutely opposed to the materialist philosophy of Thomas Hobbes, who in his monumental work *Leviathan* (1649) had rejected ghosts, dæmons and fairies as 'but *Idols, or Phantasms of the braine*, without any reall nature of their own, distinct from humane fancy'.[18] More emphasizes the corporeality – the very materiality – of ghosts, in order to make them valid subjects for scientific inquiry; but at the same time he also advances the importance of the immaterial. In fact, More found in empirical science precisely the evidence he required: the pioneering natural philosopher Robert Boyle would evacuate the air from a glass jar containing a fluttering bird, leading to the poor creature's demise; he would then allow the air back into the jar, whereupon the bird would (usually) be resuscitated. These experiments demonstrated, More argued, that 'there must be some *Immaterial* Being that exercises its *directive* Activity on the *Matter* of the World'.[19] Accordingly, More's aim is to prove the existence of the divine world of spirits and miracles through experience, testimony and experimental evidence – substantiating proofs that drew on legal principles.[20] This was the latest permutation of the long-running scholastic and humanistic attention to the relationship between body and spirit, and More's consolidated thinking would characterize the rational theology of the eighteenth century – and galvanize the later literary vampire.

A congregation of ghosts followed in the wake of More's work – although it is worth emphasizing, *pace* More, that these seventeenth-century ghosts were not the wholly intangible apparitions they would become by the nineteenth century. Like Lazarus, these ghosts usually appeared in grave shrouds and were rarely depicted as transparent; rather, they were earthly: 'fleshy and life-like', as Handley puts it.[21] Many such ghosts were raised in political debate. *A Warning Piece for the World, or, A Watch-Word to England* (1655) featured a ghost in 'bright and glittering armour', and on the eve of the Restoration, *Bradshaw's Ghost* (1659) introduced the ghost of the recently executed Charles I. There was likewise a spate of political and anti-Jesuit ghosts in the wake of the Popish Plot, and a Jacobite apparition, 'The Duchess of York's Ghost' (1691).[22] There were also plenty of supernatural ballads popular at the time, ghostly murder tales (supernaturally exposing crimes and criminals) and intriguing anecdotes, many dating from the sixteenth century and earlier: a 1661 chapbook, for example, with the unpromising title *A True and Perfect Relation from the Faulcon at the Banke-Side* includes a metamorphic ghost that was 'sometimes like a goat . . . and sometimes like a Catt'.[23] There was even an account circulating of an impaled corpse: the ghost of Robert Eliot visited Isabell Binnington, a servant girl, and revealed that he had been murdered by having a stake driven through his heart; he was now condemned to a term of 21 years of haunting. When she uncovered his remains, they were still staked and buried beneath 'a great stone', under which was found 'certain bones (*viz.*) A scalp or head; some of the teeth, and other bones'.[24] This ghost, too, appeared in various different guises – dressed, for example, in green and with flowing hair – though always in human form.[25]

By the 1690s there was so much discussion of ghosts that the journal *Athenian Mercury* was responding to readers' questions such as 'Do the deceased walk?'[26] Such accounts were also very popular among the lower social orders, and cheap print abetted the dissemination of ghost stories through popular pamphlets such as *A True Relation of the Dreadful Ghost Appearing to one John Dyer* (1691). Tales were also, of course, recounted orally: in Shakespeare's *The Winter's Tale* (1609–10), the child Mamillius begins his own winter's tale, 'There was a man . . . Dwelt by a churchyard . . .'[27] Ghostly tales were a favourite of the nursery, though the later children's publisher John Newbery thought that they could have a very detrimental effect on children.[28] The prevalence of ghost stories and supernaturalism in folklore meant that ghosts were also, unsurprisingly, mobilized as vehicles to criticize the upper classes or simply as a way to further personal interests.[29] *The Duke's Daughter's Cruelty* (1692), for instance, opportunistically reworked 'The Cruel Mother' (a ballad of double infanticide in which a mother murders her two new-born babies, who then return to haunt her and condemn her to Hell), while the antiquary John Aubrey claimed that reports of ghostly hauntings were sometimes invoked by sitting tenants to scare off rivals and thus retain their leases.[30] The whole motif of the haunted house can in any case be seen as a critique of property and wealth, which following Clara Reeve's novel *The Old English Baron* (1778) became a key feature of Gothic fiction – and especially of vampire narratives.[31] There was also, however, an alternative, more conservative tradition: in *An Account of a Most Horrid and Barbarous Murther and Robbery, Committed on the Body of Captain Brown, near Shrewsbury in Shropshire* (1694), it is a guilty servant against whom a ghost raises the alarm.

The necessity of apparitions

This seventeenth-century British ghostlore is part of a wider post-Reformation debate on resurrection and immortality, and was directed by the sectarianism that divided the Church. Opinion ranged widely. The puritan Thomas Edwards listed 11 heresies founded on claims about immortality and post-mortem being in his ramshackle work of 'heresiology' *Gangraena* (1646), while the political radical and proto-communist 'Digger' Gerrard Winstanley completely rejected any notion of an individuated, physical afterlife. On the other side of the debate, the angelologist Benjamin Camfield comprehended that ghosts might be guarantees of Christian spiritual immortality and resurrection, while the Cambridge Platonist Ralph Cudworth took this notion further, observing that 'if there be once any *Invisible Ghosts* or *Spirits* acknowledged, as Things *Permanent*, it will not be easie for any to give a reason, why there might not be one *Supreme Ghost* also, presiding over them all, and the whole world'.[32]

There were also more pragmatic positions. In 1658, Thomas Bromhall had argued in *A Treatise of Specters* that dismissing ghosts was ungodly and led to immorality, and that ghost stories were part of a more general latitudinarian policy of inculcating practical values.[33] Many such examples were included in Joseph Glanvill's *Saducismus Triumphatus*, posthumously edited and published by More himself in 1681.[34] Glanvill, natural philosopher and an elected fellow of the Royal Society, investigated cases such as *The Deemon [sic] of Marleborough* (1674) and the 'Drummer of Tedworth', placing significant emphasis on witnesses and testimonies.[35] For Glanvill (somewhat bizarrely), 'The LAND of SPIRITS is a kinde of *AMERICA*, and not well discover'd *Region*.'[36] One of the most celebrated cases Glanvill related concerned Major George Sydenham and Captain William Dyke, who had a pact that the first to die would return three nights later to settle for the survivor questions concerning the nature of God and the immortality of the soul. Sydenham failed to appear to Dyke three nights after his death, but then did appear some six weeks later, with dire warnings that Dyke should mend his ways. The Sydenham–Dyke case, underwritten as it was by comradely loyalty and military honour, became a popular paradigm and was reprinted from *Saducismus Triumphatus* throughout the eighteenth century.[37] Intriguingly, though, despite Glanvill claiming that ghosts did exist and did appear, he did not suggest that they could yet be explained through contemporary religious thinking. Instead he proposed that Protestant theology was an ongoing process of investigation and discovery.[38] At the heart of his belief, then, there lay a defining, intellectually informed doubt and an emerging notion of progress.[39]

Richard Baxter, the leading Presbyterian writer of the day, corresponded over several years with More and Glanvill on the subject of ghosts – despite Glanvill's opposition to nonconformity – and he responded to their research in *Of the Immortality of Mans Soul* (1682) and later in *Certainty of the World of Spirits* (1691).[40] Baxter, who sought moral guidance and spiritual direction from ghost stories, was of the opinion that evil spirits were more common than benevolent ones, citing as an example Lieutenant-Colonel Bowen of Glamorgan, an atheist whose wife was visited by an incubus. Ghostly hauntings could therefore be taken as a warning against immoral or irreligious behaviour – hence, outbreaks of supernatural activity suggested that society was collapsing into sin.[41] Baxter, too, was a rational (and indeed a reasonable) theologian whose thinking would lead the way towards the philosophy of John Locke and deism, and more immediately to 'natural theology', or what the clergyman, horologist and fellow of the Royal Society William Derham christened 'physico-theology': the proof of God through natural and scientific laws.[42] A particular branch of physico-theology concerned the supernatural: religious truths that existed outside reason, such as the Resurrection. Theologians clearly needed to distinguish these divine verities from the evil undead.

Debate on ghosts and the invisible world persisted throughout the eighteenth century (the so-called 'Age of Reason'), and spirits of every stripe haunted theological disputes across the spectrum of belief. Some commentators, such as William Assheton, author of the tract *The Possibility of Apparitions* (1706), embraced the supernatural as an inevitability of Christianity, reiterating the arguments that immortality and resurrection were 'evident and Consequential upon the Truth of Apparitions' ('Apparitions' being 'Souls Departed') to the extent that there was actually a doctrinal necessity for ghostly manifestations.[43] Likewise, Josiah Woodward in *Fair Warnings to a Careless World* (1707) provided several recent and well-attested examples of apparitions in England to confirm the existence of ghosts.[44]

Others were more circumspect. In response to the scientific rationalism of the Royal Society there was a move towards a deistic natural religion: one that could be empirically proven and which operated according to natural laws.[45] Such thinking was typified by Anthony Ashley Cooper, the earl of Shaftesbury.[46] Shaftesbury warns against supplementing a belief in biblical miracles with 'Old-Wives Storys'. Enthusiasm – by which he means religious fanaticism – is fomented by melancholy; it is, then, a symptom of psychological disturbance and physical ill-health, of 'strange Ferments in the Blood' or incipient plague. Shaftesbury observes that enthusiasm is a 'Disease' of mass panic, comparable to rabies ('*Hydrophoby*') and spread by 'the snappish spirit' – by figuratively biting and infecting victims; enthusiasm is also at the same time an 'Apparition'.[47] What is remarkable about Shaftesbury's account, written as early as 1708, is that it outlines vampirism before vampires had been explicitly recognized: the mix of blood and pestilence, the triggers in delusion and disease, the tangibility of teeth and the immateriality of phantasm – and all seasoned with scepticism towards religious extremism.

Shaftesbury was writing against the background of the religious intolerance of seventeenth-century Puritanism that persisted (albeit in a more mellow form) in nonconformity and dissent. More immediately, the 'French Prophets' had arrived in London in 1707, a Huguenot (French Protestant) sect gifted with falling into ecstatic trances and performing almost medieval mortifications of the flesh. A contemporary reported that:

> their Countenance changes, and is no longer Natural; their Eyes roll after a ghastly manner in their Heads, or they stand altogether fixed; all the Members of their Body seem displaced, their Hearts beat with extraordinary Efforts and Agitations; they become swelled and Bloated, and look bigger than ordinary; they Beat themselves with their Hands with a vast Force, like the miserable Creature in the Gospel, cutting himself with Stones; the Tone of their Voice is stronger than what it cou'd be Naturally; their Words are sometimes broken and interrupted; they speak without knowing what they speak, and without remembering what they have Prophesied.[48]

Despite the fearful scepticism (and Francophobia) inspired by the Prophets, they were nevertheless the heralds of the 'Great Awakening': the fundamentalist Protestant revival that ignited in Britain in the 1730s in the context of another ecstatic sect, the Demoniacks, and the passing of the Witchcraft Act – a state declaration of enlightened thinking, denying the existence of witches and thereby making persecution on such grounds illegal.[49] By 1740, Methodism had taken definite hold in England.[50] At its core was a thoroughgoing confidence in the validity of supernatural experience and the prevalence of diabolical hazards. Ghostly encounters were valued among Methodists, as they offered a rarefied form of subjective testimony. Indeed, the faith of Methodism's founder John Wesley in the afterlife was stirred by his conviction as a child that he had been selected by Providence, and this calling was confirmed by his personal (if indirect) experience of Old Jeffrey, a Jacobite ghost who haunted his parents' rectory at Epworth in Lincolnshire. Wesley later published his sightings and dealings with spirits in the *Arminian Magazine*: his ghost stories validated the gospels and the promise of a divine afterlife.

Signs or intimations of immortality were already a cornerstone of the dissenting tradition, as exemplified by John Bunyan's *Grace Abounding to the Chief of Sinners* (1666) – a spiritual autobiography that details the divinely supernatural calling Bunyan received on Elstow village green in Bedfordshire. There were other supernatural beings, too, that manifested the kindliness of God, such as guardian angels. Ghosts also had a more practical function, uniting religious communities at a time when dissent and individualistic faith were on the rise. Indeed, sermons on ghosts could be topical and entertaining, and were even deployed to tempt Dissenters towards Anglicanism: Richard Jago, poet and vicar of Harbury, published his sermon of 4 May 1755 with the tantalizing – and enticing – subtitle, 'On occasion of a Conversation said to have pass'd between one of the Inhabitants, and an Apparition, in the Church-Yard belonging to that Place'.[51]

The mainstream Anglican clergy in any case nourished the popular belief in ghosts. Archibald Cockburn, for instance, pointed to the biblical precedent of the Witch of Endor and the cast-iron testimony of reliable witnesses in order to prove the existence of phantoms, determining that 'whosoever discredits such a Relation, may equally condemn all Proofs but Sense and Demonstration'.[52] For Cockburn, phantoms were not 'Sanguiferous [cardiovascular] Bodies', but immaterial, having relinquished flesh and bones; but neither were they lost souls, as the soul abided in the vital union between blood and life: ghosts were instead 'impermanent and incarnous [incorporeal] Bodies'.[53]

The relationship between testimony and material evidence had been exercising commentators since the end of the previous century and added a further complication to the corroboration of proofs. In 1705, the philosopher Samuel Clarke, for example, had rebutted materialist objections to the existence of God through the elusive concept of immateriality, inspired by Sir Isaac Newton's groundbreaking work on light and optics. Clarke argued that

the Power of seeing Light or Colour, is to a Man Born Blind, altogether as incomprehensible and absolutely beyond the Reach of all his Ideas, as either the Operations and Perceptions, or even the Simple Essence of a Pure Immaterial Substance or Spirit, can be to any of us. If therefore the Blind Mans want of Idea's [*sic*] be not a sufficient Proof of the Impossibility of Light or Colour; how comes our bare want of Idea's, to be a Demonstration of the Impossibility of the Being of Immaterial Substances? A Blind Man, they will say, has Testimony of the Existence of Light: Very true; so also have we, of the Existence of Immaterial Substances.[54]

The Scottish Enlightenment philosopher David Hume also considered testimony in detail in his essay 'Of Miracles' (1748). Religious faith for Hume is necessarily based on belief in miracles, which are events that violate natural laws. However, he argues that it is a general maxim that 'no Testimony is sufficient to establish a Miracle, unless the Testimony be of such a Kind, that its Falshood would be more miraculous, than the Fact, which it endeavours to establish'.[55] He goes on to point out that miracles can actually destroy the credit of the testimony, and furthermore that the principle of testimony destroys itself – it is always at a remove: no matter how reliable or extensive the testimony, it cannot ultimately represent an event in itself.[56] As was later to become uncomfortably apparent, this was indeed the case in vampire inquiries.

Ghost stories were clearly ubiquitous, saturating British intellectual life and popular culture, and they provided a key focus for understanding the metaphysical and the immaterial. They continued to be traditionally told at Christmas throughout the period, and indeed both the first account of the renowned case of the ghost of Mrs Veal, which appeared in *The Loyal Post* in 1705, and Horace Walpole's inaugural Gothic novel *The Castle of Otranto* (1764) appeared on Christmas Eve.[57] Inevitably, the case of Mrs Veal was subsequently investigated with a scientific and rationalist eye for circumstantial detail in *A True Relation of the Apparition of one Mrs. Veal, the Next Day after her Death* (1706), a pamphlet attributed to Daniel Defoe.[58] But any time of the year was a good time for a ghost story. The Whig literary grandee Joseph Addison entertained the likelihood of spirits in several essays for the *Spectator*, including one in which his favourite fictional mouthpiece, Roger de Coverley, mentions that his mother and his servants believe his estate to be haunted.[59] Although Addison dismissed the oracular revelations of the classical sybils – 'always seeing Apparitions, and hearing Death-watches' – as resulting from attacks of the 'Vapours', he nevertheless later wrote a play based on Glanvill's account of the 'Drummer of Tedworth': *The Drummer; or, The Haunted House* (1715).[60]

Ghosts were also already popular in the theatre, not least as they afforded an opportunity for audacious special effects. They were also one of the most recognizable features of Shakespeare's plays, and thereby influenced culture both on and off stage; the young Samuel Johnson for one was so terrified when he came to read the appearance of the ghost of Hamlet's father that he abandoned the play and fled his room in order to get among living people.[61] This fascination with supernatural apparitions continued in popular high-brow journalism, such as the *Gentleman's Magazine*, which covered accounts of ghosts, as well as fairy armies on the march on Midsummer Eve and the mysteries of dreams.[62] Literally hundreds of published works mentioned ghosts or apparitions on their title pages.[63]

Ghosts also remained on the political stage in, for instance, the 1712 squib *The Story of the St. Albans Ghost, or the Apparition of Mother Haggy*. Battlefield ghosts advanced the Protestant cause during the War of the Austrian Succession, and there were similar anti-Jacobite ghosts in the aftermath of the Battle of Culloden. Meanwhile at sea the anti-Spanish ghost Admiral Hosier famously addressed Admiral Vernon (1740), and Admiral Byng (court-martialled and executed in a travesty of legal justice in 1757) appeared as an anti-government ghost. The conjuration of unearthly powers was a way of rallying generally anti-Catholic (whether against the French or the Spanish or the Jacobites) and anti-egalitarian sentiments into a unifying declaration of national identity, driven by supposedly Protestant moral imperatives: as such, this blend of Whig politics and historical drama laid the foundations for Gothic literature.[64]

Dust to dust

Inevitably, ghosts roamed through poetry, too. Melancholic verse, morbidly introspective and self-absorbed, caught the mood of a country in the grip of an evangelical revival. Churchyards were traditionally festive spaces, and there was much folklore associated with graveyards; but now they became sites of meditation and the contemplation of mortality, historical processes and the vagaries of human existence.[65] So it was that Edward Young's *The Complaint, or, Night-Thoughts on Life, Death, and Immortality* (1742–45), Robert Blair's *The Grave* (1743) and Mark Akenside's *The Pleasures of Imagination* (1744) caught the mood of the country and inaugurated the 'Graveyard' or 'Mortuary' school of poetry.[66] In Blair's exemplary poem, the scene is ghastly, riven with the supernatural horror of howling wind, creaking doors, ominous cries of birds and cavernously echoing churches. The dead inevitably emerge from their tombs to walk again, soundlessly pacing:

> Rous'd from their Slumbers
> In grim Array the grizly Spectres rise,
> Grin horrible, and obstinately sullen
> Pass and repass, hush'd as the Foot of Night.[67]

The churchyard is filled with the undead lurking by graves:

> Of horrid *Apparition*, tall and ghastly,
> That walks at Dead of Night, or takes his Stand
> O'er some new-open'd *Grave*; and, strange to tell!
> Evanishes at Crowing of the Cock.[68]

This horror of the grave is visceral: 'it makes one's Blood run chill', and evokes primal fears born of grim folklore and occult wisdom:

> Strange Things, the Neighbours say, have happen'd here:
> Wild Shrieks have issu'd from the hollow Tombs,
> Dead men have come again, and walk'd about,
> And the Great Bell has toll'd, unrung, untouch'd.[69]

Such revenants and spectral manifestations had remained in the English tradition of songs and ballads, later formally revived by Thomas Percy in his influential anthology *Reliques of Ancient English Poetry* (1765), and even appearing in idiosyncratic love poetry of the 1730s. Indeed, one of the most enduring poems of the period was, of course, a graveyard poem: Thomas Gray's *An Elegy Wrote in a Country Churchyard* (1751).

This saturnine vogue for tarrying in graveyards not only inspired macabre sentimentality, but also had the side-effect of focusing attention on the sickly foetidness of burial places.[70] Blair himself described the 'low-brow'd misty Vaults, / (Furr'd around with mouldy Damps, and ropy Slime)'[71] and the already-putrefying carcass carried away by the undertakers that 'in the Nostril / Smells horrible'.[72] Miasmatic theory suggested that pestilences could be spread through the air, which in turn drew attention to the disposal of bodies and the need for public health policies.[73]

Ghosts, meanwhile, continued to walk. 'Scratching Fanny', or the Cock Lane ghost, was believed to be the restless spirit of one Fanny Lynes. Although she had apparently died of smallpox in 1760, the knocking sounds by which her wraith made itself known (she was never seen) were interpreted as sinister evidence that she had in fact been poisoned by her husband-to-be, a stockbroker and creditor by the name of William Kent. It transpired that the whole thing was a bizarre plot against Kent over an unpaid debt, involving Richard Parsons (a parish clerk), his wife Elizabeth, their maidservant Mary Frazer and the Revd John Moore (a Methodist preacher). All four were convicted of conspiracy, but not before the case had attracted much coverage in the press. It also captured the attention of Horace Walpole, and Samuel Johnson was even invited by the lord mayor of London to be part of an independent inquiry to investigate the events.[74] Although both Walpole and Johnson were metropolitan cognoscenti who ridiculed the incident and mocked the credulity of the faithful, Walpole was not above including an undead friar in his novel *The Castle of Otranto*.[75] Johnson, meanwhile, famously pronounced of ghosts:

> It is wonderful that five thousand years have now elapsed since the creation of the world, and still it is undecided whether or not there has ever been an instance of the spirit of any person appearing after death. All argument is against it; but all belief is for it.[76]

Also responding to the Cock Lane ghost was *Anti-Canidia*, an anonymous diatribe published in the same year as the affair. The title *Anti-Canidia* refers to the Roman witch Canidia, invoked by the poet Horace in his *Epodes* and *Satires*, and notorious for, among other offences, trespass, desecration, child torture and murder, and bloodsucking (*empusa*) – a folkloric element later enlisted in tracing the supposed genealogy of the vampire.[77] The subtitle of *Anti-Canidia* lists a selection of the 'vulgar superstitions' it promises to confute: 'witches, spirits, demons, magick, divination, omens, prognostications, dreams, augurys, charms, amulets, incantations, astrology, oracles, &c.'[78] *Anti-Canidia* is clearly a rationalist attack on the supernatural credulity of the Methodists, firm believers in this sort of paranormal activity. But the very fact that the author of *Anti-Canidia* felt the need to explode these fancies (and to remain anonymous) is testament to their credibility at the time for many.[79]

But where are the vampires in all this magical thinking? Although the discourse on ghosts clearly frames eighteenth-century vampire debate – and more specifically helped to shape later depictions of vampires – vampires themselves did not form part of it. Protestants were greatly concerned to demonstrate how ghosts were proof of the afterlife and the immortality of the soul, and could act as divine agents of moral enforcement. But in all these considerations they could not afford to allow the Devil too much authority; for while the Devil incontrovertibly existed, his powers were severely restricted and anyway counterfeit. Through beguiling and bewitching, the Devil might ensnare the unwary into *believing* that the dead walked in order to prey upon the living; but the Devil could not actually raise the dead: that was God's prerogative, as demonstrated through the exceptionality of Christ's resurrection and in anticipation of the Day of Judgment (the exploits of the Witch of Endor and the restoration of Lazarus notwithstanding). But vampires were tangible – the physical risen dead – so vampirism was deliberately avoided by Protestant theologians, who were in any case increasingly fascinated by intangible phenomena. Vampirism, seemingly engineered by the Devil and his demonic minions, smacked too much of Catholic superstition – which is one of the reasons why in Britain it became historicized as ancient legend and dark folklore (rather than acknowledged as the uncomfortably modern phenomenon it really was), and also why later accounts of measures for dealing with vampires drew on archaic customs in an attempt to confine them to a remote Catholic past. In contrast, Catholic theologians found themselves in a deadly embrace with vampires. The key thinker here is Dom Augustin Calmet, a Benedictine abbot renowned for his 26-volume commentary on the Bible, and the most distinguished theologian of eighteenth-century France.[80] It is to him that we now turn.

CHAPTER 4

THE COVENANT OF THE UNDEAD

Catholicism and Enlightenment, Sanctity and Danger

How arise the dead? With what bodies come they in?

1 Corinthians 15:35[1]

'I will come,' the priest answered, 'for I have read in old books of these strange beings which are neither quick nor dead, and which lie ever fresh in their graves, stealing out in the dusk to taste life and blood.'

Francis Marion Crawford (1905)[2]

O, blood, blood, blood!

William Shakespeare (1604)[3]

The Roman Catholic Church took a particularly keen interest in the eighteenth-century vampire plague, as did Enlightenment thinkers such as the French *philosophes*. For Catholic as well as Protestant theologians, vampires were potentially evidence of some sort of afterlife and, like miracles, proof of the supernatural. But in these fundamental areas of Christian faith, Catholicism differed profoundly from Protestantism. With regard to ghosts, for instance, Protestants regarded them as entities sent from Heaven or Hell as, respectively, visitations of angelic compassion or demonic malice. In Catholic thinking, by contrast, ghosts occupied the transitory realm of

73

Purgatory, the interlude between perpetual bliss or endless suffering. They were disembodied souls, capable of little more than making signs of repentance or admonition. Although they were known to be capable of delivering moral guidance, most were content to visit their surviving family as a reminder that masses be dedicated to them to expedite their progress to Heaven. These purgatorial ghosts were also quite distinct from divine or diabolical apparitions – appearances of the Blessed Virgin Mary or the oppressions of incubi – which accounted for their impermanence and limited agency. As such, ghosts were held up as proof of the Catholic afterlife, just as Protestants defended them as confirming godly intervention in human affairs.[4]

Yet vampires, despite sharing various traits with ghosts – most obviously by belonging to the order of the undead – were not demonstrably and unarguably simply Catholic or Protestant. Although they were, like some Protestant ghosts, colossally malevolent and more than capable of causing actual physical harm, they were also clearly corporeal. For Catholics, they might not be purgatorial ghosts, but could they be diabolical illusions? If so, they risked conceding more power to the Devil than modern theology allowed for. Were they instead, then, something else entirely: preternatural monsters or visceral demons? Vampires consequently tested the differences in thinking within the Christian Church by presenting a challenge to both the Protestant and the Catholic creeds and the logic of their thought. Although this resulted in an uneasy agreement between the two about the non-existence of vampires, each tackled the problem in entirely different ways. While Protestant theologians resolutely ignored vampires, their Catholic counterparts did endeavour to accommodate them within their world view and attempt to make them consistent with their beliefs. At the same time, the vampire phenomenon also confronted the leading European philosophers of the Enlightenment engaged in epistemology and ascertaining the laws of nature. Vampires gave much food for thought not only to monks, archbishops and even the pope, but also to Voltaire, Jean-Jacques Rousseau and Denis Diderot.

Spiritual biology

In 1739, Giuseppe Davanzati, archbishop of Trani, wrote his *Dissertazione sopra i Vampiri* (*Dissertation Regarding the Vampires*) about the events of the

1720s. Although this discursive treatise was not published until 1774, well after Davanzati was dead, it nevertheless circulated in manuscript, and the fact that vampires remained a live theological subject is shown by the work going into a second edition some 15 years later.[5] Just as rational empiricism characterized Protestant inquiry into ghosts – and despite the fact that there was little cross-pollination between the two churches – so Davanzati was part of a rationalist drive in Roman Catholicism that sought explanations based on natural laws for apparently supernatural occurrences.[6] In the case of vampirism, reason and faith had to work together against this new threat.

Although Davanzati toys with the idea that vampires might be linked with the *monaci* and *monacelle* (elves and fairies) of southern Italian folklore, he remains committed to rational explanation and argues against attributing inordinate powers to the Devil, or to those seductive, suffocating demons such as incubi and succubi. Davanzati explicitly denies that the Devil is able to contravene natural laws, and so he cannot raise the dead, effect miraculous cures or cause illness, transform humans into animals or transmute inanimate materials, have the gift of ubiquity, see into the future or summon partner demons; the Devil even has only limited powers when it comes to conjuring up apparitions. Davanzati also relies on natural laws to explain the whole host of well-attested mysterious phenomena, such as incorruptible cadavers, corpse lights and the postmortem vitality of cadavers growing hair and nails: all can be explained according to natural science.[7] However, in following this logic Davanzati allows that the physical body must retain a vestige of life – at least in some fashion – even after the soul has departed. This created a significant theological and philosophical dilemma, as it blurred the fundamental distinction between life and death, and thereby the whole superstructure of ritual and pattern of the afterlife. Rationalizing vampirism by explaining away the supernatural entirely therefore risked undermining the spiritual foundations of faith; but then treating vampires as magical and malignant demons disturbed the supremacy of God over the Devil. It is precisely in this no-man's land between sacred faith and secular rationalism that vampires found a congenial habitat.

Davanzati's strategy, therefore, is to place vampires firmly within the new union of rational Catholicism. Vampires cannot be a species of ghost because they are evil, and neither are they denizens of Hell, as the Devil's power has itself been exaggerated. So either they are not as murderous and contagious as they are reputed to be (and are therefore purgatorial ghosts touring remote Orthodox communities) or, alternatively, because they serve no divine purpose, they do not actually exist at all. Ultimately – and like other Italian commentators such as Girolamo Tartarotti, author of *Del Congresso Notturno delle Lammie* (*Night-Time Coven of Witches*, 1749) – Davanzati puts vampires down to the imagination, whose darkling and corporeal powers, sometimes admittedly exploited by the Devil, were increasingly held responsible for what had once been understood as super-natural, malefic or even miraculous. They do not actually have a physical state: that simply is the mind playing tricks. In Davanzati's words, 'If imag-ination with the vehemence of its spirits has the power to operate physically as well inside the subject as outside of it, this means it can produce real and physical effects in [the subject's] own body and in those of others.' This being the case, he goes on to argue, does not the imagination therefore have 'the force to cause in us a simple ephemeral and purely imaginary operation, such as the simple representation of one image in the place of another?'[8]

Vampires were thus manifested as a collective and communicable delirium that proliferated and circulated as a plague of baleful fantasies, and Davanzati's reasoning very much chimes with the predominant Catholic logic of the time. Although his work enjoyed only limited circula-tion, it is not impossible that Pope Benedict XIV, celebrated both for his cultural erudition and his knowledge of science, saw Davanzati's text or heard his arguments, as he himself later dismissed vampire beliefs in similar terms as '*deceptæ phantasiæ figmentum habentur*' – 'fictions that have deceived the imagination'.[9] But whatever the case, Davanzati's *Dissertazione* usefully encapsulates the quandary that vampires posed to Catholic theo-logians. The central problem was whether vampires could be rationally explained by recourse to natural laws, or whether they were supernatural agents that demanded theological justification. If neither of these approaches proved adequate, there was also the possibility that the reports of vampirism, for all their attention to detail, were somehow mistaken or deluded, and that the value of testimony was in question; certainly, it would be reasonable to question scrupulously the validity of these reports.

Davanzati's treatise accordingly anticipates the most sustained account of vampirism of the time, written by the French Benedictine Dom Augustin Calmet. Calmet's research was published in France in 1746, rapidly going into second and third editions, and appeared in English in 1759 as *Dissertations upon the Apparitions of Angels, Dæmons, and Ghosts, and Concerning the Vampires of Hungary, Bohemia, Moravia, and Silesia.*[10] In one sense a trailblazing collection of ghost stories, his book is also a comprehensive body of antiquarian research and philosophical debate that scrutinizes the conditions and extent of popular belief in the supernatural, and methods for ascertaining the actual existence (or otherwise) of vampires and their ilk. Calmet admits that as there are instances in the Bible of the dead miraculously rising and walking, the phenomenon should neither be explained as an uncomplicated natural event, nor rejected out of hand. However, he distances the integrity and authenticity of biblical apparitions from contemporary cases of the supernatural, and – crucially – maintains the omnipotence of God throughout. Initially, Calmet adopted the position that vampires existed as a form of celestial punishment, but by the second edition of 1749 he had come to the conclusion that they were fantasy – although his discussion retains many of the arguments of his earlier conviction, and his change of opinion may in any case have been directed by Pope Benedict, who would within a few years publicly denounce belief in vampires.

Like the seventeenth-century divine Henry More, Calmet mixes evidential history, theories of natural philosophy and disputations into theological truth. But whereas More, Glanvill and other commentators had discussed apparitions and miracles at length, Calmet's investigation is the first sustained analysis of vampires using deductive theological reasoning, as opposed to medical analysis. Although they had spectral qualities, vampires were embodied, tangible revenants, and this had implications for Catholic traditions of the materiality of human flesh. The undecayed corpse of a vampire was a direct reflection (or evil twin) of the Incorruptibles – the fresh and pliant bodies of the saints – which has persisted as a major bone of contention between Protestant and Catholic beliefs since the Reformation, and which continues to characterize Catholic hagiography through the cult of relics, the physical remnants of saints' bodies and chattels.[11]

In 1738, two years before he became Pope Benedict, Prospero Lambertini had published *De Servorum Dei Beatificatione et Beatorum Canonizatione*, one of the crowning texts of the rationalist Catholic movement. This all-encompassing handbook on canonization remains in use today. From 1708, Lambertini had been *promotor fidei* – the 'Devil's advocate' – a role that required him to come up with arguments to block petitions for beatification or canonization. He was therefore well versed in the significance attached to the incorruptibility of saints' bodies and the spectrum of post-mortem states, and much of Book IV of *De Servorum Dei Beatificatione* is given over to the topic. This is not to say that incorruptibility was an absolute guarantee of sainthood, though, and miracles – understood to be a consequence of godliness rather than an inspiration to virtuousness – remained crucial for canonization. Nor did Catholic theology in the period deny the possibility that non-putrefaction may have natural causes, which ranged from deliberate or accidental embalming compounds, to being struck by lightning, or even to being born on 27 or 30 January or 13 February – unaccountably understood to be days that bestowed protection from decay. Furthermore, it could be one of the Devil's wiles to meddle with the natural processes of decomposition, and indeed Johann Heinrich Zopf of the Essen Gymnasium postulated that the non-decomposition of vampire bodies may be a diabolical ruse to mock the Catholic belief in the Incorruptibles. To complicate matters further, according to some schools of theological thought (notably the Eastern Orthodox Church), the bodies of excommunicants also remain uncannily fresh. Nevertheless, in the contest between faith and reason, it should be remembered that, from the Roman Catholic perspective, incorruptibility was a theological confirmation of saintliness, not a scientific verification of the holy.

Vampires mirrored saints, too, in that they were put to death multiple times. The megalomartyrs in particular, such as St George and St Catherine of Alexandria, were repeatedly executed by diverse methods; similarly, vampires were usually slain by some combination or sequence of decoronation, decapitation and cremation. More generally, vampires were an inversion of the Eucharist. The ingestion of blood was a calculated perversion of the communion sacrament – turning blood into wine, rather than wine into blood – and their consumption of this sacrament was gluttonous rather than sparing: postprandial vampires were bloated, weeping blood. Their transubstantiation, then – if it can indeed be called that – was the conversion of living humans into undead vampires. In early accounts this was the result of contamination with disease, but it soon became the result of the vampire ingesting and infecting the blood of their victims and thereby transfiguring them to become part of the vampire brood.

Moreover, whereas the blood of Christ was shared among communicants, and bread had a bodily symbolism, protection from vampires was conferred by eating bread infused with vampiric blood. Staking the corpse of a suspected vampire also seems to be a distortion or brutal mockery of the crucifixion, transforming the vertical impalement of a living body by its extremities into the horizontal impalement of a dead body through the heart (literally). In fact, Calmet does come close to reading vampires as a symbolic attack on the Church, and the French literary historian Marie-Hélène Huet has since interpreted the whole Arnod Paole case as the life of Christ in reverse, emphasizing the 40 days He spent fasting in the wilderness and resisting the Devil – 40 days being (by some accounts) the delay before Paole was raised as a vampire (and also almost exactly the time it took Major Sydenham to return and warn Captain William Dyke). For the vampire Paole, this is a reanimation into secular society rather than a resurrection into everlasting life; gorging and indulging in feasts of blood rather than fasting and abstaining; and infecting his victims with ghastly corruption rather than converting them into eternal disciples.[12]

Calmet notes that the recent accounts of vampirism in the Habsburg Empire are detailed and consistent, attested by professional witnesses and investigators, and that the depositions are legally sound and reliable. He observes that, unlike ghosts and witches, vampires are a modern phenomenon, although wizards of old were sometimes bloodsuckers, and excommunicants (again, beings in Limbo) are occasionally said to have risen from the dead. He notes that spectres had sometimes been resuscitated after months or years to torment the living by sucking their blood and causing death, often 'appearing in their former clothes to their own families' – a telling detail.[13] He cites authorities such as Karl Ferdinand Schertz's *Magia Posthuma*, as well as the considerably more elusive *Philosophicæ et Christianæ Cogitationes de Vampiriis*, supposedly by Johann Christoph

Harenberg, both of which argue that vampirism is a sign of mental derangement.[14] He is most sceptical of manducation, although the book is haunted by fears of premature burial and anecdotes of unfortunates who, awaking in their coffins, are compelled to eat themselves in a grisly effort to stay alive. In particular, Calmet wrestles with the question of how lifeless carcasses can leave and return to their graves, ultimately deciding that this is impossible and that vampires should not therefore be numbered among the dead.[15]

Calmet approaches the problem of vampires from the long perspective of Catholic thinking about the risen dead. As Davanzati had pointed out, vampires hardly served a divine purpose, and so if only God could resurrect the body, how could vampires be accounted for? Calmet's considered opinion was that 'If these vampires are not really raised to life again, nor their bodies refined and spiritualised, . . . I am afraid we shall have nothing left, but to deny absolutely, that they ever come again.'[16] But if apparently reliable testimonies were tainted by hallucinations, how did that account for the corporeal nature of vampires, such as bleeding copiously when staked? Calmet is correspondingly both sceptical of the testimony and able to provide examples of post-mortem activity in which corpses retain a trace of animation. The biggest issue is how they leave and return to their graves: how their bodies can 'lengthen, diminish, and rarefy . . . so as to enable them to insinuate themselves through the earth, or to pass through windows and doors'.[17] Calmet's reluctance to dismiss vampires reflects his sense that such a dogmatic insistence would risk casting a shadow of doubt over the apparitions, resurrections and miracles recorded in the Bible and credited to the saints (Calmet reported that St Stanislaus, for instance, raised a man who had been dead for three years). Indeed, the prevalence of the risen dead in both theological deliberations and on the borders of the Habsburg Empire caused Benito Jerónimo Feijóo, professor of theology at Oviedo University and – like Calmet – a Benedictine monk, to observe in 1753 with justifiable archness that certain regions of Europe had apparently witnessed more resurrections in the past few decades than the entire Christian world had in nearly two thousand years.[18]

Calmet's work was heavily criticized because he did not uncompromisingly explode the vampire phenomenon as a modern myth – despite the fact that this scepticism mirrored the caution of the earlier medical researchers. Instead, he remains somewhat refreshingly doubtful and undogmatic to the last, and the inconsistencies in his account suggestively reflect the complexities of the vampire problem. Ironically, Calmet's plurality of methods also cast considerable doubt on the value of testimony, and he was roundly attacked by Voltaire and the French *philosophes* precisely for making a virtue of testimony, which now appeared to encourage naïve trust and effectively endorsed taking folklore and superstition seriously. But overall, Calmet's *Dissertations* are valuable in charting social issues such as a fear of the dead and anxieties concerning the spread of infection in what amounts to a culture of mortal discrimination: a culture in which the dead are ritually expelled from society and made invisible. Under such conditions, all the dead posed the threat of being vampires-in-waiting, returning to disrupt and contaminate normality.[19]

Vampirosophy

Voltaire's attack on Calmet was only a part of the philosophical response to vampirism. Just as theologians were bewitched by vampires, so several Enlightenment philosophers were drawn into the controversy. In part, this was one element of a wider debate on defining human identity in an increasingly materialistic world. In the preceding century, René Descartes had promulgated in his *Discourse on Method* (1637) the idea that a machine with the appearance and physiology of a monkey would, to all intents, be a monkey. He argued that it is possible to replicate the essence of a monkey because the monkey is purely mechanized material. Animals were effectively clockwork automata, with no capacity to reason and therefore no soul. The human soul, in contrast, was the instrument of reason, which distinguished the human from the animal. The essence of the human therefore lay beyond the material in language and in powers of deductive reasoning – features that are recognizable and that exist, for Descartes, independent of history and institutions such as politics. Hence a human assemblage would not be human, however well it was constructed, as it could not be infused with reason.

This had far-reaching implications. On the one hand it inspired counter-theories of life and consciousness in which not only animals but human beings as well were considered to be no more (or less) than elegantly sophisticated biological mechanisms – as exemplified by Julien Offray de La Mettrie in his radical work *L'Homme Machine* (1747).[20] But there was another, more disturbing side to this thinking. Descartes had also argued that pain could only be felt with understanding. If animals could not reason, then they could not feel pain (at least as it was understood by humans), and so they did not require undue protection. A monkey felt no more pain than a machine, and neither was qualified to have rights – both were automata. And so this provided the intellectual justification for vivisection.

Philosophers from Jeremy Bentham to Voltaire were profoundly aware of the urgent need to rethink human–animal relations. Under the entry for 'Beasts' in *A Philosophical Dictionary*, Voltaire wrote feelingly of dogs fretting because they cannot find their masters, and of their joy on being reunited. However,

> Some barbarians seize this dog, who so prodigiously excels man in friendship, they nail him on a table, and dissect him living, to show the mezarian veins. You discover in him all the same organs of sentiment which are in yourself. Answer me, machinist, has nature arranged all the springs of sentiment in this animal that he should not feel? Has he nerves to be incapable of suffering? Do not suppose this impertinent contradiction in nature.[21]

Descartes had himself performed vivisections on dogs.[22]

On the face of it, vampires could once again be seen to occupy a problem space in contemporary thinking: they were at least originally human, but once vampire did they exercise reason or were they driven by bestial instincts to feed and kill and infect? Did they remain human in any sense? In his *Discours sur l'Origine et les Fondements de l'Inégalité parmi les Hommes* (*Discourse on the Origin and Basis of Inequality among Men*, 1755, known as the *Second Discourse*), Jean-Jacques Rousseau discussed the '*homme sauvage*' or 'natural' man, and crucially considered this figure in relation to apes, in particularly the orangutan (by which he means the great apes more generally, taxonomy being in its infancy). Orangutans appeared to share many qualities with primitive or savage humans. Indeed, racial theories of the time were usually brutally sanctimonious about primitive societies, dismissing native peoples as, for example, 'perfectly stupid' – although this at least meant that they were human and at least potentially capable of reason.[23] Rousseau has accordingly been described as the first Enlightenment thinker 'to suppose that there might be a temporal and sequential relation between particular species in the natural chain' and the first to suggest that 'the relation between apes and men . . . might be one of genetic continuity'.[24] Although he had never seen an orangutan and was obliged to rely instead on travellers' sightings and descriptions, by narrowing the gulf between humankind and the animal kingdom, his work provoked much thought – as well as scorn. Rousseau was described by one anonymous detractor as an orangutan himself, and those inspired by his ideas, such as the primitivist theorist and advocate James Burnett, Lord Monboddo, were comprehensively derided. Samuel Johnson, for instance, declared that Monboddo 'talked a great deal of nonsense'; and although he considered that Rousseau also talked nonsense, 'Rousseau *knows* he is talking nonsense', whereas sadly 'Monboddo does *not* know that he is talking nonsense'.[25] Monboddo, who lived a primitivist life forgoing luxury and taking frequent cold-water baths and naked 'air baths' at four in the morning, and who regularly spent the autumn affecting the lifestyle of a tenant farmer, attempted to develop Rousseau's ideas by proposing that orangutans walk on two legs, use weapons and tools, build huts and live in societies, and even capture humans and force them to work for them.

The notion that 'orang-utans' were bipedal was repeated by naturalists from Samuel Purchas (1625) to Georges-Louis Leclerc, comte de Buffon (1766), while others noted their impressively decent table-manners when introduced to western etiquette. As for Monboddo,

it appears certain, that they are of our species, and though they have made some progress in the arts of life, they have not advanced so far as to invent a language; and accordingly none of them that have been brought to Europe could speak, and, what seems strange, never learned to speak.[26]

They are, however, vegetarian, do not hunt and have a sense of justice. Monboddo also describes an orangutan that had learned to play the pipe and the harp.[27] Besides, according to Monboddo's classical sources, humans were originally wild animals with tails (Rousseau and Buffon also mention primitive humans equipped with tails of up to a foot long).[28] These caudate anthropods had fortuitously developed language, which in turn led to society and culture. Yet despite Monboddo being an object of ridicule for decades – Thomas Love Peacock was still satirizing him in 1817 in his novel *Melincourt*, in which an orangutan (Sir Oran Haut-Ton) is elected to Parliament – by the mid-nineteenth century he was recognized as a proto-Darwinist: in other words, part of the evolution of the theory of evolution.[29]

In any case, in these rudimentary anthropological studies, orangutans seem considerably more civilized than vampires, which appear to be degenerate anthropomorphic primates in comparison: while vampires huddle in graves, orangutans create shelters; whereas vampires hunt their prey and are without exception flesh-eaters, orangutans are gatherers of the fruits of the forest, and also enjoy elegant and gentle music. Both are, however, immensely strong and a threat to humans, whom they enslave – which, as the comte de Buffon coolly argued, could actually be considered to be a defining human characteristic.[30] These evolutionary debates exploded in the next century, of course. But in fact Rousseau also discussed vampires – if not directly comparing them with orangutans. And in many ways vampires matched Rousseau's model of 'natural man': they were physically powerful, agile, solitary and insensible beings; whether they were healthy was, however, open to question, and they were certainly not vegetarian.[31]

Rousseau had no doubt that vampires did not exist, and so the supernatural dimensions of vampirism held no interest for him. The various peculiarities – such as fresh blood in vampire coffins – could reasonably be explained by simply being 'pieces in the dead body which, by nitrous particles fermenting with them, could be brewed into a liquor rather resembling blood'.[32] But what was troubling – or intriguing – was the amount of testimony and sustained intellectual attention that vampirism had attracted from medical scientists, the military, the government and the Church:

There is not an historical fact in the world more fully attested, than that of the Vampires. It is confirmed by regular information, certificates of Notaries, Surgeons, Vicars, and Magistrates. And yet, with all this, who believes in Vampires? And shall we be all damned for not believing? . . . My constant experience, as well as that of mankind in general, is much more convincing in this respect than the testimony of individuals.[33]

It was this that might bear on the relationship of vampires to 'natural man'.

Hence Rousseau considers vampire tales to be fables. His novel *Émile* (1762) includes a dialogue between a 'Believer' and a 'Reasoner' on the subject of the supernatural:

Reasoner. Supernatural! What is the meaning of that word? I do not understand it.

Believer. Changes in the order of nature, prophecies, miracles, prodigies of every kind.

Reasoner. Prodigies! Miracles! I never saw any.

Believer. Others saw them for you. Clouds of witnesses . . . The consent of nations . . .

Reasoner. Is the consent of nations in the supernatural order?

Believer. No; but when unanimous, it is incontestable.

Reasoner. There is nothing more incontestable than the principles of reason; and it is impossible to support an absurdity by human testimony. Once more I ask you, where are the supernatural proofs? for the testimony of all the world does not go beyond nature.[34]

Vampires hang over this dispute, as they do in Rousseau's more forthright account of miracles that prefaces this dialogue:

Who can pretend to tell me, how many ocular witnesses are necessary, to render a miracle worthy of credit? If the wonders you have performed in proof of your doctrine, stand in need of a proof themselves, of what use are they? We might as well have none.[35]

But that still did not explain why vampires persisted, outside of reason and theology. They existed in the twilight of apprehension, where faith and superstition, reason and imagination were undecided. So they did exist, at least in the minds of those who believed in them, and according to the institutions represented by 'Notaries, Surgeons, Vicars, and Magistrates'. They were instruments of power and control. And they disproved proof.

Others joined the debate – though seldom with the subtlety of Rousseau. The physician and deist Protestant Louis de Jaucourt, for example, wrote a brief entry on vampires for Diderot's *Encyclopédie* (1765; de Jaucourt was the most assiduous contributor to the *Encyclopédie*) and duly dismissed them as '*prétendus démons*' ('pretended demons') that appeal to superstitious minds.[36] A similar entry, approvingly citing Calmet though dismissing vampirism as '*une espèce de fanatisme épidémique*', appeared in Diderot's primary competitor, the Jesuit *Dictionnarie de Trévoux* (1771), and interestingly distinguished between active and passive vampires: between predators and victims.[37] Nonetheless, at the same time the *Gazette Françoise* carried a news report that the 'madness of Vampires' had struck a small town in Moldavia, and rumours were circulating advising that the most effective protection against contracting vampirism was to rip out the teeth from infected corpses and suck the blood out of the gums.[38]

With considerably more sophistication, Voltaire similarly disputed the value of testimony, if he predictably cloaked his account of vampires with ridicule of the Roman Catholic Church. For Voltaire – Enlightenment deist, defender of freedom of faith and scourge of institutionalized religion – all superstition is false, as is anything that violates God's natural laws. His discursive entry on 'Vampires' for his *Questions sur L'Encyclopédie* (1772) begins incredulously:

> WHAT! is it in our eighteenth century that vampires exist? Is it after the reigns of Locke, Shaftesbury, Trenchard, and Collins? Is it under those of D'Alembert, Diderot, St. Lambert, and Duclos, that we believe in vampires?[39]

Having duly marshalled his rational sceptics, he then provides a droll account, in which vampires enjoy a comfortable residence in Poland,

Hungary, Silesia, Moravia, Austria and Lorraine, where they satisfy an 'excellent appetite' by sucking the blood from the living. Of the Paole case, for instance, Voltaire notes that when he was exhumed, 'They found him in his coffin, fresh and jolly, with his eyes open, and asking for food.' Voltaire cites Tournefort and d'Argens in outlining vampire belief, and importantly recognizes it as a modern phenomenon, pointing out that there are no vampires in the Bible and that for analogies commentators have tended (incongruously) to cite miraculous instances of resurrection. He also notes that feeding the dead is a shared belief across different cultures: light foods such as 'sweetmeats, whipped cream, and melting fruits' nourish the soul, while heavier foods – 'roast beef, and the like' – sustain the body.

Vampires are, then, a fantastical epidemic, a delusion of crowds: 'Nothing was spoken of but vampires, from 1730 to 1735; they were laid in wait for, their hearts torn out and burnt.'[40] For Voltaire, they are a perfect Enlightenment storm, rushing across the continent in the face of reason: 'After slander, nothing is communicated more promptly than superstition, fanaticism, sorcery, and tales of those raised from the dead.' The belief was a madness comparable to religious zealotry. Vampires on the one hand resembled 'the ancient martyrs – the more they were burnt, the more they abounded'; on the other hand, their sudden rise and equally sudden disappearance is comparable to extremist waves, such as the Demoniacs and Convulsionnaires, the latter being a radical cult that started in the late 1720s in which votaries exhibited violent convulsions and practised extreme mortifications of the flesh – such as crucifixion. 'The result of all this is, that a great part of Europe has been infested with vampires for five or six years, and that there are now no more . . .'

Voltaire ultimately puts the origins of vampires down to fundamentalist Greek Orthodox Christianity and the belief that excommunicants do not decay – 'precisely the contrary' to Roman Catholics, 'who believe that corpses which do not corrupt are marked with the seal of eternal beatitude'.[41] However,

The Greeks are persuaded that these dead are sorcerers; they call them 'broucolacas', or 'vroucolacas' . . . The Greek corpses go into houses to suck the blood of little children, eat the supper of the fathers and mothers, drink their wine, and break all the furniture. They can only be put to rights by burning them when they are caught. But the precaution must be taken of not putting them into the fire until after their hearts are torn out, which must be burnt separately.

For Voltaire, Catholics were gullible enough to be taken in by this fairy-tale nonsense. Calmet (who had died in 1757) comes in for especial venom. Despite having more or less consistently argued that vampires do not exist, he is scathingly attacked for even entertaining doubt and weighing the evidence. Voltaire, who had taken much from Calmet's commentaries (and indeed his library) in amassing his evidence to attack the Bible, witheringly brands him the 'historiographer' of vampires, and claims that he 'treated vampires as he treated the Old and new Testament, by relating faithfully all that has been said before him'. Calmet's moderation was distorted to imply that he believed in the whole ensemble of vampirism. In fact, the Church itself was little more than a nest of vampires: 'the true vampires are the monks, who eat at the expense of both kings and people'. Exit Count Calmet.

But if vampires are absurd Orthodox superstitions from the edges of Europe that could mesmerize Catholic theologians, they are nevertheless telling figurative metaphors:

We never heard speak of vampires in London, nor even at Paris. I confess, that in both these cities there were stock-jobbers, brokers, and men of business, who sucked the blood of the people in broad daylight; but they were not dead, though corrupted. These true suckers lived not in cemeteries, but in very agreeable palaces.[42]

In Hungary, Sámuel Tessedik later likewise saw vampires as economic marauders, describing rich peasants and tax-collectors as 'vampires', and Gábor Klaniczay makes the point that 'Whilst in earlier centuries it was imaginary magical conflicts that served to resolve or release real social and cultural tensions, now it was social and cultural conflicts that began to assume a somewhat magical dimension.'[43] The political vampires of England – legislators, entrepreneurs and commissioned officers – found associates among the ecclesiastical officials, stock-jobbers, brokers and businessmen on the continent. They were already a world away from the folklore of Eastern Europe.

Demonic mystical body

In the medical journal *The Lancet* in 1829, the Irish physician Peter Hennis Green, writing as 'Erinensis', criticized imports of Irish cadavers to British medical schools. The 'resurrectionists' or body-snatchers having exhausted graveyards in England, Scotland and Wales for medical science were now seeing profitability in Irish graveyards. This commercial initiative was made possible by the traffic in steamboats across the Irish Sea; however, even then the corpses could be in transit in the warm hold of a vessel for two or three weeks. Wilson Rae, a retired naval surgeon, was the mastermind behind this ghastly trade, harvesting up to 2,000 corpses a year. Green describes him as a 'wholesale vampire', emptying graves and leaving them open, and getting 'the dead to march for the convenience of the living'. Rae smuggled the cadavers in piano-cases, and, in a gruesomely erotic twist, also involved his 'respectably-dressed' wife in the trade. He was eventually arrested and imprisoned in Newgate. But Green called for a more apt penalty to be meted out on the vampiric miscreant:

> The punishment imposed by Mezentius on the soldiers of Æneas should be inflicted, by coupling him to one of his own corses and parading him through the streets, until his carcass and its companion were amalgamated by putrefaction.[44]

Green's call, though hardly serious, refers to a grotesque form of Etruscan torture and execution favoured by the named tyrant Mezentius and described in Virgil's *Aeneid*. It involved a living victim coming literally face to face with death by being bound to a corpse. In John Dryden's translation:

> The Living and the Dead, at his Command
> Were coupled, Face to Face, and Hand to Hand:

Till choak'd with Stench, in loth'd Embraces ty'd,
The ling'ring Wretches pin'd away, and dy'd.[45]

By the sixteenth century, this deadly communion had become medicalized as a horrific emblematic figure, in which a woman is depicted as being bound to a syphilitic man and inevitably succumbing to the putrid disease.[46] This sickening matrimony, the *Nupta Contagioso* or *Nupta Cadavera*, was a forced union with the dead that clearly prefigured fears of vampirism, and so maps further the constellation of dreads and confusions that surround the condition.

The Etruscan torture was not only physically nauseating, but was also mentally appalling as it exposed the hideous truth that the body was already rotting. Nigredo – the post-mortem blackening of a corpse – spreads from the dead to make the living not so much undead as unliving, as well as liquefying individual integrity and identity into slime: the blackening bestowed by the corpse bride is less an 'infestation' than a 'revelatory catalyst'.[47] Death and the processes of decay become the norm; life is a mere aberration, a stage on the way of extinction and rottenness; and the body is merely a corpse-in-waiting. Aristotle had already argued that growth was a defining quality of life – but so was decomposition.[48] Indeed, for Aristotle the whole science of being was based on putrefaction, which was a fugitive process that allowed amalgamation and incorporation:

> beings must undergo necrosis and decay in order to remain in being and the Ideas must be founded on an intensive necrosis and an extensive decay in order to remain in their essence and to synthesize with other Ideas.[49]

By the beginning of the nineteenth century, natural scientists exhibited a highly progressive interest in putrefaction, which seemed to be engaged in a macabre dance with the forces of life. According to the pioneering chemist Humphry Davy, the discipline of chemistry could explain 'the conversion of dead matter into living matter by vegetable organs', and so he consequently claimed that 'the study of the simple and unvarying agencies of dead matter ought surely to precede investigations concerning the mysterious and complicated powers of life'.[50] Life, it appeared, could emerge from foul ooze.

The strangeness of vampirism, then, is that it encapsulates the perverse human desire to rot in the grave. Vampires do not decay, so post-mortem putrefaction is a guarantee that one is (or one's mouldering remains once were) human – unless one is so impossibly conceited as to claim to be an Incorruptible – and indeed there were articles on this very topic published at the time in the popular press.[51] In this context, vampires are 'things' that by bringing us literally face to face with death act as a chilling reminder that human life aspires to death and rottenness rather than to changeless permanence.[52] But this also links vampires to another theological concept that was itself entangled in politics and anatomy: the 'mystical body'. This, the *corpus mysticum*, is a spiritualized version of the body politic, an anatomized body of faith that realizes the implications of fleshly embodiment. It is proposed by St Paul in his First Letter to the Corinthians and expounded by St Augustine and St Jerome.[53] St Paul catalogues the necessary multiplicity of the body: 'the eye cannot say unto the hand, I have no need of thee: nor again the head to the feet, I have no need of you'. The repeated point he makes is that 'the body is not one member, but many', in which manifold and disparate parts cohere in a divine unity.[54]

The idea of the mystical body – 'the *body in mystery*, immediately connected to a *mystery of the body*' – distinguishes 'the sacramental body from the historical body [that is] the crucified body . . . [i.e.] the sacrament of the Passion from the Passion itself'.[55] Thus the anatomical body becomes a living metaphor for the Church, the Incarnation and the Eucharist. In other words, the tangible reality of the human body can be understood as inseparable from its Christianization and symbolism within the faith.[56] But the vampire is effectively a 'demonic mystical body'. Vampirism is chaotically disruptive, unrestrained by worldly and otherworldly thresholds, and physically terrorizing: in contrast, then, it is an undead metaphor for the disarray and collapse of secular society; for unbridled and intangible contagion; and for the horrid corporeality of the human body (which is sucked dry of blood) and the disorder of the grave (which is neither an eternal nor a serene place of rest).[57] What is drily disguised in the funeral service of the Anglican Book of Common Prayer as the body crumbling to dust and ashes

(ashes being an archaic synonym for dust) is recast as the sodden blood-thirstiness of the restless vampire. As such, the vampire, in all its inexplicability and multiplicity, reveals a world oblivious of human explication.[58]

It is precisely these implications of the living reality of the body that are so challenged by vampirism. It is not enough to claim that the bread and wine of the Eucharist is somehow cannibalistic and vampiric – that is a sensationalist and superficial reading of the communion. Rather, the vampire, as a 'demonic mystical body', is 'blasphemous life . . . the life that is living but that should not be living'.[59] Though this outlandish life form may have possible scientific explanations, it nevertheless persists in being 'utterly incomprehensible'. It is not so much, then, that the vampire emerges from 'an epistemological void' between life and death that cannot be bridged either by science or by religion, as that it insists on an alien concept of 'life' itself that 'mediates between theology and horror' and that resists comprehension and interpretation by single methods of reasoning.[60] Vampires are thus 'wicked problems' on the nature of being.

Thinking about vampires in these ways aligns vampirology with the occult neo-Platonic mystic Dionysius the Areopagite, whose 'negative theology' is based on a notion of the divine as 'shadowy, dark, and absent . . . not because it is lacking in anything, but because it is superlatively beyond human comprehension'. The contemporary philosopher of horror, Eugene Thacker, christens this the 'black illumination':

The black illumination is a degree zero of thought, inaccessible to the senses, unintelligible to thought, impossible to experience – all that is left is the residue of a minimal, frozen thought of an enigmatic epiphany . . . In the black illumination, thought does not exist, but instead subsists, persists, and even resists. In the black illumination, all experience leads to the impossibility of experience, from the fullness of fear to the emptiness of thought.

Hence Thacker and fellow thinkers such as Graham Harman claim that the literature of horror is concerned with the same questions of the unearthly and the ineffable that have in the past been the focus of religion and mysticism. Yet, like medical science, Enlightenment philosophy and rational theology, horror writing exists within a secular and empirical world 'that ultimately questions the ability of humans to know anything at all'.[61] Although Thacker barely mentions vampires – and certainly does not historicize his understanding of horror – this point is nevertheless crucial for grasping the vampiric import. Vampires are not like other, earlier supernatural monsters or undead apparitions: they are quite different, because they are Enlightenment beings. They exist – *have* to exist – in a modern and rational world. We might describe this world as a complex of ecosystems and human–vampire–animal relations; in the eighteenth century, however, it would have been described in the context of, for example, empirical science, forensic medicine, competing theologies of the supernatural, ratiocination, the value of testimony, definitions of the human, and social politics. Taken out of these frames, vampires are little more than primordial Gothic fiends – shadows of a lost world. The unearthly vampire requires an earthly body, a biology and an environmental logic; it is not simply a haunting, but a set of physical signs and symptoms. Vampires thus bring a black illumination to the Enlightenment, by challenging the epistemological foundations of rationalism and empirical knowledge. They are both real and unreal; physical yet possessing immaterial potentialities; and of course wholly non-anthropocentric. So it is that vampires, by occupying radically uncertain positions in medical science, in questions of evidence, in the rationalist turn in both Protestant and Catholic theology, and in philosophical accounts of the human, draw uncomfortable and disturbing attention to the fissures and shortcomings in contemporary ways of thinking; in so doing, they inspired generations of writers.

PART II

COAGULATING
THE NINETEENTH CENTURY TO THE PRESENT

CHAPTER 5

THE CULTURES OF DEATH
Gothic Romanticism, Deathly Words

If you slice off the pointed end of the heart in a live dog, and insert a finger into one of the cavities, you will feel unmistakeably that every time the heart gets shorter it presses the finger, and every time it gets longer it stops pressing it.

René Descartes (1647–48)[1]

I have been half in love with easeful Death.

John Keats (1819)[2]

These reanimations are vampire-cold.

Thomas Lovell Beddoes (1825)[3]

For nearly a century, the vampire was a medical, sociological and political reality – or disputed reality – of Eastern Europe, as well as a theological conundrum. Then it came to Britain and was transformed. Vampires flashed through Romanticism like lightning, driven on by the obsessively necrophiliac imagination of the period, from John Keats's repeated deathly wooings to Thomas De Quincey's scandalous assertion that murder was a 'fine art'. Vampires were animated by sublime terror and abject horror to become comprehensively supernaturalized, even figures of inspiration, and they therefore have a place in theories of the Romantic imagination – from the influence of psychology and the understanding of monstrosity to questions of self-identity and the emotions.[4] At the same time, vampires began to accumulate a vast panoply of morbid imagery that was gathered from the vaults of the English past, and so they were simultaneously Gothicized. The cult of the vampire thrived within the emerging Gothic, as the figure was a perpetual and literal reminder that the past cannot be laid to rest, but will forever haunt the present.

Yet accounts of vampires also remained rooted in the concerns of contemporary medical and natural science, and thus in physical matter and the stuff of the world. For this reason, they also became part of an increasingly materialistic taste, gripped by crime narratives and contemporary villainy, as well as spellbound by the newly discovered mysteries of the natural world. Hence writers increasingly depicted vampires as more life-like, more human – part of nineteenth-century capitalist society; at the same time, the natural world became more magical, more eerie. And although in one sense the vampire threat was partly defused by writers who treated them as fictions, there remained considerable wariness about dismissing them too hastily, and there were repeated references to the earlier attested reports. Even as Gothic avatars, then, vampires are not simply restless shades serving as reminders of the crimes of history. They are bundles of history themselves: buried in the ground or immured in tombs, they are dug up to reveal histories inside history – histories that are complex, disturbing and dangerous; histories that are apparently real and make reality unreal.

Bloodlines

The vampire first emerges in poetry in Germany. Heinrich August Ossenfelder's poem 'Der Vampir' was published in the scientific journal *Der Naturforscher* (*The Natural Scientist*, 1748). It derives directly from the Arnod Paole case, via the marquis d'Argens' account of Johann Flückinger's report, which had just been reprinted in the same journal by the editor, Christlob Mylius.[5] Ossenfelder's short 22-line verse depicts the vampire as a male sexual predator, threatening to suck away the lifeblood of the symbolically named maiden Christiana while she sleeps. Although the poem had little immediate impact, it is striking that it appeared in a scientific journal based in Leipzig (the heart of eighteenth-century German vampire debate) and identifies the vampire as being Hungarian (specifically mentioning the River Tisza and the wine-producing Tokaj region – details taken from d'Argens). However, Ossenfelder explicitly avoids scientific or medical debate and theological or philosophical dilemmas. The poem is secular, sinister and darkly erotic – a fantasy of love and death, of *Liebestod*.[6]

This theme of sexual violence and the dazzling power dynamics that it conjures up produced a decisive shift in depictions of the vampire, and is the crucial literary bequest to the figure. For a few years, the allure of carnality and cruelty, steeped in blood, was the key cultural motif of vampirism, even while it continued to be described as East European folklore and a staple of travellers' tales, often in an uneasy relationship with empirical explanations. And although Ossenfelder's vampire was superseded by other, later incarnations, they were of the same kin and shared the same fatally seductive blood-line. Gottfried August Bürger's 'Lenore' was the most renowned of this brood.[7] Although Bürger continued in the same sexual vein as Ossenfelder, his lines were also inspired by Thomas Percy's collection *Reliques of Ancient English Poetry* (1765) – an anthology of traditional and national songs and ballads that included several supernatural revenant pieces, such as 'Sweet William's Ghost'. Indeed, 'Lenore' was itself purported to have originated as a traditional German ballad. Whatever the case, Bürger's *Kunstballade* (art ballad) certainly set the tone of the emerging movement of *Sturm und Drang* ('storm and stress'): writings of extreme states, unrestrained passion and imaginative excess that conjured the supernatural back into mainstream literary culture and led directly to Gothic Romanticism.

'Lenore', first published in 1774 in the literary annual *Göttinger Musenalmanach*, was a *succès de scandale* across Europe, attracting praise from critics such as Wilhelm August von Schlegel (if also causing the *Göttinger Musenalmanach* to be banned in Vienna). The demon lover in this 32-verse poem is Wilhelm, a soldier who fails to return home following the 1757 Battle of Prague, an engagement in the Seven Years' War. Is he tarrying, or has he been killed in the conflict? Both scenarios, it transpires, are true; and when he does then return, he does so as a harbinger of death. The dead man seizes – rapes – his betrothed Lenore, and carries her alive to the grave, accompanied by a ghastly train of spirits and a chilling refrain that would echo through vampire tales: '*die Todten reiten schnell*' ('the dead ride fast').[8] Wilhelm is revealed to be Death himself, carrying the archaic symbols of mortality: an hourglass and a scythe. Once revealed, he becomes rancid flesh before his lover's eyes.

Yet 'Lenore', despite its East European orientation, is not strictly a vampire ballad; it is really a Gothic revival of the medieval cult of the macabre and a lurid reworking of the northern ballad tradition. Nonetheless, in its turn, 'Lenore' inspired Johann Wolfgang von Goethe's pagan vampire poem 'Die Braut von Korinth' ('The Bride of Corinth', 1798). 'Die Braut' was far more explicitly concerned with bloodsucking demons. Goethe's poem is based on the ancient Greek myth of Philinnion, as told by Phlegon and later Proclus, in which a she-demon lover returns from the dead to woo the youth Makhartes and is consequently immolated by the townspeople.[9] In Goethe's poem, the unnamed bride of Corinth is a *femme fatale*, whose threat is implicit in a thirst for wine accompanied by an abstention from food. Ominously, 'Her pale lips quaff[ing] the blood-red wine' hint at what is to come: she drains her lover of life –

> While in her lover's bosom prest,
>   The blood that stirs
> In his veins warms hers,
> But, oh! no heart throbs in her breast![10]

And yet although she literally sucks the blood of his heart ('*Und zu saugen seines Herzens Blut*'), she is not explicitly named as a vampire in the poem.

Both 'Lenore' and 'Die Braut von Korinth' were popular in Britain – and proved to be abiding influences on Gothic Romanticism. 'Lenore' was first translated into English by William Taylor of Norwich in March 1796, and subsequently by many others, including Walter Scott in his first publication (also 1796); over the next century over 30 different translations left the press.[11] These German poems certainly cast a profound shadow over Samuel Taylor Coleridge's uncanny faerie verse *Christabel*, begun in 1798 (though not published until 1816). The bewitching character Geraldine in this poem is undoubtedly vampiric, if again not actually a vampire. She preys on the young Christabel in mysterious ways, feeding from the young girl until 'her girded vests / Grew tight beneath her heaving breasts'. She has an unnerving reptilian quality: her own breasts are scaly and she has large, bright, wild and mesmerizing eyes that flash upon Christabel and cause her to screw up her own eyes into snaky cavities.[12] Vampirism haunts Coleridge's other work of the period, too. At the same time as he was beginning *Christabel*, he was also completing *The Rime of the Ancient Mariner*, in which the Mariner drinks his own blood ('I bit my arm, I sucked the blood') and a ship of the undead bears down upon the Mariner's own vessel.[13] Yet despite these allusions, it was really Coleridge's friend and ally Robert Southey who first unequivocally gathered vampires to English poetry.[14]

Like Coleridge, Southey had encountered vampires through sensationalist German *Sturm und Drang* literature; but for his Islamic epic *Thalaba the Destroyer* (first published in 1801) he reworked the Hungarian phenomenon through orientalism. Oneiza, Thalaba's bride, dies on their wedding day, but when he visits her tomb she appears as a spirit enveloped in strange fire:

> 'Now, now!' cried Thalaba;
> And o'er the chamber of the tomb
> There spread a lurid gleam,
> Like the reflection of a sulphur fire;
> And in that hideous light
> Oneiza stood before them. It was She, . .
> Her very lineaments, . . and such as death
> Had changed them, livid cheeks, and lips of blue;
> But in her eyes there dwelt
> Brightness more terrible
> Than all the loathsomeness of death.[15]

Her 'vampire corpse' is straightaway impaled by a spear, releasing her spirit. Yet despite locating the poem in the lands described in the *Arabian Nights*, Southey provided ten pages of notes on East European vampires, conspicuously reprinting the marquis d'Argens' text *Lettres Juives* (detailing Arnod Paole), Tournefort's account and Louis-François Cassas's Istrian travel narrative.[16]

But the first poem in English completely devoted to the vampire is probably 'The Dead Men of Pest', which was published in *The Athenæum* ('A Magazine of Literary and Miscellaneous Information') in April 1807. Its very subtitle – 'A Hungarian Legend' – hints at its sources, but the verse also commences with an 'argument' that explicitly refers to the eighteenth-century Slavonic cases, the ensuing intellectual debate between 'learned divines and physicians', and which directly refers to the work of Henry More and the digests reported in the pages of the *Gentleman's Magazine*. The author, John Herman Merivale, was a regular contributor to the *Monthly Review* and had discussed vampires with Byron; he was, however, a thoroughgoing sceptic and so sees fit to write his poem as an antiquarian pastiche in ballad metre imitating Percy's *Reliques* and Thomas Chatterton's 'Rowley' poems (and consequently – if doubtless inadvertently – reviving the debate on authentic evidence via recent controversies on literary forgery).[17]

Despite this anachronistic historicizing, the poem has some force. An English traveller visits the cosmopolitan 'Towne of Peste' on the River Danube (part of what is now Budapest). It is filled with 'towering Mosques', but the Christian faith seems to have died: bells do not ring on Sundays and churchyards are barred – as if Judgment Day has already been and gone. An aged and skeletal old man recounts the fate of the townspeople as a howling dog passes by, falls into an eerie silence and slinks away. The narrator is unsettled, for the old man has a magnetic charisma akin to that of Coleridge's 'Ancyent Marinere' (a poem which, in its first incarnation, also imitated archaic poetry):

> I felt my verie bloud creepe in my vaynes;
>> My Bones were icie-cold; my Hayr on ende.
> I wishd myself agen uponn the Playnes,
>> Yet cold not but that sadde old Man attende.

His tale is sobering. He is not an aged retainer, but is desperately old before his time, both his young daughters – like most of the townsfolk – having died in the past seven weeks, all growing 'pale and sadd' and deathly cold. So it was that

'One miserable Wight did pyne and wane,
  And, on the seaventh Daye gave upp the Ghoste;
His Corse was oped by a Chirurgeon of fame
  Who found that evrie dropp of bloud was loste.'

The surgeon's dissection foreshadows what is to come.

Hundreds die, despite the rabid consumption of ox meat and Tokay wine. This 'straunge Disease' at last reaches the family of the (not so) old man – in the form of a tailor who had died some 12 months previously and is now caught 'lumbering upp the Stayres' to his daughter, the very clatter of his coming indicating that he was no mere ghost – 'A Noyse more hevie than a Tunne of Ledde'. Bloated with her blood, he staggers out even heavier than before. When the old man himself witnesses this disaster, he straightaway goes to a priest, and they visit the churchyard and the grave of the tailor: 'We stopped – we brought a Mattocke and a Spade'. They dig up the coffin and open it, tearing away the shroud to reveal the corpse:

The Veynes seemed full of Bloud, the Lipps distained,
  All dripping with my Daughter's new suck'd gore.

The priest confirms that this is 'The Vampyre', and so further corpses are exhumed – and every one proves to be a vampire, heavy with engorged flesh and the blood of its victims. Even before the tale has been told, the narrator's own blood is freezing in his veins. Yet all the attempts to deal with the menace are wholly inadequate – purification rituals of incense and Ave Marias, and bolts on the churchyard. These vampires are supernaturally strong, resistant to the devices of priestcraft and – most chillingly – innumerable. The poem ends with the old man observing that

For when a Dead-Man has learn'd to draw a naile,
  He can also burst an iron Bolte in two.

The town has become a city of the undead, a twilight realm in which the aged man and the narrator are now the aliens: vampirism has been normalized in Pest as an all-embracing pestilence. The narrator flees and resolves never again to go near 'the Walles of Peste'.[18]

The cult grew. In 1813, Southey was appointed poet laureate, and in the same year the two best-selling poets of the time both introduced vampirism into their poetry. Lord Byron consolidated Southey's oriental-ized vampires in *The Giaour*, in which the Giaour (or infidel) is cursed by a Turk to rise as a vampire and suck the blood from his closest female rela-tions – daughter, sister and wife:

> But first, on earth as Vampire sent,
> Thy corse shall from its tomb be rent;
> Then ghastly haunt thy native place,
> And suck the blood of all thy race,
> There from thy daughter, sister, wife,
> At midnight drain the stream of life;
> Yet loathe the banquet which perforce
> Must feed thy livid living corse:
> Thy victims ere they yet expire
> Shall know the dæmon for their sire,
> As cursing thee, thou cursing them,
> Thy flowers are wither'd on the stem.[19]

Byron added two notes to this description. The first cites 'Honest Tournefort', as quoted by Southey, observing that 'The Vampire supersti-tion is still general in the Levant' (meaning the eastern Mediterranean) and that 'The Greeks never mention the word without horror'; Byron himself had witnessed 'a whole family being terrified by the scream of a child, which they imagined must proceed from such a visitation'. The second note gives physical details and reiterates the testimonials confirming their existence:

> The freshness of the face, and the wetness of the lip with blood, are the never-failing signs of a Vampire. The stories told in Hungary and Greece of these foul feeders are singular, and some of them most *incred-ibly* attested.[20]

Meanwhile Walter Scott wove vampirism into the British legends and lore that formed the fabric of *Rokeby*, in the shape of a fairy succubus that haunts Wilfrid:

> For, like the bat of Indian brakes,
> Her pinions fan the wound she makes,
> And, soothing thus the dreamer's pain,
> She drinks his life-blood from the vein.[21]

There were, of course, fierce sceptics. The Scottish physician John Ferriar, whose work was read by Coleridge and who reviewed Southey's poetry (negatively), attacked 'Medical Demonology', not only dismissing much of the folklore surrounding blood, but also ridiculing Calmet and declaring the vampire (or 'the *vroucolocas*, as they termed the *redivivus*') to be an 'absurdity'.[22] But although both Byron and Scott suggest how the vampire could be adapted to popular audiences – on the one hand as an exotic monstrosity; on the other as a blend of natural history and indigenous faërie – they still did not supersede the more factual East European vampire, which kept returning. In 'The Vampyre', a poem written by John Stagg, the 'Blind Bard' of Cumberland, and published in 1816, Stagg emphasized the recent vampire origins in Hungary and Germany. In the introductory 'Argument', he describes dead persons leaving their graves at night and visiting their friends 'whom, by suckosity, they drained of their blood as they slept. The person thus phlebotomised was sure to become a Vampyre in his turn.'[23] Stagg's tone is mock-antiquarian: he takes delight in tongue-in-cheek coinages (such as 'suckosity'), and interestingly describes the vampire feasting as a 'carnival', referring to the etymology of the word as 'the putting away or removal of flesh (as food)'.[24] He also summarizes earlier research, suggesting that vampirism could variously be explained by *vis vegetans* or the demonic possession of corpses.[25] The poem itself is a morbid Germanic ballad written in a wry tone of *Schadenfreude*, in which the unfortunate character Herman is wasting away, preyed on from beyond the grave by his recently deceased friend Sigismund:

> 'From the drear mansions of the tomb,
>   From the low regions of the dead,

The ghost of Sigismund doth roam,
  And dreadful haunts me in my bed!

'There, vested in infernal guise,
  (By means to me not understood)
Close to my side the goblin lies,
  And drinks away my vital blood!'[26]

Upon Herman's death his lover, Gertrude, comes face to face with the frightful Sigismund:

His jaws cadaverous were besmear'd
  With clotted carnage o'er and o'er,
And all his horrid whole appear'd
  Distent, and fill'd with human gore![27]

Sigismund's coffin is opened and he is found to be undecayed; both corpses are staked. Stagg's poem heightens the erotic pulse that characterizes poetic portrayals, by making his vampire relationship an intimacy between males, and so conspicuously homoerotic.

The prevalence of vampires and vampirism (and near-vampirism) in poetry shows how the figure was both a familiar and also a developing figure. But it was in fiction that the vampire was really to flourish. In particular, two works of the British Romantic movement not only established the figure for the remainder of the nineteenth century, but sealed its fate to the present day.[28]

Lords of iniquity

On 17 June 1816, John William Polidori recorded in his diary that 'The ghost stories are begun by all but me.'[29] Polidori was Lord Byron's physician and had accompanied the poet and hypochondriac to Switzerland, where Byron rented the Villa Diodati on the banks of Lake Geneva.[30] They had been joined there by the poet Percy Shelley, his lover Mary Godwin (whom Percy married later that year) and her half-sister Claire

Clairmont. The weather in Switzerland – indeed across the globe – was atrocious. The year 1816 was 'The Year Without A Summer': due to a gigantic volcanic eruption on the Indonesian island of Tambora the previous year, volcanic ash had been hurled into the stratosphere and remained there for years, blotting out sunlight and drastically altering weather patterns.[31] Daytrips were out of the question for much of their stay, and so the previous evening, while watching storms thundering across the lake, Byron had suggested to the assembled company that they should each write a ghost story.[32]

The next day, Polidori recorded 'Began my ghost story after tea.'[33] Mary Shelley later recalled:

Poor Polidori had some terrible idea about a skull-headed lady who was so punished for peeping through a keyhole – what to see I forget – something very shocking and wrong of course; but when she was reduced to a worse condition than the renowned Tom of Coventry, he did not know what to do with her, and was obliged to dispatch her to the tomb of the Capulets, the only place for which she was fitted.[34]

This story – if it ever existed – has not survived, but Polidori may well have been distracted by what happened later that evening. At midnight, he noted, as Mary breastfed her four-month-old baby child, the group

really began to talk ghostly. L[ord] B[yron] repeated some verses of Coleridge's 'Christabel', of the witch's breast; when silence ensued, and Shelley, suddenly shrieking and putting his hands to his head, ran out of the room with a candle. Threw water in his face and gave him ether. He was looking at Mrs. S[helley], and suddenly thought of a woman he had heard of who had eyes instead of nipples, which, taking hold of his mind, horrified him.[35]

The following day he again noted 'began my ghost-story' – presumably a different story, and perhaps influenced by the *Christabel* fiasco the previous night.[36] The new story became his unregarded novel *Ernestus Berchtold; or, the Modern Oedipus*, published in 1819.

Byron had abandoned his own story after a few pages, although nevertheless it was published (without his permission) in 1819 as 'A Fragment'. 'A Fragment' returns to the Turkish vampire figure of *The Giaour*, describing the mysterious Augustus Darvell, who is in the grip of some curious and undiagnosed wasting disease. Darvell and the unnamed narrator travel to Turkey, intending to visit the Greek ruins at Ephesus, and their journey takes them through a desolate landscape of Greek, Christian and Islamic ruins to a remote cemetery. Darvell disconcertingly murmurs, 'I have also been here before' and states that he will soon die. He demands that the narrator conceal the news of his death, throw an Arabic ring he has into certain springs on the ninth day of the month at noon, and the following day wait at a ruined temple.[37] A stork with a live snake writhing in its beak contemplates Darvell as he makes these plans, and Darvell asks to be buried where the bird is perched. The moment it flies away he dies and begins to turn black and decompose with unnatural rapidity; the narrator buries him as instructed, and there the text ends.

'A Fragment' is a curtailed vampire narrative. The metamorphosis of the flesh, the burial ground and the abnormal post-mortem state link it to the earlier eighteenth-century history of vampires, and doubtless Darvell would have risen from the dead. But Byron also introduces calculatedly exotic elements, notably the spell with the ring, and the stork and snake – a familiar enough pairing, but here suggesting a disturbing inversion of the ancient lore that storks deliver new babies. Although 'A Fragment' hardly has a prominent place in the Byron canon, its mood was transfused into Polidori's next story.

Polidori had studied medicine at Edinburgh and had written a treatise on somnambulism, and his professional interest was clearly piqued by the serious scientific interest afforded to vampires in the previous century. A shadow of vampirism lies upon his aborted story about the 'skull-headed lady' who ends up, like Juliet, in the tomb of the Capulets – Juliet of course rises vampire-like from this tomb, before discovering that Romeo, believing her to be dead, has already killed himself. Polidori would have been familiar with the notes to Southey's *Thalaba* and to Byron's own *Giaour* (if only through Byron's recollection of them) and *Christabel* presumably provoked talk of the seductive powers of the undead. So it was that Polidori discussed

Byron's aborted vampire narrative at the villa with the countess of Breuss, who urged him to write his own version. The results – Polidori's third story undertaken at the villa – were to be far from forgettable.[38]

Polidori commenced work, but then his situation changed rapidly. As the Swiss trip drew to a close in early September, an exasperated Byron fired his cantankerous physician; Polidori consequently used his tale to revenge himself on his former employer. He aimed to expose the haughty lordling as a cruel seducer – Mary Shelley's half-sister Claire Clairmont being pregnant at the time with Byron's child, and hardly the first victim to fall for his diabolical charms. His portrait of Lord Ruthven was therefore of a sexual delinquent and predator, powerfully attracted to the virtuous and the virginal. He drew on anti-heroes such as the rapist Robert Lovelace from Samuel Richardson's epistolary novel *Clarissa* (1747–48), the malevolent monk Schedoni of Ann Radcliffe's novel of terror *The Italian* (1797), and the repugnant libertines who inhabit the marquis de Sade's repellent novel *Juliette* (1797–1801), such as the cannibal giant Minski (who has furniture made of human bones) and the obsessive necrophiliac and criminally depraved Cordelli.[39] He also drew on Lady Caroline Lamb's scandalous novel *Glenarvon* (1816). Byron had deserted Lamb in the midst of their passionate affair, and Lamb exacted her revenge by basing the novel's pitiless anti-hero on her former lover; Lord Glenarvon's name is Clarence de Ruthven.

Polidori's portrait is not conventionally erotic: Ruthven has a 'dead grey eye' that seems not to perceive character or humanity; he is cadaverous and the 'deadly hue' of his face is never lit with vivacity; and he all but ignores women as an inferior species. Yet he has strong features and a compelling voice, and his apparent indifference to women carries a masochistic allure. He is also wealthy and perversely generous, sharing his wealth in the most decadent ways possible: by financing the dissolute in their pursuit of vice and leading them into disgrace – or to the gallows. He is a lone wolf, subverting morals. And then his dead eyes fall upon women, his tender prey.

Ruthven dies in Greece after being shot by robbers. He has already started rotting before his death, but has time to swear his companion, the protagonist Mr Aubrey, to keep silent about him for a year and a day. His body is placed on a summit to catch the first rays of the moon, whereupon it disappears.[40] Aubrey then discovers through forensic deduction that

Ruthven must have killed his Greek paramour Ianthe, who was found with blood on her neck and breast, 'and upon her throat were the marks of teeth having opened the vein'. As Aubrey sinks into delirium, Ruthven rises from the dead and seduces Aubrey's innocent young sister, who is likewise found to have glutted his thirst for fresh blood. As if in ironic sympathy to the plight of both his lover and his sister, Aubrey dies from a haemorrhage. Lord Ruthven, meanwhile, escapes; he is, as is clear from the title of the story, 'The Vampyre'.

Inspired by Gothic poetries, then, Polidori literally romanticizes the vampire into an enthralling outrage of sexual bloodlust.[41] But that was not the end of it. Polidori's tale was delivered to the countess of Breuss and nothing was heard of it for two-and-a-half years. Then, on 1 April 1819, it was published in the *New Monthly Magazine* as 'A Tale by Lord Byron'. It had been sent to the publisher Henry Colburn with a note that certain tales had been written by Byron, Polidori and Mary Shelley; Colburn inferred that the story in question was by Byron and, in order to capitalize on his notorious reputation, published it as such.[42]

Polidori was livid: Byron had apparently stolen his story. He immediately wrote to Colburn, insisting it is '*not* Lord Byron's, but was written *entirely* by me at the request of a lady'.[43] Polidori admitted that Byron's 'Fragment' had provided particular incidents – 'his Lordship had said that it was his intention of writing a ghost story, depending for interest upon the circumstances of two friends leaving England, and one dying in Greece, the other finding him alive, upon his return, and making love to his sister' – although, of course, Byron's 'Fragment' never reached the point of the dead man rising and seducing the sister. Polidori accordingly requested a correction, proper attribution and compensation, and insisted that any further publication be suppressed. He himself supplied a statement correcting the claims made about the tale.[44] Notwithstanding this, 'The Vampyre' continued to be attributed to Byron throughout the century – and was celebrated across the continent as further proof of his wayward genius.[45]

'The Vampyre' was not only attributed to Byron, though; it was also supplemented in the *New Monthly Magazine* and subsequent reprintings by prefatory material about Byron and the Villa Diodati retreat (including the episode regarding the effect of *Christabel* on Percy Shelley), together with an account of vampirism.[46] This description of vampires locates them in Arabia and Greece (following Southey and Byron), as well as in Hungary, Poland, Austria and Lorraine (following Ossenfelder and Bürger). It gives details of blood-engorged corpses taken from the earlier medical reports, and the account of Paole given in Britain in *The Craftsman* (1732). The sexual content of the tales is underlined – they rise from their graves to 'feed upon the blood of the young and beautiful' – and instructions for slaying vampires are provided: staking, decapitation and cremation. This self-proclaimed 'monstrous rodomontade' concludes with a long quotation from *The Giaour*, and references to *Thalaba*, 'the veracious Tournefort' and Calmet – again. It has to be said that the concise details given in this note concerning 'this singularly horrible superstition' were to prove at least as influential as Polidori's narrative.[47]

Polidori, in presenting the vampire as a depraved and amoral English aristocrat, triggered a cultural sensation.[48] Rather than being at the borders of Europe, the vampire was at the debauched edges of society, a Byronic anti-hero.[49] But although he was careful not to over-stress the medical aspects of vampirism, Polidori's vampire nevertheless helped to reignite interest in the scientific phenomenon of vampirism from a new perspective. In 1819, the *Imperial Magazine* published a feature on vampires that discussed Polidori's tale, reprinted Polidori's letter and the account of vampirism given by the *New Monthly*, and considered whether vampires were fictitious or not. The anonymous author argues that the leading idea of the literary vampire is that the vampire is a supernatural fiction, but a thread of fey doubt runs through the language:

The Vampyre is represented as a mere creature of the imagination; to which have been ascribed fictitious powers, corresponding, in their application, with those which we attribute to sylphs, fairies, elves and genii . . . Under its imposing aspect, the mind of the reader is insensibly transported into a region of enchantment . . . Awakened from this poetic delirium, when we reach the conclusion of the tale, reason once more regains its dominion over fancy; but, unfortunately, instead of following that steady light, which is necessary to all just discrimination, we suddenly fall into an opposite snare, and hastily conclude that the

Vampyre has no kind of existence, except in the dreams of poets, and the fables of romance.[50]

The writer is aware that literature inoculates readers against vampires, but recognizes that despite this they maintain some sort of presence, a state of unbeing that carries a trace of reality. They are more than mere fictions.

Unnatural history

To refute the classification of vampires as mere figments of the imagination, the *Imperial Magazine* followed the discussion of Polidori's 'Vampyre' with a letter from a correspondent on vampire bats. This account, gleaned from natural history and travel reports, drew attention to the *Vampyrum spectrum*, the name adopted by Carl Linnaeus in 1758 to designate South American spectral vampire bats reputed to suck blood (Linnaeus's false vampire bat, which was first recorded in Ecuador).[51] Various species of bat were considered to be carnivorous, from vampire bats to the enormous flying foxes of Malaysia. The correspondent, 'P.G.', claims that their wing-span can reach up to six feet, that they swarm like bees and their colonies can reach five hundred individuals, and that they are found from Brazil to Java. Like the incubus, these creatures come at night to suck blood, and have even been known to kill their hosts:

> The Bat is so dextrous a bleeder, as to insinuate its aculeated tongue into a vein without being perceived, and then suck the blood till it is satiated, all the while fanning with its wings, and agitating the air, in that hot climate, in so pleasing a manner as to throw the sufferer into a still sounder sleep.

'P.G.' also repeats John Stedman's account in his *Narrative of a Five Years Expedition against the Revolted Negroes of Surinam* (1796) of being bitten in Surinam by 'a Bat, of a monstrous size' and waking up 'weltering in congealed blood'.[52] Stedman's account had moreover been placed alongside his notorious and appallingly horrific images of slaves being tortured and executed among scattered human skulls. The clear conclusion of 'P.G.'

is that vampire beliefs derive from actual examples of predatory blood-suckers in the natural world, where vampires not only certainly do exist, but also cast a disturbing light on human cruelties.

Popular interest in the natural history of vampires enlivened travel narratives. The pioneering Roman Catholic explorer and taxidermist Charles Waterton, for instance, had what amounted to a vampire death-wish while journeying through South America. He was clearly delighted by his adopted bat, the 'nocturnal surgeon', and observed it at close quarters: 'He frequents old abandoned houses and hollow trees; and sometimes a cluster of them may be seen in the forest hanging head downwards from the branch of a tree.' One night, he shares a billet on the Pomeroon River with a Scotsman who claims he was virtually sucked to death by the 'infernal imps' of the vampire bats. Waterton notes that 'the Vampire had tapped his great toe' and makes a joke comparing the dozen ounces of blood lost to the nugatory cost of a physician letting the same amount; at this the dour Scot takes offence. Waterton then relates that the unfortunate Scotsman later gorged on the local delicacy of crabs and retired to the privy, whereupon his nether regions came under attack from an army of red ants. The poor fellow suffered an 'indescribable martyrdom'.

It was the irrepressible Waterton's ambition to be vampirized. 'I have often wished to have been once sucked by the Vampire,' he wrote, 'in order that I might have it in my power to say it had really happened to me.' He saw no danger: 'There can be no pain in the operation, for the patient is always asleep when the Vampire is sucking him, and as for the loss of a few ounces of blood, that would be a trifle in the long run.' Accordingly, 'Many a night have I slept with my foot out of the hammock to tempt this winged surgeon, expecting that he would be there; but it was all in vain.' Sadly for Waterton, 'the Vampire never sucked me, and I could never account for his not doing so, for we were inhabitants of the same loft for months together'.[53] Charles Darwin also encountered vampire bats in South America, recording that in Chile they bit horses on their withers, but that any subsequent inflammation resulted from the rubbing of saddles on the wound, rather than from loss of blood.[54] These vampires were harmless creatures, notable as much for their peculiar 'quadrupedal gait' as for their modest appetite for blood.[55]

Back in Europe, though, the contemporary history of the vampire could not be so easily forgotten or forgiven. In northern Greece, 'Colonel' William Martin Leake returned to Tournefort's account of the *vrykolakas* in his *Travels* of 1835, describing it as 'an example of the most barbarous of all those [Greek] superstitions'. He derives the name 'Vrukólaka' from the Illyric (Illyria being part of the Balkan peninsula), in particular 'the barbarians of Sclavonic race'. The description has familiar contours:

> The Devil is supposed to enter the Vrukólaka, who, rising from his grave, torments first his nearest relations and then others, causing their death or loss of health. The remedy is to dig up the body, and if after it has been exorcised by the priest, the demon still persists in annoying the living, to cut the body into small pieces, or if that be not sufficient, to burn it.[56]

Like Tournefort, Leake dismisses the superstition. However, immediately preceding this account he describes a practice of the mountain shepherds of Kiepína, who protect lambs from wolves by sewing part of the fibula (calf bone) of a dog into the flesh of their thigh. This is supposed to make them healthy and strong, and their meat unsavoury to predators.

In the context of vampirism, however, such cross-species transplantation is a reminder of the overlaps between folkloric superstition and medical science at the time, notably in concerns surrounding vivisection, transfusion, transplantation and inoculation: the key medical innovations of the period. The extraction and implantation of human teeth by barber-surgeons, for instance, had been permitted in law during the reign of Henry VIII, and there is evidence that it was practised in the ancient world. But it was the eighteenth-century physician and antiquary John Hunter who was the first to publish a treatise on tooth transplantation in 1771.[57] Hunter avoided theological issues and did not refer to the supposedly divine integrity of the human body: he focused on empirical experimentation.[58] Hunter preferred 'live' teeth (removed from living donors) and also favoured young female teeth – often forcibly taken from servants.[59] As there were some ethical concerns about using living donors, Hunter also recommended keeping a collection of dead teeth, and many of those killed at Waterloo had their teeth removed and sold to dentists at

£2 each. Likewise, grave-robbers would extract teeth if the corpse was not worth fully exhuming. Charges for such dentistry were five guineas for implanting a tooth from a living donor, three for a human tooth on a gold bridge, and two for implanting a dead donor's tooth. The operation was not without its risks, though, and recipients feared diseases such as syphilis being transmitted through donated teeth.[60] Ignorance of basic hygiene among doctors also meant that unsuccessful implants could lead to septicaemia and death. As the *Gentleman's Magazine* warned, 'Beware, ye young, of dentists! – beware of transplantation!'[61]

Indeed, as early as 1804, Dubois de Chémant had warned against the 'criminal and unnatural operation of transplanting teeth, taken either from a living person or a dead body', as transplanted teeth never take.[62] Teeth from infected donors could cause venereal infection, scrofula or smallpox, and the 'strange blood' of non-human teeth could activate latent conditions in the human blood and raise inflammations.[63] Consequently, de Chémant advocates replacing dead teeth with artificial false teeth fashioned from elephant ivory or 'sea-horse' (walrus) or hippopotamus tusks, as well as ox and calf molars. But he also warns against using 'animal substances', and instead proposes bespoke teeth made from 'mineral paste' (a form of porcelain) and gold pivots.[64] De Chémant's amalgam could further be used to reconstruct chins and noses, and alongside his cosmetic dentistry he even found time to patent a design for a heated table.

Notwithstanding de Chémant's advances in developing false teeth, human tooth transplantation continued for the next half-century. Philippe Frédéric Blandin, for example, recommended that prosthetic teeth should either be from a hippopotamus, or ideally a human – the hippopotamus tusk being likely to turn blue. Human teeth were best acquired from battlefields, being those of healthy young men and less likely to be infected than those taken from patients who had died in hospital. Neither had Blandin any objection to using porcelain teeth, which he interestingly styles as 'incorruptible teeth' – though he did advise 'never to use the teeth found in grave-yards', which regrettably suggests that this was the habit of some dentists.[65] So teeth were not only articles of cosmetic dentistry, but also examples of cross-human and cross-species medical transplantation, and furthermore the cause of infections of the blood – effectively operating as vampirism in miniature. Many of those alive at the time had major dental problems; by contrast, vampires had extraordinarily healthy teeth – long, sharp and dazzlingly white, and in at least one story there is some discussion of dentistry.[66] Teeth were little fetish objects and appear as such in Edgar Allan Poe's horrible tale of 'Berenice'. In this study of odontophilia – the erotic obsession with teeth – a whole set is extracted from the corpse of a beautiful woman, who (this being Poe) turns out to have been committed to the tomb somewhat prematurely . . .[67]

In any case, as described above, whole human corpses could be harvested for profit – an economic imperative that also fuelled fears of vampirism. Indeed, one of the most gruesome accounts of grave-robbing detailed is chilling in its matter-of-fact detail about the assets that could be stripped from the body after death. On Monday, 24 March 1794, the *London Packet* reported:

> The church-yards of Lambeth, St John's, Westminster, Whitechapel and Hampstead have lately been plundered of their dead. In a house lately demolished near Whitechapel, as the receptacle of stolen bodies, the mysteries of this detestable traffic were found out: – that they were boiled in large coppers – the fat was skimmed off for candle-makers – the flesh disposed of for dog's meat, and feeding wild beasts – and the bones of course disposed of to the surgeons as usual; so that these dealers in human flesh now make, upon an average, five guineas of every corpse they plunder from its grave.[68]

Aside from teeth, inoculation – the most significant medical story of the time – was another form of cross-species medicine that shared the same bizarre incongruity of modern medical science. It was also a form of cross-species experimentation that had effectively become an invisible transaction. Inoculation against smallpox was a widespread – if highly controversial – practice. Edward Jenner had examined the spread of cowpox infection from horses to cows to humans in *An Inquiry into the Causes and Effects of the Variolæ Vaccinæ*, published in 1798.[69] This was not simply a case of the infection jumping across species, for as Jenner pointed out 'what renders the Cow-pox virus so extremely singular is, that the person who has been thus affected is for ever after secure from the infection of the Small Pox'.[70] The unavoidable conclusion to be drawn was that human subjects should be deliberately infected with animal diseases. Inevitably, scare stories of patients metamorphosing into bulls abounded.[71] One notable report described 'a child at Peckham, who, after being inoculated with the cowpox, had its former disposition absolutely changed to the *brutal*, so that it ran upon all fours like a BEAST, bellowing like a cow, and butting with its head like a bull'.[72] Other accounts depicted vaccinated persons sprouting horns and tails, acquiring leather hides and chewing the cud. But beyond the possible benefits for world health lay an equally profound issue: such scientific discoveries seriously eroded distinctions between the human and the non-human, and vampires are physiologically much closer to humans than cattle. Vampires have had an earlier human existence and can still recognize their family relations – even if this acknowledgement is murderous.[73]

By the beginning of the nineteenth century, vampires had plural identities. They were an established, if barely credible, feature of East European regional folklore; they were political metaphors; they provided food for thought for theologians and philosophers; they were a wonder of the natural world; they haunted the latest medical advances; and they were literary tropes, often associated with power and sexuality. They certainly were not simply fictional entities, and defied classification. The imperceptible qualities of vampirism through its association with contagion persisted: in his natural history poem 'Loves of the Plants' (1791), Erasmus Darwin – grandfather of the naturalist Charles Darwin – figured malaria as vampiric: 'Fierce from his fens the Giant AGUE springs, / And wrap'd in fogs descends on vampire-wings.'[74] But the most arresting portrayal, which gathers together their elusive natural history with the dilemmas they pose to reason, occurs in the last lines in Percy Shelley's final and unfinished poem, 'The Triumph of Life' (1822). The vampire bats that swarm are a tide of night, bringing a 'Strange night upon some Indian isle'; bewildering shadows – 'Shadows of shadows' – variously compared with eaglets and elves, falcons and flies, snowflakes and dust, clouds, and apes and vultures.[75] They lack precise definition – or rather they teem with much too much irreconcilable definition, so that they perplex and confound understanding. Such otherworldly discordance would continue to be their most abiding trait.

CHAPTER 6

MORTAL PATHOLOGIES
Being Bestial, Living Lies

[T]hat which does comprehend the doctrine of Diseases, whether they be natural or preternatural is to be called Pathology.

William Harvey (1653)[1]

Murder is not just killing. Murder is a lust to get at the very quick of life itself, and kill it – hence the stealth and the frequent morbid dismemberment of the corpse, the attempt to get at the very quick of the murdered being, to find the quick and to possess it.

D.H. Lawrence (1923)[2]

Pathologie, *The doctrine of the passions.*

Thomas Willis (1681)[3]

Within a few years at the beginning of the nineteenth century, vampires were becoming the stuff of thought. They had survived the ratiocination of the Enlightenment and the mystifications of Romanticism, retaining both their corporeal bodies and their ethereal powers. They were walking impossibilities – simultaneously medical prodigies and Gothic monsters, physical entities and strange nightmares. They suffused thought and writing, from pioneering science

118

fact and fiction to the growing taste for sensation and horror. Vampires keep returning, either explicitly invoked or implicitly through the oozing of suspect blood – whether in true-crime narratives or in medical debates on the ethics of experimentation. They were compelling, charismatic and contagious.

The Promethean blaze

'A Fragment' and 'The Vampyre' were not the only vampire tales written at the Villa Diodati during the dark summer of 1816. Mary Shelley's iconic novel *Frankenstein; or, The Modern Prometheus* was also inspired by the ghost-story challenge, and it is a novel that reverberates with vampire thinking. Indeed, during the course of his confession, the scientist Victor Frankenstein considers the near-human Being which he has crafted from the dead and animated 'nearly in the light of my own vampire, my own spirit let loose from the grave, and forced to destroy all that was dear to me'.[4] 'Vampire' here means both a murderous monster and the more figurative use of a malignant and loathsome person who preys ruthlessly upon others; and in fact this meaning reveals an odd coincidence in the Shelley circle. On 20 November 1814, Percy Shelley's first wife Harriet had written that her husband had been seduced to betray her by both William Godwin's philosophy and his bewitching daughter Mary: 'In short, the man I once loved is dead. This is a vampire. His character is blasted for ever.'[5] Percy Shelley – who called himself Victor and on whom Mary part-based her protagonist – had already been vampirized.

Other figurative uses of vampirism are also suggested in the novel. The 'Bloody Code' of the law, for instance, is invoked several times; the Being describes the 'laws of man' as 'sanguinary', meaning bloodthirsty, and later as 'bloody'; he also learns to appreciate that political power is rooted in 'noble blood'. By manipulating forensic evidence, the Being frames Justine for the murder of William, and visiting the unfortunate victim in prison, Elizabeth criticizes the legal system:

> when one creature is murdered, another is immediately deprived of life
> in a slow torturing manner; then the executioners, their hands yet

reeking with the blood of innocence, believe that they have done a great deed. They call this *retribution*.[6]

Elizabeth later reflects on the 'miserable death of Justine' as a horrifying revelation of a vampiric contagion: 'I no longer see the world and its works as they before appeared to me . . . misery has come home, and men appear to me as monsters thirsting for each other's blood.'[7]

But a novel as visceral as *Frankenstein* also makes a more literal and inexorable use of blood. Victor's tutor Monsieur Waldman alerts him to the scientific discovery of cardiovascular circulation, and henceforth he can feel the blood running through him.[8] With William and Justine dead, Victor's guilt oppresses him, mixing medical signs with psychiatric disturbance: the 'blood flowed freely in my veins, but a weight of despair and remorse pressed on my heart, which nothing could remove . . . I wandered like an evil spirit, for I had committed deeds of mischief beyond description horrible . . .' His blood is chilled – literally. When he comes to make the She-Being, he admits 'I went to it in cold blood, and my heart often sickened at the work of my hands'; and later he uses the phrase 'cool blood'.[9] The shadow of vampirism seems to lurk throughout the book.

But the most striking effect of Victor's blood is when he has a premonition that something dreadful has befallen his fiancée Elizabeth on their wedding night: 'I could feel the blood trickling in my veins, and tingling in the extremities of my limbs'; there is a hint of cruentation transferred to Victor here in the intuition of his own blood. He hurries back into the bedchamber:

> She was there, lifeless and inanimate, thrown across the bed, her head hanging down, and her pale and distorted features half covered by her hair. Every where I turn I see the same figure – her bloodless arms and relaxed form flung by the murderer on its bridal bier.[10]

Elizabeth's twisted corpse is reminiscent of the drugged and deranged female in Henry Fuseli's renowned painting *The Nightmare*, first exhibited in 1782, which depicts the infernal visit of an incubus.[11] Elizabeth has been strangled by the Being: 'The murderous mark of the fiend's grasp was on her neck, and the breath had ceased to issue from her lips.' The child William, too, is found 'stretched on the grass livid and motionless: the print of the murderer's finger was on his neck'. So is Henry Clerval: 'He had apparently been strangled; for there was no sign of any violence, except the black mark of fingers on his neck.'[12] The Habsburg military surgeon Johann Flückinger had noticed a mark on the neck of Stanoicka, a victim of Paole's: a bruise the length of a finger on the right side of her neck under her ear.[13] So the marks left on the Being's victims – as well as Elizabeth's bloodless limbs – can be seen as evidence of vampire killings: the vampires Plogojowitz and Paole were both stranglers who then drained their victims' blood. The Being is not a vampire in the modern sense, and neither is he a Polidorian vampire – a salacious aristocrat; but the scene is positively steeped in the psychotic aura of Eastern European vampirism.

Like vampires, the Being also exhibits hideously supernatural strength, such as in his dizzyingly rapid ascent of the Salève.[14] He travels rapidly and by night ('the dead ride fast') through a traumatized and collapsing environment – 'Nature,' he observes, 'decayed around me'.[15] His targets are, like a vampire's, Victor's closest kin and dearest friends, and the Being's threats against his father-creator are a bloodlust: 'I will glut the maw of death, until it be satiated with the blood of your remaining friends.'[16] For his part, Victor describes the Being's crimes as 'deeds of blood' which have not yet 'satiated' him, and kisses the earth in the superstitious belief that it will protect him.[17] In both the grip of an over-identification with the Being and a fit of Messianic delusion, Victor wishes his own blood could redeem the deaths he claims to have caused:

'I am not mad,' I cried energetically; 'the sun and the heavens, who have viewed my operations, can bear witness of my truth. I am the assassin of those most innocent victims; they died by my machinations. A thousand times would I have shed my own blood, drop by drop, to have saved their lives; but I could not, my father, indeed I could not sacrifice the whole human race.'[18]

There is in any case something wrong with the blood of the Being. The confrontation with the De Laceys gives him 'a fever of my blood', and in contrast to Victor's 'cold blood', the Being claims that his blood 'boils'. Where does his blood come from? We are in fact told by Victor of 'the horrors of my secret toil, as I dabbled among the unhallowed damps of the grave', and that he 'tortured the living animal to animate the lifeless clay'. The Being has animal blood. It is an unsettling coincidence that in 1818, the year in which *Frankenstein* was published, James Blundell announced the results of experimental blood transfusions given to dogs, which led directly to his experiments on human subjects.[19] Arthur Coga's transfusion of lamb's blood followed speculation that the temper of dogs could be manipulated by mixing a cocktail of the blood of different breeds, and introducing lamb's blood into Coga's veins was calculated to calm his immoderate temper.[20]

In *Frankenstein* too, then, blood has sentience: that is how Victor has a portent of Elizabeth's death (she is close to him in blood); meanwhile the Being's bestial blood may be responsible for his literally inhuman ferocity. The novel is in any case itself like a transfusion – or contagion – of the blood. Walton's blood is chilled not simply by the extreme cold, but by the extreme accounts he hears from Victor and the Being. He writes to his sister, 'You have read this strange and terrific story, Margaret; and do you not feel your blood congealed with horror, like that which even now curdles mine?' Mary Shelley could not resist transfusing this same image into her introduction to the 1831 edition, describing her story as 'One which would speak to the mysterious fears of our nature, and awaken thrilling horror – one to make the reader dread to look round, to curdle the blood, and quicken the beatings of the heart.'[21]

The vampiric stigma of the Being may also help to explain why he cremates himself. Cremation was not properly legalized in Britain until 1885, and so the Being's act is both pagan and illegal – but it is also a conventional way of destroying a vampire, and therefore a dutiful final act that moves him closer to the human, even as it distances him. This is the question at the heart of *Frankenstein* – what is the nature of the human? The Being, like a vampire, is a threat to an anthropocentric world view, and the novel is indeed troubled by humanity being sidelined. The Alps, for instance, are described as belonging to 'another earth, the habitations of another race of beings'; and Percy Shelley, visiting the Mer de Glace glacier on 25 July 1816, shortly after Mary had commenced *Frankenstein*, wrote that 'One would think that Mont Blanc was a living being & that the frozen blood forever circulated slowly thro' his stony veins.'[22] Mary Shelley recognizes what has been described as the 'agency, and sometimes even subjectivity, of nonhuman nature', thereby displacing the human.[23]

The unholy brotherhood of Polidori's 'Vampyre' and Shelley's *Frankenstein* proved immensely influential, not least on the stage. Indeed, the celebrity of both the figure of the vampire and Victor Frankenstein's Being was unquestionably the result of their ubiquity in the theatres in both Britain and France, rather than of the original tales. Moreover, it was not only through a string of dramatic adaptations that these two figures gripped the popular imagination in the 1820s, but also because they were often paired in an early 'double-bill' of horror theatre. The French writer Charles Nodier adapted Polidori's narrative for the theatre stage and in 1821 published his own vampire story *Smarra, ou les Démons de la Nuit*, a 'fantastique' dream tale. James Planché produced a 'Romantic Melodrama', *The Vampire, or, The Bride of the Isles* (1820, scored by Joseph Hart), derived from Nodier's adaptation, which sensationally featured the 'Vampire trap', an innovative sprung trapdoor which gave the impression that characters could disappear through floors and walls.[24] The renowned actor Thomas Cooke appeared at the Lyceum Theatre as Ruthven, the central character in Planché's adaptation *The Vampire*, before taking the role of '------', the Being in *Presumption, or, The Fate of Frankenstein* (1823), Richard Brinsley Peake's celebrated adaptation of Mary Shelley's novel.[25] Meanwhile, Hugo John Belfour wrote an Egyptian melodrama *The Vampire, A Tragedy in Five Acts* (1821), before he abandoned the life of the theatre to become a curate in Jamaica.[26] In the wake of Polidori's tale, theatres were overrun with vampires; but despite – or because of – their popularity, these adaptations lacked the intellectual weight of vampire literature: they were comic and loaded with topical references in the tradition of pantomimes and knockabout farce.[27] Nevertheless, burlesques on vampires were still running at the Royal Strand Theatre over 50 years later.[28]

This sudden craze for vampires in melodrama ran alongside the pervasive vampire influence on poetry and prose. More poems followed. Some merely hint at vampirism, such as Keats's *Lamia* (written 1819, published

1820). This was, like Goethe's 'Die Braut', inspired in part by Philostratus's story of Menippus Lycius, which Keats had read in Robert Burton's *Anatomy of Melancholy* (1621):

a young man 25 yeares of age, . . . going betwixt *Cenchreas* and *Corinth*, met such a phantasme in the habit of a faire gentlewoman, which taking him by the hand, carried him home to her house, in the suburbs of *Corinth*, and told him she was a *Phœnician* by birth, and if hee would tarry with her, *he should heare her sing and play, and drinke such wine as never any dranke, and no man should molest him; but she being faire and lovely, would live and dye with him, that was faire and lovely to behold.* The young man a Philosopher, otherwise staid and discreet, able to moderate his passions, though not this of love, tarried with her a while to his great content, and at last married her, to whose wedding amongst other guests came *Apollonius*, who by some probable conjectures, found her out to be a serpent, a *Lamia*, and that all her furniture, was like *Tantalus* gold described by *Homer*, no substance but meere illusions.[29]

As for Lamia herself,

She seem'd, at once, some penanced lady elf,
Some demon's mistress, or the demon's self.[30]

Lamia is a demonic she-serpent – dazzlingly beautiful and sensuously virginal – and her eyes are enthralling:

her eyelids open'd bland,
And, like new flowers at morning song of bees,
Bloom'd, and gave up her honey to the lees.
Into the green-recessed woods they flew;
Nor grew they pale, as mortal lovers do.[31]

The glimmer of her glance 'if her eyes could brighter be' casts the young Lycius into a trance:

> He sick to lose
> The amorous promise of her lone complain,
> Swoon'd, murmuring of love, and pale with pain.[32]

Keats's eerie ballad 'La Belle Dame Sans Merci' also portrays a predatory female figure. 'La Belle Dame' materializes more like the sinister fay
of Scott's *Rokeby* than the illusive and reptilian Lamia to steal away the life
from her male victims. Her prey, the knight-at-arms and the warriors that
have foundered before him, are anguished, feverish and pale, caught in the
glare of her 'wild wild eyes'. Like the succubus, she rides through dreams
– the knight seeing in his sleep her emaciated victims: 'death-pale' warriors
with 'starved lips'.

The Polidorian English 'vampyre' had only just been constituted and
neither of these enchantresses is strictly a vampire, yet both are undoubtedly vampiric, and also show Keats playing out vampirism in both English
Gothic folklore and Ancient Greek classicism in entangled, catachthonic
pasts, where spirits such as 'La Belle Dame' emerge from history to reveal
more history in visions and transfused memories.[33] Just as the vampire
disturbs territorial borders, so it disrupts temporality. But Keats's she-
vampires do manifest what was to become the key characteristic of the
nineteenth-century figure. From Lord Ruthven's 'dead grey eye' to
Geraldine's 'large bright eyes', the vampire in English culture was exemplified less by its bite than by its gaze.

Exhibiting atrocity

Vampirism extends the workings of crime and punishment into the here-
after, and so the emphasis on testimony described in earlier chapters also has
a legal context as a criminological method underpinning early investigations
into vampires. The vampire is an inflection of the exercise of post-mortem
power, insisting that even beyond the grave bodies are governed by discourses
such as the medical, theological and legal. So, as well as being medically
and theologically aberrant, the vampire is also a criminal – a grave-robber
(of itself), usually violent, often sexually abusive and consistently a mass
murderer. Hence the horrified fascination at the time with vampiric

bloodletting is part of the craving for crime writing, known in Britain as 'Newgate Calendars'. Meticulous accounts of shocking homicides were particularly popular – much as they are again today – and shared the same bloodcurdling details as the vampire narratives. In 1708, Ann Edgbrook was murdered by John Barns: 'with her throat cut from ear to ear, her stomach cut down throughout like a sheep, and her bowels and heart taken out and put into a tub'.[34] In 1717, Richard Davis was murdered by Richard Griffith: 'the deceased was found in a dunghill without a head'; the skull was subsequently recovered, 'picked clean to the very bone, which . . . might have been done by the hogs, which were in the field'.[35] In 1726, Catherine Hays and her two lovers murdered her husband John, decapitated and dismembered the body, and scattered his remains. The head was discovered and, so as to identify the victim, was displayed – first on a post in the street and then pickled in a jar; Mrs Hays was burnt at the stake for her pains.[36] Even more suggestive was the celebrated case of James Hall, who murdered his master, John Penny, in 1741. Hall stove in Penny's skull; then, to avoid staining his clothes, stripped himself stark naked, drained Penny's blood into a chamber pot (filling the vessel five times), and threw the withered body into the privy or 'bog-house'.[37] A souvenir etching of the crime includes a graphic frame of the bloodletting: Hall is positively vampiric, crouching naked in the candlelight over the prone body. He bears a diabolical expression, watching gleefully as the blood pours into the pot from a livid gash in Penny's throat.[38] Ironically, though, in all these grisly cases it is the victim who, through the agency of the law, ultimately reaches back from beyond the grave to condemn the living murderer and consign him (or her) to execution; for the killers themselves, there is no return from the dead.

The romantic essayist Thomas De Quincey was an avid reader of the cases in the *Newgate Calendar* and similar reports, and was spellbound by the Ratcliffe Highway murders of 1811. The murderer in this case was believed to be one John Williams, held responsible for two separate incidents that took place in London over less than a fortnight in December 1811. Seven victims were left dead. The first attack took place around midnight on Ratcliffe Highway in the East End of London. Williams broke into a warehouse and slaughtered a linen-draper and his wife, their apprentice and their three-month-old baby son. The victims were all killed in the same way: 'the skull was first shattered' with a shipwright's mallet, and then 'uniformly the throat was cut' – in some instances cut to the bone.[39] Williams escaped. The bodies of the victims were exhibited on the premises and 30,000 mourners attended the burials. Twelve days later, Williams went on the rampage again, breaking into the King's Arms, a public house in the same area, and murdering the publican, his wife and their maid. The landlord was thrown downstairs and had his throat slashed; the two women had their skulls pulverized, before their throats were cut. However, a lodger escaped and raised the alarm, and the family's young granddaughter in one of the upper rooms miraculously remained unscathed. Williams was quickly arrested, but before the case could go to trial he hanged himself in his cell. He was found guilty regardless, and on New Year's Eve his body was paraded along Ratcliffe Highway in an 'immense cavalcade' led by local dignitaries and constables with drawn cutlasses. On either side of Williams' head, like grim laurels, were fixed his instruments of murder: the maul and the 'ripping chisel'. The procession halted at the scenes of the crimes, before delivering Williams to a cross-roads, where he was buried in a deliberately narrow and unmarked grave, 'so formed as not to admit [his corpse] of being laid at length'. The killer was immediately staked through his heart 'amidst the shouts and vociferous execrations of the multitude', and the earth was stamped down onto his corpse: 'And over him drives for ever the uproar of unresting London.'[40]

De Quincey returned to the case several times.[41] His response was outrageous, presenting Williams as an artist in blood – evident in the title of his most notorious essay, 'On Murder Considered as One of the Fine Arts' (1827). This essay was presented as the 'Williams Lecture', delivered to 'The Society of Connoisseurs in Murder' (or 'Murder-Fanciers'). It discusses characters such as Cain, the Old Man of the Mountains (leader of the *Hashishin*, or 'assassins'), several philosophers who are figurative murderers – and, of course, Williams himself.

Williams is obviously not a vampire – and neither does De Quincey claim that he is; but De Quincey's fascination with Williams exemplifies the public mania for serial killers, and his ghoulishly playful analysis of murder as an artistic category does go some way towards explaining and justifying that popular obsession. In fact, for all his irony and *Schadenfreude*,

De Quincey's philosophical and aesthetic consideration of murder is a continuation of the theological and philosophical attention given to vampires in the previous century. As the posthuman philosopher David Roden argues, the question is whether mass murderers and psychopaths (or indeed vampires) qualify as human in phenomenological terms. If we accept them as human, we may consequently expect them to be capable of an empathy they do not – and cannot – entertain. Yet despite this, these figures 'exercise a continuing allure' within culture and journalism.[42] These deviant, non-human beings are attractive because they challenge the moral absolute that indiscriminate mass murder is wrong – an absolute that it should not be possible to challenge. In doing so they destabilize other, less certain moral certainties – that lying is always wrong, that greed is immoral – by suggesting that these are simply social conventions and therefore relative, as well as being part of a shared moral system and thus somehow connected to mass murder. Hence De Quincey's preposterous declaration:

> From Murder . . . you will soon come to highway robbery; and from highway robbery it is but a short step to petty larceny. And when you are got to *that*, there comes in sad progression Sabbath-breaking, drunkenness, and late hours; until the awful climax terminates in neglect of dress, non-punctuality, and general waspishness. Many a man has begun with dabbling a little in murder, and thought he would stop there, until from one thing to another he has been led so far that in a few years he has become generally disrespectable.[43]

The philosophy of mass murder is highly suggestive for thinking about vampires. Mass murderers are, at least physically, human beings – they conform to the 'genre' (or *genus*) of the human while remaining outside it.[44] Vampires, however, have the same physical consanguinity with humans but are clearly biologically distinct – their monstrosity is organic. Both mass murderers and vampires have a radically different consciousness in that they lack basic moral coordinates, making them phenomenologically alien; and this alienated consciousness in turn disturbs the assumption that the world is essentially anthropocentric – that it is defined by human needs, desires and experience. Roden's proposal, then, is that we are drawn to the serial killer not because we admire their actions or identify with their prey, but because they intimate a reality deeper or more capacious than our parochial human world. The hyperbolically powerful serial killer may, then, entice us with the prospect of a weird transcendence, hidden in the defiles of an inhuman nature.[45]

Writers and readers, film-makers and audiences are drawn to vampires for the same reason: they present a world in which the human no longer has dominion, or reliable understanding, and so offer a sublime glimpse of a wider, if unknowable, world.

Of course, that is precisely what the Promethean, dæmonically inspired Romantic artist attempts, driven by occult powers of the imagination to create new worlds. As Mary Shelley described the composition of *Frankenstein*: 'My imagination, unbidden, possessed and guided me, gifting the successive images that arose in my mind with a vividness far beyond the usual bounds of reverie' – and in *Frankenstein* the immaterial imagination has physical consequences.[46] Artists and killers are both driven, and in some instances the behaviour within these roles overlaps. The Romantic art critic Thomas Griffiths Wainewright was, as Oscar Wilde suggested, an artist in 'pen, pencil and poison': a writer, aesthete and murderer – and certainly on the spectrum of De Quincey's homicidal connoisseurship.[47] Similarly, the vampire is made an aristocrat, an aficionado and an artist. In other words, vampires, like aesthetes, live through the lives of others: they represent the dark side of artistic endeavour – but a side of artistic endeavour nonetheless. They create themselves through the destruction of others.[48] Vampires did not properly become a subject for literature until literary composition was conceived to be conducted through inspiration and possession: in that sense, they are essentially creatures of Romantic Gothicism and could not have been imagined in the same ways under the eighteenth-century culture of Augustanism, characterized as it was by classical models of mimesis and imitation rather than creative originality.[49]

To return to De Quincey. I have written that De Quincey does not present Williams as a vampire. In his later 'Postscript' he does, however, depict Williams as undead – as a vampire in all but name. The scene of his crimes is a bloodbath:

the carnage of the night [was] stretched out on the floor, and the narrow premises so floated with gore, that it was hardly possible to escape the pollution of blood in picking out a path to the front-door.[50]

So one may be prepared for a vampire. Williams is not the bloated animated corpse of Hungarian medical science, but a blood-brother of Lord Ruthven. He is certainly no aristocrat – Williams was a sailor – but he is lean and lithe, with striking bright blonde hair. And like Ruthven – and Augustus Darvell, too – his skin is ashen and his eyes are dead. De Quincey observes that his face was 'cadaverous' and 'wore at all times a bloodless ghastly pallor'. He goes on to describe how an eyewitness had stated that 'You might imagine . . . that in his veins circulated not red life-blood, such as could kindle into the blush of shame, of wrath, or pity – but a green sap that welled from no human heart.' His eyes, moreover, are 'glazed' and 'rigid', and seem 'rightfully belonging to a corpse, when one glance at them sufficed to proclaim a death warrant'; elsewhere he is 'the diabolic man, clothed in mystery'. Notwithstanding this, 'the oiliness and snaky insinuation of his demeanour' makes him attractive to 'inexperienced young women'.[51] The kinship with Ruthven is remarkable.

Williams is a vampire in all but name, and is an example of how the literature of extreme crime feeds on supernatural images. Indeed, in De Quincey's similarly detailed description of the murders committed by the McKean brothers, the dead nearly do rise. The brothers spend a night at the Jolly Carter, an inn on the road to Manchester, where they molest a maidservant, Elizabeth 'Betty' Bate; when she objects, they cut her throat. She screams faintly, then falls to the floor. The other servant, a young boy, makes a daring escape by vaulting over the bannister to the ground floor and bolting from the butchery; and the landlady, though stabbed in the face as the brothers flee, manages to survive the attack. The McKeans are caught a week later, tried for killing Betty Bate and executed. However, an uncanny detail reveals again the shadow of the undead that lies across true-crime writing. When Betty's throat is cut, she sinks to the floor; then,

Solemnly, and in ghostly silence, uprose in her dying delirium the murdered girl; she stood upright, she walked steadily for a moment or two, she bent her steps towards the door . . .[52]

Betty manages to stagger to the club room before she finally dies, but the 'dreadful spectacle' of her reanimation creates an opportunity for the young lad to get away. He is saved by ministries from beyond the grave.

Williams' staking was thoroughly in accordance with English law at the time. Suicides were *felos de se* (felons to themselves); they were impaled through the chest with ash stakes, buried at crossroads and had their property confiscated. The despicable Daniel Quilp in Charles Dickens' *The Old Curiosity Shop* (1842), set in about 1825, is 'buried with a stake through his heart in the centre of four lonely roads' after his drowning is deemed to be suicide.[53] However, Dickens was being anachronistic: in 1823, the Suicide Act outlawed staked burials at crossroads. Instead, those found *felo de se* were to be buried within 24 hours of the coroner's inquest, between the hours of nine and twelve at night in consecrated ground, but without religious solemnities, with the coroner providing 'instructions for the private interment of such remains without any stake being driven through the body of such persons'.[54] As commentators have pointed out, the 'recurring similarity in the treatment of the criminal and the vampire body after death is the desire to ensure its complete dissolution, which often calls for the burning of bodies and the grinding of bones, followed by the scattering of ashes into a river or to the four winds'.[55] The law thus attempts to obliterate the criminal body, and the Murder Act of 1752, for 'better Preventing the horrid Crime of Murder', allowed the bodies of executed criminals to be given up for public dissection rather being than gibbetted (publicly hung in chains).[56] Thus they would literally be disappeared. The vampire embraces this imperceptibility deliberately, adopting invisibility, mistiness and distortions in shadows, in reflections and in photographs as part of its power to terrify. Having been annihilated, the dead can return as a vampire – as a nothingness, a hunger that then seeks to slake its lust on the living.[57]

Nineteenth-century readers were captivated by violent crime. The antiquarian and author Revd Sabine Baring-Gould was the first lycanthropologist in Britain, publishing his *Book of Werewolves* in 1865 and drawing attention to the folklore and history of inter-species affinities. This was a systematic account covering werewolf beliefs from classical times, in Norse legend and myth and in medieval hagiography – noteworthy, for instance, is St Boniface's rebuke to those who entertained belief in '*strigas et fictos lupos*' ('witches and the werewolf').[58] Baring-Gould focuses on a number of gruesome case studies. In one, Pierre Bourgot and Michel Verdung pledge allegiance to the Devil, and following a Black Mass smear themselves with a metamorphic salve. 'I was at first somewhat horrified at my four wolf's feet, and the fur with which I was covered all at once,' recalled Bourgot, 'but I found that I could now travel with the speed of the wind.'[59] He and Michel run riot, tearing to pieces a woman while she gathers peas, a man who comes to her rescue, and at least four small girls – one of whom they strangle before lapping up her blood.

Baring-Gould claims that the werewolf is known as *vrkolak* among the Bulgarians and Slovakians, and *vlkoslak* by the Serbs, and although he is mistaken in these terms (the modern Serbian for werewolf being *vukodlak*), he is right to point out that the same word is used for the vampire:[60]

> The lycanthropist falls into a cataleptic trance, during which his soul leaves his body, enters that of a wolf and ravens for blood. On the return of the soul, the body is exhausted and aches as though it had been put through violent exercise. After death lycanthropists become vampires. They are believed to frequent battlefields in wolf or hyæna shapes, and to suck the breath from dying soldiers, or to enter houses and steal the infants from their cradles. Modern Greeks call any savage-looking man, with dark complexion, and with distorted, misshapen limbs, a βρύκολακας [*vrykolakas*], and suppose him to be invested with power of running in wolf-form.[61]

Baring-Gould also records instances of cruelty against fellow humans and animals, down to him witnessing 'an accomplished young woman of considerable refinement . . . string flies with a needle on a piece of thread and watch complacently their flutterings'.[62] He notes that a Hungarian noblewoman bathed in the blood of young girls, who were usually beaten to death before being sliced up with razors, and at one point she bit a victim; the fresh blood rejuvenated her.[63] A craving for blood was also sometimes the result of pregnancy, and Baring-Gould notes that in 1553 a wife in this condition cut her husband's throat, and gnawed the nose and the left arm, whilst the body was yet warm. She then gutted the corpse, and salted it for future consumption.[64]

The latest example of such cannibalism had been in 1845. Other causes were psychosis, drugs and hallucinatory fevers, such as typhus, in which 'it is not uncommon for the sick person, with deranged nervous system, to believe himself to be double in the bed, or to be severed in half, or to have lost his limbs'.[65] Baring-Gould also covers astral projection, metempsychosis (the transmigration of souls) and the reputed medicinal properties of human tissue, and describes in detail the fifteenth-century mass murderer Gilles de Laval (also known as Gilles de Rais, or 'Bluebeard') and the recent notorious case in Paris of the army officer François Bertrand (1848–49). Bertrand periodically lost his wits and went on violent excursions in which he desecrated graves and dug up corpses, mutilating them horribly if they were women:

Some he chopped with the spade, others he tore and ripped with his teeth and nails. Sometimes he tore the mouth open and rent the face back to the ears, he opened the stomachs, and pulled off the limbs.[66]

Although Baring-Gould omits to mention it, Bertrand was christened by the press 'The Vampire of Montparnasse'.

Much of Baring-Gould's *Book of Werewolves* is written in the style of sensation fiction. It was followed by other fables of beasts, such as Prosper Mérimée's horror fantasy *Lokis* (1869), in which the Lithuanian Countess Szemioth is allegedly raped by a bear; her son develops a taste for blood and eventually kills his bride on their wedding night by biting her throat.[67] Julian Osgood Field's vampire story 'A Kiss of Judas' (1893, written under the cipher 'X.L.'), meanwhile, includes a particularly disturbing and bestial male vampire in a narrative that covers Eastern Europe, crime and forensics, madness and illness – notably leprosy. Kinship between vampires and werewolves was close: in an early, cancelled chapter for *Dracula*, later published as 'Dracula's Guest', Bram Stoker combines the vampirism of the Count with the primal horror of being eaten alive by a carnivorous animal. The narrator strays into a graveyard on *Walpurgisnacht* (30 April), enters a tomb and passes out, before being awoken by a huge wolf about to rip open his throat. He is rescued by a company of soldiers.[68]

There was also a medical aspect to this consideration of animals, in particular to the ethics of animal experimentation. In the same year that *The Book of Werewolves* was published, Claude Bernard argued in favour of vivisection in *An Introduction to the Study of Experimental Medicine*, proposing that animals should be vivisected after cadavers have been dissected 'to uncover the inner or hidden parts of the organisms and see them work'; moreover, 'to learn how man and animals live, we cannot avoid seeing great numbers of them die, because the mechanisms of life can be unveiled and proved only by knowledge of the mechanisms of death'.[69] Not content with this, Bernard also gives a historical account of experiments on living people, expressly defending experiments on humans condemned to die, noting that 'a helminthologist [concerned with the study of parasitic worms] had a condemned woman without her knowledge swallow larvæ of intestinal worms, so as to see whether the worms developed in the intestines after her death'.[70] Bernard's tone becomes almost vampiric (and certainly reminiscent of Victor Frankenstein): one definition of vivisection being 'only an autopsy on the living . . . only anatomical dissection of the living'.[71] Clearly, vampires sucking blood is a form of nutritive vivisection on living donors, reflecting fears that medical researchers can reduce human beings – like animals – to the subject of a scientific experiment, just as vampires (and werewolves and other beasts) redefine them as prey. Vampire writing is then in part concerned with anxieties over the progress of science: at what cost is human bioscientific knowledge to be gained? But for Bernard, objections to the march of medical science are merely faddish nonsense:

> A physiologist is not a man of fashion, he is a man of science, absorbed by the scientific idea which he pursues: he no longer hears the cry of animals, he no longer sees the blood that flows, he sees only his idea and perceives only organisms concealing problems which he intends to solve.[72]

In 1873, John Scott Burden Sanderson, professor of physiology at University College, London, had described animal experimentation in detail in his *Handbook for the Physiological Laboratory*. However, the next year a prosecution of wanton cruelty was brought against a French physiologist who had injected two dogs with alcohol, and against the three doctors who had organized the experiment at Norwich Medical Association. In 1875, a royal commission reported on vivisection. Some of the responses were shocking: the bacteriologist Emanuel Edward Klein (a contributor to Sanderson's *Handbook*) admitted that he very rarely used anaesthetics, and when asked what he felt towards the animals used in his experiments, simply responded, 'No regard at all.'[73]

The Cruelty to Animals Act was passed in 1876, and vivisectors were demonized. The social reformer and animal rights advocate Frances Power Cobbe assembled hair-raising horror stories from the *Handbook for the Physiological Laboratory*, *Transactions of the Royal Society* and the *Journal of Physiology*, involving

> Sawing across the backbone, dissecting out and irritating all the great nerves, driving catheters along the veins and arteries, inoculating with the most dreadful diseases, cutting out pieces of the intestine, baking, stewing, pouring boiling water into the stomach, freezing to death, reducing the brain to the condition of a 'lately-hoed potato field'; these and similarly terrible experiments form the staple of some of them, and a significant feature in all.[74]

She then quotes the Russo-French physiologist Elie de Cyon, who in 1876 had declared that:

> The true vivisector must approach a difficult vivisection with *joyful excitement* . . . He who shrinks from cutting into a living animal, he who approaches a vivisection as a disagreeable necessity, may be able to repeat one or two vivisections, but he will never be an artist in vivisection . . . The sensation of the physiologist when, from a gruesome wound, full of blood and mangled tissue, he draws forth some delicate nerve thread . . . has much in common with that of a sculptor.[75]

There are disquieting echoes of De Quincey on murder in this passage, as well as of the refined vampire preparing to feed. As the medical historian

W.F. Bynum points out, the anti-vivisection movement raised a number of salient issues

> about the price of experimental knowledge; about its validity in human settings, given its origin in animal models and preparations; about the relationship between experimentation on animals and more subtle forms of experimentation on patients, particularly women and paupers; about gender roles in medicine, especially women scientists and vivisectors; about cruelty to animals manifesting itself in cruelty to patients; about medical education as a form of indoctrination; about medicine as a materialistic and, ultimately atheistic, endeavour; about medical motives and medical trustworthiness.[76]

Supernatural connoisseurship

Coleridge's Christabel confirmed the vampire as a female predator: a challenge to marriage, social stability and child-bearing – and a threat to young women. Indeed, most nineteenth-century vampires were female.[77] 'The Vampire Bride' (1833), a poem by the Scottish nobleman Henry Thomas Liddell, was inspired by a tale included by Scott in *Minstrelsy of the Scottish Border* (1802–03) and Southey's *Thalaba*.[78] In this ballad, the young bridegroom Albert inadvertently summons a she-vampire with his wedding ring; the creature then possesses him in his marriage bed in place of his true love, sucking his blood and soaking the matrimonial linen in his gore. His servant is sent to the monster, but encounters trees swaying in still air, a meteor,

> And the bats unclean, with leathern skin,
>   Flapp'd heavily around;
> And a strange dog did howl, while shriek'd the owl,
>   And like a grave smell'd the ground.[79]

His mortal wife, however, discovers the lair of the monster: a coffin buried five yards down, where she lies naked and undecayed beneath a blood-stained shroud, her eyes staring:

Her veins accurs'd seem'd ready to burst,
　　She was gorged with infernal food;
And the vampire mouth foam'd with crimson froth;
　　Her very pores oozed blood.[80]

She is duly staked, whereupon all her blood spurts out in a vast fountain. Her body is thrown to the wolves, a storm ensues, and although Albert is free, his scar weeps blood every year on the anniversary of the encounter.

Liddell's poem demonstrates that the vampire was open to reworking, but that many features, such as the corpse being swollen, the necessity of staking and the implied metamorphosis of the creature into a 'strange dog', were already well established and could be adapted to British folk motifs. The physicist James Clerk Maxwell similarly makes the vampire a folkloric revenant: in 'The Vampyre' (1845), written in archaic Scottish vernacular (and when he was still a teenager), Maxwell depicts the vampire as a lady forsaken by a false knight who inevitably meets him again and wreaks her vengeance on him:

Hee saw hir lipps were wet wi' blude,
　　And hee saw hir lyfelesse eyne . . .
And the vampyr suckis his gude lyfe blude,
　　Sho suckis hym till hee dee.[81]

There were, of course, male vampires too – indeed, the most popular vampire of the 1840s (and arguably of the entire century) was *Varney the Vampyre or, The Feast of Blood*, a 'Penny Dreadful' or 'Penny Blood' published in 109 weekly parts from 1845, and then in 1847 as a collected 220-chapter book. By any standards, *Varney* was a publishing sensation and a runaway success, generously illustrated with inventive offset layout. The story is set in about 1730 and haunted by memories of the Civil Wars and the splitting of the Commonwealth. Sir Francis Varney, the Varney of the title, had originally been a Cromwellian double agent whose death and vampiric afterlife is therefore intimately tied to the Interregnum and Restoration – a typical Gothic trope of the ramifications of national history and political bloodshed.[82] But by the end of the very first chapter, Varney's predilections are clear: he is a die-hard bloodsucker, and far more explicit in his feasting than either Lord Ruthven or Augustus Darvell:

> With a sudden rush that could not be foreseen – with a strange howling cry that was enough to awaken terror in every breast, the figure seized the long tresses of her hair, and twining them round his bony hands he held her to the bed. Then she screamed – Heaven granted her then power to scream. Shriek followed shriek in rapid succession. The bed-clothes fell in a heap by the side of the bed – she was dragged by her long silken hair completely on to it again. Her beautifully rounded limbs quivered with the agony of her soul. The glassy, horrible eyes of the figure ran over that angelic form with a hideous satisfaction – horrible profanation. He drags her head to the bed's edge. He forces it back by the long hair still entwined in his grasp. With a plunge he seizes her neck in his fang-like teeth – a gush of blood, and a hideous sucking noise follows. *The girl has swooned, and the vampyre is at his hideous repast!*[83]

Yet in the course of his manifold adventures, Varney plays many different roles, not all villainous; and although slain many times, he can always be revived through the agency of moonlight. In fact, this reference to Polidori's 'Vampyre' is one of the few debts to the high cultural vampire tradition in *Varney*: instead, *Varney the Vampyre* is really inspired by popular stage adaptations. So there is none of the Eastern European folklore or Habsburg medical science in *Varney*, little of the weighty denominational theology or Enlightenment philosophy, and scant attention to the cultural import of the figure. At best, the origins of the vampire are garbled into a mish-mash of Northern European and Near Eastern legends – although possibly the shadows of Tournefort, Southey and Byron hang over at least one exchange in the book:

> 'You have, of course, heard something,' said Henry to the doctor, as he was pulling on his gloves, 'about vampyres.'
> 'I certainly have, and I understand that in some countries, particularly Norway and Sweden, the superstition is a very common one.'
> 'And in the Levant.'

'Yes. The ghouls of the Mahometans are of the same description of beings.'[84]

Moreover, in addition to the dark memories of the Civil War there are occasional moments of veiled social politics. In a postscript to a letter, Samuel Johnson's dictionary-definition of the 'vampire' is given. 'Vampire' does not, of course, appear in Johnson's *Dictionary* (1755–56), but the pastiche is well-wrought and evocatively presented as a critique of Hanoverian patronage:

> VAMPYRE (a German blood-sucker) – by which you perceive how many vampyres, from time immemorial, must have been well entertained at the expense of John Bull, at the court of St. James, where nothing hardly is to be met with but German blood-suckers.[85]

The entry, supposedly in a standard – if partisan – reference work, is barbed enough to call genuine eighteenth-century satire to mind.

If there is an overall theme to *Varney*, though, it is to make the eponymous vampire the vehicle for an enduring melodrama on the curse of immortality. As the almost interminable narrative goes on, the anti-hero himself tires of his own epic and eventually commits suicide through a definitive self-cremation: by throwing himself into the volcanic crater of Mount Vesuvius.[86] He has, of course, died and revived many times before this; but intriguingly – and in a rare philosophical moment – when at one point Varney has been shot and is believed dead, his slayer wonders whether he has actually committed murder: 'He is one of God's creatures if he were ten times a vampire.'[87] Such questions go some way towards aligning *Varney* with the intellectual currents of the Enlightenment and Romanticism; and although it has been claimed that the tale enables the reader to empathize 'with the vampire's desolation and despair', such moments are buried deep within more than a thousand pages of text. *Varney the Vampyre* should therefore really be recognized as an early example of popular vampirism, in which the figure of the vampire is introduced into a whole variety of social situations: in other words, it is the cradle of the vampire cult in popular fiction, television and film that dominates today.[88]

Notwithstanding the popularity of *Varney*, however, it was the she-vampire that was queen of the nineteenth century. Several of the American writer Edgar Allan Poe's stories and poems have noticeable vampiric elements attached to female characters, if none actually feature out-and-out vampires: the nightmarish mix of erotic obsession and catalepsy in 'Berenice' (1835), the return of the dead in 'Morella' (1835) and 'Ligeia' (1838), catalepsy (again) and premature entombment in 'The Fall of the House of Usher' (1839) and the transference of life into art in 'The Oval Portrait' (originally 'Life in Death', 1842). Poe also repeatedly wrote on premature burial – another of his stories bears that very title (1844). The writer D.H. Lawrence specifically referred to 'vampire lust' in Poe's stories, and vampires seeking vengeance on life, while his reading of 'The Fall of the House of Usher' treats Roderick Usher as a vampire sucking the life out of his sister Madeline; 'And she is asking to be sucked.'[89] Charles Baudelaire, meanwhile, was unflinching in presenting a prostitute as a vampire in his poem 'Metamorphoses of the Vampire', written in 1852 (though it was expunged from the first edition of *Les Fleurs du Mal*, 1857). Germany also retained its association with the figure, linking the vampire to Anglo-Germanic heritage as an alternative to the classical superstitions of the Mediterranean. Charlotte Brontë, for instance, describes the mixed-race Bertha Mason's face thus: 'the lips were swelled and dark; the brow furrowed: the black eyebrows widely raised over the bloodshot eyes', reminding Jane Eyre 'Of the foul German spectre – the Vampyre' (1847).[90]

Several writers drew overtly on the medical and philosophical connotations of vampirism. Mary Fortune's 'The White Maniac: A Doctor's Tale' (1867) focuses on a female psychiatric patient who is sent into a bloodthirsty rage by the colour scarlet, ultimately attempting to rip out the throat of the narrator. Mary Elizabeth Braddon also focused on psychiatry and medicine, particularly pollution and sanitation in 'Herself' (1894), in which death appears in a mirror, while her acclaimed tale 'The Good Lady Ducayne' (1896) concerns blood transfusion – blood hypodermically stolen from servants to prolong the protagonist's life. Sabine Baring-Gould's own 'Margery of Quether' (1884), another seductress, represents a different side of Enlightenment vampirism in exploring the legal rights of the vampire in marriage and, crucially, property ownership and inheritance. In contrast,

VERBES OF CRVEL
Mortuus non mordet. ex Plutarcho in Vita

M. Michael Ranfts
Diaconi zu Nebra,

TRACTAT

von dem

Kauen und Schmatzen

der Todten

in Gräbern,

Worin die wahre Beschaffenheit
derer Hungarischen

VAMPYRS

und

Blut-Sauger

gezeigt,

Auch alle von dieser Materie bißher
zum Vorschein gekommene Schrifften
recensiret werden.

Leipzig, 1734.
Zu finden in Teubners Buchladen.

1 Frontispiece and title page of Michael Ranft's *Tractat von dem Kauen und Schmatzen der Todten in Gräbern* (1734), the earliest compendium of vampirism. The illustration is of a satyr, the half-human half-goat of Greek mythology, as a symbol of beings that were near-human (early accounts of orangutans sometimes described them as 'satyrs'); and Wisdom personified as a woman who has discarded the hourglass of time to contemplate the alchemical symbol of the ouroboros, the tail-swallowing serpent that represents renewal and rejuvenation.

2 The Devil taunts passers-by by beating a tattoo in Joseph Glanvill's *Saducismus Triumphatus* (1681). Uncanny noises were often characteristic of ghostly occurrences, from the 'Drummer of Tedworth' to 'Scratching Fanny', and in vampire lore were manifested in reports of hearing manducation or 'grave-eating' from beneath the earth.

3 Sir Edmund King and Dr Richard Lower's first-hand account of blood transfused to Arthur Coga from a sheep on 23 November 1667, achieved by means of quills, silver pipes and a porringer. The report was published in *Philosophical Transactions* shortly afterwards, on 9 December.

4 The barber's shop as a political satire on ignorance and credulity (*c.* 1730–45). A monstrous congregation assembles for blood-letting and tooth-extraction (and reading from the *Grub Street Journal*), and in doing so abandon their humanity; the only fully human figure is behind them and leaves the surgery as a maimed double-amputee.

5 The gruesome 'reward' of the hanged murderer Tom Nero in William Hogarth's series *The Four Stages of Cruelty* (1751) is to be publicly dissected before an unfeeling audience of professional physicians.

THE DEAD ALIVE!

6 *The Dead Alive!* by Henry Wigstead (1784): Mr Gripe groggily emerges from his coffin to startle his wife who is poring over his business accounts; a bowl, flask and goblet litter the floor, which may suggest that he has been poisoned.

7 *Terrour or Fright,* from the series *Caricatures of the Passions* by Wigstead's friend and collaborator Thomas Rowlandson (1800). A countryman is terrified by an apparition, though the accompanying text suggests that this may be a hoax. Ghosts were usually depicted clothed in winding sheets or shrouds, but this specimen is unusual in having long, post-mortem nails as well as fangs, which links the image to the emergent cultural vampire.

8 The title page of Dr John Polidori's inaugural *The Vampyre: A Tale* (1819). It was originally published as being by Lord Byron and, despite Polidori's protests, continued to be attributed to Byron throughout the nineteenth century.

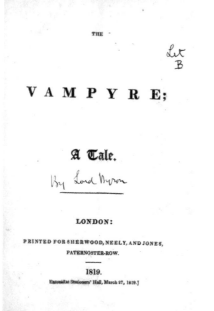

9 The title page of James Malcolm Rymer's bestselling 'Penny Dreadful' *Varney the Vampire or, The Feast of Blood* (1845–47). Varney is a hideous incarnation of the undead – shrouded, skeletal and fanged – while his prey is a typically 'vulnerable' young woman, asleep but with 'wanton ringlets' playing across her bedclothes.

10 Charles Darwin's sketch of the vampire bat *Desmodus* caught feeding on a horse in Chile in 1832. His report, recorded during his voyage to South America on the *Beagle*, was the first confirmed instance of a vampire bat sucking blood.

11 The naked murderer James Hall drains blood from the corpse of his master John Penny, having stoved in Penny's head with the oaken staff now lying beside him. Hall spent the rest of the night attempting to remove all traces of blood from the scene, but without success. He was charged on the forensic evidence of bloodstains, confessed, and was hanged on the central London thoroughfare The Strand on 14 September 1741.

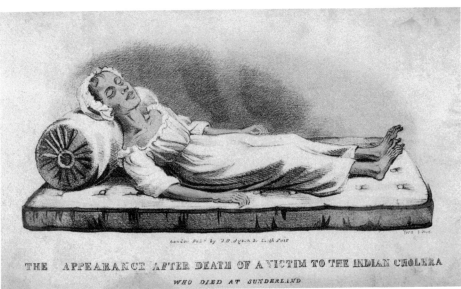

12 The so-called 'blue stage' of cholera from a victim in Sunderland, 1832, by 'I.W.G.'. Extreme dehydration has caused blood vessels to collapse, resulting in the skin turning blue and giving the appearance of sudden and premature ageing. The progress of the disease was thus horribly and distinctively apparent.

13 Henry Fuseli's iconic painting *The Nightmare* (1781) represented a rejection of the natural world in favour of the psychology of the supernatural – in proof of which a bottle of laudanum stands on the table. According to the *Art Journal*, Fuseli 'complained that nature put him out – that is, he could not draw what he saw before him, and rather blamed nature than blamed himself; and he was one of those who thought that not to copy nature is the rule for attaining perfection'.

14 In the absence of cadavers, breathtakingly lifelike waxworks were popular for teaching anatomy. These figures, often built around actual skeletons, were modelled on dissections of executed felons – a side-effect being the proliferation of the mutilated criminal body.

15 David Henry Friston's illustration for Joseph Sheridan Le Fanu's vampire tale (1871–72): another prone female with disarrayed hair, another undead predator – this time the arachnidan Carmilla.

16 Gothic politics in *Punch* (1885): the Irish National League, figured as a huge vampire bat with the face of the Irish nationalist politician Charles Stewart Parnell, threatens to wreak havoc on the prostrate Hibernia (Ireland) through Home Rule.

17 In contrast, the vampire of capitalism, riding on wings of religious hypocrisy and party politics, sucks the life from labour, while the Angel of Socialism sounds the alarm (*c.* 1880). The artist, Walter Crane, while best known for his illustrations of children's stories was also a close friend of William Morris and was committed to the international socialist movement.

18 & 19 Madeleine Lemaire's Ophelia (1880), left, is poised precariously at the water's edge; her hair is elfed in knots and she gathers flowers to her – that much can be gleaned from Shakespeare – but her daringly exposed breasts and shocking expression of a knowing and libidinous madness is something disturbingly new. By contrast, Antoine-Auguste-Ernest Hébert's Ophelia (1890s) burns with homicidal wrath: her glowering cascade of fiery hair and fathomless eyes reveal her to be nothing less than a coiled serpent who will strike with lethal power.

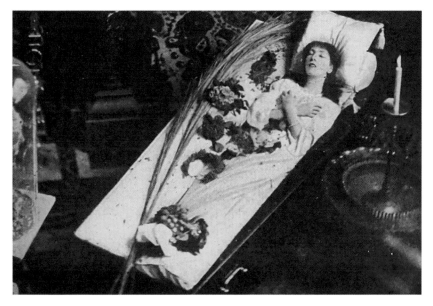

20 The renowned actress Sarah Bernhardt posing in her coffin, where she preferred to learn her lines and where she regularly slept. This photograph from 1873 appeared in her autobiography, *Memories of My Life* (1907).

21 *À un Dîner d'Athées* (*At a Dinner of Atheists*), by the decadent artist Félicien Rops (1873), later included in *Les Diaboliques* (*The She-Devils*), Barbey d'Aurevilly's collection of short stories of women, revenge and death (1874). 'À un Dîner d'Athées' is a tale of blasphemy, sexual violence and the mummified heart of a child; the book was immediately condemned.

22 Aubrey Beardsley's illustration of 'X.L.'s (Julian Osgood Field's) vampire story 'A Kiss of Judas' (1893), contrasting a bestial, satyr-like male with an otherworldly female. The sexual tension between beast and beauty is accentuated by Beardsley's characteristically unforgiving monochrome style.

23 Albert von Keller, *Im Mondschein* (*In the Moonlight*, 1894). The reclining, dying, dead female finds new undead life writhing on the cross in a sado-erotic fantasy as a radical feminization of Christ, or as a she-vampire bathed in moonlight and tied down before being slain.

24 Edvard Munch's *Love and Pain* (1893–95), later known as *Vampire*. Despite maintaining that this simply portrayed a woman kissing a man, Munch obsessively repainted this searing image, and the woman's incandescent hair and overpowering stance strongly suggest something far more sinister than a merely human embrace.

25 Philip Burne-Jones, *The Vampire* (1897: the year of *Dracula*). Philip was the son of the Pre-Raphaelite artist Edward Burne-Jones; this, his most famous work, inspired Rudyard Kipling's appalled poem of sexual abhorrence, 'The Vampire'.

26 Dracula as a bat, from the first paperback edition of Bram Stoker's *Dracula* (1901). The original text reads: 'I saw the whole man clearly emerge from the window and begin to crawl down the castle wall over that dreadful abyss, face down, with his cloak spreading out around him like great wings.'

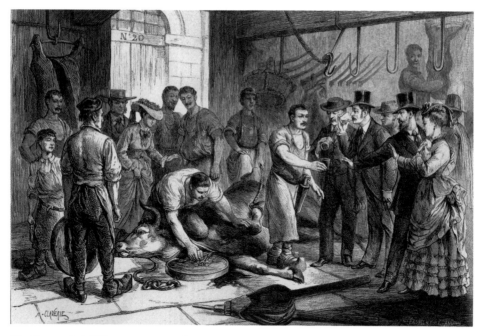

27 *Abattoir de la Villette: Les Buveurs de Sang* (Paris, late nineteenth century). Warm blood from a freshly slain ox is promoted as a fashionable cure for fatigue and listlessness, and consequently attracts both the affluent and the anaemic, both men and women. Some, however, are horrified at the prospect of drinking blood.

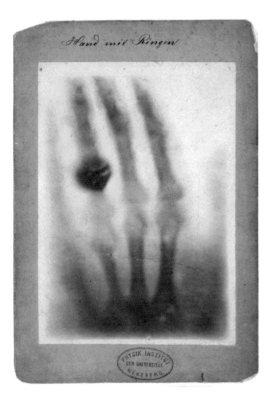

28 Wilhelm Röntgen X-rayed his wife's hand ('Hand mit Ringen') on 22 December 1895, inspiring a craze for X-ray photography. Within a year the first radiology department had opened and travelling carnivals were offering X-ray images made by slot-machines. Meanwhile, legend has it that the first X-ray subject, Anna Röntgen, declared, 'I have seen my death' – and refused to take part in any further experiments.

29 Madeleine Wallis's vampire fashion for the House of Paquin (1921): a black satin cloak with lined hood and red sash. Jeanne Paquin was a pioneering female couturier whose signature colour was red, and who helped to re-establish black as a chic choice after decades of Victorian mourning.

30 The stunning Theda Bara playing Rosa in the 1915 silent movie *Sin* – both her character and the film were notorious for glamourizing crime, lust and suicide. Despite its popularity, no prints of the film appear to have survived.

31 The incomparable Maila Nurmi in the film *Plan 9 from Outer Space* (1959). The movie (originally titled *Grave Robbers from Outer Space*) attempted to combine sci-fi apocalypse with ghoulish Gothic, aided by Nurmi's instantly identifiable 'Vampira' look and posthumous footage of Béla Lugosi, who had died in 1956. The film has since achieved cult status as the worst movie ever made.

32 Patricia Morrison's Goth credentials are impeccable: she has been bassist in The Gun Club, Fur Bible (with Kid Congo Powers, later of The Bad Seeds), The Sisters of Mercy and The Damned. Andrew Eldritch allegedly wrote the vampire anthem 'Lucretia, My Reflection' (*Floodland*, 1987) about Morrison.

33 *Weird Tales* was a left-field pulp fiction magazine that in recent years has been recognized as a crucible for experimental horror writing of the 1920s and 1930s. Major authors such as Robert Bloch (*Psycho*), Robert E. Howard (Conan) and H.P. Lovecraft and August Derleth (the Cthulhu mythos) published their work in *Weird Tales*, which also featured the alluring vampirism of Thorp McClusky.

34 The chameleon seventies rock star David Bowie plays the part of a sub-vampire in *The Hunger* (1983), the first scene of which features post-punk Goth band Bauhaus performing their genre-defining single 'Bela Lugosi's Dead'. Style, cinema and music thus combine in a New York club to create a super-classy vampire film for the HIV-threatened generation – presided over by the domme-vampire Catherine Deneuve.

35 Vampire-slaying kits were acknowledged stage props in the twentieth century and have subsequently become desirable collectors' items, especially those associated with filmmakers such as Hammer Productions. This example was made around 1970 and is in the collection of the Royal Armouries Museum, Leeds.

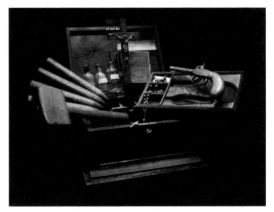

Mme de St Croix in *Bones and I* (1869) by G.J. Whyte-Melville features a Hungarian beauty preying more insidiously on men, who waste away in her company, falling into ruin and decay. Similarly, in Phil Robinson's 'Medusa' (1889), politics and disease come together in the beguiling figure of Mrs Tierce, whose eyes have a hypnotic allure. But as one of her victims warns,

> She is not a woman; she is not human. Yes, I know how beautiful she is . . . You will think me mad . . . What else should you think when a stranger comes into your chambers and tells you that in these matter-of-fact nineteenth-century days there exist beings who are not human – who have more than human attributes, and that one of these beings is the woman whom you love?[91]

The motif was later taken up by Dick Donovan in 'The Woman with the "Oily Eyes"' (1899), which features a parallel character to Mme de St Croix with an equally eerie gaze.[92] A chilling version of the fear of feminine seduction was written by Eliza Lynn Linton in 1880: in 'The Fate of Madame Cabanel', an innocent English governess is lynched by a mob of French peasants who believe she is a vampire by virtue of her good health, rosy cheeks and red lips. In response, Rudyard Kipling's panic-stricken poem 'The Vampire' (written in 1897) is a forthright warning against predatory women, who are imagined as abject fiends: 'a rag and a bone and a hank of hair'.[93]

One of the most unnerving of these medical she-vampire tales is Robert Louis Stevenson's 'Olalla' (1885), in which the Scottish narrator is sent by his doctor to Spain for a therapeutic treatment for blood renewal. The stifling atmosphere of the story is heavy with congenital debility. He finds himself within a family of degenerates: the mother and son have infantile and bestial intellects, and while the daughter Olalla carries the same genetic predisposition, she appears to be relatively normal – yet despite her intoxicating beauty, she will never marry and instead spends her time immersed in ancient Latin texts. The narrative is replete with vampire motives – from the luminous dead eyes of the mother to the mephitic 'black wind' that blows from 'malarious lowlands' – and when the narrator encounters Olalla 'she passed through my veins: she was one with me'.[94]

This imagery of blood is decanted throughout the text, and indeed the mother falls into a frenzied biting fit when she glimpses blood seeping from a cut on the narrator's wrist; but the word 'vampire' is never audibly uttered – instead, it is only ever hinted at through half-puns and allusions.[95] But what characterizes the unspoken family curse is that the family blood is impoverished: 'the wheel has gone backward with my doomed race' declares Olalla.[96] Vampirism here is a 'genetic inheritance' understood through Darwinian theory – a loss of oneself, an enforced abdication of free will through indefinable hereditary coding (much as Dr Jekyll loses himself through chemical medication in Stevenson's most renowned story): 'the cause of becoming a vampire is not infection, the consumption of blood, or mortal death, but rather the secret logic of the genes'.[97]

In the same year that Kipling shrank from the unbearable threat of the female, Florence Marryat published *Blood of the Vampire* (1897).[98] In spite of its arresting title, this novel presents a far less sensational – but no less deadly – female vampire. Harriet Brandt is from Jamaica and of mixed race, but her skin is strangely 'colourless', her eyes are hooded – 'long-shaped, dark, and narrow, with heavy lids and thick black lashes which lay upon her cheeks' – and her lips are of 'a deep blood'.[99] Her father was a scientist, slaver and experimental vivisectionist; her mother a black slave:

> They declared that when her slave mother was pregnant with her, she was bitten by a Vampire bat, which are formidable creatures in the West Indies, and are said to fan their victims to sleep with their enormous wings, whilst they suck their blood. Anyway the slave woman did not survive her delivery, and her fellows prophecied [*sic*] that the child would grow up to be a murderess.[100]

As the reference to the vampire bat suggests, she is perceived as a peculiarity of natural history, comparable to the deadly (if fictitious) 'upas tree'. Although she thirsts for blood, it is the invisible, intangible breath she takes from her victims, sucking out the life 'by lulling him into a sleep from which he never wakens'.[101] She is therefore inimical to human relationships and the whole future of the species, a web of aberrant identities that crystallize nineteenth-century fears of racial difference, miscegenation, female emancipation, experimental science, invasive flora and fauna, and impropriety. When she is diagnosed as vampiric by a physician, her response to her condition is seemingly plaintive: 'Doctor Phillips said I was not fit for marriage,' she laments,

> that I should always weaken and hurt those whom I loved most – and that I should draw from them, physically and mentally, until I had sapped all their strength – that I have the blood of the vampire in me, the vampire that sucks its victims' breaths until they die![102]

But at the same time, the response to her from Mme Gobelli after the death of her son is utterly venomous:

> 'It is *you* 'oo 'ave killed 'im,' screamed the Baroness, shaking her stick, 'it's your poisonous breath that 'as sapped 'is! I should 'ave seen it from the beginning. Do you suppose I don't know your 'istory? Do you think I 'aven't 'eard all about your parents and their vile doings – that I don't know that you're a common bastard, and that your mother was a devilish negress, and your father a murderer? Why didn't I listen to my friends and forbid you the 'ouse?'[103]

Harriet Brandt is, like Olalla, a vampire born: her vampirism is her genetic inheritance.

The central she-vampire of the nineteenth century is, however, indubitably Carmilla, in Joseph Sheridan Le Fanu's story of the same name (1871–72).[104] 'Carmilla' is certainly open to readings based on Le Fanu's Calvinism, Ireland's politics and the Irish role in driving the British Empire in the nineteenth century.[105] Yet in the immediate context of vampires, it is striking how faithful Le Fanu is to the Enlightenment vampire: along with the other vampire tales mentioned, 'Carmilla' readily resolves the narrative possibilities of medical diagnosis and empirical inquiry. The story is set in Styria, a state of Inner Austria, though the narrator Laura's father is English, having worked for 'the Austrian service' – an officer of the Habsburg Empire.[106] This has enabled him to retire to a schloss with a Gothic chapel close to a deserted village and ruined church – a ruined church that regrettably turns out to be the lair of the vampire Carmilla, who preys on young women in the village. Laura first encounters Carmilla when she is a little girl, apparently dreaming. She recalls, 'I was awakened by a sensation as if two needles ran into my breast very deep at the same moment', though there is no visible puncture wound.[107] Laura later dreams that she is visited in the night by a monstrous black feline creature that sinks its fangs into her: 'a stinging pain as if two large needles darted, an inch or two apart, deep into my breast'.[108] The cat metamorphoses into the beautiful Carmilla, who appears and disappears at Laura's bedside, sometimes soaked in blood. The rational explanation is that Carmilla is a somnambulist – a sleepwalker – though this does not explain how she is able to pass through locked doors.

Carmilla herself is in any case an enigma – both adorable and abhorrent – and a blood-sister to Laura: 'if your dear heart is wounded, my wild heart bleeds with yours'.[109] Like many vampires of the period, Carmilla has a bestial ferocity that simmers just below her exquisite looks: when livid, she clenches her teeth, one of which is noticeably 'long, thin, pointed, like an awl, like a needle'.[110] Her devotion to Laura is passionately invigorated by Laura's own growing weakness, 'like a momentary glare of insanity'; she also possesses startling physical strength.[111] But like Polidori's Lord Ruthven, Carmilla is an aristocrat, and she approaches her bloodsucking 'with the refinement of an epicure'.[112]

As Laura falls ill, she details her symptoms: misty dreams (like the mist over the landscape), physical sensations, a breathlessness as if she were being asphyxiated:

Certain vague and strange sensations visited me in my sleep . . . This was soon accompanied by dreams that seemed interminable, and were so vague that I could never recollect their scenery and persons . . . But they left an awful impression, and a sense of exhaustion, as if I had passed through a long period of great mental exertion and danger. After all these dreams there remained on waking a remembrance of having been in a place very nearly dark, and of having spoken to people whom I could not see; and especially of one clear voice, of a female's, very deep, that spoke as if at a distance, slowly, and producing always the same sensation of indescribable solemnity and fear. Sometimes there came a sensation as if a hand was drawn softly along my cheek and neck. Sometimes it was as if warm lips kissed me, and longer and more lovingly as they reached my throat, but there the caress fixed itself. My heart beat faster, my breathing rose and fell rapidly and full drawn; a sobbing, that rose into a sense of strangulation, supervened, and turned into a dreadful convulsion, in which my senses left me, and I became unconscious.

It was now three weeks since the commencement of this unaccountable state. My sufferings had, during the last week, told upon my appearance. I had grown pale, my eyes were dilated and darkened underneath, and the languor which I had long felt began to display itself in my countenance.[113]

A doctor visits Laura and discovers a small contusion 'about the size of the tip of your little finger'; like her symptoms, the bruise is consistent with the account given in Flückinger's report.[114]

General Spielsdorf, the voice of military authority in the tale, then gives an account of the nocturnal raids conducted on his daughter by one 'Millarca', which exactly mirror those of Carmilla. Predictably, the ordeal of his daughter reflects that of Laura:

She was at first visited by appalling dreams; then, as she fancied, by a spectre, sometimes resembling Millarca, sometimes in the shape of a beast, indistinctly seen, walking round the foot of her bed, from side to side. Lastly came sensations. One, not unpleasant, but very peculiar, she said, resembled the flow of an icy stream against her breast. At a later time, she felt something like a pair of large needles pierce her, a little below the throat, with a very sharp pain. A few nights after, followed a gradual and convulsive sense of strangulation; then came unconsciousness.[115]

Dreams and suffocation: this is the incubus effect common to early vampire assaults, followed by the intravenous bloodsucking. The needles penetrate deep, and eventually the victim dies.

It transpires that Carmilla is actually Countess Mircalla Karnstein, as apparent from a portrait of 1698. This leads the general to visit the ruined chapel of the Karnsteins to locate her tomb. In the face of disbelief and ridicule the tomb is opened – not broken into – and the countess's body is exhumed by imperial officials. It is found to be fresh and 'tinted with the warmth of life'; her eyes are open and 'the leaden coffin floated with blood'.[116] She is accordingly decapitated, staked and cremated. A formal report is subsequently filed, testifying to the operation and authenticating Laura's account:

> My father has a copy of the report of the Imperial Commission, with the signatures of all who were present at these proceedings, attached in verification of the statement. It is from this official paper that I have summarized my account of this last shocking scene.[117]

Laura further validates her narrative by noting that vampires (*pace* the Flückinger report) tend to be fresh-faced, and that 'the deadly pallor attributed to that sort of *revenants*, is a mere melodramatic fiction'.[118] She also brings up Calmet's problem as to how they are able to quit and resume their place in the grave, which 'has always been admitted to be utterly inexplicable', but leaves that question unanswered.[119] She further sketches the character of the vampirologist of the story, Baron Vordenburg, whose library includes ' "*Magia Posthuma*", "*Phlegon de Mirabilibus*", "*Augustinus de curâ pro Mortuis*", "*Philosophicæ et Christianæ Cogitationes de Vampiris*" by John Christofer Herenberg; and a thousand others' – some of the familiar and reputed works of eighteenth-century vampirology.[120] In fact, this textual verification is a feature of the tale, which is allegedly based on a medical manuscript written by Dr Hesselius, and which includes letters from General Spielsdorf as well as reported speech. The exhumation, staking, decapitation and cremation of Carmilla is all performed in accordance with Flückinger's inquest: 'Carmilla' is an Enlightenment episode dramatized for the nineteenth century. For all the new permutations of vampirism, true vampires still remained at large.

CHAPTER 7

BLEEDING GOLD
Gothic Capitalism and Undead Consumerism

What I was once, alive, I still am, dead!

Dante (fourteenth century)[1]

Gold runs in our blood.

Virginia Woolf (1931)[2]

Soon we will drink blood for wine.

'The Revolutionary of the Upper Rhine' (sixteenth century)[3]

L
ike vampires themselves, interest in blood was hardly likely to fall away in the nineteenth century. If anything, its status as a funda-mental image of life and wellbeing was intensified. John Hunter's researches into blood had established it as the matter of life itself (the *materia vitae*) and indicative of a range of conditions, from fevers to gout. Blood, in other words, 'was in a dynamic relationship with the organs and tissues of the body'.[4] Blood therefore remained both a central concern and a central symbol, and it seeped into fields such as female physiology and theories of degeneration, adding a tantalizing (if often overstated) sexual allure to the figure of the vampire. But images of blood and bloodsuckers also continued to run through political science, providing a body of images

for the expanding world of capitalism and consumerism. Commodities sucked the life out of shoppers, substituting their identities with identikit facsimiles of the ideal consumer and alienating them from their fellow beings. Meanwhile global capitalism spawned a verminous social underclass: the 'masses'. The vampire aesthetic was, then, inescapably capitalist: Voltaire had already compared vampires in Paris and London to stockjobbers on the markets; but the longevity and pervasiveness of the metaphorical figure of the political vampire is noteworthy. Not only does politics saturate vampire tales, but it has remained an abiding feature of portrayals of the vampire, from its very first appearance in Britain to the present day. And again, vampire thinking also continued to be reflected in medical sciences, especially in developing new theories of contagion.

In the nineteenth century, then, vampires entangle medical and political thinking with literature, dissolving the gap between fiction and theories of medicine and the social sciences. Whereas in the eighteenth century they had been a medical riddle, they now became a more pervasive influence on the apprehensions that occupied physicians, economists and writers.

Blood science

The nineteenth century was an era nigh on besotted with blood and blood science, from experiments into intravenous transfusion to bloodstock and hereditary disease. The philosopher Immanuel Kant believed that the characteristics of European nationalities were inherent in the blood – 'innate, natural character, which, so to speak, lies in the composition of the person's blood' (1798); while in Thomas Hardy's novel *Jude the Obscure* (1895), Drusilla Fawley warns her nephew, 'There's sommat in our blood'.[5] That 'sommat' could, however, be fixed. Slaughterhouses attracted regular 'blood drinkers', and Ferdinand Joseph Gueldry's painting of the fashion for imbibing fresh blood proved sensationally popular. As the editor of *The Magazine of Art* described it in 1898:

one of the most popular pictures of the year is undoubtedly Monsieur Gueldry's gorge raising representation of 'The Blood-Drinkers,' in which a group of consumptive invalids, congregated in a shambles, are

drinking the blood fresh from the newly-slain ox lying in the fore-
ground – blood that oozes out over the floor – while the slaughterers
themselves, steeped in gore, hand out the glasses like the women at the
wells. What gives point to the loathsomeness of the subject is the figure
of one young girl, pale and trembling, who turns from the scene in
sickening disgust, and so accentuates our own.[6]

So the folkloric faith in the restorative qualities of blood continued to be
promoted throughout the century as a scientific reality, and human-to-
human blood transfusions became increasingly popular – the largest series
of the time being led by the surgeon John Duncan at Edinburgh, from
1885 to 1892.[7]

This fascination with blood went hand in hand with the growing popularity of vampire tales. Women were particularly prone to anaemia, and
with the improvement of microscopes in the 1830s the preparation of
slides of blood samples became widespread, and instruments such as the
haemoglobinometer were used to diagnose the condition.[8] Women also
lost blood through menstruation, and their blood was in any case thought
to be thinner than men's. All this associated women with vampirism, and
the vampires themselves increasingly shifted from the ruddy and replete
beings of Eastern European cases to the pale and cadaverous features of
corpse-like *femmes fatales*.[9] As the decadent poet Arthur Symons put it in
his poem 'The Vampire' (1894), it was a

> white bloodless creature of the night,
> Whose lust of blood has blanched her chill veins white,
> Veins fed with moonlight over dead men's tombs.[10]

So the monstrosity of Carmilla, for example, was no surprise: women
were already formed in the image of the vampire, with a supernatural lineage
in Lamia and Lilith. The feminist viragoes deemed to be sisters of these
monstrosities were the 'New Women', promoters of a late-nineteenth-
century social and political emancipatory movement: they dressed casually,
smoked, rode bicycles and even – horror of horrors! – educated themselves
and pursued professional careers. As the art historian Bram Dijkstra suggests:

the Lamia of myth was thought to have been a bisexual, masculinized, cradle-robbing creature, and therefore to the men of the turn of the century perfectly representative of the New Woman who, in their eyes, was seeking to arrogate to herself male privileges, refused the duties of motherhood, and was intent upon destroying the heavenly harmony of feminine subordination within the family. The same was certainly true of Lilith.[11]

Of the serpentine Lamia, Keats had already detailed the voluptuous danger of her inhuman sexuality. Likewise Lilith: according to Dante Gabriel Rossetti, 'Not a drop of her blood was human, / But she was made like a soft sweet woman.'[12] And at the same time as they were being literally demonized, women could also be simply, metamorphically bestial: comparing women to cats was 'virtually endemic by the 1890s'.[13] It appeared that women were not merely a separate species from men: they were an alien life-form.

Female physiology was held to be partially responsible for these characteristics – and this physiology was, in one sense, characterized by blood and bleeding. Henry Maudsley, the leading psychiatrist of the time, argued in *Body and Mind* (1870) that mental conditions had physical and biological causes – what he called 'the effects of organic sympathies in the causation of mental disorders'. In other words, 'the derangement of an internal organ, acting upon the brain, may engender, by pathological sympathy, morbid feelings and their related ideas'. Inevitably, 'The monthly activity of the ovaries which marks the advent of puberty in women has a notable effect upon the mind and body; wherefore it may become an important cause of mental and physical derangement.' This could lead to 'a direct explosion of insanity' and cause epilepsy – the archetypal condition best alleviated by fresh blood (the alternative was to be treated to a bilateral oophorectomy – the surgical removal of both ovaries).

Maudsley's account of the symptoms of delusion and psychological derangement are strikingly similar to those associated with vampirism in the previous century:

When positive insanity breaks out, it usually has the form of profound melancholia, with vague delusions of an extreme character, as that the

150

world is in flames, that it is turned upside down, that every thing is changed, or that some very dreadful but undefined calamity has happened or is about to happen. The countenance has the expression of a vague terror and apprehension.[14]

Associated syndromes included hyperaesthesia, or morbid sensitivity (the equally cold-blooded remedy for which being clitoridectomy).

The criminologists Cesare Lombroso and Guglielmo Ferrero took a slightly different perspective, deeming that women had infant brains: having 'many traits in common with children; . . . their moral sense is deficient; . . . they are revengeful, jealous, inclined to vengeances of a refined cruelty'.[15] Yet despite this congenital immaturity, delinquency in women was viewed with marked abhorrence:

the born female criminal is, so to speak, doubly exceptional, as a woman and as a criminal. For criminals are an exception among civilised people, and women are an exception among criminals, the natural form of retrogression in women being prostitution and not crime . . . As a double exception, the criminal woman is consequently a monster.[16]

Prostitution – marketing the female as a commodity and a sexual plaything – was explicable in a way that other crimes committed by women were not. And this equation of sex and consumption was also itself vampiric.

Having been comprehensively medicalized in the eighteenth century, in the next century vampirism became emblematic of a constellation of conditions and indeed fears connected with the female body, derived from the conviction that loss of menstrual blood had potentially catastrophic physical and mental consequences. But these effects were not confined to individuals: they posed a threat to the whole of western civilization. The later nineteenth century lived in dread of evolutionary reversion, or degeneration to a bestial, primaeval state. The first theorist of degeneration was Bénédict Morel in 1857 with *Traité des Dégénérescences Physiques, Intellectuelles et Morales de l'Espèce Humaine*, a book that mixed Catholicism with Lamarckian theories of heredity. Madness, to give one example, was the result of physiological damage or immoral behaviour, and could become a transmissible condition carried down to later generations. Psychiatry was therefore rooted as much in the body as it was in behaviour – bloodlines could communicate insanity.[17] The criminal anthropologist Lombroso built on Morel's ideas in *L'Uomo Delinquente* (*Criminal Man*, first published in 1876), arguing that criminals actually constituted a separate race – a more primitive, subhuman racial type.

In one sense, then, degeneracy for Lombroso was backwards evolution, the 'criminal man' was ape-like, a throwback, a perverse proof that Darwinian evolution could be both progressive and regressive. Their reversion to rudimentary states was both mental and physical, and consequently had recognizable characteristics: they 'exhibit numerous anomalies in the face, skeleton, and various psychic and sensitive functions, so that they strongly resemble primitive races'.[18] In addition, there were various cultural indicators, such as a liking for tattoos, and sociopathic behaviour encompassing 'excessive idleness, love of orgies, and the irresistible craving for evil for its own sake, the desire not only to extinguish life in the victim, but to mutilate the corpse, tear its flesh, and drink its blood'.[19]

For his own part, Lombroso was not beyond ransacking burial grounds for anatomical specimens, and was once caught with a sack stuffed with pillaged skulls – but clearly he did not consider this sort of behaviour to be on the spectrum of crimes against the dead. Tellingly, however, one consequence of Lombroso's argument that criminality amounted to a species distinction was that crime was literally in the blood of felons, and that blaming and punishing them for anti-social offences was tantamount to holding a mad dog morally culpable: such a brute might have to be destroyed, but it could hardly be held responsible in human terms for its canine brutality. In this context, vampire writing poses the problem of alternative evolutionary strands, effectively presenting vampires as a competing species.[20]

In his position of biological positivism, Lombroso was profoundly influenced by Darwin – and although his application of natural selection and genetic variation to sociology and anthropology was fundamentally flawed, it proved highly influential and could be applied across a wide range of personality types. In 1864, he published an essay arguing that genius effectively fell under the categorization of degeneration – an idea that was eventually developed into the books *L'Uomo di Genio* (*Man of Genius*, 1888) and *Genio e Degenerazione* (*Genius and Degeneration*, 1897).[21] The physician, social scientist and Zionist intellectual Max Nordau in turn derived *Degeneration* (first published in Germany in 1892, English edition 1895) from Morel and Lombroso (to whom it was dedicated) in order to diagnose what he described as the 'moral sea-sickness' of contemporary society and taste.[22]

Nordau studied such pernicious deviants as lawbreakers, homosexuals, New Women and Pre-Raphaelite artists. Everything from trendy fashions and women dyeing their hair to particularly noxious perversions such as chic furniture, naturalistic literature and impressionism was appalling evidence of utter moral decay. Such degeneracy was in part due to physical causes:

> narcotics and stimulants in any form (such as fermented alcoholic drinks, tobacco, opium, hashish, arsenic), which partakes of tainted foods (bread made with bad corn), which absorbs organic poisons (march fever, syphilis, tuberculosis, goitre), begets degenerate descendants who, if they remain exposed to the same influences, rapidly descend to the lowest degrees of degeneracy, to idiocy, to dwarfishness, etc.[23]

But it was also a consequence simply of living in the nineteenth century. In other words, the problem was modernity itself. Nordau cited statistics on railways, publishing and the postal service in cataloguing the dire challenges of modern life, which included such desperate ordeals as receiving unexpected visitors. His breakdown is little short of hysterical:

> All these activities, . . . even the simplest, involve an effort of the nervous system and a wearing of tissue. Every line we read or write, every human face we see, every conversation we carry on, every scene we perceive through the window of the flying express, sets in activity our sensory nerves and our brain centres. Even the little shocks of railway travelling, not perceived by consciousness, the perpetual noises, and the various sights in the streets of a large town, our suspense pending the sequel of progressing events, the constant expectation of the newspaper, of the postman, of visitors, cost our brains wear and tear.[24]

In effect, vampires are not a cause or sign of degeneracy: it is the entire modern world that is degenerate, and vampires – as thoroughly modern beings inhabiting the modern world – consequently share in the trauma of degeneracy. Furthermore, Nordau claims that 'The enormous increase in hysteria in our days is partly due to the same causes as degeneracy.'[25] So the world is likewise *mundus hystericus*, and the vampires, like the people, are part of its hectic ferocity.

Female physiology and degeneracy evidently share the same blood in the nineteenth century, and account in part for the eruption of vampire stories and their subject matter; and it is tempting to add racial politics to this cocktail – in particular the 'blood libel' raised against the Jews. This baleful accusation – that the blood of Gentiles was customarily used in Jewish rituals, such as making matzos – first arose in 1144 in the case of William of Norwich, as reported by Thomas of Monmouth in 1150.[26] The allegation that individual witches or vampires stole blood could also obviously be levelled at groups such as gypsies or the Jews: 'others', foreign and invasive.[27] The persecution of Jewish minorities by Christian societies may only be a remote echo of the theological debates on vampires that had gripped Enlightenment thinking a century before, but it is a powerful reminder that Christian theology is dripping with the blood of Christ and the martyrs, effectively constituting a whole haemodynamic discourse.[28] In the case of the Jews, the blood libel offered a focus for fears that a supposedly dead religion (Judaism) could return from the grave to sap Christianity of its vitality, literally draining the blood from Christian believers and making it into unleavened bread – a derisive inversion of the whole sacrament.[29] No matter that the Hebrew Bible prohibited the ingestion of blood, whereas Christianity made it a central tenet of its symbolism.[30]

The medieval blood libel was indeed revived in the nineteenth century, in 1840 in Damascus, following the disappearance of Thomas, a Capuchin friar, and his Muslim servant; the Capuchins accused the Jews of the city of double murder in order to obtain blood for Passover rituals. A confession was extracted by torture from a Jewish barber that the victims had been killed by a Jewish gang:

the body [of Friar Thomas] was suspended head down; one held a tub to collect the blood while the other two applied pressure to facilitate the flow. Then, once the source of blood had dried up, all of them, maddened, threw themselves on the corpse, cutting it to bits.[31]

These innocents were rounded up and tortured, in the process of which two died and one converted to Islam. News spread across Europe and provided newspapers with plenty of copy that could draw on alleged cases of historical ritual slaughter by Jewish communities. In London, *The Times* was markedly confrontational, thundering that the affair was

one of the most important cases ever submitted to the notice of the civilized world . . . Admitting for the moment [the accusations to be true] . . . then the Jewish religion must at once disappear from the face of the earth . . . We shall await the issue, as the whole of Europe and the civilized world will do, with intense interest.[32]

But while the revival of the Jewish blood libel certainly helped to stir up anti-Semitism in the period, in England there were more domestic issues at stake. In the decade following the Damascus Blood Libel, it was the Jewish ritual slaughter of livestock that came under attack in the 1850s – criticism that was led by animal-rights activists and anti-vivisectionists, and which was only gradually enlisted into racist politics.[33] In part, this was due to the prominence of public figures such as Benjamin Disraeli, chancellor of the Exchequer and leader of the House (and later prime minster), who, though baptized a Christian, had led the first 12 years of his life as a Sephardic Jew and later campaigned for the right of Jews to sit in Parliament (granted in 1858).[34] So although Jewish historian David Biale remarks that 'the same kind of anxieties over race, nationalism, and sexuality that pervade modern vampire stories can certainly be seen in the context of the blood libel against the Jews', the gradual revival of the blood libel accusation was only tangentially connected to the growing number of vampire tales.[35] Vampires tend to be (sometimes quite plainly) lone wolves, whereas the allegations of ritual murder and theft of Christian blood made against the Jews usually involved small communities, a synagogue, ceremonial practice and the wherewithal to make matzos. In the same way that 'vampirophobia' is not, in Britain, at heart a fear of 'reverse colonialism' (Eastern Europe never having been part of the British Empire), the assumption that these are anti-Semitic texts also risks distorting them. Vampires are not relentlessly Jewish or inevitably pretexts for the persecution of Jews.[36]

If there is a connection between vampires and Jews, it is one predicated on capitalism. In 1845, the socialist-Zionist philosopher Moses Hess described money as 'the coagulated blood of those who suffer, that itself brings to market its unalienated character, its own means, its life activity, in order to exchange its own dead head (*caput mortuum*) for a so-called Capital and to cannibalistically suck nourishment from its own fat'. Hess, as will become apparent, adopts a distinctive vampiric language in describing humans as 'social beasts of prey' who have evolved into carnivorous predators by being blooded with money:

> We are no longer *grass eaters*, like our good-natured ancestors, who were also social animals but not yet social beasts of prey; who, in the majority, merely let themselves be *fed* like good-natured domestic animals – we are *bloodsuckers* who *maltreat and consume each other*. Just as the animal enjoys its own life in the blood, in an *animal-like, brutal* manner – in the same way man enjoys his own life through money in a *brutal, animal-like, cannibalistic* way. Money is the social blood, but the externalized, the *spilled blood*.[37]

Blood and toil

Vampirism had already been identified with commerce, trade and stock-broking by Nicholas Amherst, Charles Forman, Voltaire and Jean-Jacques Rousseau, but this association went far further in the next century. Markets were a favoured habitat of the vampire: the Scottish poet Robert Burns described the victimized figure of the 'Bard' as prey to 'Vampyre book-sellers [that] drain him to the heart', while the Irish poet Thomas Moore attacked the bribery and corruption of the British government:

That greedy vampire, which from Freedom's tomb
Comes forth, with all the mimicry of bloom
Upon its lifeless cheek, and sucks and drains
A people's blood to feed its putrid veins![38]

Anglo-Irish landlords were, in the words of both Romantic poet Percy Shelley and the later Irish MP William O'Brien, 'bloodsuckers', while fellow Irish MP Michael Davitt branded them 'the brood of cormorant vampires that have sucked the life-blood out of the country'.[39] The political economist and modernizing Catholic Charles Stanton Devas quoted Davitt to attack international free trade in precisely the same terms, while even in the early twentieth century Prime Minister David Lloyd George was reviled by the economist John Maynard Keynes as someone 'rooted in nothing . . . a vampire and a medium in one'.[40]

But the most influential political usage of vampirism in the nineteenth century (and indeed of the Gothic more generally) is undoubtedly Karl Marx. As the Marxist critical theorist Terry Eagleton puts it,

> Capital is a phantasmal body, a monstrous *Doppelgänger* which stalks abroad while its master sleeps, mechanically consuming the pleasures he austerely forgoes. The more the capitalist forswears his self-delight, devoting his labours instead to the fashioning of his zombie-like *alter ego*, the more second-hand fulfilments he is able to reap. Both capitalist and capital are images of the living dead, the one animate yet anaesthetized, the other inanimate yet active.[41]

In fact, motifs of the dead and the undead are scattered throughout Marx's writing, most obviously in *The Communist Manifesto* (1848) – 'A spectre is haunting Europe' (possibly a clue as to his bedtime reading).[42] In *The Class Struggles in France* (1850), the French National Assembly is described as 'a vampire living off the blood of the June insurgents'; similarly, in the *Eighteenth Brumaire of Louis Bonaparte* (1852) – in a reversal of Edmund Burke's language condemning the French Revolutionaries – 'the bourgeois order . . . has become a vampire that sucks out its [the rural workers'] blood and brains and throws them into the alchemist's cauldron'.[43] The image is elaborated in his notes towards the *Grundrisse* (written 1857–58), which highlights the elusive and metamorphic nature of capital:

> Capital posits the permanence of value (to a certain degree) by incarnating itself in fleeting commodities and taking on their form, but at the same time changing them just as constantly . . . But capital obtains this ability only by constantly sucking in living labour as its soul, vampire-like . . . sucking its living soul out of labour.[44]

Marx also reiterated the bureaucratic dimensions of vampirism in *The Civil War in France* (1871), in which 'the notary, advocate, executor, and other judicial vampires' of the French legislature are all described as 'bloodsuckers'.[45] In a bureaucracy, Marx wrote, 'real life appears dead'.[46] Citizenship is a post-mortem state.

Marx's most famous use of vampire imagery, however, lies in *Capital* (1867), in which he argues that 'capital is dead labour which, vampire-like, lives only by sucking living labour, and lives the more, the more labour it sucks'.[47] He claims that the extension of the working day into night time 'only slightly quenches the vampire thirst for the living blood of labour', and also quotes from Friedrich Engels' article 'The English Ten Hours' Bill' (1850), presenting capital as ruthlessly rapacious: 'the vampire will not let go "while there remains a single muscle, sinew or drop of blood to be exploited"'.[48] (Engels had in fact already used the image in his 1845 *Condition of the Working Class in England*, describing landlords as the 'vampire property-holding class'.)[49] In his 'Inaugural Address of the International Working Men's Association' (published in 1864), Marx proposes that 'British industry . . . vampire-like, could but live by sucking blood, and children's blood too.'[50]

These explicit uses of vampire imagery (as well as Marx's invocation of the werewolf, and arguably the figure of Vlad the Impaler, too) reveal that the vampire was a common touchstone in the culture and society of the time.[51] Moreover, his writing is strewn with vampire allusions more generally. As the critical and political theorist Mark Neocleous suggests,

> if one also explores [Marx's] text for comments that appear to *derive* from the vampire motif but fail to mention the vampire explicitly, one

finds a wealth of additional material. Capital 'sucks up the worker's value-creating power' and is dripping with blood. Lacemaking institutions exploiting children are described as 'blood-sucking', while US capital is said to be financed by the 'capitalized blood of children'. The appropriation of labour is described as the 'life-blood of capitalism', while the state is said to have here and there interposed itself 'as a barrier to the transformation of children's blood into capital'.[52]

Most striking, perhaps, is Marx's statement that, 'If money comes into the world with a congenital blood-stain on one cheek', then 'capital comes dripping from head to toe, from every pore, with blood and dirt'.[53] This directly evokes the past century and a half of vampirology, the vampire weltering in gore and mired in the mud of the graveyard – a corporeal horror, rather than a spectral menace. It is no surprise that Marx planned to write an essay on 'The Vampires of the Mosel Region'.[54]

Vampire metaphors were evidently key devices with which Marx could describe and diagnose capitalism. But as suggested by that last, unequivocal example, he actually shifts vampire language from the figurative back into the realm of the literal. As the legal theorist Terrell Carver has observed, Marx's attitude to the vampire was 'every bit as rationalist as one would expect, having its roots in the *philosophes* themselves'.[55] In other words, Marx's vampirology derives from Enlightenment philosophy rather than the escalating popular appetite for supernatural fiction. What is more, it was in the *philosophes*' distrust of testimony and personal verification, alongside the tendency of (as Rousseau suggested) institutions such as 'Notaries, Surgeons, Vicars, and Magistrates' to use vampires as a means of control, that Marx's theory of ideology and false consciousness took root.[56]

According to Marx, in capitalist economies 'the realization of labour appears as a *loss of reality* for the worker, objectification as *loss of and bondage to the object*, and appropriation as *estrangement*, as *alienation*'.[57] This '*loss of reality*' is key: Marx was not alone in describing consumer society as insubstantial, unreal, wraithlike: 'The world looks often quite spectral to me', wrote the polymath Thomas Carlyle in 1835.[58] But as radical philosopher Slavoj Žižek suggests, 'The paradox of the vampires is that, precisely as "living dead", they are *far more alive* than us.' The real 'living dead' are we 'common mortals': consumers 'mortified by the symbolic network'.[59] For Žižek, vampires are not part of our 'reality', because our reality is merely a fabrication constructed by psychological, socio-economic and political forces (the 'symbolic'); rather, vampires are 'returns of the Real' – in other words, things that have an existence that we know, but do not (or cannot) believe.[60] The Žižekian 'return of the Real' is then a traumatic episode that disrupts everyday life by exposing the short-comings of the ways in which we make sense of our experience.[61]

Vampires are horribly real because capital has more reality and substance than our own lives – in the words of the influential Marxist thinker Franco Moretti, the vampire is 'capital that is not ashamed of itself'.[62] This economic being again confirms the vampire as a characteristically modern phenomenon. Although it is often claimed that nineteenth-century vampires are ancient nobility, and that representing them as undead reveals the aristocracy to be antiquated and obsolete, such readings have deep-seated shortcomings. Vampires are, more usually, often oddly classless. Lord Ruthven, for instance, may be an aristocrat, but his lifestyle is not markedly lavish or luxurious, and he travels without servants. Vampires are presented as being more individual and entrepreneurial: on the dark side of contemporary finance – rogue traders.

In this way, vampires are in effect 'living' metaphors that expose the undead nature of consumerism. Capital itself is the monster consumer now, with a life of its own enabled by conspicuous expenditure. For Marx,

> Everything which the political economist takes from you in terms of life and humanity, he restores to you in the form of *money* and *wealth*, and everything which you are unable to do, your money can do for you: it can eat, drink, go dancing, go to the theatre, it can appropriate art, learning, historical curiosities, political power, it can travel, it is *capable* of doing all these things for you.[63]

This roaming independence of capital is, for Marx, intimately linked to aesthetics and connoisseurship, as signalled by his examples: eating, drinking, dancing, theatre-going, investing in art or historical curiosities, and travelling. In such contexts, the vampire is manifest capital, an insatiable arch-consumer who combines ultra-predatory instincts with the operation of 'monstrous capital'.[64] High culture is hyper-consumerist, and, as we shall see, the supposed benefits of the arts are themselves complicit in vampirism. Sex, too, is a metaphor for consumption, not *vice versa*. As early as in his notes towards *The German Ideology* (written 1845–46), Marx derided the Hegelian philosophers Bruno Bauer and Max Stirner, but does seem to have been struck by a comment of Bauer's that 'sensuousness, like a vampire, sucks all the marrow and blood from the life of man'.[65] It is all too easy to over-sexualize vampire tales; but in the light of Marx's thinking, it should be clear that sexual tensions are actually expressing anxieties about consumption redefining the human – and more directly, anxieties about being consumed. This runaway consumerism is also driven by technology, and nineteenth-century vampire tales are literally on the button here as well, replete with typewriters and railway timetables, newspapers and telegrams, phonographs and cameras.[66]

It is tempting, too, to see vampirism as coloured by attitudes towards drug abuse. Yet once more it should be clear that describing the vampire as a blood addict is overly simplistic.[67] Likewise, vampire tales are not straightforward allegories of orientalism that demonize the East (that is, Turkey and beyond) as, say, the source of opium. Certainly drugs, hypodermic injections and narcotics do permeate vampire literature; but again, this is because drugs are a commodity – and a particular sort of commodity: they are neither food nor medicine, and their consumption compels the consumer to consume more simply for the sake of the drug itself.[68] If vampires are fanatic consumers, and drugs are the ultimate commodity, then the two together are an unholy pairing, two sides of the same coin.[69] Both stalk their quarries, transforming and destroying their victims; both are simultaneously tangible (the vampire has a corporeal body; the drug a material state) and intangible (the vampire – if it indeed exists – can dematerialize; the effects of drugs are impalpable and indefinable); both are otherworldly, anti-Catholic forms of transubstantiation. And drugs also return us to medicine.

Sickening filth

In 1832, Sligo in the west of Ireland was hit by an outbreak of cholera. Some years later, Charlotte Stoker recalled the events in a letter to her son. There was a biblical intensity to the experience of those affected:

One action I vividly remember. A poor traveller was taken ill on the roadside some miles from the town, and how did those samaritans tend him? They dug a pit and with long poles pushed him living into it, and covered him up quick, alive. Severely, like Sodom, did our city pay for such crimes . . .

The plague was insatiable and unstoppable:

One evening we heard that a Mrs Feeny, a very fat woman who was a music teacher, had died suddenly and, by the doctor's orders, had been buried an hour after. With blanched faces men looked at each other and whispered 'Cholera!'; but the whispers next day deepened to a roar, and in many houses lay one, nay two or three dead. One house would be attacked and the next spared. There was no telling who would go next, and when one said goodbye to a friend he said it as if for ever.

In a very few days the town became a place of the dead. No vehicles moved except the cholera carts or doctors' carriages. Many people fled, and many of these were overtaken by the plague and died by the way . . .

The town became a hallucinatory place of premature live burial:

The habit was when a new batch arrived for whom there were no beds, to take those who were stupified [sic] from opium and nearest death and remove them to make room for the new arrivals. Many were said to be buried alive. One man brought his wife to the hospital on his back and, she being in great agony, he tied a red neck handkerchief tightly round her waist to try and relieve the pain. When he came again to the hospital in the evening he heard that she was dead, and lying in the dead house. He sought her body to give it more decent burial than could be given there (the custom was to dig a large trench, put in forty or fifty corpses without coffins, throw lime on them and cover the grave). He saw the corner of his red handkerchief under several bodies which he removed, found his wife and saw there was still life in her. He carried her home and she recovered and lived many years.

Other victims were rescued from the grave in more violent ways:

> There was a remarkable character in the town, a man of great stature,
> who had been a soldier and was usually known as 'long Sergeant Callen'.
> He took the cholera, was thought dead, and a coffin was brought. As the
> coffin maker had always a stack of coffins ready on hand, with the
> burials following immediately on the deaths, they were much of a
> uniform size and, of course, too short for long Sergeant Callen. The men
> who were putting him in, when they found he would not fit, took a big
> hammer to break his legs and *make* him fit. The first blow roused the
> sergeant from his stupor, and he started up and recovered. I often saw
> the man afterwards.

Despite the fact that 'Long' Sergeant Callen's legs were to be broken in
order to make him fit in the coffin, there is a sinister shadow of the deviant
burials of vampires here, who were hamstrung, staked or mutilated in
various ways to prevent them from leaving their graves. The letter continues,
still haunted by the undead:

> At night many tar barrels and other combustible matters used to be
> burned along the street to try to purify the air, and they had a weird,
> unearthly look, gleaming out in the darkness. The cholera carts and cots
> had bells, which added to the horror, and the coffin maker, a man named
> Young, used to knock on the doors to inquire if any coffins were wanted.

Eventually, the family decides to flee:

> All went well until we got within a mile of a village about four miles
> from Ballyshannon, when the coach was met and stopped by a mob of
> men armed with sticks, scythes and pitchforks. They were headed by a
> Dr John Shields, who was half-mad. He was the son of one of the first
> physicians and most respected men in the county, but he did not take
> after his father. The coach was stopped and we were ordered out, our
> luggage taken off, and no entreaties could prevail on those men to
> allow us to pass. Fear had maddened them.[70]

The remainder of Charlotte Stoker's account describes the starving family wandering through their native Ireland like exiles: feared and reviled – pariahs in their own land. Over 40 years after the event, her letter still conveys the terrors of the epidemic, and fears that the living were being buried alongside the dead.

Cholera was a terrible disease. In stark contrast to aesthetically attractive and languorous (if also admittedly mortal) illnesses such as tuberculosis, once the signs of cholera presented, the end was often stupefyingly swift. The disease could kill within 12 hours. And that was not all: within that short time, it turned its subjects into abject beings. It was a most humiliating condition, in which victims suffered from severe diarrhoea and dehydration, incessant vomiting, the possibility of seizures and delirium, coma and hypovolemic (haemorrhagic) shock. As the medical historian Ian Morley puts it,

> When coupled with its ability to defy conventional medicine, it engineered unparalleled fear. The disease, a frightening silent spectacle, was unlike anything known before it. It was a psychological sledgehammer to material progress and all the perceived benefits of modernity. With its air of mystery, defiance, and with such minimal explanation as to its cause, cholera recalled the memory of the Middle Ages' plagues. It shocked society like no other illness had done in recent times and generated everything from general unease to riots. In light of the rise of statistical analysis and contemporary ways of thinking about the social nature of disease, cholera became a compelling propagandist for urban betterment, and warranted both political stability and social justice.[71]

Cholera, a bacterial infection spread through infected water and infected persons (who could carry the disease for up to two weeks before they exhibited any symptoms), had originated in India, and had spread to Afghanistan and Russia along trade routes. It was a plague driven by capitalism. In the words of the historian Sir Richard Evans,

> Once in Europe, it moved rapidly along the waterways and, later, railways, which were the main arteries of the rapidly expanding commerce

of the nineteenth century. As it arrived in the mushrooming towns and cities of a society in the throes of rapid urbanisation, it took advantage of overcrowded housing conditions, poor hygiene and insanitary water supplies with a vigour that suggested that these conditions might almost have been designed for it.[72]

There were major cholera pandemics in more than half the years of the nineteenth century – 1826–37, 1841–59, 1863–75, 1881–96 – as it engulfed Europe and navigated the Atlantic to North America. Outbreaks also coincided with – and were hastened by – wars and the political turmoil of the early 1830s and 1848, such as the passage of the Great Reform Bill and the 'Year of Revolutions'. These were peculiarly modern contagions, then, associated not with meteors or divine visitations, but with barges and ships, railways, markets and fairs, and mass movements and assemblies of people – be they marching troops, escaping refugees or crowds gathered at political rallies and popular demonstrations.[73] In tune with the modernity of the disease, traditional scapegoats such as witches and Jews escaped blame; instead, it was the medical profession who were first held responsible.[74] Not only was fear of doctors and physicians endemic in Britain at the time, but there were cholera riots in 1832 in which medical practitioners were actually physically attacked.[75] Medicine was, in a sense, a monstrous occupation: the fears of cholera echoed earlier fears about body-snatching and the activities of Burke and Hare, who murdered the poor in order to procure cadavers for dissection.[76] The 'kiss' of cholera, as Charlotte Stoker hauntingly described it – a 'bitter strange kiss' – was quickly perceived to be vampiric, and indeed Julian Osgood Field's story 'A Kiss of Judas' (1893) explicitly compares the kiss of the vampire with rabies and cholera.

Evidently the association of vampires with virulent contagion continued from the eighteenth century throughout the nineteenth century, changed only by the more modern contexts of medical theory and practice, as well as diversifying into the genetic vampirism of the fictional tale 'Olalla' and its sister-texts. Epidemics were still understood to be spread by bad air, or 'miasma', which emanated from filth and decay. 'Miasma' was derived from the Greek word for contamination or stain, and in any case words such as 'infectious' and 'contagious' originally carried implications of 'pollution, taint, and defilement, moral as well as physical'.[77] These fears that the miasmatic ooze of the dead threatened health and wellbeing were highly pertinent in the urban projects necessitated by the industrial revolution, which had spawned the housing disaster of the city slums.[78] Many towns and cities were overpoweringly insanitary. In London, for instance, the social reformer Henry Mayhew described the Jacob's Island slum in south London as hellish:

> The water of the huge ditch in front of the houses is covered with a scum . . . and prismatic with grease . . . Along the banks are heaps of indescribable filth . . . the air has literally the smell of a graveyard.[79]

The voice of the slum-dwellers themselves was also occasionally heard. In 1849, *The Times* published a heart-breaking letter from St Giles, the worst 'rookery' or slum in London, just off Tottenham Court Road:

> Sur, – May we beg and beseach your proteckshion and power, We are Sur, as it may be, livin in a Willderniss, so far as the rest of London knows anything of us, or as the rich and great people care about. We live in muck and filthe. We aint got no priviz, no dust bins, no drains, no water-splies, and no drain or suer in the hole place. The Suer Company, in Greek St., Soho Square, all great, rich and powerfool men, take no notice watsomedever of our cumplaints. The Stenche of a Gully-hole is disgustin. We all of us suffur, and numbers are ill, and if the Colera comes Lord help us.[80]

In *Old and New London* (1878), Edward Walfourd noted that the rookery of St Giles had 'passed into a byword as the synonym of filth and squalor'.[81]

The vampire was already an emblematic vector of disease and so thrived in these atrociously congested conditions; in consequence, vampires haunted urban spaces, the underside of the industrial city, blighting the modern built environment. The ways of countering the vampire threat were equally modern and technological: cremation, for example – that mainstay of vampire slaying – was a public health issue and a solution to overflowing cemeteries; but it only became legal in 1885.[82] The Public

Health Act 1848 and successive legislation inspired by Edwin Chadwick's *Report from the Poor Law Commissioners on an Inquiry into the Sanitary Conditions of the Labouring Population of Great Britain* (1842) focused on the regulation of urban areas by introducing 'drains, cess pools, refuse, burial grounds and slaughter houses'.[83] These laws made medicine and health the responsibility of government, as well as establishing the legal right to sanitary living conditions and good health. But in fact these measures – admirably hygienic as they are – were really continuations of eighteenth-century theories of fever. Typhus epidemics of the late eighteenth century were, for example, considered a constitutional ailment caused by poor diet and anxiety, and exacerbated by bad air – notably, by confinement. The physician Southwood Smith argued that exhalations of those suffering from fever were analogous to marsh miasma – 'poison derived from the putrefaction of animal matter': 'The room of a fever-patient, in a small and heated apartment in London, with no perflation of fresh air, is perfectly analogous to a stagnant pool in Ethiopia, full of the bodies of dead locusts.'[84] So it was not only the rookeries that were toxic sites: heated city apartments were, too. Just as vampires were spawned by the conditions and attitudes of modernity, so the whole city was septic and a breeding ground for vampirism.

Thus fevers were treated by ventilation rather than by bloodletting, which was reserved for inflammations. But by the mid-nineteenth century opinion had shifted: fever was held to be an inflammatory condition, and that, too, required bleeding, often by leeches. Fever (it was now believed) was caused by 'gaseous products, decomposing matter which infected the patient', in which 'other fever patients could here count as a special case of decomposing matter'.[85] The popularity of vampire tales therefore parallels the prevalent medical thinking of the nineteenth century by embodying this fear of bloodsucking.

At the same time, there was a shift from 'bedside' medicine towards 'hospital' medicine, the latter concentrating on 'disease as localised, anatomical changes, detected by physical examinations, illuminated by post-mortem examination'.[86] Vampires were often depicted as hanging over their victims like bedside physicians – as well, of course, as making private house visits. But the threat of the vampire was not necessarily an expression of nostalgia for an earlier form of medical treatment, because private practice – favoured by the bourgeoisie and aristocracy – continued the tradition of personal bedside treatments (albeit informed by hospital practices). It was the poor or seriously ill who were objectified in hospitals as collections of signs and symptoms; for the affluent infirm, private medicine at home remained the norm. In other words, medical treatment, good health and indeed life were an index of class and wealth – a connection exposed by the vampire by turning private bedside medicine into a threat.

Germ theory replaced miasma theory in the second half of the nineteenth century in part, according to cultural historian Laura Otis, because 'cultural developments made the idea of infectious germs believable', and by the 1880s microbial theory was widely accepted.[87] She argues that while the notion that disease is caused by living parasites has classical origins, it was reworked in the context of imperial politics and international affairs from 1870 to 1914, so that by the 1880s, 'because of their minuscule size and deadly effects, bacteria became a metaphor through which one could articulate fears about all invisible enemies, military, political, or economic'.[88] This theory of microbial infection is already implicit in decades of vampire tales, earlier eighteenth-century attempts to make sense of vampire contagion, and even earlier theories of plague and contamination. The compelling figure of the vampire consequently added momentum to a reconsideration of infection. Reflecting this shift further, later Victorian vampire tales dwell on minute forensic traces (tiny lesions in the skin, dust) or invisible forces (mesmerism, psychic and psychological effects, and telepathy).[89] Contagion and the body, blood and the economy, political power, the invisible and vampirism thus co-existed in the Victorian imagination. Nowhere is this better demonstrated than in Bram Stoker's novel *Dracula*.

CHAPTER 8

THE COUNT, *DRACULA*
Smoke and Mirrors – Pen, Paint and Blood

. . . the very weirdest of weird tales . . .

Punch (1897)[1]

There is work to be done.

Bram Stoker (1897)[2]

For the blood is the life.
Marketing slogan for 'Clarke's World-Famed Blood Mixture' (*c.* 1860s)[3]

B ram Stoker's *Dracula* is like a black hole that irresistibly attracts other texts – indeed whole fields of literature – and engulfs them. It exercises a vampiric genealogy, casting earlier writings as a mere foretelling of its later, iconic status, while infecting its successors with its own blood, part of its own brood. It also is peculiarly receptive to diverse readings and interpretations, and is persistently being reinvented through the prism of criticism. *Dracula*, first published in 1897, has had a seismic influence. Indeed, it is no exaggeration to suggest that vampirology 'After *Dracula*' ('AD') will never fully escape the clutches of Stoker's iconic text.[4] Cultural history and literary criticism also find themselves in the same predicament. But the vampire clearly existed before *Dracula* as a species of Enlightenment thinking in the contexts of medical science, theology, empiricism and politics, and it was this figure that both thrived in the nineteenth century and was adapted by Stoker.

Dracula is the climax to over 70 years of vampire tales, themselves pre-dated by (and predating upon) a further century of attested reports, reasoned theories and systematic debate. And although in its wake *Dracula* would be restlessly reworked in thousands of ways – not only in literature, but also on the big screen and the small screen, on stage and on the catwalk, as well as by late-twentieth-century Goths and early-twenty-first-century Emos – the novel remains a remarkable document of state-of-the-art 1890s vampirology. Indeed, the *Dracula* that was published in 1897 is an uncanny novel: familiar today through its multiform variations and deviations, but also unexpectedly strange and curious – grounded in the rich blood and deep soil of darker understandings of corporeal matter, spiritual mystery and social havoc. This *Dracula* is a perturbing entity that brings us face to face with an inevitable horror from which we cannot escape: the horror of being here now.

Black books

Stoker researched his book carefully, and spent several years drafting and redrafting the narrative. As earlier chapters have shown, the eighteenth-century context of Calmetian vampirology was in the nineteenth century disseminated through the supplementary material to poems such as Southey's *Thalaba the Destroyer* and Polidori's 'The Vampyre', and the proliferation of vampire tales. Literary intensity was mixed with empirical reasoning – and vice versa. In his study of *Popular Superstitions*, the physiologist Herbert Mayo, for instance, dramatizes the perilous threat to believers and cynics alike in his sensationalist, second-person, present-tense narration:

> Your scepticism will abate pretty considerably when you see him stealthily entering your room, yet are powerless under the fascination of his fixed and leaden eye – when you are conscious, as you lie motion-less with terror, of his nearer and nearer approach – when you feel his face, fresh with the smell of the grave, bent over your throat, while his

keen teeth make a fine incision in your jugular, preparatorily to his commencing his plain but nutritive repast.[5]

He notes preventive measures, such as smearing oneself with vampire blood and eating earth from the grave; slaying vampires by staking or beheading, and cremation; and summarizes the virulence of eighteenth-century outbreaks: 'The facts are matters of history: the people died like rotten sheep.'[6] Drawing on Flückinger's report, he describes the 'perfectly authenticated' Paole case in considerable detail, dramatizing the relationship between Paole and his fiancée Nina in direct speech, before recounting the death, burial and disinterment of Paole in a grave overshadowed by a stone 'ornamented with grotesque Gothic carvings'.[7]

For Mayo, this is evidence of live burial through the condition of '*apparent death*' or 'suspended animation', or what Mayo terms 'death-trance' – a physiological condition of which he provides further attested examples, including passing evidence of unfortunates awaking in the tomb and gnawing their own arms for sustenance: manducation.[8] Mayo is also at pains to demonstrate that this is a contemporary phenomenon, noting that under an ordinance of 1829 to deter premature burial, the New York dead were stored in their coffins for eight days above ground, their heads exposed and with little alarm bells attached to their hands and feet. Out of 1,200 corpses retained in this way, apparently six of the dead returned to life, suggesting that the premature burial rate was as high as 1 in 200. Mayo then goes on to give examples of autopsies inadvertently performed on living subjects, their still-beating hearts being removed, the desperate victims reviving and vainly attempting to fend off the knives of the surgeons. Mayo's solution – consistent with contemporary opinion – is that putrefaction is the only sure sign that a body is lifeless. In fact, when, after the publication of *Dracula*, Stoker was interviewed about vampires for the *British Weekly*, Jane Stoddard (writing under the name of 'Lorna'), asked: 'Is there any historical basis for the [vampire] legend?'

Stoker's reply was unequivocally Mayonian:

'It rested, I imagine, on some case such as this. A person may have fallen into a death-like trance and been buried before the time.

Afterwards the body may have been dug up and found alive, and from this a horror seized upon the people, and in their ignorance they imagined that a vampire was about.'[9]

Such questions were very much international news. The year before *Dracula* was published, an article on 'Vampires in New England' had appeared in the *New York World* reporting that 'Dead bodies are dug up and their hearts burned to prevent disease.'[10] The article focused on the survival of rural vampire superstitions in Rhode Island, combining the natural history of bloodsucking bats with East European settlers' memories of the vampiromania of the eighteenth century. Stoker kept a cutting of the piece among his notes for *Dracula*, rooting his knowledge of vampires in rational explanation and the scientific encounter with folklore.[11]

Stoker's research thus led him along similar intellectual paths travelled by earlier vampirologists, most notably in regional identity, political history, medicine and psychology, and natural history.[12] He made notes on the Magyar language of Hungary, its racial history and geography from the travel writings of Nina Elizabeth Mazuchelli; folk beliefs and demonology from Isabella Bird; landscape, observations on local dress, folklore and habitual customs from Andrew Crosse; racial history – in particular how the Goths were driven out of Eastern Europe by the Huns – as well as the political history of annexation, and local details of food and clothes from Major E.C. Johnson; Transylvanian politics from Charles Boner; and practical advice from Baedeker's, the universal travel guide (of which, as manager of the actor Henry Irving, Stoker had a thorough working knowledge).[13] Consequently, within the first two pages of the novel, Jonathan Harker is pondering subjects from train timetables to East European racial migration.

Stoker consulted the Hungarian consul William Wilkinson's *Account of the Principalities of Wallachia and Moldavia* (1820), in which he found the name 'Dracula' and from which he took the racial and political history of the region – some parts of Voivode history being copied almost verbatim.[14] He discovered the word 'nosferatu' in Emily de Laszowska Gerard's article on 'Transylvanian Superstitions' (1885), where he also encountered information on the ability of vampires to cause drought.[15] He would have been reminded of the word '*vrykolakas*' in Rennell Rodd's *Customs and Lore of*

Modern Greece (1892). Though it is, of course, mentioned elsewhere, Rodd states that the 'genuine vampire is the Vourkólakas', though 'the word itself is undoubtedly of Sclavonic origin.'[16] Stoker encountered the legend of Elizabeth Báthory and other grisly material in Baring-Gould's *Book of Werewolves*, and there are several sources where he may have come across Vlad Țepeș in German, Russian and Romanian legends.[17]

The entry on vampires in the 1888 *Encyclopædia Britannica* includes much Eastern European folklore, as well as references to Calmet's researches, Ranft on manducation, and Waterton and Darwin on blood-sucking bats; and Stoker may also have received additional information from Ármin (Arminius) Vámbéry, who had written the entry. Vámbéry was a professor of oriental languages, a traveller and translator, and a spy working for the British government by informing on the machinations of the Ottoman emperor (and possibly a double-agent for the sultan of Turkey as well); he was also a friend of Stoker's.[18] If nothing else, Vámbéry was an insistent reminder that vampire lore was bound up with the polit-ical intricacies of Eastern Europe.

In contrast to the influence of high political intrigue, Stoker also took copious notes from Robert H. Scott's *Fishery Barometer Manual*, as well as on windspeed and sailing, Whitby maritime lore and legends, wrecks off Whitby, Whitby dialect and Whitby gravestones and memorials.[19] These notes on Whitby were made when Stoker visited the former whaling town and trading port in the summer of 1890 – indeed, it was in Whitby Library that he read Wilkinson's *Account of the Principalities of Wallachia and Moldavia*. But Stoker had never travelled to Eastern Europe, Greece or Turkey himself, and so much of his reading was focused on these territories – territories that loomed large in the nineteenth-century imagination. Turkey, for instance, was particularly demonized at the time – as it is in *The Giaour* and 'The Vampyre' – and Stoker's decision to have Dracula emerge from these remote regions has been interpreted as embodying national disquiet over international trade and Near Eastern politics. Certainly, in Thomas De Quincey's *Confessions of an English Opium Eater* (first published in 1822) the importation of opium into the British Empire is both person-ified and 'orientalized' as the infiltration of a single, fateful Malay who terrorizes the author. But *Dracula* is not a fable of the trade in drugs or fear and guilt over the Far East, or of migration – and still less of Anglo-Irish colonialism. Eastern Europe was already established as the habitation of vampires, and Stoker's research accordingly delved into the history of international power politics in the area.

Stoker thought of setting the novel in Germany; but, just as the first vampires were brought into the contemporary world from the turbulent borders of the Habsburg Empire, he revised the setting to Styria (after 'Carmilla'), before establishing Dracula's residence in Transylvania.[20] His bloodline and genealogy place him among the Wallachian resistance to both the Ottoman and the Habsburg empires, while also situating him within the Gothic 'hive of nations' that peopled Eastern Europe, Germany and (according to some) England. Dracula expressly arises from 'the whirlpool of European Races', seething with independence and rebellion, leading Van Helsing to declare that he rides on the wings of violent conquest – 'He have follow the wake of the berserker Icelander, the devil-begotten Hun, the Slav, the Saxon, the Magyar.'[21] He exhibits then a malign Gothic hybridity, reflected in the different words for 'vampire' that Stoker gives in the novel: 'Ordog' (*Ördög*: Hungarian for 'Satan'), 'pokol' (Hungarian for 'hell'), 'stregoica' (according to Stoker, this is Romanian for 'witch', but is in fact a likely error for *strigoi*, meaning 'ghost'), 'vrolok' (a cognate of the Serb *vukodlak*) and 'nosferatu' (an older Romanian term for the Devil).[22] Dracula is not simply defined as 'vampire' – Van Helsing at one point calls him 'very polyglot': he can pass unnoticed and is shrouded under a swarm of strange and baffling names.[23]

This linguistic confusion reflects a deeper chaos. Transylvania was at the centre of the 'Eastern Question', the byzantine complex of Balkan affairs that became the stage on which the major European states played out their games of diplomacy; a sideshow that eventually led to the Great War in 1914.[24] It was a turbulent theatre, in which international politicking merged with the region's recent vampire phenomenon. In the Crimean War sonnet 'Austrian Alliance' (1855), the 'spasmodic' poet Sydney Dobell, for example, wrote of the Habsburg 'Vampyre', torn

> from the breathing throat
> Of living Man, and he leaps up and flings
> Thy rotten carcase at the heads of Kings.[25]

Dracula is, in other words, less a representative of a decayed and decadent aristocracy than a symbol of strategic power-brokering. That is why he goes to London, to Piccadilly, to be within yards of Whitehall and Buckingham Palace: he is a reminder that Britain is not just an island and that European affairs are at the very heart of government. The might of the Empire will be rallied in defence against the vampire threat: most of the band pitted against Dracula – the 'Defenders of the Light' – have colonial experience (Harker even carries a Gurkha kukri knife) and all are in some sense English.[26] It is the blood of Europe that seeps through politics, in both the bloodshed of war and the bloodlines of race. And the very ground of the novel is manured with blood – 'there is hardly a foot of soil in all this region that has not been enriched by the blood of men, patriots or invaders'.[27] Such enriched – or contaminated – earth is moved around, and bloody soil circulates like corrupted blood. There's an intense materiality to this blood: it is not enigmatically animated by vitalism or galvanic theory – it is a physical reality.

This tangibility extends to the form of the novel. *Dracula* is a mass of papers – a scrapbook of textual proofs that reflect the earlier emphasis on evidence and authenticity. It is made up of diaries, letters, logbooks, legal receipts, accounts, way-bills, title deeds, memoranda, notes, newspaper cuttings and miscellaneous other writings 'knitted' together. It is also a patchwork of printed texts – from Shakespeare's *Hamlet* to Baedeker's to the Bible. And it draws on heterogeneous languages and alphabets – from dialect and slang to shorthand and Latin.[28] There is much reading and writing and signing in the book – even Dracula writes by hand – and this emphasis on verifying, witnessing and testifying is a constant reminder of the criminal aspects of the novel. Indeed, in 1888, the Lyceum Theatre in London had cut short the run of its adaptation of Robert Louis Stevenson's *Dr Jekyll and Mr Hyde* following rumours that it was inspiring the Jack the Ripper killings in Whitechapel; Stoker was manager of the Lyceum at the time. As a contemporary report in the *East London Advertiser* put it:

> it is so impossible to account . . . for these revolting acts of blood, that the mind turns as it were instinctively to some theory of occult force, and the myths of the Dark Ages rise before the imagination. Ghouls, vampires, bloodsuckers, and all the ghastly array of fables which have

been accumulated throughout the course of centuries take form, and seize hold of the excited fancy.[29]

Stoker later stated that Jack the Ripper was a source for *Dracula*, and the Count is ultimately classified as a 'Lombrosian' criminal type who can be intellectually outwitted through deductive reasoning.[30]

There was also less-tangible evidence that coloured the phantasmic atmosphere of much of the novel – a novel in which characters spend much of their time sleeping, dreaming, hypnotized or comatose.[31] Stoker had encountered reports of cataleptic states and the 'nephritic complaint' of a man who 'had power of dying and coming to life at pleasure' in Robert Gray's *Theory of Dreams* (1808).[32] Gray surveyed ancient philosophers such as Macrobius, Simonides, Pliny and Aristotle; but it was the much more recent thinking of the seventeenth-century English physician and antiquarian Sir Thomas Browne that particularly captivated Stoker and inspired him to transcribe a passage on sleep quoted by Gray from Browne's *Religio Medici* (first published in 1642):

> It (sleep) is a death whereby we live. A middle moderating point between life and death, and so like death <and as like death> I dare not trust it without my prayers, and an half adieu to the world, and take my farewell in a colloquy with God. After which, I close my eyes in security, content to take my leave of him, and sleep unto the resurrection.[33]

Browne's troubling compound of sleep and death is less a Shakespearean conceit or early Romantic impulse than it is a philosophical reckoning with identity.[34] It transpires that more recent thinkers have also had sleepless nights considering this problem. According to the French philosopher Emmanuel Levinas,

> In insomnia one can and one cannot say that there is an 'I' which cannot manage to fall asleep. The impossibility of escaping wakefulness is something 'objective,' independent of my initiative. This impersonality absorbs my consciousness; consciousness is depersonalized. *I do not stay awake: 'it' stays awake.*[35]

Dylan Trigg accordingly argues that Levinas's emphasis that '*I do not stay awake: "it" stays awake*' captures the 'double bind between identity and non-identity converging in the same body'.[36] And this is perhaps what attracted Stoker – and why vampire tales are so drowsy with sleep and stirred by somnambulism: the vampire is, again, the thing that inhabits one's body but is not oneself ('the foul Thing', as Stoker describes it).[37] The haziness of sleep merging in and out of death states is reflected in the inseparability of conjoined blood types – the human and the vampiric.

In Dracula's castle, then, Harker is roused from sleep (or rather is in an uncertain state between dreaming and waking) when the three she-vampires glide into his room. This malevolent trinity are a corruption of the threefold femininity that the pioneering French social scientist Auguste Comte had argued was essential to the wellbeing of the male soul: mother, wife and daughter; they are also a perverted trinity; and they are the Weird Sisters.[38] They come not to succour, but to devour him:

> The fair girl went on her knees and bent over me, fairly gloating. There was a deliberate voluptuousness which was both thrilling and repulsive, and as she arched her neck she actually licked her lips like an animal, till I could see in the moonlight the moisture shining on the scarlet lips and on the red tongue as it lapped the white sharp teeth. Lower and lower went her head . . . I closed my eyes in a languorous ecstasy and waited – waited with beating heart.[39]

This is not the thrill of illicit sexual gratification, but the dynamics of the market expressed through bodily desire and physical need. The transaction can work both ways: in a comparable act of enforced consumption, the Count compels Mina to drink blood –

> he . . . seized my neck and pressed my mouth to the wound, so that I must either suffocate or swallow some of the – Oh, my God, my God! What have I done?[40]

Being sucked and sucking blood are both part of the same haemodynamic economy that threatens to merge donor and recipient into a single cardiovascular system of shared blood, analogous to the compromising exchange of dirty money. Moreover, when the golden-haired she-vampire licks her teeth and lips, Harker hears the 'churning sound of her tongue': repellently voluptuous, menacingly carnivorous – an echo of diabolical manducation and the entire rational discourse of vampirology.[41]

Bram Stoker's Count Dracula is a player in international finance and real-estate investment, both the 'arch-consumer' and at the same time the CEO of an international corporate occultism – and his financial reserves are literally unclean.[42] Ever since the early eighteenth century, accounts of vampires had endowed them with legal and commercial interests and property portfolios; they are adroit with inheritance laws, with the written word and with deeds – indeed, the solicitor Jonathan Harker comments that Count Dracula 'would have made a wonderful solicitor' himself; and to counter the Count, Abraham Van Helsing is 'a lawyer as well as a doctor'.[43] Dracula's very title is a reminder of the frequency of the 'counting' in the novel: accounting, recounting, countering, comparing accounts.[44] Counting is potentially endless, and Dracula can be understood as the embodiment of an unregulated capitalism: according to the critic Franco Moretti, he is 'impelled towards a continuous growth, an unlimited expansion of his domain: accumulation is inherent in his nature'.[45] In *Dracula*, then, profiteering appears to be as natural as blood and biology, as elemental as primordial folklore.

Through this shared conceptual language, blood and money are twinned circulatory systems, and capital flows in Dracula's blood: when Harker slices through Dracula's coat, a stream of gold coins pours out. Is this moment a covert racial slur, implying that Dracula has stereotypical Jewish traits of avarice? Does it slyly recast Shylock's line in Shakespeare's *Merchant of Venice*, 'If you prick us, do we not bleed?'[46] Although Dracula may have a 'beaky' nose (conforming to other nineteenth-century racial characterizations of Jewishness), his other features do not chime with the stereotype: once rejuvenated, he sports a luxuriant black moustache; and in any case, he describes to Harker in detail his impeccable Wallachian ancestry, which implies an Orthodox faith.[47]

Moreover, Dracula's spending is not aimed at establishing himself in high society, and he cuts an anomalous figure in London, wearing a curiously unfashionable hat. Stoker's attention to Dracula's clothing is in fact another allusion to Calmet and earlier accounts. Calmet notes that spectres have sometimes been resuscitated after months or years to torment the living by sucking their blood and causing death, often 'appearing in their former clothes to their own families'.[48] Dracula, however, takes some of Harker's clothes, and so his unfashionable hat may in fact be Harker's unfashionable hat: an artfully sly Stoker joke and, like much of the humour in the novel, in preposterously bad taste.[49]

A lust for life

Circulation – in many forms – is the key theme of *Dracula*: 'movements of blood, money, and energy, all of which are related to each other and the flow of data'.[50] These currents flow to and from characters: Dracula, for example, sails on tides, drains blood, injects money into the property market; Lucy meanwhile has thoughts and emotions flowing through her, to say nothing of the blood of four different men, as well as Dracula's own tainted blood. The novel includes several human blood transfusions and haematological analysis, as well as drugs such as laudanum and morphine, both ingested and introduced into the blood hypodermically. And so, if – like many nineteenth-century vampire tales – the novel gives voice to folk memories regarding the dread of plague and the standard operation of bloodletting, it is also a reflection of contemporary medical practice concerning patients, diagnosis, treatment and invasive surgery. *Dracula* is a medical drama, an organic endgame and a perpetual deathbed scene. If vampirism was first treated as a genuine disease in the eighteenth century, and then as a mass delusion of peripheral and backward communities, *Dracula* reverses this flow. Harker is initially wary of East European superstitions, but the characters gradually recognize that vampirism is indeed a genuine – and worse than fatal – condition. Hence there is a clinical attention to such physical characteristics as the colour of eyes, the touch of teeth, the caress of breath, the beating of the heart. All are tiny indicators of health or sickness, but they also serve as unbearably sinister clues to illness (or crime). There are tiny puncture wounds on Lucy's throat that do not heal; her gums shrink back and her teeth appear to lengthen, and so it appears that she will echo the earlier encounter with the she-vampires.[51]

Hermann von Helmholtz had proposed the principle of the conservation of energy in 1847; consequently, Dracula's activities can be understood as 'a thermodynamic as well as a biological threat'.[52] In other words, he incorporates or absorbs what flows to him, stockpiling his power – the earth of his homeland, the blood of his victims and the masonry of his properties – in an attempt to defy entropy. Information flows, too, and Stoker shows how communications networks can be exploited: in the words of the historian of science and culture Laura Otis, 'Future battles between good and evil, Stoker suggests, will be struggles to control information.'[53] Textual exchanges, too, are circulations of information that parallel the transference of blood.[54] The latest up-to-the-minute communications media are central to the plot of *Dracula*, and the book is suffused by occult new technologies. Mina is a medium, a receiver tracking Dracula's movements – as is Renfield the fly-eater, in a more garbled or riddling fashion (Renfield is actually described as 'a sort of index to the coming and going of the Count').[55] Radio communication is the same bandwidth as telepathy, as inexplicable as Mina's transmissions under hypnosis (another weird science) or Lucy's somnambulism and dreamlife: as Van Helsing declares, 'Let me tell you my friend that there are things done today in electrical science which would have been deemed unholy by the very men who discovered electricity – who would themselves not so long before have been burned as wizards.'[56]

Wilhelm Röntgen discovered X-rays in late 1895, photographing his wife's hand on 22 December of that year. X-rays rapidly became worldwide news – as did the fashion of replaying Röntgen and having X-ray photographs taken of one's own hand.[57] Ultraviolet light rays were first used in treatment in 1896, and radiation was discovered by Henri Becquerel in the same year.[58] Psychology is another science of the invisible – of thoughts and impulses and emotions, and the lunatic asylum is a key site in the novel and a focus for paranormal activity; it is run by Dr John Seward, who as a medical researcher is an advocate of vivisection.[59] The world is inundated by invisible powers, presided over by vampires.

At the same time, Van Helsing also, of course, relies on the efficacy of consecrated communion wafers and wild garlic. Dracula, meanwhile, has extrasensory powers of telepathy; moreover, he can control the dead and creatures such as rats, owls, bats, moths, foxes and wolves, and he can influence the weather. The Count has more decidedly supernatural powers, too: he has superhuman strength and can climb sheer surfaces; he has the ability to shape-shift into a wolf or a bat, as well as to make himself larger or smaller – or to disappear altogether; he can dematerialize into stardust and be carried by moonrays.[60] However, he requires to be invited across a threshold; is only able to use his powers between dusk and dawn (though he can shape-shift at noon); can only cross running water at high or low tide; and can be checked by crucifixes and garlic. He can also be slain simply with two daggers. Stoker thus sets modern science against folklore, and occult arts against technological science: the novel is conspicuously packed with the latest hardware – portable typewriters, phonographs, Kodak cameras and Winchester rifles. It is an uneasy juxtaposition, prompting Otis to suggest that 'While Stoker relies on contemporary comparisons of technological and organic thought transmission, his novel raises serious doubts about whether artificial information systems will ever surpass living ones.'[61] The upshot of a telegram arriving late, for example, is that Lucy Westenra is vampirized and her mother killed.[62]

One of the core tenets of the British Society for Psychical Research (founded 1882) was that thoughts could be communicated in the same way that telegraph signals travelled.[63] The invisible forces of electromagnetism, telegraphy, telepathy and clairvoyance consequently pervaded both science and parapsychology at the time, and psychic theorists wrote at length on vampires, since they appeared to connect the observable world of flesh and bone to the inscrutable domain of the paranormal, while also serving as reminders that meddling in the occult carried great risks.[64] In *The Key of the Mysteries* (1861), for example, Eliphas Lévi claims that when 'one creates phantoms, one is putting vampires into the world, and one will have to feed these children of a voluntary nightmare with one's blood, with one's life, with one's intelligence and one's reason, without ever satisfying them'.[65] This idea of psychic blood sacrifice was developed by the theosophical magus Madame Helena Petrovna Blavatsky in her lengthy discussion of vampires in *Isis Unveiled* (1877), and in 1891 her associate Colonel Henry Steel Olcott penned an essay on 'The Vampire' for the journal *The Theosophist*.[66]

Blavatsky argues that vampires are 'depraved and wicked' souls that are only annihilated over centuries – in the meantime they subsist as ghouls and vampires and possess a certain grisly charisma as 'the leading "stars" on the great spiritual stage of "materialization"'.[67] Blavatsky quotes Lévi on blood – 'the first incarnation of the universal fluid . . . the materialized *vital light* . . . the great arcanum of being' – and reiterates its magical properties of being able to beget phantoms and to animate life. She also cites Indian mystics, Old Testament prophets, neo-Platonists and Siberian shamans to demonstrate the universal potency of blood in generating and sustaining life, the strict taboos against ingesting it, and the eldritch powers it can command:

> It is during the sacrifices of blood, which take place at night, that the Yakuts call forth the wicked or *dark* shadows, to inquire of them what they can do to arrest their mischief; hence, *blood is necessary*, for without its fumes the ghosts could not make themselves clearly visible, and would become, according to their ideas, but the more dangerous, for they would suck it from living persons by their perspiration.[68]

In the case of vampires, Blavatsky agrees that there are sufficiently reliable witnesses testifying to their existence, and she deals with Calmet's quandary over how they are able to quit and resume their graves with theosophical reasoning, explaining that their bodies are in 'a state of *half-death*' that allows their astral soul to roam abroad. Their life is 'bicorporeal': while the body is buried and cataleptic, the astral spirit or æthereal form, attached to the body by a cord, is free to 'rob the life-blood from living persons'.[69]

So not only was the esoteric theory of the time steeped in the language of blood, but it was also gripped by the figure of the vampire. Again, vampires galvanized thinking, demonstrating the continuity between the physical and biological sciences and occult science.[70] Hence it was hypothesized that vampires could be explained by invisible physical forces, such as magnetism, preying upon the '*magnetic emanations*' of the young 'in the shape of *volatilized* blood'.[71] Or did they feed on more elusive emotional energies? In 1904, A. Osborne Eaves warned of the dangers of tiresome acquaintances in *Modern Vampirism* (helpfully subtitled *Its Dangers, and*

How to Avoid Them): 'many persons are so constituted that they have, unconsciously to themselves, an extraordinary faculty for sucking the life-principle from others'.[72] Vampires had fast become everyday hazards. Althea Gyles, the Irish poet and artist, once obtained a hair from the head of the occultist Aleister Crowley. The poet William Butler Yeats employed the strand in his spells, which resulted in Crowley being harassed by a 'vampire for ten nights'.[73]

Psychic vampirism does, however, retain the vampiric principle of mixing the mutually incompatible – the organic demon with the spiritual human – which is the driving force of Dracula's power of metamorphosis and a reminder of the incongruous shape-shifting of earlier spectres. Metamorphosis is another blood science: it is lubricated by blood. Dracula can either become animal (a moth, bat, dog, wolf or a horde of rats) or inorganic haze, smoke and particles. Mist and fog are endemic in *Dracula*, and while meteorological obscurity sets the scene in many Gothic novels and supernatural tales, here it is elemental to the vampire. Not only were vampires believed to be able to control weather – 'milking the clouds' – but vapour, like blood, seeps into places that should be secure – out of coffins and into Lucy's bedroom.[74]

The movement of vampires across land and sea, through streets and into houses, is akin to a creeping epidemic, an oozing disease. Indeed, there is something alarmingly distasteful about the spread of ooze through the novel.[75] Ooze is both a fundamental constituent state and a way in which humans can be alienated from the world. In such a world, vampires represent a viable alternative to the human: they possess a 'dark vitalism'.[76] So it is that in *Dracula* they cannot be allowed even a bestial status. When Mina muses on the nature of Dracula, she supposes 'one ought to pity anything so hunted as is the Count. That is just it: this Thing is not human – not even beast.'[77]

XXX vampires

Dracula is played out in a world dominated by women. It subsequently inspired a mania for sexualizing the vampire, already foreshadowed in Romantic vampire works and later tales such as 'Carmilla'.[78] But the whole nature of the vampire has been rewritten as a protracted sado-masochistic sexual fantasy, appealing to every kink and sex-crime, from voyeurism to seduction, from paedophilia to gang rape. There are only hints of this in the history of the vampire; but just as the vampire was supernaturalized in the early nineteenth century, so in the late nineteenth and early twentieth century it was forcefully sexualized – by the psychoanalyst Sigmund Freud, the pioneering sexologist Richard von Krafft-Ebing and in the profound prurience and objectification encouraged by the mesmerizing glamour of the moving image in early cinema.[79] Vampires on the screen were agents of forbidden desire, and as such were eagerly embraced in the next century. Hammer Film Productions, in particular, identified a demand for shlock-horror movies, which became a marketable aspect of the 1960s sexual revolution. Since then, vampires have tended to be lustful, depraved and super-sexy: models of transgression, avatars of forbidden fantasies and fallen angels of the death drive. But this is a recent reworking, and there is little of it in *Dracula*. As I have suggested, when it comes to desire, *Dracula* is much more focused on the fetishization of commodities.

Three of Stoker's brothers were doctors. One of them, Sir William Thornley Stoker, was an early brain surgeon, and he provided the writer with notes on head trauma, recording 'I have seen a patient in profound coma, begin to move his limbs and curse and swear during the operation', and Stoker's novel does actually include invasive brain surgery.[80] None of his siblings, however, was a sexologist, and there is nothing in Stoker's notes to indicate that he researched sexual and psychosexual conditions (though, as a married man and father, it would probably be more surprising if he *had* kept any notes on female sexuality). Yet the apparent need to sexualize Dracula is almost overpowering.

Even from a medical-historical perspective, there is a wealth of material. An inflammation of the ovaries or the uterus, defined in 1708 as '*Furor Uterinus*', was believed to cause hypersexuality, later known as nymphomania.[81] Nymphomania was also linked to hysteria, or the migrations of the womb around the female body – a condition that could (like the incubus) cause suffocation, and which was also believed to deplete the blood.[82] Hence the physician and moralist William Acton wrote of female desire in *The Functions and Disorders of the Reproductive Organs* (1857):

I should say that the majority of women (happily for society) are not very much troubled with sexual feeling of any kind. What men are habitually, women are only exceptionally. It is too true, I admit, as the Divorce Court shows, that there are some few women who have sexual desires so strong that they surpass those of men . . . I admit, of course, the existence of sexual excitement terminating even in nymphomania, a form of insanity that those accustomed to visit lunatic asylums must be fully conversant with.[83]

Intense sexual desire in women was, for Acton, evidence that they were clinically insane. The diagnosis was confirmed by Henry Maudsley's definition of nymphomania in *Body and Mind*: 'the irritation of ovaries or uterus . . . is sometimes the direct occasion of *nymphomania* – a disease by which the most chaste and modest woman is transformed into a raging fury of lust'.[84] Gustave Bouchereau likewise defined 'Nymphomania' in *A Dictionary of Psychological Medicine* (1892) as 'a morbid condition peculiar to the female sex' ('erotic insanity'), adding that it could be exacerbated by using drugs such as 'opium, morphia, and haschish', causing 'a condition in which their imagination dwells in consequence, upon erotic ideas and images'.[85] Nymphomania exercised an irresistible fascination for male psychoanalysts.

Such women (or rather, such heterosexual male fantasies) were wildly promiscuous with 'polyandrous instincts', making them 'more insatiable than men'.[86] They were monsters, vampires in all but name: according to Nicholas Francis Cooke in *Satan in Society* (1871), these women are 'more merciless, more bloodthirsty than men'.[87] In addition to vampire tales, there was a fashion for often perverse depictions of powerful, violent women, from the imperious flagellatrix Wanda in Leopold von Sacher-Masoch's *Venus in Furs* (*Venus im Pelz*, 1870) to paintings of Delilah shearing Samson's locks, Circe dominating Odysseus's crew, fabulous creatures such as the inscrutable Sphinx and Medusa and the Gorgons, Keats's Isabella mourning the severed head of her lover Lorenzo, the Maenads tearing apart Orpheus, and the decapitations ordered by Salome and performed by Judith.[88] And if all this was not warning enough of the latent condition of women, simply having long hair was considered symptomatic of mental incapacity, dissipated immorality and bloodlust – the she-vampire

Carmilla had 'wonderful' hair: 'I never saw hair so magnificently thick and long.'[89] That was sufficient proof of licentiousness.

This is the stuff of temptation. Lucy Westenra's behaviour is arguably consistent with nymphomania. She entertains fantasies of polyandry – 'Why can't they let a girl marry three men, or as many as want her?' – and she is symbolically infused with the blood of Arthur Godalming, John Seward, Quincey Morris and Abraham Van Helsing (not to mention having her blood infected by the Count).[90] This prompts Van Helsing to remark upon this artificial insemination with prurient humour – and after her death: 'Ho, ho! Then this so sweet maid is a polyandrist, and me . . . am bigamist.'[91] But then Lucy is in any case one of the reviled 'New Women' – already degenerate.[92] Moreover, the pallor and listlessness that follow Dracula's assaults on her also suggest other vices:

> The symptoms which enable us to recognize or suspect this crime are the following: A general condition of languor, weakness, and loss of flesh; the absence of freshness and beauty, of color from the complexion, of the vermilion from the lips, and whiteness from the teeth, which are replaced by a pale, lean, puffy, flabby, livid physiognomy; a bluish circle around the eyes, which are sunken, dull, and spiritless; a sad expression, dry cough, oppression and panting on the least exertion, the appearance of incipient consumption.[93]

This is how Cooke exposed the female masturbator in *Satan in Society*. Later accounts compounded all of these symptoms into a physical condition of aberrant femininity and sexual incontinence:

> the frequent exercise of the act of copulation leads directly to anaemia, malnutrition, asthenia of the muscles and nerves, and mental exhaustion. Immoderate persons are pale and have long, flabby or sometimes tense features. They are melancholic and not fit for any difficult and continued corporeal or mental work.[94]

Pallor, sleep and psychic decay inevitably aroused suspicion. In such circumstances, extreme violence against women was condoned. To ease the male conscience in handling women thus, Cesare Lombroso and Guglielmo Ferrero claimed that 'normal woman is naturally less sensitive to pain than a man', while Krafft-Ebing went so far as to suggest that really women just want to be beaten. Simply put, sadism was normalized and rape was justifiable by such pseudo-scientific discourses.[95] Lucy, who is 'pale', with a 'drawn, haggard look under her eyes' and 'languid and tired', returns to normality once she has been staked, and as a direct result of her extermination she does make a lovely corpse, with a 'face of unequalled sweetness and purity' – at least until her mouth is stuffed with garlic and she is decapitated.[96]

The vampire certainly haunted such sexualized thinking – or rather influenced it. Dr William J. Robinson, head of the department of genito-urinary diseases and dermatology at the Bronx Hospital, described the 'hypersensual woman' as 'a great danger to the health and even the very life of her husband':

> It is to her that the name vampire can be applied in its literal sense. Just as the vampire sucks the blood of its victims in their sleep while they are alive, so does the woman vampire suck the life and exhaust the vitality of her male partner – or victim. And some of them – the pronounced type – are utterly without pity or consideration.[97]

In *Psychopathia Sexualis* (1886), meanwhile, Krafft-Ebing even recounted literal cases of vampirism – thereby somatizing the condition.[98] But the vampire came first, and the diagnosis of the sexually rapacious woman follows those earlier issues of power, life sciences and identity that had already dominated vampirology for decades. In other words, vampire tales helped to mould the sexual taboos of the era.

Neither was the female vampire complex confined to sexually rapacious viragoes – it also applied to the victims of vampires: the supine female form represented a paragon of passivity and was aestheticized and medicalized as an ideal condition, which along the way fetishized the intimate and tender skin around the throat.[99] Lucy Westenra spends much of *Dracula* as a recumbent invalid: delicately incapable and exquisitely ailing. This was very much in harmony with the mood of the time: the bloodless, dying female being an object of both professional and aesthetic scrutiny. Emaciation was a sign of femininity (what one might call 'femininity'), and so restores the presumptuous 'New Woman' Lucy to her properly 'old woman' submissive role. Women were thus 'vampirized' by men. Artworks focused on sickly women, such as Frank Dicksee's morose and gloomy 'The Crisis' (1891). The actress Sarah Bernhardt, already emaciated and physically frail, went one better than the bedridden beauties and by the 1870s had already posed for a photograph in a coffin. Such images of prone and defenceless women not only mixed the morbid with the sensual: they were also frank invitations to sexual abuse.

Shakespeare's Juliet was a popular subject for fine artistry, but the drowned Ophelia became virtually iconic in the period: pallid when alive and bloodless when dead. Madeleine Lemaire's *Ophelia* (1880s) was a fey bloodsucker, and the eyes of Antoine-Auguste-Ernest Hébert's *Ophelia* (1890s) betrayed an unearthly lunacy. This wanton sprite was described in the French magazine *Je Sais Tout* as

> truly that helplessly abandoned ideal creature, whose hallucinating eyes see nothing more than what is within, and who, hair loosened and streaming down, will in a few moments enter gently into the stream which will carry her – a cut flower among other cut flowers – away to that world beyond whereof her madness is already an expression.[100]

It seems far more likely that she is planning to slash the jugular vein of a passing gentleman and sate herself on his gore.

Women were also portrayed as regarding and objectifying themselves.[101] They gazed at their autoerotic beauty in mirrors, corroborating their superficiality and inauthenticity, their passivity – while simultaneously inviting the viewer to join the spectacle as a passive voyeur. If mirrors possessed the ability to fascinate the beholder with her own beauty, they were also instruments of wider power – often used against female dominion. In classical myth, the mirror is weaponized in the trial of Perseus against the Medusa, enabling him to avoid her petrifying gaze and so behead her; for Eve in John Milton's *Paradise Lost* (1667), the reflection she glimpses of herself is narcissistic and incapacitating.[102] Mirrors as objects therefore condemn women, either figuratively or literally. But that is not the case with vampires, who represent the revenge of the reflection. Mirrors do not record the presence of the vampire; nor can vampires be photographed or painted (or even reliably recognized); they leave no trace when they pass through dust and they cast no shadow. Just as a jumble of alien words cannot fully characterize vampires, so they lack a graphic definition. Stoker evidently mulled over these elusive qualities. In his 'Count Wampyr' memoranda (early notes on the planned novel made in 1890), he jotted down the optical peculiarities of vampires:

> no looking glasses in Count's house
> never can see him reflected in one – no shadow?
> lights arranged to give no shadow . . .
> see in the dark . . .[103]

The second memo elaborates further:

> painters cannot paint him – their likenesses always like some one else
> . . .
> Could not codak [*sic*] him – come out black or like skeleton corpse.[104]

Dracula is an 'unmirrorable image', akin to the traditionally faceless figure of Death in which one cannot recognize one's own mortality, Dracula cannot be captured by either objects or artists – neither the human hand nor technology is able to record him – and so Stoker uncannily anticipates X-ray radiography in describing the results of trying to photograph vampires. Dracula's absent shadow reveals that he is removed from the material world, but he also lacks a soul and so is likewise estranged from the domain of the immaterial. One might say that he is strangely devoid of vanity and thereby inartificial. Yet in lacking such an image, a visual reality, Stoker's vampire confirms that one can only be authentically human if one is threatened by or risks inauthenticity; can only love another if one acknowledges self-conceit; can only be real and unique if countless superficial depictions can exist – and *Dracula* is, of course, among other things a love story.[105] In this sense, Wilde's novel *The Picture of Dorian Gray* shares Stoker's concerns – along with a central problem of how individuals can be perceived and recognized. *Dorian Gray* was first published in 1890, just as Stoker seriously began work on *Dracula*, and Wilde's exploration of the symbiotic relationship between the ageless, incorruptible and vampiric Dorian and his ever-changing, rotting and shrouded image may have influenced Stoker's Count. Stoker had not only known Wilde, a fellow Irishman, for years, but had married Florence Balcombe, who had previously partnered Wilde.[106] Dorian becomes a wraith because he is both all-image and, like the vampire, lacks a true image; instead he is – as Basil says of his living portrait – a 'thing'.[107]

Female sexuality was, then, simultaneously medicalized, commodified and Gothicized, and this inspired an extreme aestheticization of feminine (or rather *feminized*) beauty in art. This vampirography is at the very heart of the art-for-art's-sake movement, of *fin-de-siècle* decadence – as typified by *Dorian Gray*. The foundational text for art-for-art's-sake aesthetes in the United Kingdom – and across Europe – was Walter Pater's collection of fine-art criticism, *The Renaissance* (1873); and at the core of *The Renaissance* was Pater's awestruck reading of Leonardo da Vinci's *La Gioconda* (the *Mona Lisa*). For all Pater's audacious mannerisms, this reading is a consummate literary evocation of a painting – a painting that few of his readers would ever actually see, except in coloured prints and black-and-white photographs:

> The presence that rose thus so strangely beside the waters, is expressive of what in the ways of a thousand years men had come to desire. Hers is the head upon which all 'the ends of the world are come,' and the eyelids are a little weary. It is a beauty wrought out from within upon the flesh, the deposit, little cell by cell, of strange thoughts and fantastic reveries and exquisite passions. Set it for a moment beside one of those white Greek goddesses or beautiful women of antiquity, and how would they be troubled by this beauty, into which the soul with all its maladies has passed! All the thoughts and experience of the world have etched and moulded there, in that which they have of power to refine and make expressive the outward form, the animalism of Greece, the lust of Rome,

the mysticism of the middle age with its spiritual ambition and imaginative loves, the return of the Pagan world, the sins of the Borgias. She is older than the rocks among which she sits; like the vampire, she has been dead many times, and learned the secrets of the grave; and has been a diver in deep seas, and keeps their fallen day about her; and trafficked for strange webs with Eastern merchants[;] and, as Leda, was the mother of Helen of Troy, and, as Saint Anne, the mother of Mary; and all this has been to her but as the sound of lyres and flutes, and lives only in the delicacy with which it has moulded the changing lineaments, and tinged the eyelids and the hands. The fancy of a perpetual life, sweeping together ten thousand experiences, is an old one; and modern philosophy has conceived the idea of humanity as wrought upon by, and summing up in itself, all modes of thought and life. Certainly Lady Lisa might stand as the embodiment of the old fancy, the symbol of the modern idea.[108]

Oscar Wilde could not resist quoting this passage virtually word for word in his scintillating essay, 'The Critic as Artist' (1891): manifestly Pater's appraisal of *La Gioconda* was still momentous news in the 1890s. As Pater reflects, 'like the vampire', *La Gioconda* has 'been dead many times, and learned the secrets of the grave'. When Lucy is vampirized, then, it is not an expression of her incipient or current nymphomania (or other latent sexual deviations – much as many critics would like to imagine). Instead, she aspires to a super-abundant condition of female beauty: a condition perceived – in its wild aestheticism – to be morally tendentious, to be decadent. Thus, for all Stoker's research in folklore, political history, medicine and the sciences, his vampires also have a very immediate textual, literary and cultural presence. That presence remains with us today.

CRAWLING AND CREEPING
LIVING WITH VAMPIRES

From 1730 to 1735, all we hear about are vampires.

Gilles Deleuze and Félix Guattari (1987)[1]

Everyone knows the phenomenon of trying to hold your breath under-water – how at first it's alright and you can handle it, and then as it gets closer and closer to the time when you must breathe, how urgent the need becomes, the lust and the hunger to breathe. And then the panic sets in when you begin to think that you won't be able to breathe – and finally, when you take in air and the anxiety subsides . . . that's what it's like to be a vampire and need blood.

Francis Ford Coppola (1992)[2]

Defined by their categorical ambiguity and troubling mobility, vampires do not rest easy (or easily) in the boxes labeled good and bad. Always transported and shifting, the vampire's native soil is more nutritious, and more *unheimlich*, than that.

Donna Haraway (1997)[3]

The vampire has become universalized, primarily through Bram Stoker's epoch-making *Dracula* and the sprawling cultural industry it has spawned. As a figure that questions the very being of what it is to be human – combining medical science with theology and philosophy, politics and social science – the vampire has flourished for nearly two centuries. Throughout its dissident existence, the figure of the vampire has embraced contradictions between rational belief and supernatural agency, the impossibilities in defining an authentic selfhood, the insoluble dilemmas of medical science in experimentation and physical and psychological pathologies, the morbid fears and fantasies of consumption, and the insoluble complexities of establishing social and political legitimacy. Vampires are not simply another Gothic entity, but utterly weird *things*, 'catachthonic': catalysts of new and vertiginous ways of imagining history and art, technology and ideology. Vampires, as I have argued, are enmeshments of history that escape their interment to reveal deeper histories – histories more complex, more disturbing, more dangerous and more present. They were then, and they are now.

This is certainly the case in a novel such as *Dracula*, but how far does it apply to the AD world and especially the prevalence of vampires in the twenty-first century? Echoing the reception of Polidori's 'Vampyre', Stoker's *Dracula* inspired both stage adaptations (one of which was hastily prepared by Stoker himself) and considered historical analysis of the figure. By 1914, Dudley Wright had condensed nineteenth-century antiquarian discussion into a world history of bloodsuckers, *Vampires and Vampirism*, and following the Great War of 1914–18, the maverick priest and demonologist Montague Summers produced two studies, *The Vampire, His Kith and Kin* (1928) and *The Vampire in Europe* (1929) that prepared the way for his pioneering two-volume account of the Gothic novel (1938–40). Vampires also attracted attention from the influential Freudian psychoanalyst and neurologist Ernest Jones in 1924.[4] But even as academia was turning its lugubrious gaze towards the vampire, the creature was already a movie star. The extraordinary growth of the vampire cult was, not surprisingly, in large measure due to the rise of film in the twentieth century and its prominence as the quintessential cultural medium of our time.[5]

Béla's not dead

The vampire was at the forefront of this cultural watershed in experimental films such as F.W. Murnau's *Nosferatu, A Symphony of Horror* (1922) – an early German expressionist masterpiece that was brilliantly inventive in its groundbreaking special effects and visual narrative, if not an immediate commercial success due in part to Florence Stoker, Bram's widow, endeavouring to have all prints of the movie destroyed for copyright infringement.[6] But within a decade, Hollywood had turned the Hungarian actor Béla Lugosi into a global icon in Tod Browning's *Dracula* (1931), a film produced during a golden age of horror that within a few years boasted *Frankenstein* (1931) and *Bride of Frankenstein* (1935), *The Mummy* (1932) and *King Kong* (1933). Hamilton Deane's stage adaption had toured England in 1924 and a version revised by John L. Balderston hit Broadway in 1927, but as the cinema critic Jeffrey Andrew Weinstock remarks, 'the early twentieth-century American vampire narrative was primarily a cinematic affair', and American films had a global reach.[7]

Visually, vampires were extremely well suited to black-and-white film, which enabled both the uncanny chiaroscuro effects of *Nosferatu* and also encouraged cast members to dress in black in vivid contrast with their pallid, sometimes cadaverous, faces.[8] The medium consequently added momentum to a dark new image of femininity that had been smouldering since the end of the nineteenth century, and which now flared up across the world's cinema screens: the 'vamp' – a striking look that mixed pale and featureless skin with outrageously kohled eyes. The wildly exotic sex symbol Theda Bara typified this latest sex symbol – even her outlandish name had a vampiric twist to it: it was an anagram of 'Arab Death'. These vamps and vampires were arcane beings: they tended to be psychic entities rather than fanged bloodsuckers. They did not appear with blood trickling wantonly from their lips – that would only come with technicolour (even Béla Lugosi declined to appear with enhanced and sharpened teeth) – instead, these vamps extracted the vitality from their victims. At the same time, they were instantly recognizable as symbols and symptoms of classy modernity, and they swiftly migrated into other media. The cartoonist Charles Addams introduced a vamp into his *New Yorker* comic strip in 1938, and when the cartoons provided the basis for a television series in 1964, the character eventually became Morticia Addams of *The Addams Family*. By then the style had already been adopted on the small screen by Maila Nurmi for her role as 'Vampira', presenter of late-night horror films. This look has since become a standard Hallowe'en costume for those seeking to seduce rather than terrify.[9]

Neither did writers give up on the vampire. The vampire appeared across the whole range of literature, from the magazine *Weird Tales* publishing vampire stories such as Henry Kuttner's thrilling and sassy 'I, the Vampire' – appropriately enough about the vampiric relationships between movie stars and cameras in Hollywood – to the poetry of T.S. Eliot. Vampires appear in Eliot's modernist epic *The Waste Land* (1922) in a wreckage of Gothic motifs that combine nightmarish images gleaned from the paintings of Hieronymus Bosch with the despair of Romantic and Victorian horror writing (including an allusion to Dracula crawling down a wall) to create a phantasmagoric landscape of ruin and desolation:

> A woman drew her long black hair out tight
> And fiddled whisper music on those strings

And bats with baby faces in the violet light
Whistled, and beat their wings
And crawled head downward down a blackened wall
And upside down in air were towers
Tolling reminiscent bells, that kept the hours
And voices singing out of empty cisterns and exhausted wells.[10]

Vampires have continued to appear in all of these spheres – and many more – since, and it would take several volumes to detail the succession of vampire films and television series, all the literature and academic criticism devoted to them, and simply the sheer omnipresence of vampires in recent years.[11] They have remained a cinema standby, helping to establish Vincent Price, Peter Cushing and Christopher Lee as international stars following the Second World War and propelling the prolific output of House of Hammer films. They also revelled in the occasional film that escaped the niche of cult horror to become mainstream classics, such as Werner Herzog's *Nosferatu the Vampyre* (1979) and Francis Ford Coppola's *Bram Stoker's Dracula* (1992), as well as the alternative mockumentary comedy of *What We Do in the Shadows* (2014).[12] There are comic vampires, vampires with a conscience, vampires in outer space; and despite this absurd proliferation, some vampire films – such as the Iranian *A Girl Walks Home Alone at Night* (2014) – still have the power to chill.[13]

This tide shows no sign of abating. The prodigious sales of Stephenie Meyer's bestselling and remarkably chaste *Twilight* series of young-adult fiction (2005–08; unfairly dismissed by some as insipid teen glamourpuss 'sparkly vampires') captivated a generation and inevitably created a film franchise (2008–12), and vampire television series continue unchecked – from *Buffy the Vampire Slayer* (1997–2003) to *The Vampire Diaries* (2009–17), as well as *Penny Dreadful* (2014–16), which featured a melting-pot of assorted literary and historical vampires.[14] Other popular vampire classics include Stephen King's Watergate novel *Salem's Lot* (1975) and Angela Carter's Great War requiem 'The Lady of the House of Love' (1979).[15] Anne Rice's *Interview with the Vampire* was published in 1976 and has led to a multi-novel series which, among many other things, glamorizes Lestat, the key narrator of the *Vampire Chronicles*, as a rock star.

It is a telling coincidence, then, that in the very same year that *Interview with the Vampire* was published, Dave 'Vanian' (from 'Transyl-Vanian') was fronting the punk band The Damned dressed as a Béla Lugosi-style Dracula. In 1979, Bauhaus responded with the inaugural Goth single 'Bela Lugosi's Dead'; the next year The Birthday Party (led by Nick Cave, who later masterminded The Bad Seeds) recorded 'Release the Bats' (1980). Goth, as a subculture within rock music, was therefore established against an ever-mutating background of cultural vampires, and unsurprisingly bands such as The Sisters of Mercy and The Bad Seeds dwelt upon blood and predation. This music has maintained a strong international appeal, for example through bands such as Inkubus Sukkubus and the Italian group Theatres des Vampires, and retains its popularity to this day.[16]

Moreover, Goth also encompassed a variety of fashion styles, with vampire chic being high on the list: both women and men dressing as vamps.[17] This look has had a worldwide impact from Whitby to Tokyo, from catwalk fashion such as Susie Cave's label 'The Vampire's Wife' to inspired potpourri assemblages of deathly Victoriana and Gothic corpse trinkets.[18] In turn, the dazzling undead bravura of such styles of dress has generated an idiosyncratic genre of popular fantasy art that feeds back into the Goth look.[19] Vampirism can also be a lifestyle choice: there are sanguinarians who allegedly drink blood and followers of esoteric self-improvement programmes, such as the Temple of the Vampire, which claims that

> The Temple embraces only those aspects of the Vampire mythos that include a love and respect for all life, physical immortality, individual elegance, proven wisdom, civilized behavior, worldly success, and personal happiness. The Temple rejects those aspects of the Vampire mythos that are negative including any that are anti-life, anti-social, deathist, crude, gory, self-defeating, or criminal.[20]

There are also 'vampire facial' skin rejuvenation treatments available, as well as cosmetic vampire dentistry.[21]

Much of the obsession with vampires at the beginning of the twenty-first century was put down to the runaway success of *Buffy* and *Twilight*, with the claim that these books and programmes had revived the figure.[22]

But in fact vampires had never been away: not only did they survive in the relatively niche imaginations of Goths and fans of cult horror films, but they had never actually left mainstream popular culture. In comics, for example, Vampirella made her first appearance in 1969, and in 1972 Marvel launched *The Tomb of Dracula*. The original theatrical double-bills of the 1820s had regularly paired 'The Vampyre' with *Frankenstein* (the monsters were, moreover, often played by the same character), and in the twentieth century horror movies regularly inspired sequels that brought together creatures from different films. Comics therefore took their cue from stage and screen not only to confirm the place of vampires within this expanding popular universe of monsters, but to locate them at its very heart. On the screen or in comic strips, Dracula could appear with werewolves, zombies, Frankenstein's Being or even aliens from outer space. Both *House of Frankenstein* (1944) and *House of Dracula* (1945), for instance, were 'monster rallies', featuring Dracula, Frankenstein's Being, and Wolf Man.[23] This confraternity of monsters was either bent on destroying humankind or engaged in direct inter-species conflict.[24] These cross-over vampire tales were printed and reprinted in comic books, and the trend continues in contemporary graphic novels such as the erotico-political saga *The Ravening* (2016) – the main difference being that comic-book vampires today are, as they were in the nineteenth century, predominantly female.[25]

The multiplicity and plurality of vampire identity has now, therefore, extended to its entire cultural condition. Cross-fertilization is rife: Bauhaus's music influences the she-vampire film *The Hunger* (1983), which in turn influences fashion – not least as David Bowie is a sub-vampire in the movie.[26] Patricia Morrison, bass player for bands The Gun Club and later The Sisters of Mercy, perfected the Goth vamp look that was later taken up by Cassandra Peterson to create Elvira, a pop-Goth brand that continues to run. Meanwhile Bauhaus singer Pete Murphy appeared in cameo in the *Twilight* film *Eclipse* (2010). This intense and self-referential intertextuality means that it is impossible to disentangle the multitude of manifestations in which vampires today appear. They appear to all be interconnected: they are a media contagion.

At the same time, in this avalanche of popular literature, television, film and merchandising knick-knacks, vampires risk becoming commonplace, prompting the radical cultural theorist Mark Fisher to suggest drily that, 'a natural phenomenon such as a black hole is more weird than a vampire'.[27] Worse still is the tendency to treat the vampire as a 'metaphor run amuck'.[28] Critics have imbued vampires with every conceivable interpretation, as if desperate to prove Nina Auerbach's memorable claim that 'every age embraces the vampire it needs' as a justification for rampant over-analysis of the figure.[29]

But the opposite is in fact the case. Our age has reworked the vampire into an all-embracing cipher, a cosmic vessel to be filled and refilled with endless readings and re-readings – a veritable multiplicity. Yet this quality has deep historical roots – as does the vampire's neophilia for the latest media and technology. Even the focus on the body as a biological phenomenon or as the medium for fashion, tattoos, piercings and desires is one rooted in the medical and physiological discourses of the past.[30] Today's vampires retain an affinity with historical vampires – an affinity that can enhance our current relationship with the supernatural.

The remarks of the acclaimed writer Neil Gaiman that the over-exposure of the vampire has leached its eerie allure therefore deserve attention. Gaiman complains that while it is terrific that vampire tales get children reading, vampires 'like reality television contestants . . . are everywhere', and so 'The saddest thing is that it [the plague of vampires] runs the risk of making vampires not scary.'[31] Yet while it is certainly true that vampires are ubiquitous (and even arguably out of control), some considered restraint is still evident in television series such as *Being Human* (2009–13) and *True Blood* (2008–14), which both deal with the ethical and legal issues surrounding vampires attempting to co-exist with humans.

At the same time, the extreme ubiquity and hyper-adaptability of vampires is surely not to be lamented, but explained. It is the evidence of the elusive necessity of vampire thinking. But even critics of Gothicism doubt their own subject: obituaries of vampires and the end of Gothic frequently appear in the closing pages of major studies on the subject.[32] Reports of the death of vampires are, however, greatly exaggerated: the dead will always rise – until death itself dies, and then vampires will be our thought experiments in fathoming the horrors (and possible delights) of immortality. But once vampires were discovered, they did indeed infect thought. So the vampire is both pervasive and indiscernible: part of the very nature of humanity, and also then part of its undoing. And perhaps we are living not so much in the anthropocene period (as people aver more and more frequently), as in the vampirocene era – an era in which the human race has transformed the world, but in doing so has also lost its primacy.[33] In the vampirocene, the world is no longer anthropocentric; it is nihilocentric.

Truest blood

The foregoing chapters have argued that the vampire is a relatively modern phenomenon. I have tried to resist essentializing the vampire as an elemental mythic type, or turning it into a canvas on which to portray the whole spectrum of contemporary critical thinking.[34] This is because the vampire becomes more thought-provoking and more perplexing precisely if it is not reduced to a knot of, say, contemporary sexual neuroses or post-colonial anxieties – valuable as these approaches might be in other ways.[35] Even the great Slavonic vampirologist Jan Perkowski was tempted to elucidate the case of Arnod Paole as a symbolic engagement with tenth-century Bogomilism:

> Quite evident are several dualist motifs . . .: an evil force, – the vampire – hounding men and women and sapping their strength; an evil force active only at night; the migration of souls; the association of corpses with the evil force; symbolic interplay of water, fire, and earth; and the association of light (day) and fire with the god of good. Soul migration in both cases is limited until the fortieth day. The piercing of the heart and removal of the head, seen as repositories of emotion and the mind (the soul) were perpetrated to exorcise the evil spirit or soul, which has been motivating the body to do evil. Three of the four elements occur: water (blood), earth, and fire. The final cure of cremation brings about the ultimate separation of elements belonging to the force of good and those belonging to the force of evil.[36]

Such readings may hum with intellectual vibrancy, but they lack historical specificity.

In fact, in 2014 the author Hilary Mantel published a medicophobic short story 'Harley Street', which deals with the phenomenon of vampirism in a way that is far closer to the historical vampire. It is a deceptively light tale of social manners set at a private medical practice laced with covert vampire references: death and the undead, the drug datura, cosmetic dentistry, graves, underground sites (the clinic's phlebotomist works in the basement and tries to protect herself with a crucifix), vivisection, forensic attention to mouths and nails, debilitation, pallor and blood. Of the three female characters, one is a vampire, the other two – including the narrator – are her victims. Mimicking current sexual obsessions, Mantel misdirects the reader to imply that this is a tale of repressed sexuality rather than vampiric predation. The narrator does not realize that she is being preyed upon, despite her preternaturally heightened senses and foreboding and enervating dreams:

> I was coming or going: the pavement was stained – sunrise or sunset – and I saw that all the Harley Street railings had been filed to points . . . Then a big hand came out, and pushed me towards them.[37]

The story ends with a sly pun that reveals to the reader – if not the narrator herself – that this is a modern medical vampire story in the tradition of Mary Braddon's 'The Good Lady Ducayne'.[38]

Mantel's subtle and elegant tale admirably demonstrates how a complex cultural symbol such as the vampire can be mobilized in preternatural medical fiction, and vampires also continue to play a role today in geopolitics, protest and identity formation. In the mid-twentieth century on the South Africa–Mozambique border, for example, rumours spread that blood was being forcibly taken from locals by state firemen and policemen for the treatment of rich Europeans.[39] This pharmacophobia, or fear of medication, was based on memories of colonial medicine, and patently mirrored the stress-related traumas of Austro-Hungarian vampiromania and the subsequent medicalization of the psychological condition. Likewise, there are contemporary analyses of vampire films and Reaganomics, vampires participating in American consumer culture (*The Lost Boys* (1987) in the shopping mall), queer Goths and techno-vampires in Japan – so perhaps the best response to Gaiman's complaint about the over-vampirism of contemporary culture is to focus on such trouble-spots as sites of alleged vampire activity, knitting recent concerns into past memories of turbulent political trauma and the ordeals of social identity.[40]

The nations of Eastern Europe – like many other oppressed peoples – still lie under the shadow of the political vampire; but here it has a history – it is in the very ground, so to speak. Romanian President Nicolae Ceaușescu attempted to revive the memory of Vlad Țepeș as a national hero at a time when he was firmly associated with Count Dracula – a strategy that could be interpreted as vampiric terrorism against non-communist states; following the revolution, Ceaușescu was callously executed by his own people in 1989.[41] In direct contrast, in 2001 Mlađan Dinkić, governor of the Serb National Bank, said that Slobodan Milošević, president of Serbia, was 'politically dead' but will still 'suck the blood of Serbia'.[42] Accordingly, on the first anniversary following his death in 2006, attempts were made to stake Milošević and prevent him from rising as a vampire.[43] In December 2017, meanwhile, nine people were killed and over 250 were arrested following rumours of vampire attacks in Malawi, which borders Mozambique. The epidemic of blood-sucking *anamapopa*, which targeted tourists and the wealthy, was put down to unrest over social inequalities fomented by opposition to the government.[44] Paraphrasing the philosopher Eugene Thacker, one might point out that the vampire is inseparable from a process of vampirization, and that this process is as much political as it is religious or philosophical. Yet we should not be too quick in explaining away outbreaks of apparent vampire activity, especially when they lead to mob rule and public lynchings.[45]

Vampires have consequently maintained a presence in challenging political films such as Faye Jackson's *Strigoi* (2009) – a black comedy on the Romanian revolution, the execution of the Ceaușescus and the historical background of war – and in Guillermo del Toro and Chuck Hogan's novel *The Strain* (first published in 2009 and at present continuing as a television series), exemplifying the fear of occult administration, worldwide conspiracy and alien superpowers.[46] Kouta Hirano's manga comic *Hellsing*, meanwhile, enlists vampires into the ranks of the Nazis – Nazis being particularly appealing in vampire narratives due to their credo of 'Blood and Soil'. Adolf Hitler's Lamarckian theories of blood memory, cultural purity and race pollution were promulgated in *Mein Kampf* (1925) and repeated in a speech to the Nazi party in 1933: 'Blood mixture and the resultant drop in the racial level is the sole cause of the dying out of old cultures.'[47] These reminders are crucial in dealing with the politics of vampires in the twenty-first century: there is an established tradition of legal process and intellectual justification in handling vampires, and it is worth recalling that as part of the vampirological discourse (as indeed outside it) there is a serious risk of tyranny and reigns of terror.

But the status of the vampire is not only political; it is also clearly psychological and physiological. Vampires are both super-fit and potentially immortal, if at the same time possible evidence of regression or de-evolution. As such, vampires also pose questions of conservation and ecology. What is the status of anthropovores: creatures that can only survive by preying on humans? As Suzy McKee Charnas, author of the novel *The Vampire Tapestry* (1981), said in an interview: 'I just decided that there would be something that preyed specifically on us, but in a much more rational manner than we prey on the rest of the world, putting us (I wish) to shame for our moronic clumsiness.'[48] Vampires are thus an endangered species and hunted to extinction; at the same time they propose uncomfortable ways of conceiving of ecological systems that do not privilege the human – i.e. that are non-anthropocentric. Hence fears from poisoning landscapes to the overexploitation and consumption of natural resources, as well as the general desecration of the earth can be linked to vampires rising.[49] Vampires can therefore be a reminder of the ground on which we walk, whereon we live, and upon which we rely.

The vampire is, finally then, a chthonic creature of darkness, emerging from the ground white and ashen, preferring the sublunary glimmer to daylight. Strangely, it shares certain characteristics with another subterranean dweller with origins in colonized regions outside the territorial concerns of the British Empire. It was believed to cause leprosy (just as fresh blood was believed to cure it), favoured moonlight, was strongly associated with Catholic superstition, was linked to dietary guilt, was disconcertingly human (with dead-looking eyes and cadaverous skin), was liable to spread invisibly and rhizomatically – and was even, as one critic has it, 'ambivalent, arbitrary, historically overdetermined, and opaque as any signifier'.[50] It was also the bane of Bram Stoker's Ireland and the root of the Great Hunger . . .

Unlike bread – prepared from golden wheat that has ripened in sunshine and been ruffled by the fresh air, before being leavened by the magic of yeast and enshrined in the Lord's Prayer – the potato had a darker symbolism. Potatoes were in fact rejected as a staple foodstuff by the labouring classes for decades. 'Taters' may have become standard fare on British dinner tables by the time of *Dracula*, but the Irish famine of 1845, caused as it was by potato blight, remained in the national imagination. So, the vampire was not only manifest in scientific and epistemological discourses; it was also as political as the potato. It recalled crisis, desperation, mass migration and mortality on a terrible scale. The vampire was a reminder of this modern pestilence, and the memory of it still ran in the blood of the people.

It may seem puzzling to end with the humble and homely spud, but thinking with vampires is surely a way of reminding us of the un-homely qualities of everyday objects and our experience of them, revealing that they have imperceptible potentials – making them *unheimlich*, 'uncanny'.[51] It is not only graves, or the risen dead, or bestial transformations that dwell in and shape the realm of the supernatural: so, too, do everyday mysteries such as the flow of blood and the settling mist and our unsettling dreams. Vampires moving as we do between enfleshed reality and the obscure shadows of clandestine passions and impalpable thoughts are close, very close, too close to us. Our encounter with them is impossibly intimate because they become us – or we become them. And thus, in the end, then, vampires can bring the magical back into the world – a world that in the twenty-first century has become demarcated and circumscribed by genomic mapping, market algorithms, materialist secularism and social media. We subsist in a digital datasphere, an electromagnetic shanty town.[52] That may be the reason that the prevalence and importance of vampires continues to soar; is it simply a coincidence that the year after Facebook was launched, Stephenie Meyer published the first novel in her *Twilight* series? If vampire thinking can transmute the previously implacable potato into a sinister and enigmatic entity, so it can correspondingly present the experience of being human as something lastingly cryptic.

ENDNOTES

Epigraphs

1. *The Bible: King James Version*, ed. Robert Carroll and Stephen Prickett ([1611] Oxford and New York: Oxford University Press, 1998).
2. Desiderius Erasmus, *Collected Works: Adages III iv 1 to IV ii 100*, trans. Denis L. Drysdall, ed. John N. Grant (Toronto, Buffalo, London: University of Toronto Press, 2005), Adage III vi 41, p. 145 (derived from Plutarch's *Parallel Lives*, 'Pompey'); there is also the oral tradition that Patrick, Lord Gray sanctioned the execution of Mary, Queen of Scots in 1587 by declaring '*Mortui non mordent* [*sic*]' ('A dead woman bites not').
3. Bram Stoker, *Dracula*, ed. Roger Luckhurst (Oxford: Oxford University Press, 2011), 351.

Foreword

1. Friedrich Nietzsche, *Also Sprach Zarathustra*, quoted in David Biale, *Blood and Belief: The Circulation of a Symbol between Jews and Christians* (Berkeley, Los Angeles, London: University of California Press, 2007), Biale's translation: see p. 216 n.18.
2. In one of the anonymous reader reports on this very work . . .
3. For the Gothic, see my book *The Gothic: A Very Short Introduction* (Oxford: Oxford University Press, 2012), especially 96–99.
4. Moreover, some readers will recognize concepts of continental philosophy and speculative realist theory in certain sections; these ideas have provoked various lines of thought and I am therefore happy to acknowledge their influence. Although in a sense these fields go against the grain of this book by often being naïvely ahistorical and reductionist, it would be overly dogmatic to reject this thinking – which if nothing else has afforded horror writing an intellectual credibility, and which is in any case entertaining to read and usually thought-provoking.
5. Reading all the secondary literature on *Dracula* alone would itself devour a lifetime.
6. The conceit of 'thinking with vampires' developed in the Introduction obviously draws on Stuart Clark's monumental work, *Thinking with Demons: The Idea of Witchcraft in Early Modern Europe* (Oxford: Clarendon Press, 1997). The 'magical thinkers' who have also influenced this book and who may not be directly cited in references are legion, but include Willem de Blécourt, Marion Gibson, Ronald Hutton, Joanne Parker and the late Gareth Roberts.

Note on the Etymology of the Word *Vampire*

NB Transliteration conventions are necessarily mixed in this Note as they follow the preferences of the individual authors cited.

1. Samuel Pegge, *Anonymiana; or, Ten Centuries of Observations on Various Authors and Subjects* (London: John Nichols and Son, 1809), V. vi (p. 182).

2. Aleksandr N. Afanasev, 'Poetic Views of the Slavs Regarding Nature', (trans. Jan Louis Perkowski), in Jan Louis Perkowski, *Vampire Lore: From the Writings of Jan Louis Perkowski* (Bloomington, IN: Slavica Publishers, 2006), 195–211, at 199.

3. Jan Louis Perkowski, *The Darkling: A Treatise on Slavic Vampirism* (1989), reprinted in Perkowski, *Vampire Lore*, 317–488, at 347–50.

4. Kazimierz Moszyński, 'Slavic Folk Culture' (trans. Perkowski), in Perkowski, *Vampire Lore*, 213–17, at 216.

5. Peter Mario Kreuter, 'The Name of the Vampire: Some Reflections on Current Linguistic Theories on the Etymology of the Word *Vampire*', in Peter Day (ed.), *Vampires: Myths and Metaphors of Enduring Evil* (Amsterdam and New York: Rodopi, 2006), 57–63.

6. Brian Cooper, 'The Word *Vampire*: Its Slavonic Form and Origin', *Journal of Slavic Linguistics*, 13 (2005), 251–70, at 253. Other studies include Katharina M. Wilson, 'The History of the Word "Vampire"', *Journal of the History of Ideas*, 46(4) (1985), 577–83, which makes unsubstantiated claims and is unfortunately strewn with errors.

7. The *OED* cites Franz Miklosich's *Lexicon Palaeoslovenico-Graeco-Latinum* (Vienna: Wilhelm Braumüller, 1862–65).

8. Gábor Klaniczay, *The Uses of Supernatural Power: The Transformation of Popular Religion in Medieval and Early-Modern Europe* (Cambridge and Oxford: Polity Press, 1990), 148, 166.

9. Rennell Rodd, *The Customs and Lore of Modern Greece* (London: David Stott, 1892), 188 (see also 127, and 187–97); Rodd also gives the Albanian variant '*Wurwolakas*', as well as the Cretan '*Katakhanás*', the Tinian '*Anakathouménos*' and the Cyprian '*Sarkoménos*'.

10. Agnes Murgoçi, 'The Vampire in Roumania', *Folklore*, 37 (1926), 320–49, at 322; this essay is quoted at length by Montague Summers in *The Vampire, His Kith and Kin* (London: Kegan, Paul, Trench, Trubner & Co., 1928) with further variants.

11. Perkowski, *The Darkling*, 351–68: for all of which, see below.

12. Perkowski, *The Darkling*, at 332 (citing *Srpski Mitološki Rečnik* (Beograd: Nollit, 1970), p. 51); see also T.P. Vukanović, 'The Vampire' (trans. Perkowski), in Perkowski, *Vampire Lore*, 230–59, at 233: considering Kosovo-Metohija, Vukanović argues that vampires are equivalent to werewolves.

13. Klaniczay, *Uses of Supernatural Power*, 178; Klaniczay also mentions the Silesian shoemaker in 1591 (described by More: see chapter 2 of the present study); a Bohemian case in 1618 described by Martin Zeiler in *Trauergeschichten* (1625); and a Polish case in 1624 recorded in Gabriel Rzączyński, *Historia Naturalis Curiosa Regni Poloniæ, Magni Ducatus Litvaniæ, Annexarum; Provinciarum, in Tractatus XX Divisa . . .* (Sandomir, 1721).

14. Mary Edith Durham, 'Of Magic, Witches, and Vampires in the Balkans', *Man*, 23 (1923), 189–90.

Introduction

1. Unless stated otherwise, all biblical quotations are from the King James Bible.

2. Robert Burton, *The Anatomy of Melancholy*, ed. Thomas C. Faulkner, Nicolas K. Kiessling and Rhonda L. Blair, 3 vols (Oxford: Clarendon Press, 1989–94), Pt 1, Sect. 2, Memb. 3, Subs. 1 (vol. i. p. 279).

3. Friedrich Nietzsche, *The Gay Science with a Prelude in Rhymes and an Appendix of Songs*, trans. Walter Kaufman (New York: Vintage, 1974), §109.

4. George Sinclar [Sinclair], *Satans Invisible World Discovered; or, A Choice Collection of Modern Relations, proving evidently against the Saducees and Atheists of this Present Age, that there are Devils, Spirits, Witches, and Apparitions, from Authentick Records, Attestations of Witnesses, and [sic] Undoubted Verity* (Edinburgh, 1685) (Relation xxx) (italicized thus in original); see also 'R.B.', *The Kingdom of Darkness: or The History of Dæmons, Specters, Witches, Apparitions, Possessions, Disturbances, and other Wonderful and Supernatural Delusions, Mischievous Feats, and Malicious Impostures of the Devil* (London, 1688), 96–97.

5. It was also associated with Christian martyrdom: several saints were depicted as cephalophores, that is, martyrs carrying their own severed heads (see Nicola Masciandaro's thought-provoking essay '*Non potest hoc Corpus Decollari*: Beheading and the Impossible', in Larissa Tracy and Jeff Massey (eds), *Heads Will Roll: Decapitation in the Medieval and Early Modern Imagination* (Leiden and Boston, MA: Brill, 2012), 15–36).

6. See Stanislaw Frankowski, 'Post-Communist Europe', in Peter Hodgkinson and Andrew Rutherford (eds), *Capital Punishment: Global Issues and Prospects* (Winchester: Waterside Press, 1996), 215–41, especially 215–16.

7. Dudley Wright, *Vampires and Vampirism* (London: William Rider and Son, 1914), 7.

8. *The Bible: A New Translation*, trans. James A.R. Moffat (London: Hodder & Stoughton, 1922); and *The Old Testament Newly Translated from the Latin Vulgate*, trans. Ronald Knox, 2 vols (London: Burns Oates & Washbourne, 1949). Isaiah 34:14 mentions '*strygia*', which though translated as 'screech owl' in the King James Bible, has also been proposed as a reference to the vampire: see the Greco-Italian *striges*.

9. See Matthew Beresford, *From Demons to Dracula: The Creation of the Modern Vampire Myth* (London: Reaktion Books, 2008).

10. Claudian, *De Bello Gothico: The Gothic War*, trans. Maurice Platnauer, 2 vols, Loeb Classical Library (Cambridge, MA, and London: Harvard University Press, 1963), ii. 143.

11. Quoted by John Man, *Attila the Hun: A Barbarian King and the Fall of Rome* (London: Bantam, 2006), 144.

12. Jordanes, *The Gothic History*, trans. Charles Christopher Mierow (Princeton, NJ: Princeton University Press, and London: Oxford University Press, 1915), 123 (ch. xlix).

13. See William Sayers, 'The Alien and Alienated as Unquiet Dead in the Sagas of the Icelanders', in Jeffrey Jerome Cohen (ed.), *Monster Theory: Reading Culture* (Minneapolis, MN and London: University of Minnesota Press, 1996), 242–63, at 242.

14. See Montague Summers, *The Vampire in Europe* (New York: University Books, 1968), 78; William Morris, 'The Story of Grettir the Strong', in *The Collected Works of William Morris*, ed. May Morris, 24 vols (London: Longmans Green and Company, 1911 [1910–15]), vii. 1–279; and *Grettir's Saga*, ed. and trans. Jesse Byock (Oxford: Oxford University Press, 2009); see also 'Sagann af Kyrielax Keysara', British Library Add MS 4859 (Icelandic Sagas, Sir Joseph Banks Collection, 1693–97).

15. See *Eyrbyggja Saga*, ed. and trans. Hermann Pálsson and Paul Edwards (London: Penguin, 1989); and Julian D'Arcy and Kirsten Wolf, 'Sir Walter Scott and *Eyrbyggja Saga*', *Studies in Scottish Literature*, 22 (1987), 30–43; for Scott, see below pp. 100, 105.

16. The claim that there is an Anglo-Saxon poem *A Vampyre of the Fens* is, in fact, a misreading of an 1855 article on *Beowulf* in *Household Words*: see Carol A. Senf, 'Daughters of Lilith: Women Vampires in Popular Literature', in Leonard G. Heldreth and Mary Pharr (eds), *The Blood is the Life: Vampires in Literature* (Bowling Green, OH: Bowling Green State University Press, 1999), 199–216, at 199.

17. This was a Gothic practice: a sixth-century Visigothic cemetery at Estagel contained the grave of child with an iron stake through its heart (see E.A. Thompson, *The Goths in Spain* (Oxford: Clarendon Press, 1969), 56).

18. Geoffrey of Burton, *Life and Miracles of St Modwenna*, ed. Robert Bartlett (Oxford: Oxford University Press, 2002), xxix–xxx, ch. 47, pp. 192–99; see also David Wilson, *Anglo-Saxon Paganism* (London: Routledge, 1992), 92–93; and Elizabeth O'Brien, *Post-Roman Britain to Anglo-Saxon England: Burial Practices Reviewed* in *British Archaeological Reports*, British Series 289 (1999), 7–8, 54–55, 173–74.

19. Willelmi Parvi de Newburgh [William of Newburgh], *Historia Rerum Anglicarum*, ed. Hans Claude Hamilton, 2 vols (London: Sumptibus Societatis, 1856), ii. 182–90 (chs xxii–xxiv).

20. Biale, *Blood and Belief*, 101; Marsilio Ficino, *Della Religione Christiane* (Florence, 1568), 59; see Piero Camporesi, *Juice of Life: The Symbolic and Magic Significance of Blood*, trans. Robert R. Barr (New York: Continuum, 1995), 36–37.

21. Richard M. Titmuss, *The Gift Relationship: From Human Blood to Social Policy* (London: George Allen & Unwin, 2002), 17n.

22. See entry on 'Vampires in World Folklore' in S.T. Joshi (ed.), *Encyclopedia of the Vampire: The Living Dead in Myth, Legend, and Popular Culture* (Santa Barbara, CA, Denver, CO, and Oxford: Greenwood, 2011).

23. Thomas Middleton, *A Tragi-Coomodie* [sic], *called The Witch; long since acted by His Maties Servants at the Black-Friers* (London, 1778), 24; see Summers, *The Vampire in Europe*, 165.

24. John Webster, *The Duchess of Malfi*, in *The Duchess of Malfi and Other Plays*, ed. René Weiss (Oxford: Oxford University Press, 2009), V. ii. 5–6 (p. 180); see Brett D. Hirsch, 'Lycanthropy in Early Modern England: The Case of John Webster's *The Duchess of Malfi*', in Yasmin Haskell (ed.), *Diseases of the Imagination and Imaginary Diseases in the Early Modern Period* (Turnhout: Brepols Publishers, 2011), 301–40.

25. William Shakespeare, *The Tragedy of King Richard III*, in *The Oxford Shakespeare: The Complete Works*, gen. eds Stanley Wells and Gary Taylor (Oxford: Clarendon Press, 1988), I. ii. 55–56 (p. 187).

26. John Webster [and Thomas Heywood], *Appius and Virginia. A Tragedy* (London, 1659), V. i. (p. 59); see MacD.P. Jackson, 'John Webster and Thomas Heywood in *Appius and Virginia*: A Bibliographical Approach to the Problem of Authorship', *Studies in Bibliography*, 38 (1985), 217–35.

27. James VI, *Daemonologie* (Edinburgh, 1597), Bk III: see Brian P. Levack (ed.), *The Witchcraft Sourcebook*, 2nd edn (London and New York: Routledge, 2015), 160–61 (see also Summers, *The Vampire in Europe*, 100).

28. [*Cobbett's Complete Collection . . .*] T.B. Howell, *A Complete Collection of State Trials and Proceedings for High Treason and Other Crimes and Misdemeanors from the Earliest Period to the Present Time*, 21 vols (London: T.C. Hansard, 1816), xiv. cols 1325–26.

29. *Cobbett's Complete Collection*, xiv. col. 1328.

30. On cruentation, see Malcolm Gaskill, *Crime and Mentalities in Early Modern England* (Cambridge: Cambridge University Press, 2000), 203–40; and Margaret Ingram, 'Bodies That Speak: Early Modern European Gender Distinctions in Bleeding Corpses and Demoniacs' (MA Thesis: University of Oregon, 2017), 158–59; see also Robert P. Brittain, 'Cruentation in Legal Medicine and in Literature', *Medical History*, 9 (1965), 82–88; Winston Black, 'Animated Corpses and Bodies with Power in the Scholastic Age', in Joëlle Rollo-Koster (ed.), *Death in Medieval Europe: Death Scripted and Death Choreographed,* (London: Routledge, 2017), 71–92; and Nancy Mandeville Caciola, *Afterlives: The Return of the Dead in the Middle Ages* (Ithaca, NY: Cornell University Press, 2016); see also Paul Barber, *Vampires, Burial, and Death: Folklore and Reality*, 2nd edn (New Haven, CT, and London: Yale University Press, 2010), 122.

31. For a wide-ranging account, see Chris Cooper, *Blood: A Very Short Introduction* (Oxford: Oxford University Press, 2016).

32. Pliny, 'Remedies from Animals', in *Natural History*, trans. W.H.S. Jones, 10 vols, Loeb Classical Library (Cambridge, MA: Harvard University Press, and London: William Heinemann, 1963), viii. 5 (see Bks XXVIII–XXIX, which list hundreds of applications of blood). See Hermann L. Strack, *The Jew and Human Sacrifice (Human Blood and Jewish Ritual): An Historical and Sociological Inquiry*, trans. Henry Blanchamp ([1891; first translation of rev. 8th edn] London: Cope and Fenwick, 1909), 50, 52, 62–65); and especially Richard Sugg, *Mummies, Cannibals, and Vampires: The History of Corpse Medicine from the Renaissance to the Victorians* (London and New York: Routledge, 2011), 278–85. On Elizabeth Báthory see Raymond McNally, *Dracula was a Woman: In Search of the Blood Countess of Transylvania* (New York: McGraw-Hill, 1983); see also Strack, *The Jew and Human Sacrifice*, 89–91 (from an account published in Vienna in 1796); and Sabine Baring-Gould below, pp. 132, 173.

33. Biale, *Blood and Belief*, 100–01.

34. Strack, *The Jew and Human Sacrifice*, 62.

35. Strack, *The Jew and Human Sacrifice*, 54–55.

36. Strack, *The Jew and Human Sacrifice*, 70–76.

37. Strack, *The Jew and Human Sacrifice*, 70–71. Strack gives further examples of this practice in Germany in the years 1755, 1823, 1844, 1859 and 1862.

38. See Kathy Stuart, *Defiled Trades and Social Outcasts: Honor and Ritual Pollution in Early Modern Germany* (Cambridge: Cambridge University Press, 1999), 158–59; Strack, *The Jew and Human Sacrifice*, 73–76; Francesca Matteoni, 'The Criminal Corpse in Pieces', *Mortality*, 21 (2016), 198–209; Peter Linebaugh, 'The Tyburn Riot against the Surgeons', in Douglas Hay, Peter Linebaugh, John G. Rule, E.P. Thompson and Cal Winslow, *Albion's Fatal Tree: Crime and Society in Eighteenth-Century England* (New York: Pantheon Books, 1975), 65–118; and, for a thorough account, Owen Davies and Francesca Matteoni, *Executing Magic in the Modern Era: Criminal Bodies and the Gallows in Popular Medicine* (Basingstoke: Palgrave Macmillan, 2017).

39. Stuart, *Defiled Trades and Social Outcasts*, 149–85, especially 156: as Biale puts it, 'Here the "polluted" trade of executioner took on a paradoxical healing function, as did the blood of criminals' (*Blood and Belief*, 100).

40. Strack, *The Jew and Human Sacrifice*, 157–58, 105–17. The use of the hearts of unborn children perhaps inspired M.R. James' chilling tale, 'Lost Hearts'.

41. See William Brockbank, 'Sovereign Remedies: A Critical Depreciation of the 17th-Century London Pharmacopoeia', *Medical History*, 8 (1964), 1–14.

42. Stuart, *Defiled Trades and Social Outcasts*, 160–61; see also Sugg, *Mummies, Cannibals, and Vampires*, 38–66.

43. Strack, *The Jew and Human Sacrifice*, 82–83.

44. Strack, *The Jew and Human Sacrifice*, 92–95.

45. Strack, *The Jew and Human Sacrifice*, 43.

46. See Klaus Oschema, 'Blood-Brothers: A Ritual of Friendship and the Construction of the Imagined Barbarian in the Middle Ages', *Journal of Medieval History*, 32 (2006), 275–301. The notion of blood-brethren has strong Christian significance in bonding through the blood of Christ; it is mentioned in the fourteenth-century English poem *Piers Plowman*.

47. Camporesi, *Juice of Life*; see also Cooper, *Blood*. Interestingly, the literal meaning of *haemophilia* is affection of or love for blood.

48. See, from a comparable – if different – perspective, G. David Keyworth, 'Was the Vampire of the Eighteenth Century a Unique Type of Undead-Corpse?', *Folklore*, 117 (2006), 241–260. For a kaleidoscopically wide-ranging account of folklore and physiology, see Barber, *Vampires, Burial, and Death*.

49. Vukanović, 'The Vampire', 234.

50. For a thorough account of Slovene blood-lore (with some passing Slovakian references), see Mojca Ramšak, 'Folk Explanations of Blood-Lands: The Map of Massacres and Bestial Cruelties', *Slovenský Národopis / Slovak Ethnology*, 64 (2016), 423–46.

51. Afanasev, 'Poetic Views of the Slavs', 197.

52. From Friedrich Lorentz, *The Cassubian Civilization* (London, 1935): see Jan Louis Perkowski, 'Vampires, Dwarves, and Witches Among the Ontario Kashubs' (1972), in *Vampire Lore*, 1–54, at 16–17 (also 207); see also Moszyński, 'Slavic Folk Culture', 214. Remarkably, Perkowski researched Kashubian daemonology by interviewing members of the Slavic Kashub diaspora in Canada, discovering that 'All of the lore found in Canada was imported from Europe' (6).

53. See Moszyński, 'Slavic Folk Culture'. There is also evidence that priests used an exorcism ritual from the 'Book of Thunder', but this volume has not been traced.

54. Afanasev, 'Poetic Views of the Slavs', 197.

55. Afanasev, 'Poetic Views of the Slavs', 199.

56. Afanasev, 'Poetic Views of the Slavs', 203.

57. Strack, *The Jew and Human Sacrifice*, 97.

58. Perkowski, *Vampire Lore*, 248–49; the term 'gypsies' is used in the original source and hence is followed here and in later chapters. Saints Cosmas and Damian were noted for their medical miracles, such as transplanting the leg of a dead Ethiopian to a European patient; accordingly, they were often made patrons of medical schools and hospitals.

59. Wright, *Vampires and Vampirism*, 107–08.

60. G.F. Abbott, *Macedonian Folklore* ([1903] Cambridge: Cambridge University Press, 2011), 217–21.

61. See L'upcho S. Risteski, 'Categories of the "Evil Dead" in Macedonian Folk Religion', in Gábor Klaniczay and Éva Pócs (eds), *Christian Demonology and Popular Mythology: Demons, Spirits, Witches*, vol. ii (Budapest and New York: Central European University Press, 2006), 202–12, at 207, quoting Tanas Vrazhinovski, Vladimir Karadzhoski, L'upcho S. Risteski and Lola Shimoska, *Narodna Demonologia na Makedonskite* ['Macedonian folk demonology'] (Skopje – Prilep: Knigoizdatelstvo 'Matitsa Makedonska' – Institut za Staroslovenska Kultura, 1995), 98.

62. Strack, *The Jew and Human Sacrifice*, 96–97.

63. Perkowski, *Vampire Lore*, 241.

64. Summers, *The Vampire in Europe*, 1.

65. *Encyclopædia Britannica* online: http://encyclopedia.jrank.org/TUM_VAN/VAMPIRE.html (accessed 10 October 2017): quoted by Dudley Wright, *Vampires and Vampirism*, 2nd edn (London: William Rider and Son, 1924), 2.

66. See, for example, Edward Ward, *The London-Spy Compleat* (London, 1700), pt iv, p. 1 (for February 1699) (see also my chapter 'Draining the Irish Sea: The Colonial Politics of Water', in Nicholas Allen, Nick Groom and Jos Smith (eds), *Coastal Works: Cultures of the Atlantic Edge* (Oxford: Oxford University Press, 2017), 20–39, at 25–26).

67. See Charles Davenant, *A Postscript to a Discourse of Credit, and the Means and Methods of Restoring it* (London, 1701); Johnson's *Dictionary* quotes 'Swift on Modern Education'.

68. In 1673, William Cave described 'man's life' as a 'fluid and transitory condition' (*Primitive Christianity: or, The Religion of the Ancient Christians in the First Ages of the Gospel*, ii. 31: see *OED*).

69. See Ben Woodard, *Slime Dynamics: Generation, Mutation, and the Creep of Life* (Winchester and Washington, DC: Zero Books, 2012), 17–18.

70. C.F. L'Homond warns that 'One single bad book is enough to pervert a thousand young people. It passes through a variety of hands; the contagion circulates, and infects a whole family' (*Theophilus, or The Pupil Instructed in the Principles, the Obligations, and the Resources of the Roman Catholic Religion*, trans. the Revd Appleton (also published as *Pious Lectures, explanatory of the Principles, Obligations and Resources, of the Catholic Religion*) (Wolverhampton, 1794), 225; see also Thomas Grady, *An Impartial*

View, of the Causes leading this Country to the Necessity of an Union; in which the Two Leading Characters of the State are Contrasted; and in which is contained, a History of the Rise and Progress of Orange Men; A Reply to Cease your Funning, and Mr. Jebb, 3rd edn (Dublin, 1799), 24.

71. Eugene Thacker, 'Ambient Plague', in *In the Dust of This Planet* [*Horror of Philosophy*, vol. 1] (Winchester and Washington, DC: Zero Books, 2011), 104–07, at 106.

72. Rosemary Horrox (ed. and trans.), *The Black Death* (Manchester: Manchester University Press, 1994), 182.

73. Horrox, *The Black Death*, 173–77, at 174; see Bishop of Aarhus, *A Litil Boke the whiche Traytied and Rehersed Many Gode Thinges necessaries for the . . . Pestilence . . . made by the . . . Bisshop of Arusiens . . .* [London, 1485?], facsimile ed. Guthrie Vine (Manchester: Manchester University Press, and London: Bernard Quaritch, and Sherratt and Hughes, 1910).

74. Horrox, *The Black Death*, 183–84.

75. Horrox, *The Black Death*, 184.

76. Horrox, *The Black Death*, 182–84, at 183–84.

77. Gabriele de' Mussis, in Horrox, *The Black Death*, 14–26, at 17 (quoted by Thacker, *In the Dust of This Planet*, 106).

78. Horrox, *The Black Death*, 184.

79. See Thacker, 'Ambient Plague', *In the Dust of This Planet*, 106; see also Emily Martin, *Flexible Bodies: Tracking Immunity in American Culture from the Days of Polio to the Age of AIDS* (Boston, MA: Beacon, 1994); Laura Otis, *Membranes: Metaphors of Invasion in Nineteenth-Century Literature, Science, and Politics* (Baltimore, MD: Johns Hopkins University Press, 1999); Ed Cohen, *A Body Worth Defending: Immunity, Biopolitics, and the Apotheosis of the Modern Body* (Durham, NC: Duke University Press, 2009); and Terence Ranger and Paul Slack (eds), *Epidemics and Ideas: Essays on the Historical Perception of Pestilence* (Cambridge: Cambridge University Press, 1992).

80. De' Mussis, in Horrox, *The Black Death*, 17.

81. Gideon Harvey, *A Discourse of the Plague* (London, 1665), 2.

82. Harvey, *Discourse of the Plague*, 16.

83. Harvey, *Discourse of the Plague*, 9, 7, 16.

84. Harvey, *Discourse of the Plague*, 8.

85. Paracelsus (Theophrastus Bombast von Hohenheim, 1493–1541) was a Swiss physician, alchemist and mystic who emphatically rejected classical medicine, replacing herbal remedies and humoural theory with pharmaceuticals (and incidentally claiming that the buckles on his shoes were more learned than Galen and Avicenna). According to the trenchant account of Paracelsus given by Elizabeth O'Mahoney, 'Drawing upon astrology, alchemy, metallurgy, folk medicine, Hermeticism, Gnosticism and Christianity, Paracelsus proposed a unique, if incoherent, chemical vision of the universe' ('Representations of Gender in Seventeenth-Century Netherlandish Alchemical Genre Painting', 2 vols (PhD thesis: University of York, 2005), i. 110). Nonetheless, this vision laid the foundations of later chemical science, distinguishing it from alchemy and traditional Galenic theories. (I owe this point to one of my anonymous readers for the press.)

86. N.S.R. Maluf, 'History of Blood Transfusion', *Journal of the History of Medicine*, 9 (1954), 59–107 (60); the first plausible account of blood transfusion was at Coburg, Saxony, in 1615 (59).

87. Titmuss, *The Gift Relationship*, 17.

88. Samuel Pepys, *The Diary of Samuel Pepys*, ed. John Warrington, 3 vols ([1906] London, Melbourne and Toronto: J.M. Dent and Sons, 1978), i. 362 (14 November 1666); see Alastair H.B. Masson, *A History of Blood Transfusion in Edinburgh* (Edinburgh: Blood Transfusion Service, n.d.), 1.

89. Letter from Henry Oldenburg to Robert Boyle, 25 November 1667, in *The Works of the Honourable Robert Boyle*, new edn, 6 vols (London, 1772), vi. 250 (Oldenburg gives the payment as a guinea); see Charles Richard Weld, *A History of the Royal Society, with Memoirs of the Presidents*, 2 vols (London: John W. Parker, 1848), i. 220–22.

90. Pepys, *Diary*, iii. 113 (21 November 1667).

91. See Edmund King, 'An Account of the Experiment of *Transfusion*, Practised upon a *Man* in *London*', *Philosophical Transactions*, 30 (9 December 1667), 557–59; see also Maluf, 'Blood Transfusion', 65; for Coga's comment see Thomas Birch, *The History of the Royal Society of London for improving of Natural Knowledge, from its First Rise*, 4 vols (London, 1756–57), ii. 214–16.

92. Coga's letter is printed in Pete Moore, *Blood and Justice: The Seventeenth-Century Parisian Doctor who Made Blood Transfusion History* (Chichester: John Wiley & Sons, 2003), 136–37; see Mary de Young, *Encyclopedia of Asylum Therapeutics, 1750–1950s* (Jefferson, NC: McFarland & Co., 2015), 58.

93. Titmuss, *The Gift Relationship*, 17.

94. Titmuss, *The Gift Relationship*, 18.
95. David Hamilton, *A History of Organ Transplantation: Ancient Legends to Modern Practice* (Philadelphia, PA: University of Pittsburgh Press, 2012), 29–30.

Chapter 1

1. King James Bible.
2. William Shakespeare, *King Lear*, in *Complete Works*, ed. Wells and Taylor, IV. ii. 25 (pp. 931, 965).
3. Thomas Hardy, 'What Did It Mean?', in *Late Lyrics and Earlier*, in *The Collected Poems of Thomas Hardy*, 4th edn (London: Macmillan and Company, 1930), 524–661, at 618.
4. For the most useful accounts, see primarily Barber, *Vampires, Burial, and Death*; other crucial accounts include Peter J. Bräunlein, 'The Frightening Borderlands of Enlightenment: The Vampire Problem', *Studies in History and Philosophy of Biological and Biomedical Sciences*, 43 (2012), 710–19; Erik Butler, *Metamorphoses of the Vampire in Literature and Film: Cultural Transformations in Europe, 1732–1933* (Rochester, NY: Camden House, 2010), especially 31–34; Christopher Frayling, *Vampyres: Lord Byron to Count Dracula* (London: Faber and Faber, 1991), 19–36; Klaus Hamberger, *Mortuus Non Mordet: Dokumente zum Vampirismus 1689–1791* (Vienna: Turia & Kant, 1992); Gábor Klaniczay's chapter 'The Decline of Witches and the Rise of Vampires under the Eighteenth-Century Habsburg Monarchy', in *Uses of Supernatural Power*, 168–88 (also published in *Ethnologia Europaea*, 17 (1987), 165–80), and his longer paper, 'Witch-Trials in Hungary (1520–1777): The Accusations and the Popular Universe of Magic', in Bengt Ankarloo and Gustav Henningsen (eds), *Early Modern European Witchcraft: Centres and Peripheries* (Oxford: Oxford University Press, 2001), 219–55; Elizabeth McCarthy, ' "Death to Vampires!": The Vampire Body and the Meaning of Mutilation', in Day (ed.), *Vampires*, 189–208; and Perkowski, *Vampire Lore*, especially Vukanović, 'The Vampire', 230–59.
5. Johann Weikhard von Valvasor recorded the case in his encyclopaedia *Die Ehre Deß Hertzogthums Crain: Das ist Wahre Gründliche und Recht eigendliche Gelegen- und Beschaffenheit dieses in manchen Alten und Neuen Geschicht-Büchern zwar rühmlich berührten doch bishero nie annoch recht beschriebenen Römisch-Keyserlichen herrlichen Erblandes: Anjetzo Vermittelst einer Vollkommenen und Ausführlichen Erzehlung aller seiner Landschafften . . . deß Welt-Berühmten Cirknitzer Wunder-Sees . . . ungemeiner Natur-Wunder imgleichen der Gewächse Mineralien Bergwercke Edelgesteine alter Müntz-Stücken Thiere . . . auch der Gebiete Herrschafften Schlösser Städte Märckten . . . Einwohner Sprachen Sitten Trachten Gewerben Handthierungen Religion . . . wie auch der Lands-Fürsten Jahr-Geschichte alter und neuer Denckwürdigkeiten* ['the glory of the Duchy of Carniola . . .'], 15 vols (Laybach and Nuremberg, 1689), ii. 335–36 (see also Perkowski, *Vampire Lore*, 417–18); contextualizing another early-eighteenth-century incident, see Stephen Gordon, 'Emotional Practice and Bodily Performance in Early Modern Vampire Literature', *Preternature: Critical and Historical Studies on the Preternatural*, 6 (2017), 93–124, at 104.
6. See Gordon, 'Emotional Practice and Bodily Performance', 104; and Beresford, *From Demons to Dracula*, 99: Beresford cites Wayne Bartlett and Flavia Idriceanu, *Legends of Blood: The Vampire in History and Myth* (Stroud: Sutton, 2005).
7. Klaniczay, *Uses of Supernatural Power*, 179.
8. Quoted by Perkowski, *Vampire Lore*, 419, from Ján Mjartan, 'Vampírske Povery v Zemplíne', *Slovenský Národopis*, 1 (1953), 133; according to Gordon, 'Emotional Practice and Bodily Performance', 'Recent excavations at Drawsko in northwest Poland (ca. 1600–1700) . . . have uncovered six deviant or "vampire" burials from a cemetery of over 330 bodies' (108).
9. University of Leipzig, 16 August 1679: see Summers, *The Vampire in Europe*, 178–206; shroud-eating is already noted in the *Malleus Maleficarum*: see Heinrich Kramer (alias 'Henricus Institoris') and Jacob Sprenger, *The Malleus Maleficarum*, ed. and trans. P.G. Maxwell-Stuart (Manchester and New York: Manchester University Press, 2007), pt 1, qu. 15, at p. 103.
10. Summers quotes at length from Phillip Rohr, *Dissertatio De Masticatione Mortuorum* (University of Leipzig, 16 August 1679): see *The Vampire in Europe*, 178–206, especially 184 and 196, and see also 198–99; Summers also notes further biblical precedents.
11. See discussion in Summers, *The Vampire in Europe*, 201–06; narrative structures of later Gothic novels are frequently embroiled in issues of authentication and veracity.
12. Roger North, *The Life of the Honourable Sir Dudley North, Knt. . . . and of the Honourable and Reverend Dr. John North . . .* (London, 1744), 125.

13. This elusive book was published in Olmütz in 1704 (not, as stated, on the title page, 1706; the MS is dated 1703): see Giuseppe Maiello, *Vampyrismus & Magia Posthuma: Vampyrismus v Kulturních Dějinách Evropy* (Prague: Nakladatelství Epocha, 2014); see also Giuseppe Maiello, 'Racionalismus Karla Ferdinanda Schertze a *Magia Posthuma*' ('Karl Ferdinand Schertz's Rationalism and *Magia Posthuma*'), *Slavica Litteraria*, 5 (2012), 215–22. Calmet (1751) seems to have popularized the volume (Dom Augustin Calmet, *Dissertations upon the Apparitions of Angels, Dæmons, and Ghosts, and Concerning the Vampires of Hungary, Bohemia, Moravia, and Silesia* (London, 1759), 33–36 – currently available in English in a reprint of the nineteenth-century translation, *The Phantom World: Concerning Apparitions and Vampires* (London: Wordsworth Editions, 2001).

14. Schertz's rationalism influenced Calmet (see below, pp. 79–80), through whose work *Magia Posthuma* became a standard (if rarely read) reference point for vampirological treatises – indeed Sheridan Le Fanu refers to *Magia Posthuma* in his narrative 'Carmilla' (see below, p. 146): see Maiello, 'Racionalismus Karla Ferdinanda Schertze a *Magia Posthuma*', 219–20; Calmet's copy of *Magia Posthuma* survives in the Bibliothèque municipale de Nancy.

15. *Pestis Dacicae anni 1709 Scrutinim e Cura* (*Examination and Relief of the Plague of 1709 in Dacia*), cited by Matei Cazacu, *Dracula*, ed. Stephen W. Reinert, trans. Nicole Mordarski, Stephen W. Reinert, Alice Brinton and Catherine Healey (Leiden and Boston, MA: Brill, 2017), 282.

16. Joseph Pitton de Tournefort, *A Voyage into the Levant: perform'd by Command of the late French King*, 2 vols (London, 1718; reprinted in 3 vols London, 1741), i. 103–07 (3 vol. text: i. 142–48), at i. 103; for an interesting and idiosyncratic reading of Tournefort, see Gordon, 'Emotional Practice and Bodily Performance', 93–124. The phenomenon of the *vrykolakas* is first recorded in the mid-seventeenth century: see Leo Allatius, *De Quorumdam Graecorum Opinationibus* (1645), and Fr Francois Richard, SJ, *Relation de l'Isle de Sant-Erini* (1657), cited by Keyworth, 'Was the Vampire a Unique Type of Undead-Corpse?', 249.

17. Tournefort, *Voyage into the Levant* (1718), i. 144.

18. W.F. Bynum, *Science and the Practice of Medicine in the Nineteenth Century* (Cambridge: Cambridge University Press, 1994), 59.

19. See 'A Note on the Etymology of the Word *Vampire*', above pp. xv–xvii.

20. Rzączyński, *Historia Naturalis Curiosa Regni Poloniæ*, 365 (section II): see Perkowski, *Vampire Lore*, 430–31.

21. Hamberger, *Mortuus Non Mordet*, 8.

22. Barber, *Vampires, Burial, and Death*, 9: 'still other wild signs (which I pass by out of high respect)'; Sam George and Bill Hughes (eds), *Open Graves, Open Minds: Representations of Vampires and the Undead from the Enlightenment to the Present Day* (Manchester and New York: Manchester University Press, 2013), 10–11; Bräunlein, 'Frightening Borderlands', 713; see Hamberger, *Mortuus Non Mordet*, 43–46 (Hamberger has 'Vanpiri'). Plogojowitz's name is variously spelt. On 31 March 1725, a report began into a female undead bloodsucker that was terrorizing the Romanian village of Herinbiesch; though the report was completed on 10 April, this case did not attract the same publicity: see https://www.shroudeater.com/cherinb.htm and http://equiamicus.blogspot.co.uk/2008/09/kisolova-1725-die-geburtsstunde-des.html (accessed 13 February 2018).

23. Barber translates the text of the case, taken from 1728 (*Vampires, Burial, and Death*, 6–7); the second skin is a post-mortem effect known as 'skin slippage' (13).

24. Summarized by Calmet, *Dissertations*, 198–99; see also Summers, *The Vampire in Europe*, 147–49 (although Summers misquotes the name).

25. After Egbert van Heemskerck: see British Library, call number 1866,0407.52.

26. For a description of the filthiness of the dissecting room some years later, see the Introduction to Mary Shelley, *Frankenstein; or, The Modern Prometheus*, ed. Nick Groom (Oxford: Oxford University Press, 2018), xxi.

27. Paul Ricaut, *The Present State of the Greek and Armenian Churches* (London, 1679), 276–83, at 277–78.

28. Ricaut, *Present State of the Greek and Armenian Churches*, 280.

29. Ricaut, *Present State of the Greek and Armenian Churches*, 282–83.

30. Richard Gough, *Sepulchral Monuments in Great Britain applied to illustrate the History of Families, Manners, Habits, and Arts, at the Different Periods from the Norman Conquest to the Seventeenth Century*, 2 vols (London, 1786–96), i. lxxvi–lxxxii: this could be attributed to post-mortem saponification causing spontaneous mummification, or to the related putrefaction process of adipocere formation of wax; Gough himself goes on to describe the ossuaries and crypts of the Capuchins, renowned for their funerary art (see Matthew Lewis, *The Monk*, ed. Nick Groom (Oxford: Oxford University Press, 2016), 356n.).

31. John Maubray, *The Female Physician, containing all the Diseases incident to that Sex, in Virgins, Wives, and Widows; together with their Causes and Symptoms, their Degrees of Danger, and respective Methods of Prevention and Cure* (London, 1730), 373–74, 375.

32. Maubray, *The Female Physician*, 376–377.

33. 'Arminius', 'On Some Popular Superstitions, more particularly on that relating to Vampyres or Blood-Suckers', *The Athenæum*, 2 (July 1807), 19–26, at 22–23.

34. Variously appearing as Medveyga or Meduegna, and in other forms (see below), none of which are either Serbian or Hungarian spellings; also rendered 'Metwett' in German; in fact it is Medvedja, near Svetozarevo, formerly Jagodina, in Serbia.

35. Perkowski, *The Darkling*, at 29–30; see also Barber, *Vampires, Burial, and Death*, 16.

36. Spelt thus in 'Putoneo' [J.C. Meinig], *Besondere Nachricht von denen Vampyren oder so genannten Blut-Saugern* (Leipzig, 1732), but again there are variations in spelling: Siedel, for instance, also appears as Sigel.

37. Official Habsburg military report by 'Putoneo' [J.C. Meinig], *Von denen Vampyren*, 8–15; Barber translates a text from 1732 (*Vampires, Burial, and Death*, 16–18).

38. Barber, *Vampires, Burial, and Death*, 16–18; see also Summers, *The Vampire in Europe*, 149–56: again, there are some variations in names.

39. Flückinger's report was dated 7 January 1732; Lt-Col. Büttener and J.H. von Lindenfels of the Honourable Alexandrian Regiment countersigned the document (26 January 1732).

40. See Antoine Faivre, 'Du Vampire Villageois aux Discours des Clercs', in [collective work] *Les Vampires* (Paris: Albin Michel, 1993), 45–74.

41. Michael Ranft, *De Masticatione Mortuorum in Tumulis (oder von dem Kauen und Schmatzen der Todten in Gräbern,) liber singularis: Duas Exhibens Exceritationes, quarum Prior Historico-Critica Posterior Philosophica* (Leipzig, 1725); it was reprinted in 1728.

42. Morawa is the river Morava, or Moravia. Michael Ranft, *Tractat von dem Kauen und Schmatzen der Todten in Gräbern, worin die wahre Beschaffenheit derer Hungarischen Vampyrs und Blut-Sauger gezeiget, Auch alle von dieser Materie bißher zum Vorschein gekommene Schrifften recensiret werden* (Leipzig, 1734), a revised and expanded edition of his two-part work *De masticatione mortuorum in tumulis*: see Vukanović, 'The Vampire', in Perkowski, *Vampire Lore*, 234.

43. Calmet, *Dissertations*, 202.

44. For translations of the report on Paole see Wright, *Vampires and Vampirism*, 2nd edn (1924), 95–105; and Perkowski, *Vampire Lore*, 345; for use of the term 'gypsies', see above p. 211n.

45. Barber, *Vampires, Burial, and Death*, 18.

46. Letter of 13 February 1732 to the editor of *Commercium Literarium ad Rei Medicae et Scientiae*: see Bräunlein, 'Frightening Borderlands', 714; and Hamberger, *Mortuus Non Mordet*, 54–55 (translated by Bräunlein and Emma Spary).

47. Milan V. Dimić, 'Vampiromania in the Eighteenth Century: The Other Side of Enlightenment', *Man and Nature / L'Homme et la nature*, 3 (1984) 1–22.

48. Among others, Johann Christian Stock, *Dissertatio de Cadaueribus Sanguisugis* (Jena, 1732); *Relation von den Vampyren oder Menschensaugern* (Leipzig, 1732); *Relation von denen in Servien sich erzeigenden Blutsaugern* (1732); *Besondere Nachricht von denen vampyren oder Sogenannten Blut-Saugeren* (1732); *Uisus et repertus über die sogenannten Vampyren* (Nuremberg, 1732); Johann Christoph Rohl and Johann Hertel, *Dissertatio de hominibus post mortem sanguisugis, vulgo dictis Uampyrea* (Leipzig, 1732); Johann Heinrich Zopf (and Christian Friedrich van Dalen), *Dissertatio de Vampyris Serviensibus* (Duisberg, 1733); Ranft, *Tractat*; Johann Christoph Harenberg, *Von Vampyren* (1739): see Summers, *The Vampire in Europe*, 132–33 (list revised; however, some of these titles seem to have been taken from earlier bibliographies, such as Johann Georg Theodor Grässe, *Bibliotheca Magica et Pneumatica oder wissenschaftlich geordnete Bibliographie der wichtigsten in das Gebiet der Zauber-, Wunder-, Geister- und sonstigen Aberglaubens vorzüglich älterer Zeit einschlagenden Werke: mit Angabe der aus diesen Wissenschaften auf der Königl. Sächs. Oeff. Bibliothek zu Dresden befindlichen Schriften; ein Beitrag zur sittengeschichtlichen Literatur* (Leipzig: Engelmann, 1843), 20–24, but are currently untraced); see also Hamberger, *Mortuus Non Mordet*, 271–86.

49. Bräunlein, 'Frightening Borderlands', 715.

50. Lewis Walpole Library, MSS 1b (Series I) Box 21, Folder 3 (photostat of letter to Upper Ossory, Anne (Liddell) Fitzroy Fitzpatrick, Countess, 16 Jan 1785; original in private hands (1965); modernized version printed in *Horace Walpole's Correspondence with the Countess of Upper Ossory*, II, ed. W.S. Lewis and A. Dayle Wallace, with Edwine M. Martz (New Haven, CT: Yale University Press, and London: Oxford University Press, 1965), 508 (*Horace Walpole's Correspondence*, ed. W.S. Lewis, et al. 48 vols

(New Haven, CT: Yale University Press, and London: Oxford University Press, 1937–1983), xxxiii). George II's interest may have reflected the fact that he was Elector of Hanover and so maintained strong German connections.

51. See 'Caleb D'Anvers' [Nicholas Amhurst], *The Craftsman*, 14 vols, no. 307 (Saturday, 20 May 1732), ix. 120–29, at 120; 'Heyducken' is an error, turning '*hajduk*' into the name of a place. For other notices see *Gentleman's Magazine*, 2 (March 1732): 'From *Medreyga* in *Hungary*, That certain dead Bodies called *Vampyres*, had kill'd several Persons by sucking out all their Blood' (681); and the *Gentleman's Magazine*, 2 (May 1732), which reprints the report from *The Craftsman*, 307 (20 May) and refers back to the *London Journal* (11 March) (750–52).

52. 'D'Anvers', *The Craftsman*, ix. 124.

53. 'D'Anvers', *The Craftsman*, ix. 127.

54. *Applebee's Journal* (27 May 1732): reprinted in the *Gentleman's Magazine*, 2 (May 1732), 755.

55. *The Political State of Great Britain*, 43 (1732), 278–80 (March); Flückinger is given as 'Flickhenger, *Surgeon Major to the Regiment of Furstemburch*', the other names may be satirical.

56. Charles Forman, *A Second Letter to the Right Honourable Sir Robert Walpole* (London, 1733), 38; see also Charles Hornby, *A Third Letter, containing some further Remarks on a Few More of the Numberless Errors and Defects in Dugdale's Baronage: with Occasional Observations on some other Authors* (London, 1738), 205.

57. Charles Forman, *Some Queries and Observations upon the Revolution in 1688, and its Consequences: Also a Short View of the Rise and Progress of the Dutch East India Company; with Critical Remarks* (London: Olive Payne, 1741), 11n. (this is briefly mentioned in George and Hughes (eds), *Open Graves, Open Minds*, 12–13; see also Butler, *Metamorphoses of the Vampire*, 52–53; and Markman Ellis, *The History of Gothic Fiction* (Edinburgh: Edinburgh University Press, 2000), 162–68).

58. Charles Hornby, *Three Letters, containing Remarks on Some of the Numberless Errors and Defects in Dugdale's Baronage: and occasionally on Some Other Authors* (London, 1738), 205.

59. Alexander Pope to William Oliver, 25 February 1740: see *The Works of Alexander Pope*, ed. Whitwell Elwin and William John Courthope, with John Wilson Croker, new edn, 10 vols (London: John Murray, 1871–89), x. 243.

60. The term 'Habsburg Empire' is used throughout this account for what was later (in 1867) known as Austria-Hungary; during this period, the Habsburg dynasty governed territories both within the Holy Roman Empire and beyond its borders.

61. Oliver Goldsmith, *The Citizen of the World; or Letters from a Chinese Philosopher, residing in London, to his Friends in the East*, 2 vols (London, 1762), i. 209, ii. 66; the essays were first published in the *Public Ledger*, 1760–61.

62. Henry Fielding, *The Debauchees: or, The Jesuit Caught* (London, 1750), 3; for Sandwich's racehorse, see John Pond, *The Sporting Calendar* (London, 1751), 31, 69; and Reginald Heber, *An Historical List of Horse-Matches Run* (London, 1752), 64, 110, 121, 124.

Chapter 2

1. William Shakespeare, *Hamlet*, in *Complete Works*, ed. Wells and Taylor, III. ii. 377–81 (p. 674).

2. The classic essay here is Stephen Arata, 'The Occidental Tourist; *Dracula* and the Anxiety of Reverse Colonization', *Victorian Studies*, 33 (1990), 621–45; see also especially Ailise Bulfin, *Gothic Invasions: Imperialism, War and Fin-de-Siècle Popular Fiction* (Cardiff: University of Wales Press, 2018). Sam George and Bill Hughes also argue that their approach 'is dominated by the figure of the undead as political metaphor in the realm of identity and difference, the trope of reflection and the sympathetic vampire' (George and Hughes (eds), *Open Graves, Open Minds*, 2).

3. See, for example, Jennifer Lipka, 'Joseph Conrad's *Heart of Darkness* as a Gothic Novel', *Conradiana*, 40 (2008), 25–37.

4. Only the Ionian Islands (1815–62) and Cyprus (1878–1960) were ever part of the British Empire.

5. Camm, Dom Bede (ed.), *Lives of the English Martyrs Declared Blessed by Pope Leo XIII in 1886 and 1895*, 2 vols (London: Burns and Oates; New York, Cincinnati and Chicago: Benziger Brothers, 1904–05), i. *Martyrs under Henry VIII*, 394; Phillip [*sic*] Stubbes, *Anatomy of the Abuses in England in Shakspere's Youth, A.D. 1583*, 2 vols in 3, ed. Frederick J. Furnivall (London: New Shakspere Society, 1877–82), i. 64 (see John Foxe, *Actes and Monuments . . .* (1583), sig. ¶ iiij [p. 23]: *John Foxe's The Acts and Monuments Online*, https://www.johnfoxe.org/).

6. See Stephen F. Schneck, 'Body Politic', in Michael T. Gibbons et al. (eds), *The Encyclopedia of Political Thought*, 8 vols [continuously paginated] (New York: Wiley-Blackwell, 2015), 362; Shakespeare uses

the image in *Coriolanus*: see, for example, Andrew Gurr, '*Coriolanus* and the Body Politic', *Shakespeare Survey*, 28 (1975), 63–70; and Mareile Pfannebaker, 'Cyborg Coriolanus/Monster Body Politic', in Stefan Herbrechter and Ivan Callus (eds), *Posthumanist Shakespeares* (Basingstoke: Palgrave Macmillan, 2012), 114–32.

7. Eugene Thacker, *Tentacles Longer Than Night* [*Horror of Philosophy*, vol. 3] (Winchester and Washington, DC: Zero Books, 2015), 37–38.

8. Henry Sacheverell, *The Political Union. A Discourse shewing the Dependance* [sic] *of Government on Religion in General: and of the English Monarchy on the Church of England in Particular* (Oxford, 1702), 50.

9. Thacker, *Tentacles Longer Than Night*, 44–48, at 46; he goes on to suggest that '*the body politic implies an anatomical framework that it is always attempting to supersede*' (47) (italicized in original).

10. Thacker, *Tentacles Longer Than Night*, 48.

11. Thacker, *Tentacles Longer Than Night*, paraphrasing 48; Thacker accordingly calls for a '*necrology* of the body politic' – the body politic as the living dead (52) (my emphasis).

12. The Treaty concluded the Seventh Ottoman–Venetian War (1714–18) and the Austro–Turkish War (1716–18). See Hamberger, *Mortuus Non Mordet*; and Jutta Nowosadtko, 'Der "Vampyrus Serviensis" und sein Habitat: Impressionen von der Österreichischen Militärgrenze', *Arbeitskreis Militär und Gesellschaft in der frühen Neuzeit e.V.*, 8 (2004), 151–67.

13. Bräunlein, 'Borderlands of Enlightenment', 712.

14. This comment is inspired by Steven Shakespeare, who suggestively quotes Friedrich Wilhelm Joseph Schelling on the notion of ground in a phrase that resonates with vampiric possibilities: 'When ground is elevated over existence "a life emerges which, though individual, is, however, false, a life of mendacity, a growth of restlessness and decay"'. See 'The Light that Illuminates Itself, the Dark that Soils Itself: Blackened Notes from Schelling's Underground', in Nicola Masciandaro (ed.), *Hideous Gnosis: Black Metal Theory Symposium I* (no place, no date; open access), 5–22, at 20 (quoting Schelling, *Philosophical Investigations into the Essence of Human Freedom*, trans. and ed. Jeff Love and Johannes Schmidt (Albany: State University of New York Press, 2006), 34); the passage goes on to discuss disease.

15. See Bräunlein, 'Borderlands of Enlightenment', especially 710–12.

16. Bräunlein, 'Borderlands of Enlightenment', 712: see Hamberger, *Mortuus Non Mordet*, 9–10 (translated by Bräunlein and Spary).

17. Zopf, *Dissertatio de Vampyris Serviensibus*: quoted by Summers, *The Vampire, His Kith and Kin*, 1; see also Johann Heinrich Zopf, *Dissertatio Physico-Theologica de eo quod Iustum est circa Cruentationem Cadaverum* (Duisburg, 1737).

18. [Anon.], 'The Travels of Three English Gentlemen, from Venice to Hamburgh, being the Grand Tour of Germany, in the Year 1734', in *The Harleian Miscellany or, A Collection of Rare, Curious, and Entertaining Pamphlets and Tracts, as well in Manuscript as in Print, found in the late Earl of Oxford's Library*, 8 vols (London, 1744–46), iv. 348–59, v. 321–45, at iv. pp. 358–59.

19. See Johann Christoph Harenberg, *Vernünftige und Christliche Gedanken über die Vampirs Oder Blutsaugende Todten* (Wolffenbüttel, 1733).

20. See C.B. Elliott, *Travels in the Three Great Empires of Austria, Russia, and Turkey*, 2 vols (London: Richard Bentley, 1838), i. *A Voyage Down the Danube, with Travels in Hungary, Wallachia, Moldavia, Southern Russia, Crim Tartary, and Turkey in Europe*, 105 (see Klaniczay, *Uses of Supernatural Power*, 183).

21. Robert Beverley, *The History of Virginia, in Four Parts*, 2nd edn (London, 1722), 121; Calmet mentions Johann Christoph Harenberg's *Philosophicæ et Christianæ Cogitationes de Vampiriis* (*Philosophical and Christian Reflections concerning Vampires*) (Leipzig, 1733; untraced), which seems to make a comparable argument (Calmet, *Dissertations*, 205): see below, pp. 79–80.

22. It is variously known as Jamestown weed or jimsonweed; angel or devil's trumpet; devil's cucumber, snare, or weed; and thorn-apple.

23. *Glaneur Historique*, 9 (1733): quoted by Calmet, *Dissertations*, 213–15, at 213.

24. John Bond, *Essay on the Incubus, or Night-Mare* (London, 1753), [vi]; see Jean Baptiste de Boyer, marquis d'Argens, *The Jewish Spy: being A Philosophical, Historical and Critical Correspondence, by Letters which lately pass'd between certain Jews in Turkey, Italy, France, &c. Translated from the Originals into French, by the Marquis D'Argens; and now done into English*, 5 vols (1739–40), iv. 122–32, at 127–28 (letter 137) (originally published as *Lettres Juives* (1737); also published as *Jewish Letters: or, A Correspondence Philosophical, Historical and Critical, betwixt a Jew and his Correspondents, in Different Parts*, 4 vols (Newcastle, 1739–44), iii. 238–47).

25. D'Argens, *The Jewish Spy*, iv. 130–31. This notion is developed by Wright, who claims that some regions have soil that preserves corpses as shown by the disinterments at a monastic chapel in Toulouse

in 1789 (see *Vampires and Vampirism*, 2nd edn (1924), 214; see also Butler, *Metamorphoses of the Vampire*, 49 n. 24).

26. See Ranft, *Tractat* (see above, pp. 35–36), cited by Klaniczay, *Uses of Supernatural Power*, 183; see Georg Oesterdiekhoff, *Traditionales Denken und Modernisierung: Jean Piaget und die Theorie der sozialen Evolution* (1992) and *Kulturelle Evolution des Geistes. Die historische Wechselwirkung von Psyche und Gesellschaft*, 2nd edn (2006), translated as *Mental Growth of Humankind in History* (open access), 265–66.

27. For Aristotle, see Noga Arikha, *Passions and Tempers: A History of the Humours* (New York: HarperCollins, 2007), 37.

28. See Perkowski, *Vampire Lore*, 400–17; Perkowski's translation is from Ante Liepopili, 'Vukodlaci' in *Zbornik za Narodni Život i Običaje Južnih Slavena*, 13 (Zagreb: Knižarnica Jugoslavenske Akademije, 1918), 277–90.

29. Perkowski, *Vampire Lore*, 408; testimonies were taken well into 1738.

30. Perkowski, *Vampire Lore*, 413–14; van Swieten later compared the spread of vampire infection in cemeteries to scabies.

31. One of the churches at which penance was to be paid was dedicated to the medical Saints Cosmas and Damian (see above, pp. 13–14).

32. Sceptics included in Italy Giuseppe Danvanzati, author of *Dissertazione sopra i Vampiri* (Naples, 1774) (see below, pp. 74–77), and Lodovico Antonio Muratori in Italy: see Klaniczay, *Uses of Supernatural Power*, 177.

33. Biale, *Blood and Belief*, 100: see Arlette Farge and Jacques Revel, *The Vanishing Children of Paris: Rumour and Politics before the French Revolution*, trans. Claudia Miéville (Cambridge, MA: Harvard University Press 1991).

34. Reay Tannahill, *Flesh and Blood: A History of the Cannibal Complex*, rev. edn (London: Abacus, 1996), 87; see Sugg, *Mummies, Cannibals, and Vampires*, 297n.

35. Klaniczay, *Uses of Supernatural Power*, 170–83.

36. Bynum, *Science and the Practice of Medicine*, 10. In 2007 the euro commemorated Gerard van Swieten.

37. Frank T. Brechka, *Gerard van Swieten and His World: 1700–1772* (The Hague: Martinus Nijhof, 1970), 132.

38. Klaniczay, *Uses of Supernatural Power*, 183, 174; see also 237n., giving van Swieten's citation of Tournefort.

39. See Gerhard van Swieten, *Vampyrismus*, ed. Piero Violante (Palermo: Flaccovio, 1988) (cited by Fernando Vidal, 'Extraordinary Bodies and the Physicotheological Imagination', in Lorraine Daston and Gianna Pomata (eds), *The Faces of Nature in Enlightenment Europe* (Berlin: Berliner Wissenschafts-Verlag, 2003), 61–96, at 78); see also Hamberger, *Mortuus Non Mordet*, 85–86.

40. Klaniczay, *Uses of Supernatural Power*, 170–71, 177.

41. Klaniczay, *Uses of Supernatural Power*, 173: translated by Klaniczay from István Weszprémi, *Magyarország és Erdély orvosainak rövid életrajza. Második száz (Short Biography of the Doctors of Hungary and Transylvania. Second hundred)* (Budapest, 1962), 110–11. Notwithstanding this, there was a spate of demoniac possession in Southern Germany in the mid-1770s.

42. H.C. Erik Midelfort, *Exorcism and Enlightenment: Johann Joseph Gassner and the Demons of Eighteenth-Century Germany* (New Haven, CT, and London: Yale University Press, 2005), 83.

43. Klaniczay, *Uses of Supernatural Power*, 171–72.

44. Klaniczay, *Uses of Supernatural Power*, 179, 175 – although here Klaniczay's thinking is somewhat blurred by trying to incorporate archaic pre-vampire cases within modern vampirological analysis. However, he does note that a handful of vampire cases were publicized across Europe while continuing witch-trials and burnings in Hungary were at the same time ignored, observing that it is a 'curious fact that the abolition of Hungarian witch-trials was related to the scandals concerning vampires' and arguing that these 'two different magical accounts of evil were related to each other'. More than two-thirds of the 1,700 known Hungarian witch-trials were held between 1690 and 1760; this was considerably later than the rest of Europe, where trials peaked during the Thirty Years' War (1618–48). Half of the Hungarian trials ended in execution or the death in prison of those convicted. There were Hungarian witch panics in the 1720s and 1730s (including a mass burning in 1728 of 14 witches in Szeged). Van Swieten's work coincided with a second wave that began in 1755 (*Uses of Supernatural Power*, 168–69). Klaniczay consequently argues that vampire beliefs provided an alternative to witchcraft, which increasingly appeared to be either fantastical or simply fraudulent. Vampirism thereby replaced superstitions of diabolical possession and orgiastic rituals with the empiricism of medical conditions, mass homicide and fears of epidemic contagion (*Uses of Supernatural Power*, 185–87; see

Keith Thomas, *Religion and the Decline of Magic: Studies in Popular Beliefs in Sixteenth and Seventeenth Century England* (Oxford: Oxford University Press, 1971), 578–79).

45. Georg Tallar, *Visum repertum anatomico-chirurgicum von den sogenannten Vampier, oder Moroi in der Wallachei, Siebenbürgen und Banat, welche eine eigens dahin abgeordnete Untersuchungskomission der löbl. K. K. Administration in Jahre 1756 erstattet hat* (Vienna/Leipzig, 1784): see Klaniczay, *Uses of Supernatural Power*, 180–81; Barber has a short translation of Tallar on decomposition (*Vampires, Burial, and Death*, 40).

46. Interestingly, Voltaire later derived vampires from Greece – not classical Greece, but schismatic Orthodox Christian Greece and the belief that corpses of excommunicants did not decay (see below, p. 31).

47. Costantino Grimaldi, *Dissertazione in cui si Investiga . . . Magia Diabolica . . . Magia Artificiale e Naturale* (Rome, 1751), 68: cited by Francesco Paolo de Ceglia, 'The Archbishop's Vampires: Giuseppe Davanzati's *Dissertation* and the Reaction of "Scientific" Italian Catholicism to the "Moravian Events"', *Archives Internationales d'Histoire des Sciences*, 61 (2011), 487–510, at 507 (trans. Ceglia and Sara Donahue).

48. Hamberger, *Mortuus Non Mordet*, 31 (translated by Bräunlein and Spary, revised by myself).

49. For the wider context here, see Nenad Ristović, 'Latin and Vernacular Relations in the Eighteenth and Nineteenth Centuries: The Serbian Case', in Gábor Almási and Lav Šubarić (eds), *Latin at the Crossroads of Identity: The Evolution of Linguistic Nationalism in the Kingdom of Hungary* (Leiden: Brill, 2015), 256–77.

50. Hamberger, *Mortuus Non Mordet*, 112: trans. Butler, *Metamorphoses of the Vampire*, 29–30.

51. Bräunlein, 'Borderlands of Enlightenment', 717; and Butler, *Metamorphoses of the Vampire*, 30. In the important chapter 'Ambient Plague', which has inspired some of the thinking here and provided salient sources, Thacker also discusses 'a generalized militarization of public health' (Thacker, *In the Dust of This Planet*, 104–07, at 105).

52. The Vlad Țepeș connection was first made in one of the earliest books of scholarship devoted to *Dracula*, Radu Florescu and Raymond T. McNally, *In Search of Dracula: A True History of Dracula and Vampire Legends* (Greenwich, CT: New York Graphic Society, 1972), though it has since been fiercely disputed. However, for the spread of the legend of Vlad Țepeș in the nineteenth century, see Cristina Artenie, *Dracula Invades England: The Text, the Context, and the Readers* (Montreal: Universitas Press, 2015) and Cristina Artenie, *Dracula: A Study of Editorial Practices* (Montreal: Universitas Press, 2016); for other stories see Sabine Baring-Gould, *The Book of Werewolves* (Stroud: Nonsuch, 2007), first published in 1865; for the later identification of Dracula with Țepeș, see Nárcisz Fejes, 'Lasting Legacies: Vlad Țepeș and Dracula in Romanian National Discourse', in Marcel Cornis-Pope and John Neubauer (eds), *History of the Literary Cultures of East-Central Europe: Junctures and Disjunctures in the 19th and 20th Centuries*, vol. iv: *Types and Stereotypes* (Amsterdam and Philadelphia, PA: John Benjamins Publishing Company, 2004), 333–42.

53. Alberto Fortis, *Travels into Dalmatia; containing General Observations on the Natural History of that Country and the Neighbouring Islands; the Natural Productions, Arts, Manners and Customs of the Inhabitants: in a Series of Letters from Abbe Alberto Fortis, to the Earl of Bute, the Bishop of Londonderry, John Strange, Esq. &c. &c* (London, 1774), 61–62.

54. Joseph Lavallée, *Travels in Istria and Dalmatia; Drawn Up from the Itinerary of L.F. Cassas* (London: Richard Phillips, 1805), 13.

55. Inigo Born, *Travels through the Bannat of Temeswar, Transylvania, and Hungary, in the year 1770*, trans. R.E. Raspe (London, 1777), 18–19.

56. Cases of vampirism on the borders of the Habsburg Empire continued into the twentieth century: see Bräunlein, 'Borderlands of Enlightenment', 718. Slavoj Žižek writes that 'borderline phenomena such as vampires and zombies are referred to as the "undead", a non-predicate that is affirmed, evidence of the "unpresentable Thing"': see 'A Hair of the Dog that Bit You', in Edmond and Elizabeth Wright (eds), *The Žižek Reader* (Oxford and Malden, MA: Blackwell, 1999), 268–282, at 270 (from Mark Bracher, et al. (eds), *Lacan's Theory of Discourse: Subject, Structure and Society* (Albany, NY: Suny Press, 1994), 46–73).

57. Butler remarks that 'all vampires share one trait: the power to move between and undo borders otherwise holding identities in place' (*Metamorphoses of the Vampire*, 1, see also 41).

58. Žižek comments that 'we resort to indefinite judgements precisely when we endeavour to comprehend those borderline phenomena that underline established differences such as that between living and being dead': see 'A Hair of the Dog That Bit You', in Wright and Wright (eds), *The Žižek Reader*, 279.

59. Thacker, *Tentacles Longer Than Night*, 51.

60. Thacker, 'Necrologies', *Tentacles Longer Than Night*, 52–57, at 55.

61. This could equally be called kinetophobia or kinesiophobia.
62. Thacker, 'Ambient Plague', *In the Dust of This Planet*, 105. As Bräunlein puts it, 'The vampire represents an epistemological void between life and death, between this side of the grave and the great beyond' ('Borderlands of Enlightenment', 711); see also Eugene Thacker, 'Biological Sovereignty', *Pli: The Warwick Journal of Philosophy*, 17 (2006), 1–17; and see Mary Douglas, *Purity and Danger: An Analysis of Concepts of Pollution and Taboo* (New York: Frederick A. Praeger, 1966).
63. Dylan Trigg, *The Thing: A Phenomenology of Horror* (Winchester and Washington, DC: Zero Books, 2014), 54.

Chapter 3

1. William Shakespeare, *Macbeth*, in *Complete Works*, ed. Wells and Taylor, III. iv. 121–25 (p. 989).
2. John Donne, 'Holy Sonnets', no. 15, in *Selected Poetry*, ed. John Carey (Oxford: Oxford University Press, 1998), 206.
3. 'A Forsaken Garden', in *The Poems of Algernon Charles Swinburne*, 6 vols (London: Chatto and Windus, 1912), iii. 22–25, at 25.
4. For a survey of some of this thinking, see E.J. Clery, *The Rise of Supernatural Fiction, 1762–1800* (Cambridge: Cambridge University Press, 1995).
5. 1 Samuel 28:7–20.
6. John 11:1–46; Mary of Bethany was at one time conflated with Mary Magdalene.
7. John 11:44.
8. Revelation 20:13–15.
9. Belief in ghosts and theology had been intertwined for some years: see Peter Marshall, *Beliefs and the Dead in Reformation England* (Oxford: Oxford University Press, 2002), esp. 12–18, 245–64.
10. See the classic work by Sasha Handley, *Visions of an Unseen World: Ghost Beliefs and Ghost Stories in Eighteenth-Century England* (London: Pickering and Chatto, 2007), which has inspired the research of the first part of this chapter; see also Ian Bostridge, *Witchcraft and its Transformations c. 1650 – c. 1700* (Oxford and New York: Clarendon Press, 1997); Lorraine Daston and Katherine Park, *Wonders and the Order of Nature, 1150–1750* (New York: Zone Books, 1998); Owen Davies, *The Haunted: A Social History of Ghosts* (Basingstoke: Palgrave Macmillan, 2007) and *Witchcraft, Magic and Culture, 1736–1951* (Manchester: Manchester University Press, 1999) (and much of his other work); Ronald Hutton, 'The English Reformation and the Evidence of Folklore', *Past and Present*, 148 (1995), 89–116 (likewise, much of his other work, including *The Witch: A History of Fear from Ancient Times to the Present* (New Haven, CT, and London: Yale University Press, 2017)); and Marshall, *Beliefs and the Dead in Reformation England*. On death (not ghosts) see Clare Gittings, *Death, Burial and the Individual in Early Modern England* (London: Croom Helm, 1984); Ralph Houlbrooke, *Death, Religion, and the Family in England, 1480–1750* (Oxford: Clarendon Press, 1988); and Ruth Richardson, *Death, Dissection and the Destitute* (London: Routledge & Kegan Paul, 2001). An excellent study of the complications and contradictions of these issues is provided by Stephen Greenblatt, *Hamlet in Purgatory* (Princeton, NJ: Princeton University Press, 2001).
11. John Strype, *Annals of the Reformation and Establishment of Religion, and Other Various Occurrences in the Church of England, during Queen Elizabeth's Happy Reign*, new edn, 4 vols in 7 (Oxford: Clarendon Press, 1824), iii. pt ii. 67.
12. The now widely used concept of 'hauntology' has its roots in Jacques Derrida's influential book, *Specters of Marx: The State of the Debt, the Work of Mourning and the New International*, trans. Peggy Kamuf (New York and London: Routledge, 1994).
13. See Ludwig Lavater, *Of Ghosts and Spirits Walking by Nyght*, ed. M. Yardley (Oxford: Oxford University Press, 1929); see also Gillian Bennett, 'Ghost and Witch in the Sixteenth and Seventeenth Centuries', *Folklore*, 97 (1986), 3–14.
14. Handley, *Visions of an Unseen World*, 23.
15. Henry More, *An Antidote Against Atheism or, An Appeal to the Naturall Faculties of the Minde of Man, whether there be not a God*, 2nd edn (London, 1655), 208–14 (Bk III ch. viii), at 210; Barber provides a version from Prussian folklore (*Vampires, Burial, and Death*, 10–13).
16. More Latinizes the name Johann Cuntze.
17. More, *Antidote Against Atheism*, 215–27 (Bk III ch. ix), at 217; Barber translates a Prussian account (*Vampires, Burial, and Death*, 102–03).
18. Thomas Hobbes, *Leviathan*, ed. C.B. Macpherson (Harmondsworth: Penguin, 1985), 629; on empirical science, see Stephen Shapin and Simon Schama, *Leviathan and the Air-Pump: Hobbes, Boyle, and the Experimental Life* (Princeton, NJ: Princeton University Press, 1989).

19. Henry More, *An Antidote Against Atheism: or, An Appeal to the Natural Faculties of the Mind of Man, Whether there be not a God*, 3rd edn (1662), in *A Collection of Several Philosophical Writings of Dr. Henry More [,] Fellow of Christ's Colledge [sic] in Cambridge*, 2nd edn (London, 1662), 43.

20. More also drifted into politics, commenting 'that Saying is not more true in Politicks, *No Bishop, No King*; then [*sic*] this in Metaphysicks, *No Spirit, no God*' (*Antidote Against Atheism*, 42).

21. Handley, *Visions of an Unseen World*, 9, 103. Thomas Groom was attacked by a ghost in Hammersmith in 1804: for 'The Hammersmith Ghosts' see *The Times* (6 January 1804), 3; and a full report in *Kirby's Wonderful and Scientific Museum; or, Magazine of Remarkable Characters; including all the Curiosities of Nature and Art, from the Remotest Period to the Present Time, drawn from Every Authentic Source*, 6 vols (London: Barnard and Sultzer, 180–182), vol. ii. (1804), 65–79.

22. For Popish Plot ghosts, see John Oldham, *Garnets Ghost, Addressing to the Jesuits, met in Private Caball, just after the Murther of Sir Edmund-Bury Godfrey* (1679); [Anon.,] *A New Apparition of S. Edmund-Bery Godfrey's Ghost to the Earl of Danby in the Tower* (1681); and [Anon.,] *Sir Edmundbury Godfreys Ghost: or, An Answer to Nat. Thompsons Scandalous Letter from Cambridge to Mr. Miles Prance, in Relation to the Murder of Sir Edmundbury Godfrey* (1682).

23. For ballads, Handley mainly uses moral ballads from the Pepys Collection: *The Two Unfortunate Lovers, A Godly Warning to all Maidens, The Suffolk Miracle* and *The Leicestershire Tragedy* (Handley, *Visions of an Unseen World*, 51–56, 56–63); and [Anon.], *Here is a True and Perfect Relation from the Faulcon at the Banke-Side; of the Strange and Wonderful Aperition [sic] of one Mr. Powel, a Baker lately deceased, and of his Appearing in Several Shapes, both at Noon-Day and at Night, with the Several Speeches which past between the Spirit of Mr. Powel and his Maid Jone and Divers Learned Men* (London, 1661); see also, for example, 'The Witches' Song', in Thomas Percy, *Reliques of Ancient English Poetry*, 3 vols (London, 1765), iii. 198–201.

24. [Anon.], *A Strange and Wonderfull Discovery of a Horrid and Cruel Murther committed Fourteen Years Since, upon the Person of Robert Eliot of London, at Great Driffield in the East-Riding of the County of York* (London, 1662), 7 (her name is also spelt 'Isabel').

25. See Todd Butler, 'The Haunting of Isabell Binnington: Ghosts of Murder, Texts, and Law in Restoration England', *Journal of British Studies*, 50 (2011), 248–76.

26. See John Dunton, et al., *The Athenian Oracle: Being an Entire Collection of all the Valuable Questions and Answers in the Old Athenian Mercuries*, 3 vols (1703–04), ii. 380.

27. William Shakespeare, *The Winter's Tale*, in *Complete Works*, ed. Wells and Taylor, II. i. 30–32 (p. 1108).

28. John Newbery, rev. Oliver Goldsmith, *The Art of Poetry on a New Plan: Illustrated with a Great Variety of Examples from the Best English Poets; and of Translations from the Ancients: Together with Such Reflections and Critical Remarks as may tend to form in our Youth an Elegant Taste, and render the Study of this Part of the Belles Lettres more Rational and Pleasing*, 2 vols (London, 1762), ii. 154; this warning against the influence of supernatural tales on children originates in John Locke's theories of identity formation in his *Essay Concerning Human Understanding* (1689) and *Some Thoughts Concerning Education* (1693).

29. Handley: 'Restoration ghost stories can . . . be understood as part of a policy of resistance against the incursions of social superiors [and] weapons used to secure social and economic survival more generally' (Handley, *Visions of an Unseen World*, 67).

30. See John Aubrey, *Remaines of Gentilisme and Judaisme*, ed. James Britten (London: Folk-Lore Society, 1881), 104, see also 53.

31. See Daniel Defoe, *An Essay on the History and Reality of Apparitions* (London, 1727), 200–01, 298–303, 373–74, 376–79; *The Old English Baron* was first published in 1777 as *The Champion of Virtue*.

32. Ralph Cudworth, *The True Intellectual System of the Universe: The First Part; wherein, All the Reason and Philosophy of Atheism is Confuted; and Its Impossibility Demonstrated* (London, 1678), 701. For angels see Benjamin Camfield, *A Theological Discourse of Angels and their Ministries wherein their Existence, Nature, Number, Order and Offices are modestly treated of: with the Character of those for whose Benefit especially they are Commissioned, and such Practical Inferences deduced as are Most Proper to the Premise* (London, 1678), Camfield quotes More on p. 172; see also Peter Marshall and Alexandra Walsham (eds), *Angels in the Early Modern World* (Cambridge: Cambridge University Press, 2006). According to Christopher Hill, Winstanley was 'groping his way towards a humanist and materialist philosophy, in which there were no outward saviours, no heaven or hell or after life, but only men and women living in society' ('The Religion of Gerrard Winstanley', *Past and Present Supplement*, 5 (1978), 56–57: quoted by Denys Turner, 'Christianity and Politics: The Case of Gerrard Winstanley', *New Blackfriars*, 62 (1981), 500–09, at 500).

221

33. Thomas Bromhall, *A Treatise of Specters, or, A History of Apparitions, Oracles, Prophecies, and Predictions* (1658), 343; however, note that as Pierre Kapitaniak has pointed out, Bromhall's book is an 'unacknowledged translation of two late-sixteenth-century works, one German and one French, with no new content whatsoever' (see Jonathan Barry, 'News from the Invisible World: The Publishing History of Tales of the Supernatural c. 1660–1832', in Jonathan Barry, Owen Davies and Cornelie Usborne (eds), *Cultures of Witchcraft in Europe from the Middle Ages to the Present* (Basingstoke: Palgrave Macmillan, 2017), 179–213, at 187).

34. *Saducismus Triumphatus: or, Full and Plain Evidence concerning Witches and Apparitions* (London, 1681) was the final version of Glanvill's investigations into witchcraft and the supernatural, beginning with *A Philosophical Endeavour towards the Defense of the being of Witches and Apparitions* (London, 1666), which was first revised as *Some Philosophical Considerations Touching the Being of Witches and Witchcraft* (London, 1667) and then as *A Blow at Modern Sadducism in some Philosophical Considerations about Witchcraft* (London, 1668), before More revised the text again. See Barry, 'News from the Invisible World', especially 184–85.

35. See Handley, *Visions of an Unseen World*, 35.

36. Glanvill, *A Blow at Modern Sadducism*, 116.

37. See, for example, Thomas Emes, *Vindiciæ Mentis. An Essay of the Being and Nature of Mind: Wherein the Distinction of Mind and Body, the Substantiality, Personality, and Perfection of Mind is Asserted; and the Original of our Minds, their Present, Separate, and Future State, is freely enquir'd into, in order to a more Certain Foundation for the Knowledge of God, and Our Selves, and the Clearing all Doubts and Objections that have been, or may be made concerning The Life and Immortality Of Our Souls* (London, 1702), 126–27; [Anon.,] *The Compleat Wizzard; Being a Collection of Authentic and Entertaining Narratives of the Real Existence and Appearance of Ghosts, Demons, and Spectres: Together with Several Wonderful Instances of the Effects of Witchcraft* (London, 1770), 55–59; and [Anon.,] *The Atheist's Reward: or, A Call from Heaven, on July the 24th, 1786* (London, 1788), 5–8.

38. See R.M. Burns, *The Great Debate on Miracles: From Joseph Glanvill to David Hume* (Lewisburg, PA: Bucknell University Press; London and Toronto: Associated University Presses, 1983), 31; see Glanvill, *Saducismus Triumphatus*, 277. As W.F. Bynum points out, 'Moral and physical, supernatural and natural explanatory schemes need not be incompatible or mutually exclusive' (*Science and the Practice of Medicine*, 60).

39. See Jeremy Gregory, *Restoration, Reformation and Reform, 1660–1828* (Oxford and New York: Oxford University Press, 2000); and Donald Spaeth, *The Church in an Age of Danger: Parsons and Parishioners, 1660–1740* (Cambridge: Cambridge University Press, 2000).

40. See Richard Baxter, *Of the Immortality of Mans [sic] Soul, and the Nature of it and Other Spirits* (London, 1682), which is subtitled 'Two Discourses, one in a Letter to an Unknown Doubter, the other in a Reply to Dr. Henry Moore's [sic] Animadversions on a Private Letter to Him, which he Published in his Second Edition of Mr. Joseph Glanvil's *Saducismus Triumphatus, or, History of Apparitions*'.

41. More's natural philosophy was also supported by the naturalist, folklorist and antiquarian John Ray in *The Wisdom of God manifested in the Works of the Creation being the Substance of Some Common Places Delivered in the Chappel [sic] of Trinity-College, in Cambridge* (London, 1691). As Handley demonstrates, ghost stories could be moral exemplars, advancing 'a practical moral theology which was favoured both by latitudinarian theologians and by Richard Baxter as a necessary supplement to an introspective faith' (*Visions of an Unseen World*, 42).

42. See William Derham, *Physico-Theology: or, A Demonstration of the Being and Attributes of God, from his Works of Creation* (London, 1713), based on his Robert Boyle lectures delivered in 1711–12, and *Astro-Theology: or A Demonstration of the Being and Attributes of God, from a Survey of the Heavens* (London, 1715).

43. William Assheton, *The Possibility of Apparitions* (London, 1706), 11, 19.

44. See Josiah Woodward, *Fair Warnings to a Careless World, or, The Serious Practice of Religion recommended by the Admonitions of Dying Men, and the Sentiments of All People in their Most Serious Hours: and Other Testimonies of an Extraordinary Nature* (London, 1707).

45. For the relationship between science and the supernatural, see the magisterial works by Stuart Clark (*Thinking with Demons*) and Keith Thomas (*Religion and the Decline of Magic*): these challenge simplistic Enlightenment definitions (e.g. Daston and Park, *Wonders and the Order of Nature*, especially 14, 20, 331).

46. See also Thomas Burnet's *The Theory of the Earth containing an Account of the Original of the Earth, and of all the General Changes which it hath Already Undergone, or is to Undergo, till the Consummation of All Things* (London, 1684), and works by Samuel Clarke, Anthony Collins and John Toland.

47. Anthony Ashley Cooper, earl of Shaftesbury, 'A Letter Concerning Enthusiasm, to My Lord Sommers' (1708), *Characteristicks of Men, Manners, Opinions, Times*, 5th edn, 3 vols (London, 1732), i. 1–55, at 6, 14, 15–16, 50, 51, also 53.

48. Marc Vernous, *A Preservative against the False Prophets of the Times: or, A Treatise concerning True and False Prophets, with their Characters: likewise a Letter to Mr. Maximilian Misson, upon the Subject of the Miracles, pretended to be wrought by the French Prophets, and their Adherents; particularly that of the Fiery Tryal, pretended to be wrought by Clary, in the Cevennes* (London, 1708), 23–24: see John Crowder, *The Ecstasy of Loving God: Trances, Raptures, and the Supernatural Pleasures of Jesus Christ* (Shippensburg, PA: Destiny Image, 2009), ch. 9.

49. For the Witchcraft Act, see Bostridge, *Witchcraft and its Transformations*, especially 180–202.

50. See Owen Davies, 'Methodism, the Clergy, and the Popular Belief in Witchcraft and Magic', *History*, 82 (1997), 252–65; for a full account of the supernatural in Methodism, see Robert Webster, *Methodism and the Miraculous: John Wesley's Idea of the Supernatural and the Identification of Methodists in the Eighteenth-Century* (Lexington, KY: Emeth Press, 2013); and more generally, Henry D. Rack, *Reasonable Enthusiast: John Wesley and the Rise of Methodism*, 3rd edn (London: Epworth Press, 2002).

51. Richard Jago, *The Causes of Impenitence Consider'd: as well in the Case of Extraordinary Warnings, as under the General Laws of Providence, and Grace* (Oxford, 1755); Jago also wrote an essay on electricity, though this does not appear to have been published: see Robert Dodsley, *The Correspondence of Robert Dodsley, 1733–1764*, ed. James E. Tierney (Cambridge: Cambridge University Press, 1988), 396 n.22.

52. Archibald Cockburn, *A Philosophical Essay concerning the Intermediate State of Blessed Souls* (London, 1722), 39.

53. Cockburn, *A Philosophical Essay*, 56, 57.

54. Samuel Clarke, *A Demonstration of the Being and Attributes of God: more particularly in Answer to Mr. Hobbs, Spinoza, and their Followers* (London, 1705), 162–63.

55. David Hume, 'Of Miracles', in *Philosophical Essays Concerning Human Understanding* (London, 1748), 173–203, 182.

56. Hume, 'Of Miracles', *Philosophical Essays*, 190.

57. See Manuel Schonhorn (ed.), *Accounts of the Apparition of Mrs Veal*, Augustan Reprint Society No. 115 (Los Angeles, CA: William Andrews Clark Memorial Library, 1965), and Horace Walpole, *The Castle of Otranto*, ed. Nick Groom (Oxford: Oxford University Press, 2014), xxx–xxxi.

58. See John Christie and Sally Shuttleworth (eds), *Nature Transfigured: Science and Literature, 1700–1900* (Manchester: Manchester University Press, 1989), 6. Defoe went on to write three substantial works on the supernatural, notably *An Essay on the History and Reality of Apparitions* (1727), in which he dismisses ghosts; there are however dissenting supernatural elements in Defoe's novels such as *Moll Flanders* and *Robinson Crusoe*.

59. See Joseph Addison, Richard Steele, et al., *The Spectator*, 8 vols (London, 1712–15), i. 38–43 (No. 7, 8 March 1711), ii. 47–52 (No. 90, 13 June 1711) and vi. 127–31 (No. 419, 1 July 1712); they are also discussed in *The Tatler* ('Isaac Bickerstaffe' [Richard Steele, Joseph Addison, et al.], *The Lucubrations of Isaac Bickerstaff Esq; Revised and Corrected by the Author*, 5 vols (London, 1712), iii. 182–88 (No. 152, 28–30 March 1710)); for Roger de Coverley's haunted estate, see Addison, et al., *Spectator*, ii. 147–52 (No. 110, 6 July 1711).

60. See Addison, et al., *Spectator*, i. 242–50 (No. 44, 20 April 1711). Children, women and the elderly were believed to be prone to such delusions, partly through distortions in their sight, again drawing on Locke (see above, n. 28).

61. Hesther Lynch Piozzi, *Anecdotes of the Late Samuel Johnson LLD.*, in George Birkbeck Hill (ed.), *Johnsonian Miscellanies*, 2 vols (London: Constable & Co. Ltd, 1966), i. 141–351, at 157–59.

62. See 'Of Credulity in Witchcraft', *Gentleman's Magazine*, 1 (January 1731), 29–30 and a similar report (August 1731), 358; 'Of Ghost, Dæmons, and Spectres' (from *Universal Spectator*, 209, 7 October), *Gentleman's Magazine*, 2 (October 1732), 1001–02; correspondence on dreams and visions, *Gentleman's Magazine*, 9 (February 1739), 74–75, 145–47; 'A Journey to Caudebec Fells, with a Map and Description of the Same', *Gentleman's Magazine*, 17 (November 1747), 522–25, at 524 (the marching fairy army was seen there on Midsummer's Eve 1735, again in 1737, and in 1745).

63. See Barry, 'News from the Invisible World', 179–213.

64. A sense of the virulence of British anti-Catholicism is evident in the title of a pamphlet: *Reasons humbly offer'd for a Law to Enact the Castration of Popish Ecclesiastics, as the Best Way to Prevent the Growth of Popery in England*, attributed to Daniel Defoe (London, 1700; Dublin, 1710).

65. See Nick Groom, *The Seasons: A Celebration of the English Year* (London: Atlantic, 2014), 115–16, 190, 212, 336 n.80; see also Will Coster and Andrew Spicer (eds), *Sacred Space in Early Modern Europe* (Cambridge: Cambridge University Press, 2005).

66. An early example being Thomas Parnell's 'A Night Piece on Death', posthumously published in Alexander Pope (ed.), *Poems on Several Occasions* (Dublin, 1722), 115–18.

67. Robert Blair, *The Grave. A Poem* (London, 1743), ll. 32–42.

68. Blair, *The Grave*, ll. 68–71.

69. Blair, *The Grave*, l. 44, ll. 50–53.

70. James Hervey's popular series of devotional letters, for instance, describes post-mortem reconciliation when bones mix in the ground and 'fall into mutual Embraces, and even incorporate with each other in the Grave' (*Meditations among the Tombs* (London and Bath, 1746), 13).

71. Blair, *The Grave*, ll. 17–18.

72. Blair, *The Grave*, ll. 171–72.

73. See John Arbuthnot, *An Essay Concerning the Effects of Air on Human Bodies* (London, 1733), 183. For public health initiatives, see John McManners, *Death and the Enlightenment: Changing Attitudes to Death among Christians and Unbelievers in Eighteenth-Century France* (Oxford: Oxford University Press, 1981), 308–19; also James C. Riley, *The Eighteenth-Century Campaign to Avoid Disease* (Basingstoke: Macmillan, 1987), 109.

74. See Sean Gaston, 'An Event Without an Object: The Cock Lane Ghost, London 1762–1763', *The Literary London Journal*, 12 (2015), 3–21.

75. See Richard Jones, *Walking Haunted London* (London: New Holland Publishers, 1999), especially 36, 66, 103.

76. James Boswell, *Boswell's Life of Johnson*, ed. George Birkbeck Hill, rev. L.F. Powell, 6 vols (Oxford: Clarendon Press, 1979), iii. 230.

77. See Maxwell Teitel Paule, *Canidia, Rome's First Witch* (London and New York: Bloomsbury, 2017); and Ellen Oliensis, 'Scenes from the Afterlife of Horace's *Epodes* (c. 1600–1900)', in Philippa Bather and Claire Stocks (eds), *Horace's Epodes: Contexts, Intertexts, and Reception* (Oxford: Oxford University Press, 2016), 219–39, especially 229–34 (interestingly, in *Epode* 3 Canidia is associated with garlic). '*Empusa*' was an ancient Greek she-demon who appears in Roman folklore as a seductress and literal man-eater; it is also the name of the vampire Count Orlok's ship in F.W. Murnau's film *Nosferatu, A Symphony of Terror* (1922).

78. For the Cock Lane ghost, see [Anon.], *Anti-Canidia: or, Superstition Detected and Exposed. In a Confutation of the Vulgar Opinion concerning Witches, Spirits, Demons, Magick, Divination, Omens, Prognostications, Dreams, Augurys, Charms, Amulets, Incantations, Astrology, Oracles, &c.* (London, 1762), 22.

79. The Unitarian Joseph Priestley also savagely attacked the science of ghostliness in *An History of the Corruptions of Christianity*, 2 vols (Birmingham, 1782).

80. Dom Augustin Calmet, *Commentaire Litteral sur Tous les Livres de l'Ancien et du Nouveau Testament*, 26 vols (Paris, 1707–17).

Chapter 4

1. *Tyndale's New Testament*, trans. William Tyndale, ed. David Daniell (New Haven, CT, and London: Yale University Press, 1989), 258.

2. Francis Marion Crawford, 'For the Blood is the Life', in *Wandering Ghosts* (New York: Macmillan, 1911), 165–94, at 190.

3. William Shakespeare, *Othello, The Moor of Venice*, in *Complete Works*, ed. Wells and Taylor, III. iii. 455 (p. 839).

4. See Thomas, *Religion and the Decline of Magic* and Francis Young, *English Catholics and the Supernatural, 1553–1829* (Farnham: Ashgate, 2013). There was, however, overlap between the two theologies: see Stuart Clark, 'Protestant Demonology: Sin, Superstition, and Society (c. 1520–c. 1630)', in Ankarloo and Henningsen (eds), *Early Modern European Witchcraft*, 45–81.

5. See de Ceglia, 'The Archbishop's Vampires', 487–510; de Ceglia notes that, remarkably, Davanzati had met Joseph Pitton de Tournefort (497n.; see above, p. 27).

6. Davanzati went so far as to praise Galileo, whose treatise on heliocentrism, *Dialogo sopra i due massimi sistemi del mondo* (*Dialogue concerning the Two Chief World Systems*, 1632), actually remained on the *Index Librorum Prohibitorum* until 1835.

7. For these explanations, Davanzati relied on Christian Friedrich Garmann's magisterial *De Miraculis Mortuorum* (Leipzig, 1709); the 1670 edition of Garmann's work was condemned by the Catholic Church in 1678 and placed on the *Index*.

8. Giuseppe Davanzati, *Dissertazione sopra i Vampiri*, ed. Giacomo Annibaldis (Bari: Besa, 1998), 107: cited by de Ceglia, 'The Archbishop's Vampires', 509, and translated by Ceglia and Donahue; Davanzati refers to the levitation of a local mystic, Giuseppe da Copertino ('The Flying Saint'), to demonstrate the power of imagination over matter (*Dissertazione sopra i Vampiri*, 97).

9. Benedicto XIV [Prospero Lambertini], *Doctrinum De Servorum Dei Beatificatione et Beatorum Canonizatione Redactum in Synopsim* (Rome, 1757), 391 (see also chapter 31, paragraphs 7–8, p. 420) (not in first edition of 1738); Book IV, chapter XXI, paragraph 4 deals specifically with the reports of vampirism in the *Commercium Literarium* of 1732; see de Ceglia, 'The Archbishop's Vampires', 507n. The bibliography *Vampiri Europeana* (http://archive.is/2PTJ, 139, 147) records that a section '*De vanitate Vampyrorum*' ('On the Vanity of Belief in Vampires') was added to the 1752 edition.

10. See, in particular, Calmet, 'A Dissertation Concerning Vampires, or the Spectres which appear in Hungary, Bohemia, Moravia, and Silesia', in *Dissertations*, 178–334. Perkowski includes translations from Calmet in *Vampire Lore*, 119–72. There is a modern edition of Calmet's *Dissertation sur les revenants en corps, les excommuniés, les oupires ou vampires, brucolaques etc.*, ed. Roland Villeneuve, 2nd edn (Grenoble: Editions Jérôme Millon, 1998); it was first published in 1986.

11. See Joan Carroll Cruz, *The Incorruptibles: A Study of the Incorruption of the Bodies of Various Catholic Saints and Beati* (Charlotte: TAN Books, 2012).

12. Marie-Hélène Huet, 'Deadly Fears: Dom Augustin Calmet's Vampires and the Rule over Death', *Eighteenth-Century Life*, 21(2) (1997), 222–32, at 227. Huet also considers that 'Arnod Paole' is not a Hungarian name and may be a coded reference to the Jansenist Antoine Arnauld: Jansenists, although professing to be Catholics, had been fiercely persecuted in Europe because of their perceived Calvinist heresy in promulgating the doctrine of predestination (228).

13. Calmet, *Dissertations*, 185; see below, pp. 178–79.

14. See above, pp. 26–27, 44.

15. See Calmet, *Dissertations*, 186, 302, 327, 331.

16. Calmet, *Dissertations*, 308.

17. Calmet, *Dissertations*, 305; later fictional vampires achieved this by virtue of transforming themselves into mists or particles.

18. Benito Jerónimo Feijóo y Montenegro, *Cartas Eruditas, y Curiosas, en que, por la mayor parte, se continua el designio Del Teatro Critico Universal . . .*, new edn, 5 vols (Madrid, 1774), cited by Vidal, 'Extraordinary Bodies and the Physicotheological Imagination', in Daston and Pomata (eds), *The Faces of Nature*, 75; see also Fernando Vidal, 'Ghosts of the European Enlightenment', in Mu-Chou Poo (ed.), *Rethinking Ghosts in World Religions* (Leiden and Boston, MA: Brill, 2009), 163–82.

19. For a more fanciful reading, see Villeneuve, '*Présentation*' to Calmet, *Dissertation sur les revenants*, 31–32, which offers a range of causes of vampirism, from catalepsis and necrophobia to schizophrenia and porphyria, this last being, in Villeneuve's partial definition, 'a hereditary blood disease frequently found in Transylvania . . . which causes cutaneous anomalies, dental malformations and creates a desire for blood' (translated by Jay L. Caplan); a more sceptical reading is provided by Ann M. Cox, 'Porphyria and Vampirism: Another Myth in the Making', *Postgraduate Medical Journal*, 71(841) (1995), 643–44. Porphyria is a very rare condition and would not account for whole graveyards filled with the blood-swelled bodies of purported vampires.

20. See William Coleman, *Biology in the Nineteenth Century: Problems of Form, Function, and Transformation* (Cambridge: Cambridge University Press, 1977), 120–23.

21. Voltaire, *A Philosophical Dictionary*, 6 vols (London: John and Henry Hunt, 1824), ii. 8–10, at 9; the 'mezarian' vein is the mesenteric.

22. See A.C. Grayling, *Descartes: The Life of René Descartes and Its Place in His Times* (London: Pocket Books, 2006), 159.

23. Both Monboddo and Smellie, Buffon's translator, use the phrase to describe the original inhabitants of Australia and New Guinea, respectively: see James Burnet[t], Lord Monboddo, *Of the Origin and Progress of Language*, 6 vols (Edinburgh, 1773–92), i. 188; and Georges-Louis Leclerc, comte de Buffon, *Natural History, General and Particular, by the Count de Buffon, Translated into English*, trans. William Smellie, 9 vols (London, 1785), iii. 151.

24. See Christopher Frayling and Robert Wokler, 'From the Orang-Utan to the Vampire: Towards an Anthropology of Rousseau', in R.A. Leigh (ed.), *Rousseau after 200 Years: Proceedings of the Cambridge Bicentennial Colloquium* ([1982] Cambridge: Cambridge University Press, 2010), 109–24, at 114.

25. Boswell, *Life of Johnson*, ii. 74.

26. Monboddo, *Of the Origin and Progress of Language*, i; (2nd edn 1774) 188; much of this volume is given over to orangutans: see in particular Bk I, chapters IV and V, pp. 270–361.

27. See Monboddo, *Of the Origin and Progress of Language*, i. 225n., 346.

28. See Monboddo, *Of the Origin and Progress of Language*, i. 262ff. Johnson inevitably pooh-poohed the idea: 'Other people have strange notions; but they conceal them. If they have tails, they hide them; but Monboddo is as jealous of his tale as a squirrel' (Boswell, *Life of Johnson*, v. 111).

29. See *ODNB*, which cites the ninth edition of the *Encyclopædia Britannica* (1875–89).

30. See Francis Moran III, 'Between Primates and Primitives: Natural Man as the Missing Link in Rousseau's *Second Discourse*', in Julie K. Ward and Tommy L. Lott, *Philosophers on Race: Critical Essays* (Oxford and Malden, MA: Blackwell Publishing, 2002), 125–44, at 133.

31. See Moran, 'Between Primates and Primitives', 134. Rousseau denies that 'natural man' has any higher intellectual or emotional capacities, such as a sense of morality.

32. Quoted by Frayling and Wokler, 'From the Orang-Utan to the Vampire', 115.

33. Jean-Jacques Rousseau, *An Expostulatory Letter from J.J. Rousseau, Citizen of Geneva, to Christopher de Beaumont, Archbishop of Paris* (London, 1763), 56. Frayling and Wokler note that in an unpublished addendum to the *Letter*, Rousseau referred to an article in the *Gazette des Gazettes* (1 November 1765) which likewise questioned the value of testimony.

34. John James [*sic*: for Jean-Jacques] Rousseau, *Emilius; or, An Essay on Education*, trans. Thomas Nugent, 2 vols (London, 1763), ii. 75.

35. Rousseau, *Emilius*, ii. 71; the section on miracles is at ii. 68–72. See also, in passing, Beresford, *From Demons to Dracula*, 16–17.

36. Frayling also quotes a passing comment by Diderot in his *Salon of 1767* (*Vampyres*, 31).

37. Antoine Furetière, 'VAMPIRE, WAMPIRE, OUPIRE & UPIRE', *Dictionnaire Universel François et Latin, vulgairement appelé Dictionnaire de Trévoux*, 6th edn, 8 vols (Paris, 1771), viii. 285.

38. *Gazette Françoise* (26 October 1770): quoted by Frayling, *Vampyres*, 35.

39. Voltaire, *A Philosophical Dictionary*, vi. 304–08, at 304 (subsequent quotations from this entry); later reprinted, e.g. by W. Dugdale in 1843, 2 vols (ii. 560–62). The essay was originally published as part of *Questions sur L'Encyclopédie, distribuées en Forme de Dictionnaire*, 2nd edn, 9 vols (London, 1772), ix. 129–35. Voltaire's comments are often wrongly attributed to his earlier *Dictionnaire Philosophique* (London [Geneva], 1764), in part as they were published in Britain in a later English translation under the title *A Philosophical Dictionary*; his *Dictionnaire Philosophique* has, however, only a passing reference to vampires (87).

40. This line is, tongue in cheek, alluded to by Gilles Deleuze and Félix Guattari in '1730: Becoming-Intense, Becoming-Animal, Becoming-Imperceptible', in *A Thousand Plateaus: Capitalism and Schizophrenia*, trans. Brian Massumi (Minneapolis, MN and London: University of Minnesota Press, 1987), 237: 'From 1730 to 1735, all we hear about are vampires' (given in quotation marks).

41. See McCarthy, '"Death to Vampires!", 189–208.

42. Voltaire, *Questions sur L'Encyclopédie*, ix. 131: literally, 'leur historiographe'; for Voltaire and Calmet, see Alfred Owen Aldridge, *Voltaire and the Century of Light* (Princeton, NJ: Princeton University Press, 1975), 325.

43. For Voltaire's figurative political use of 'bloodsucker', see Klaniczay, *Uses of Supernatural Power*, 187–88.

44. 'Erinensis' [Peter Hennis Green], 'On the Exportation of Dead Bodies from Ireland to England and Scotland', *The Lancet*, 21 March 1829 (1828–29), i. 774–78, at 776, 777 and 778 (letter dated 14 March 1829); see A.M. Lassek, *Human Dissection: Its Drama and Struggle* (Springfield, IL: Charles C. Thomas, 1958), 130.

45. Virgil, *Æneid*, Bk VIII, ll. 636–39: *The Works of Virgil: containing his Pastorals, Georgics and Æneis*, trans. John Dryden, 4th edn, 3 vols (London, 1716), iii. 614.

46. Joseph Russo, 'Perpetue Putesco: Perpetually I Putrefy', in Masciandaro (ed.), *Hideous Gnosis*, 93–103, at 101: this is quoted from Rega Negarestani, 'The Corpse Bride: Thinking with Nigredo', *Collapse*, 4 (2009), 129–60, at 131.

47. Russo, 'Perpetue Putesco', 102.

48. See Aristotle, *De Generatione et Corruptione*, I.5.321b.31 on the dead, and II.8.334b–336a on the perishable (Aristotle, *De Generatione et Corruptione*, ed. and trans. C.F.J. Williams (Oxford: Clarendon Press, 1982), 19, 51–54); and Averroes, *On Aristotle's De Generatione et Corruptione: Middle Commentary and Epitome*, ed. and trans. Samuel Kurland (Cambridge, MA: Medieval Academy of America, 1958), 18.

49. Negarestani, 'Corpse Bride', 132–33.

50. Humphry Davy, 'Discourse Introductory to a Course of Lectures in Chemistry' (*The Collected Works of Sir Humphry Davy, Bart. LL.D., F.R.S.*, ed. John Davy, 9 vols (London: Smith, Elder and Co., 1839–40), ii. 311, 313–14); Thacker, 'The Spirit of Biology', *In the Dust of This Planet*, 112–17, at 113).

51. An article on 'A Dissertation on the Uncertainty of the Signs of Death, and the Folly of Precipitant Burials, and Embalments [*sic*]', translated from Jacques Winslow, was published in the *Gentleman's Magazine* in 1745 (*Gentleman's Magazine*, 15 (June 1745), 311–13): Winslow notes that death-like states could be the result of 'apoplexy, swoonings, the true suffocation, as by strangling, stifling, drowning, close places, and noxious vapours and exhalations, and the false, or convulsive suffocation, as from hysteric and hypocondriac [*sic*] disorders, *&c.*' (312). He advocates checking for pulse, pricking, cutting, burning, concluding that 'no sign is infallible but the beginning of a putrefaction' (312) 'or till the corps [*sic*] gives a cadaverous smell' (313). The article was quoted in the *Dublin Journal* in 1747 following a report of an inadvertent live burial at Hustely, near Winchester: a man buried after lying apparently dead for two days, and having being placed in the grave, was 'rescued from it by some boys luckily playing in the church-yard! – Would people but have the patience to wait 'till the body sends forth a cadaverous smell, or shews any evident mark of putrefaction, such dire calamities could not happen' (reprinted in the *Gentleman's Magazine*, 17 (December 1747), 567–68, at 567).
52. 'Things' in the Kantian sense: as Žižek has it, 'a vampire is a Thing that looks and acts like us, yet is not one of us. In short, the difference between the vampire and the living person is that between indefinite and negative judgement: a dead person loses the predicates of a living being, yet he or she remains the same person. An undead, on the contrary, retains all the predicates of a living being without being one' ('A Hair of the Dog That Bit You', 279).
53. See Thacker, *Tentacles Longer Than Night*, 36.
54. 1 Corinthians 12:12–27, particularly verses 21, 12, 14, 20.
55. Henri Cardinal de Lubac, SJ, *Corpus Mysticum: The Eucharist and the Church in the Middle Ages*, trans. Gemma Simmons, CJ, with Richard Price and Christopher Stephens, ed. Laurence Paul Hemming and Susan Frank Parsons (London: SCM Press, 2006), 249, 250; see also Schneck, 'Body Politic', 362.
56. The *Spiritual Exercises of St Ignatius of Loyola* also recommends a comparable code of mortifying of the flesh: as Erik Butler explains, 'In the language of the Society of Jesus, the Christian soldier is *perinde ac cadaver*: "like a corpse"' ('The Counter-Reformation in Stone and Metal: Spiritual Substances', in Masciandaro (ed.), *Hideous Gnosis*, 23–31, at 25: see also terms used to describe 'submission of disciple to a spiritual master' at www.dictionaryofspiritualterms.com/public/Glossaries/terms.aspx?ID=1158%20).
57. De Lubac, *Corpus Mysticum*, 249.
58. Since Bram Stoker's *Dracula* (1897), however, vampires have increasingly been circumscribed within the Anglican Funeral Service as they literally disintegrate when slain.
59. Thacker, 'Blasphemous Life', *In the Dust of This Planet*, 101–04, at 104.
60. Bräunlein, 'Borders of Enlightenment', 711; Thacker, 'The Spirit of Biology', *In the Dust of This Planet*, 113; Hamberger, *Mortuus Non Mordet*, 167 (translated by Bräunlein and Spary: Bräunlein, 717).
61. Thacker, 'Black Illumination', *Tentacles Longer Than Night*, 126–31, at 128.

Chapter 5

1. 'Description of the Human Body and all of its Functions', in René Descartes, *The Philosophical Writings of Descartes*, ed. John Cottingham, Robert Stoothoff and Dugald Murdoch, 3 vols (Cambridge: Cambridge University Press, 1985–1991), i. 317.
2. John Keats, *Poetical Works*, ed. H.W. Garrod (Oxford and New York: Oxford University Press, 1982) 'Ode to a Nightingale', 207–09, l. 52.
3. Thomas Lovell Beddoes to Thomas Forbes Kelsall (11 January 1825), in *The Letters of Thomas Lovell Beddoes*, ed. Edmund Gosse (London: Elkin Mathews & John Lane; and New York: Macmillan & Co., 1894), 50.
4. Still useful is James B. Twitchell, *The Living Dead: A Study of the Vampire in Romantic Literature* (Durham, NC: Duke University Press, 1981); more recently see (among many examples) J. Jeffrey Franklin, 'The Economics of Immortality: The Demi-Immortal Oriental, Enlightenment Vitalism, and Political Economy in *Dracula*', *Cahiers Victoriens et Édouardiens*, 76 (2012), 127–48; Sharon Ruston, 'Has Man "Paid Too Dear a Price for his Empire"? Monsters in Romantic-Era Literature', in Raul Calzoni and Greta Perletti (eds), *Monstrous Anatomies: Literary and Scientific Imagination in Britain and Germany during the Long Nineteenth Century* (Göttingen: V&R Unipress, 2015), 133–48; and Martin Willis, 'Le Fanu's "Carmilla", Ireland, and Diseased Vision', in Sharon Ruston (ed.), *Literature and Science* (Cambridge: Boydell and Brewer, 2008), 111–30; for an overview, see Catherine Packham, *Eighteenth-Century Vitalism: Bodies, Culture, Politics* (Basingstoke: Palgrave Macmillan,

2012). The bibliography on the Gothic and Romanticism is vast and expanding exponentially; salient references are given in the following notes, but for surveys of the materials see works such as David Duff (ed.), *The Oxford Handbook of British Romanticism* (Oxford: Oxford University Press, 2018); and Catherine Spooner, Dale Townshend and Angela Wright (eds), *The Cambridge History of the Gothic*, 3 vols (Cambridge: Cambridge University Press, forthcoming).

5. See Heide Crawford, *The Origins of the Literary Vampire* (Lanham, MD: Rowman & Littlefield, 2016), 23–29; and Raul Calzoni, 'Liminal Figurations of the Vampire in the German Enlightenment, *Sturm und Drang* and Romanticism', in Calzoni and Perletti (eds), *Monstrous Anatomies*, 41–60, at 43–45. The poem appeared on 25 May 1748.

6. Klaniczay considers that the sexualization of the vampire begins with earlier Death and the Maiden imagery (see *Uses of Supernatural Power*, 183–84).

7. See Diane Long Hoeveler, *Gothic Riffs: Secularizing the Uncanny in the European Imaginary, 1780–1820* (Columbus, OH: Ohio State University Press, 2010), 163–88.

8. Taylor has 'the dead can ride apace': Taylor's version is in Oliver Farrar Emerson, *The Earliest English Translations of Bürger's* Lenore: *A Study in English and German Romanticism* (Cleveland, OH: Western Reserve University Press, 1916) [*Western Reserve University Bulletins*, new series, 18 (May 1916), *Literary Section Supplement, Western Reserve Studies*, 1], 79–85. Taylor does not include the detail of Hungary, though later translations – including Walter Scott's version 'William and Helen' – substitute Bohemia for Hungary: see Emerson. Crawford points out that this phrase has a long genealogy in northern poetry and folklore (*Origins of the Literary Vampire*, 40–43) Stoker quotes the line early in *Dracula*, and also in the cancelled chapter 'Dracula's Guest' (Stoker, *Dracula*, ed. Luckhurst, 13, 357).

9. Goethe may also have been influenced by the story of Menippus Lycius and the Lamia: see below, pp. 123–25.

10. Stanzas xiv and xix: see Johann Wolfgang von Goethe, *Faustus, A Dramatic Mystery; The Bride of Corinth; The First Walpurgis Night*, trans. John Anster (London: Longman, Rees, Orme, Brown, Green & Longman, 1835), 325–34.

11. See F.W. Stokoe, *German Influence in the English Romantic Period, 1788–1818* (Cambridge: Cambridge University Press, 1926), 65–67; Walter Scott, *The Chase, and William and Helen* (Edinburgh, 1796).

12. Samuel Taylor Coleridge, *Poems*, ed. John Beer (Everyman: London and Melbourne, 1983), (Pt II. ll. 379–380) 203; Geraldine's eyes are twice described as 'large bright' (Pt II. ll. 574, 595); the Ancient Mariner also has a 'glittering eye' (Pt I. l. 13): see 173, 208.

13. Coleridge, *Poems* (Pt III. l. 160), 135.

14. There is a passing reference in David Mallet's poem 'Zephir: or, The Stratagem' (1762), in which the vampire is glossed as 'A certain mischievous demon that delights much in human blood; of whom there are many stories told in Hungary' (David Mallet, *Poems on Several Occasions* (London, 1762), 54).

15. Robert Southey, *Thalaba the Destroyer*, 2nd edn, 2 vols (London: Longman, Hurst, Rees and Orme, 1809), Bk VIII, st. ix (vol. ii. p. 81; punctuated thus).

16. Southey, *Thalaba the Destroyer*, ii. 102–12. Later editions also included an extract from Roger North's *Life of Sir Dudley North*; Southey also half-admitted the influence of 'Lenore' (ii. 113).

17. For literary forgery and Romanticism see my own book *The Forger's Shadow: How Forgery Changed the Course of Literature* (London: Picador, 2003) and the essay 'Romanticism and Forgery' in *Literature Compass Online*, 4 (2007), online edn.

18. 'Arminius', 'The Dead Men of Pest, A Hungarian Legend', *The Athenæum*, 1 (April 1807), 362–66; a correspondent ('Scrutator') replied in the June number noting similarities with More's accounts of the undead (570–71; see above, pp. 58–61; this same correspondent had also previously written on insanity). A later version of Merivale's poem is reprinted in Caroline Franklin (ed.), *The Longman Anthology of Gothic Verse* (Harlow: Longman, 2011), 325–31.

19. George Gordon, Lord Byron, *The Giaour, A Fragment of a Turkish Tale* (London: John Murray, 1813), 23–24 (ll. 755–66).

20. Byron, *The Giaour*, 23n.–24n.; the first note was expanded in later editions to include more on variants of 'Vroucolochas' (see George Gordon, Lord Byron, *The Giaour, A Fragment of a Turkish Tale*, 10th edition (London: John Murray, 1814), 72n.).

21. Walter Scott, *Rokeby, A Poem*, 5th edn (Edinburgh: A. Constable and Co., and John Ballantyne and Co.; and London: Longman, Hurst, Rees, Orme and Brown, 1813), Canto I, xxxii, p. 43.

22. John Ferriar, 'Of POPULAR ILLUSIONS, and Particularly of MEDICAL DEMONOLOGY' (12 May 1786), in *Memoirs of the Literary and Philosophical Society of Manchester*, 5 vols (1785–87), iii. 31–105, at 86–91; Ferriar rejected the claim that drinking human blood and eating human liver could cure epilepsy,

attributing these beliefs to ancient medicine (50); he was also familiar with the reports of d'Argens and Tournefort: see, for example, Barry, 'News from the Invisible World', 208–09.

23. John Stagg, 'The Vampyre', in *The Minstrel of the North; or, Cumbrian Legends. Being a Poetical Miscellany of Legendary, Gothic, and Romantic Tales* (Manchester: Mark Wardle, 1816), 228–35, at 228; the Gothicization of the vampire is evident in the subtitle of the collection.

24. Stagg, 'The Vampyre', *Minstrel of the North*, 233; see *OED*; Thomas De Quincey also uses the word 'carnival' in this sense (see Thomas De Quincey, 'Postscript [to "On Murder Considered as One of the Fine Arts"]', *On Murder*, ed. Robert Morrison (Oxford: Oxford University Press, 2006), 95–141, at 132).

25. See above, pp. 47–48; see also Conrad Aquilina, 'The Deformed Transformed; or, From Bloodsucker to Byronic Hero – Polidori and the Literary Vampire', in George and Hughes, *Open Graves, Open Minds*, 24–38, at 25.

26. Stagg, 'The Vampyre', *Minstrel of the North*, 232.

27. Stagg, 'The Vampyre', *Minstrel of the North*, 234; 'distent', virtually obsolete, meaning 'distended' (*OED*).

28. The first vampire novel has not survived: Ignaz Ferdinand Arnold [also 'Theodor Ferdinand Kajetan Arnold'], *Der Vampir*, 3 vols (Schneeberg, 1801) (see Rebecca Tille, *Der Vampir als Element der Literaturgeschichte: Literaturwissenschaftliche Untersuchung zur schwarzromantischen Vampirmotivik* (Hamburg: Diplomica Verlag, 2013), 30). There are also other early German works, such as *Der Vampyr oder die blutige Hochzeit mit der Schönen Kroatin* (*The Vampire or the Bloody Wedding with the Croatian Beauty*) (Müller, 1812): see Crawford, *Origins of the Literary Vampire*, 59–80.

29. John William Polidori, *The Diary of Dr. John William Polidori, 1816: Relating to Byron, Shelley, etc.*, ed. William Michael Rossetti [his nephew] (London: Elkin Mathews, 1911), 125.

30. For Byron's hypochondria, see Jonathan Shears, 'Byron's Hypochondria', in Bernard Beatty and Jonathan Shears (eds), *Byron's Temperament: Essays in Body and Mind* (Newcastle upon Tyne: Cambridge Scholars Publishing, 2016), 100–17.

31. See Shelley, *Frankenstein*, xvi.

32. Byron took the idea from one of the ghost stories they had been reading, which begins with such a challenge: 'Les Portraits de famille', in [Anon.], *Fantasmagoriana, ou Recueil d'histoires d'apparitions de spectres, revenans, fantômes, etc.; Traduit de l'allemand, par un amateur*, trans. Jean Baptiste Benoit Eyriès, 2 vols (F. Schoell: Paris, 1812), i. 117–225.

33. Polidori, *Diary*, 127–28.

34. Shelley, *Frankenstein*, 175.

35. Polidori, *Diary*, 127–28.

36. Polidori's entry suggests that the first story had either been abandoned or was another tale entirely – probably his novel *Ernestus Berchtold; or, the Modern Oedipus*, which was published in 1819 (Polidori, *Diary*, 132). In the Introduction to *Ernestus Berchtold* he states that it was 'begun at Coligny, when Frankenstein was planned' (John William Polidori, *The Vampyre and Ernestus Berchtold; or, the Modern Oedipus: Collected Fiction of John William Polidori*, ed. D.L. Macdonald and Kathleen Scherf (Toronto, Buffalo and London: University of Toronto Press, 1994), 51).

37. George Gordon, Lord Byron, 'Augustus Darvell: A Fragment of a Ghost Story (1816)', in *Lord Byron: The Complete Miscellaneous Prose*, ed. Andrew Nicholson (Oxford: Oxford University Press, 1991), 58–63, at 61. 'A Fragment' was first published as appended to the poem *Mazeppa* in 1819, following the publication of Polidori's own story.

38. He had met the countess by 5 September and appears to have left the manuscript of his tale with her around 16 September: Polidori, *Diary*, 141, 152.

39. See, for example, Jolene Zigarovich, 'Courting Death: Necrophilia in Samuel Richardson's *Clarissa*', *Studies in the Novel*, 32 (2000), 112–28; and John Phillips, 'Circles of Influence: Lewis, Sade, Artaud', *Comparative Critical Studies*, 9 (2012), 61–82, at 78–79.

40. On the powers of the moon to reanimate, see Wright, *Vampires and Vampirism*, 2nd edn (1924), 217.

41. See Gregory A. Waller, *The Living and the Undead: Slaying Vampires, Exterminating Zombies* (Urbana, IL: University of Illinois Press, 2010), 49.

42. The informant was possibly Mme Gatelier.

43. Polidori, *Diary*, 15 (the letter of 2 April is at 15–17).

44. Polidori, *Diary*, 17–19.

45. See, for example, the American digest *Spirit of the English Magazines*, 5 (15 June 1819), 212–27. E.T.A. Hoffmann's short story 'Aurelia' (1819–20) begins by praising Byron for writing 'The Vampyre', and also refers to Ranft's work on manducation, see above, pp. 47–48.

46. The supplementary text was probably written by Alaric Watts, sub-editor on the magazine, with contributions from Colburn and the hack writer John Mitford.

47. See *New Monthly Magazine*, 11 (1 April 1819), 195–206 (reprinted in Chris Baldick and Robert Morrison (eds), *The Vampyre and Other Tales of the Macabre* (Oxford: Oxford University Press, 1997), 3–23, 235–45).

48. See Aquilina, 'The Deformed Transformed', 24–38.

49. See Butler, *Metamorphoses of the Vampire*, 85–100.

50. *The Imperial Magazine; or, Compendium of Religious, Moral, & Philosophical Knowledge*, 1 (1819), cols 236–39, at col. 236.

51. Also known as 'false vampires': see Barbara French, 'False Vampires and Other Carnivores: A Glimpse at this Select Group of Bats Reveals Efficient Predators with a Surprisingly Gentle Side . . .', *Bats Magazine*, 15 (1997), (online edn: accessed 20 February 2018); Buffon also identified the bat. The earliest accounts of bloodsucking bats (both sanguineous and sanguivorous) are in Aldrovandi, Shaw, Cuvier, Buffon, Geoffrey St Hilaire, Swainson, Gervais, Hensel, Goeldi and Quelch, among others (see Raymond L. Ditmars and Arthur M. Greenhall, 'The Vampire Bat: A Presentation of Undescribed Habits and a Review of its History' (1933–34), in Perkowski, *Vampire Lore*, 294–310, at 300; see also 544).

52. *Imperial Magazine*, 1 (1819), cols 241, 242.

53. Charles Waterton, *Wanderings in South America, the North-West of the United States, and the Antilles, in the Years 1812, 1816, 1820, and 1824* (London: J. Mawman, 1825), 174–79.

54. Charles Darwin, *Journal of Researches, Part One*, in *Works of Charles Darwin*, ed. Paul H. Barrett and R.B. Freeman (London: Routledge, 2016; *Works* originally published in 29 vols by William Pickering, 1986–89), ii. 21 [9 April 1832: 24/6]. The issue was discussed at length by Edward Blyth, curator to the Asiatic Society, in 'Notice of the Predatory and Sanguivorous Habits of Bats of the Genus Megaderma, with some Remarks on the Blood-Sucking Propensities of other Vespertilionide', *Journal of the Asiatic Society of Bengal*, 123 (1842), 255–62. According to Ditmars and Greenhall, 'Charles Darwin appears to have been the first scientist to observe a vampire [bat] in the act of drawing blood and note its procedure with satisfying clarity' (Ditmars and Greenhall, 'The Vampire Bat', 300).

55. The 'quadrupedal gait' of the bat is first mentioned in 1869 in the works of J.G. Wood: see Ditmars and Greenhall, 'The Vampire Bat', 301.

56. William Martin Leake, *Travels in Northern Greece*, 4 vols (London: J. Rodwell, 1835), iv. 216 (the word 'vampires' is used on p. 217); Leake observes here that 'Tournefort's description is admitted to be correct' and earlier quotes Tournefort (i. 492).

57. John Hunter, *The Natural History of the Human Teeth: Explaining their Structure, Use, Formation, Growth, and Diseases* (London, 1771); see also D.C. Schechter, 'Transplantation of Teeth', *Surgery, Gynecology & Obstetrics*, 132 (1971), 309–19 esp. 312.

58. Hamilton, *History of Organ Transplantation*, 34–45.

59. The satirist Thomas Rowlandson depicted the grim scene.

60. Hamilton, *History of Organ Transplantation*, 44–48.

61. *Gentleman's Magazine*, 58 (1785), 804: see William Watson, 'An Account of a Disease Occasioned by Transplanting a Tooth', in *Medical Commentaries*, 12 (1787), 209–17; see further Shelley, *Frankenstein*, xxii–xxiv.

62. Nicolas Dubois de Chémant, *A Dissertation on Artificial Teeth*, 4th edn (London: T. Bensley, 1804), 21.

63. Nicolas Dubois de Chémant, *A Dissertation on Artificial Teeth in General*, 1st edn (London: J. Barker, 1797), 15.

64. De Chémant, *A Dissertation on Artificial Teeth in General*, 9; see J. Robert Kelly and Paula Benetti, 'Ceramic Materials in Dentistry: Historical Evolution and Current Practice', *Australian Dental Journal*, 56 (2011), 84–96; and Colin Jones, *The Smile Revolution in Eighteenth-Century Paris* (Oxford: Oxford University Press, 2014). See also https://oldblockwriter.blogspot.co.uk/2013/01/the-mystery-of-seahorse-teeth.html and www.bbc.co.uk/news/magazine-33085031 (accessed 5 February 2018).

65. Philippe Frédéric Blandin, *Anatomy of the Dental System, Human and Comparative*, trans. Robert Arthur (Baltimore, MD: American Society of Dental Surgeons, 1845), 189–96.

66. J.S. LeFanu [*sic*], 'Carmilla', in *Best Ghost Stories*, ed. E.F. Bleiler (New York: Dover Publications, 1964), 274–339, at 296; Sugg, *Mummies, Cannibals, and Vampires*, 148–49.

67. Edgar Allan Poe, 'Berenice', in *The Complete Tales* (New York: Avenel Books, 1981), 8–13.

68. *London Packet* or *Lloyd's Evening Post*, Monday, 24 March 1794 (extracted in Cox's *Fragmenta*, x, 186 (see *Cox's Fragmenta: An Historical Miscellany*, ed. Simon Murphy (Stroud: The History Press, 2010), 61)).

69. Edward Jenner, *An Inquiry into the Causes and Effects of the Variolæ Vaccinæ, a Disease discovered in some of the Western Counties of England, particularly Gloucestershire, and known by the Name of the*

Cow Pox (London, 1798), in Tim Fulford (ed.), *Romanticism and Science, 1773–1833*, 5 vols (London and New York: Routledge, 2002), i. 103–06; for a further discussion of this, see Shelley, *Frankenstein*, xxv.

70. Fulford, *Romanticism and Science*, i. 104.
71. See 'Pamphlets on Vaccination' from *The Edinburgh Review*, 15 (1810), 324–51 in Fulford, *Romanticism and Science*, i. 131–56.
72. Fulford, *Romanticism and Science*, i. 145.
73. See the Introduction to my edition of Shelley's *Frankenstein* for a discussion, xx–xxviii.
74. Erasmus Darwin, *The Botanic Garden*, ed. Adam Komisaruk and Allison Dushane, 2 vols (London and New York: Routledge, 2017), ii. *The Loves of the Plants*, 58 (Canto II. ll. 359–60; the poem first appeared in the *Analytical Review* for 1789).
75. Percy Bysshe Shelley, 'The Triumph of Life', in *Shelley's Poetry and Prose*, ed. Donald H. Reiman and Sharon B. Powers (New York and London: W.W. Norton & Company, 1977), 455–70, at 468 (ll. 486, 488).

Chapter 6

1. William Harvey, *The Anatomical Exercises*, quoted by Bernard Lake, '*A Discourse of the Heart* by James de Back', *Medical History*, 10 (1966), 60–69, at 63 (*Discovrse*, sig. H8ᵛ).
2. D.H. Lawrence, 'Edgar Allan Poe', in *Studies in Classic American Literature*, ed. Ezra Greenspan, Lindeth Vasey and John Worthen (Cambridge: Cambridge University Press, 2003), 66–80, at 79.
3. Thomas Willis, 'A TABLE of all the hard words derived from the *Greek* and *Latin* . . .', *The Remaining Medical Works of that Famous and Renowned Physician Dr Thomas Willis . . .*, trans. Samuel Pordage (London, 1681), n.p.
4. Shelley, *Frankenstein*, 52; some points are based on the Introduction to this edition, ix–l.
5. Percy Bysshe Shelley, *The Letters of Percy Bysshe Shelley*, ed. Frederick L. Jones, 2 vols (Oxford: Clarendon Press, 1964), i. 421, 992.
6. Shelley, *Frankenstein*, 61.
7. Shelley, *Frankenstein*, 65.
8. Shelley, *Frankenstein*, 29.
9. Shelley, *Frankenstein*, 124, 127.
10. Shelley, *Frankenstein*, 149.
11. See Maryanne C. Ward, 'A Painting of the Unspeakable: Henry Fuseli's *The Nightmare* and the Creation of Mary Shelley's *Frankenstein*', *Journal of the Midwest Modern Language Association*, 33 (2000), 20–31.
12. Shelley, *Frankenstein*, 149, 48, 133.
13. A 'bloodshot blue mark, the length of a finger': see above, p. 36.
14. Shelley, *Frankenstein*, 52.
15. Shelley, *Frankenstein*, 103.
16. Shelley, *Frankenstein*, 52.
17. Shelley, *Frankenstein*, 145, 144, 154.
18. Shelley, *Frankenstein*, 141.
19. Blundell had previously lectured on animal vivisection and subsequently went on to work with human subjects; in 1828, the *Lancet* reported that he had successfully transfused blood into a human patient; see Hamilton, *History of Organ Transplantation*, 29–30; and King, 'An Account of the Experiment of Transfusion', 557–59.
20. See above, p. 19.
21. Shelley, *Frankenstein*, 175.
22. Shelley, *Letters*, i. 358; the account was published in Shelley's *History of a Six Weeks' Tour*.
23. Helena Feder, *Ecocriticism and the Idea of Culture: Biology and the Bildungsroman* (London and New York: Routledge, 2016), 18. Percy Shelley's poem 'Mont Blanc' also represents power as oblivious to the human predicament, introducing predatory and Gothic language in describing the impervious mountain: 'The glaciers creep / Like snakes that watch their prey . . . A city of death . . . a flood of ruin . . . The limits of the dead and living world, / Never to be reclaimed . . . The race / Of man, flies far in dread; his work and dwelling / Vanish, like smoke before the tempest's stream, / And their place is not known' (Shelley, *Poetry and Prose*, 91–93, at 92 (ll. 100–120)).
24. 'VAMPIRE TRAPS are folding doors made in a flat, or set scene; they are formed of whalebone faced with canvass, and through the centre the performer easily forces his body, the whalebone causing the "door"

immediately to return.' They could be either horizontal trapdoors through the stage itself or 'Upright Vampires', allowing an actor to disappear through a wall (see 'Behind the Scenes', *Paul Pry*, 20 (November 1848), 1–2).

25. Cooke played the Being 365 times: see *ODNB*.
26. Signed 'St John Dorset': see *ODNB*.
27. William St Clair, *The Reading Nation in the Romantic Period* (Cambridge: Cambridge University Press, 2004), 369–70.
28. See Roxana Stuart, *Stage Blood: Vampires of the 19th-Century Stage* (Bowling Green, OH: Bowling Green State University Popular Press, 1994), 165.
29. Keats cites this section of Burton's *Anatomy of Melancholy* at the end of the poem (Pt 3, Sect. 2, Memb. 1, Subs. 1 (Burton, *Anatomy of Melancholy*, iii. 45–46)).
30. Keats, *Lamia*, *Poetical Works*, 161–78, Pt I. ll. 55–56 (p. 162).
31. Keats, *Lamia*, *Poetical Works*, Pt I. ll. 141–45 (p. 164).
32. Keats, *Lamia*, *Poetical Works*, Pt I. ll. 292, 287–89 (p. 168); Summers makes a similar point in *The Vampire in Europe*, 5.
33. This would perhaps explain the combination of Greek and Gothic in *Lamia*, called 'confused temporality' by Robert Miles (*Gothic Writing, 1750–1820: A Genealogy* (London and New York: Routledge, 1993), 210).
34. Nick Groom (ed.), *The Bloody Register*, 4 vols (London: Routledge/Thoemmes Press, 1999), i. 135.
35. Groom, *Bloody Register*, i. 343.
36. Groom, *Bloody Register*, iii. 23.
37. Groom, *Bloody Register*, iii. 187–93, at 190.
38. [Anon.], *James Hall Footman to John Penny of Clement's Inn* (1741): BL 1953, 0411. Samuel Wale also depicted this scene in a drawing: Samuel Wale, 'James Hall Murdering Mr Penny in Clement's Inn [?], 1741' (*c. 1730–86*): BL 1953, 0411.37.
39. De Quincey, 'Postscript', *On Murder*, 114.
40. *Morning Chronicle* (1 January 1812), quoted in *Hansard*, xxvii (London: Longman, Hurst, Rees, Orme and Brown, etc., 1814), clxxxvi; De Quincey: 'in obedience to the law as it then stood, he was buried in the centre of a *quadrivium*, or conflux of four roads (in this case four streets), with a stake driven through his heart' (De Quincey, 'Postscript', *On Murder*, 141, 196n.).
41. De Quincey writes about the case in 'On the Knocking at the Gate in *Macbeth*' (1823) and 'On Murder Considered as One of the Fine Arts' (1827), to which he later added a 'Second Paper' (1839) and a 'Postscript' (1854); all of these writings are included in De Quincey, *On Murder*.
42. See David Roden, 'Aliens Under the Skin: Serial Killing and the Seduction of our Common Inhumanity', in Edia Connole and Gary J. Shipley (eds), *Serial Killing: A Philosophical Anthology* (no place: Schism Press, 2015), 9–20, at 15.
43. De Quincey, 'To the Editor of Blackwood's Magazine', *On Murder*, 155–60, at 157.
44. See Roden, 'Aliens Under the Skin', 18 (taking its cue from Jacques Derrida, 'The Law of Genre', *Acts of Literature*, ed. Derek Attridge (New York and London: Routledge, 1992), 221–53, at 227–28).
45. Roden, 'Aliens Under the Skin', 20; Roden argues that phenomenology is 'striated with "darkness" – experiencing it only affords a partial and very fallible insight into nature', 15; see David Roden, 'Nature's Dark Domain: An Argument for a Naturalised Phenomenology', *Royal Institute of Philosophy Supplement*, 72 (2013), 169–88.
46. Shelley, *Frankenstein*, 176.
47. See Aspasia Stephanou, 'Exquisite Corpse: Serial Killing and the Horripilation of Writing', in Connole and Shipley (eds), *Serial Killing*, 147–62, at 149; see also Groom, *The Forger's Shadow*, 256–92.
48. See Stephanou, 'Exquisite Corpse', 158.
49. For the classic Oedipal reading of inspiration, see Harold Bloom, *The Anxiety of Influence: A Theory of Poetry*, 2nd edn (New York: Oxford University Press, 1997).
50. De Quincey, 'Postscript', *On Murder*, 112.
51. De Quincey, 'Postscript', *On Murder*, 100–01, 119–21.
52. De Quincey, 'Postscript', *On Murder*, 139.
53. Charles Dickens, *The Old Curiosity Shop*, ed. Elizabeth M. Brennan (Oxford: Clarendon Press, 1997), 569 (ch. 73).
54. 'An Act to Alter and Amend the Law relating to the Interment of the Remains of any Person found *Felo de se*', 8 July 1823: see *A Compendious Abstract of the Public General Acts of the United Kingdom of Great Britain and Ireland: 4 Geo. IV. 1823* (London: J.W. Paget, 1823), 108 (see Wright, *Vampires and Vampirism*, 2nd edn (1924), 8–9).

55. McCarthy, ' "Death to Vampires!" ', 189–208, at 195.
56. See Elizabeth T. Hurren, *Dissecting the Criminal Corpse: Staging Post-Execution Punishment in Early Modern England* (Basingstoke: Palgrave Macmillan, 2016); Peter King, *Punishing the Criminal Corpse, 1700–1840: Aggravated Forms of the Death Penalty in England* (Basingstoke: Palgrave Macmillan, 2017); and Richard Ward (ed.), *A Global History of Execution and the Criminal Corpse* (Basingstoke: Palgrave Macmillan, 2015).
57. This obliteration of the body has a dark comedy to it, for example in Sabine Baring-Gould's 'Margery of Quether', in which the defeated she-vampire lives on as a husk.
58. Baring-Gould, *Book of Werewolves*, 47; the best account of this text is by Joanne Parker, 'Sensation and Superstition in *The Book of Werewolves*', *Transactions of the Sabine Baring-Gould Appreciation Society*, 10 (2010), 66–77.
59. Baring-Gould, *Book of Werewolves*, 57.
60. I am indebted to Clive Liddiard for this information and other linguistic points.
61. Baring-Gould, *Book of Werewolves*, 87.
62. Baring-Gould, *Book of Werewolves*, 103.
63. This is Elizabeth (Erzsébet) Báthory, whose name is given as 'Elizabeth ——' (Baring-Gould, *Book of Werewolves*, 104).
64. Baring-Gould, *Book of Werewolves*, 106.
65. Baring-Gould, *Book of Werewolves*, 108.
66. Baring-Gould, *Book of Werewolves*, 185; Baring-Gould claims that the full details 'are too revolting for reproduction' (182); these details included garlanding nearby trees and memorials with the entrails he eviscerated from the corpses, before sexually violating them. Bertrand's case helped to inspire the coining of the word 'necrophilia' in 1850: see Michel Foucault, *Abnormal: Lectures at the Collège de France, 1974–1975*, ed. Valerio Marchetti and Antonella Salomoni, trans. Graham Burchell (London and New York: Verso, 2003), 283–85 (12 March 1975); Michael Camille, *The Gargoyles of Notre-Dame: Medievalism and the Monsters of Modernity* (Chicago, IL, and London: University of Chicago Press, 2009), 144–45; and Shane Weller, 'Decomposition: Georges Bataille and the Language of Necrophilia', in Anna Katharina Schaffner and Shane Weller, *Modernist Eroticisms: European Literature after Sexology* (Basingstoke: Palgrave Macmillan, 2012), 169–94, at 169.
67. Bram Dijkstra, *Idols of Perversity: Fantasies of Feminine Evil in Fin-de-Siècle Culture* (New York and Oxford: Oxford University Press, 1986), 335–36.
68. Stoker, *Dracula*, ed. Luckhurst, 352–62, at 359.
69. Claude Bernard, *An Introduction to the Study of Experimental Medicine*, trans. Henry Copley Greene (New York: Henry Schuman, Inc., 1949), 99 (extracted in Laura Otis (ed.), *Literature and Science in the Nineteenth Century: An Anthology* (Oxford: Oxford University Press, 2002), 203–08).
70. Bernard, *Introduction to the Study of Experimental Medicine*, 102.
71. Bernard, *Introduction to the Study of Experimental Medicine*, 104; see Andrew Cunningham, *The Anatomist Anatomis'd: An Experimental Discipline in Enlightenment Europe* (Farnham: Ashgate, 2010).
72. Bernard, *Introduction to the Study of Experimental Medicine*, 103.
73. Royal Commission on Vivisection for Scientific Purposes (1875), question 3539: quoted by Bruno Atalić and Stella Fatović-Ferenčić, 'Emanuel Edward Klein – The Father of British Microbiology and the Case of the Animal Vivisection Controversy of 1875', in *Toxicologic Pathology*, 37 (2009), 708–13, at 711.
74. Frances Power Cobbe, 'Vivisection and Its Two-Faced Advocates' (*Contemporary Review*, April 1882), reprinted as *The Janus of Science* (London: Office of the Society for Protection of Animals from Vivisection, 1882), 5 (extracted in Otis (ed.), *Literature and Science*, 215–20); see also *The Times* of 11 October 1892.
75. Cobbe, *Janus of Science*, 6 (quoting from Elie de Cyon, *Methodik der Physiologischen Experimente und Vivisectionen* (1876), 15 (ellipses in original)).
76. Bynum, *Science and the Practice of Medicine*, 171; for vivisection, see, for example, Marc Bekoff, with Carron A. Meaney (eds), *Encyclopedia of Animal Rights and Animal Welfare* (London and New York: Routledge, 2013); Rob Boddice, *The Science of Sympathy: Morality, Evolution, and Victorian Civilization* (Urbana, Chicago and Springfield: University of Illinois Press, 2016); Norm Phelps, *The Longest Struggle: Animal Advocacy from Pythagoras to PETA* (New York: Lantern Books, 2007); and Deborah Rudacille, *The Scalpel and the Butterfly: The Conflict between Animal Research and Animal Protection* (Berkeley, Los Angeles and London: University of California Press, 2000).
77. See, for example, Tony Thorne, *Children of the Night: Of Vampires and Vampirism* (London: Victor Gollancz, 1999), 43, 46, 231–33.

78. 'The Young Tamlane', in Walter Scott, *Minstrelsy of the Scottish Border*, 3 vols (London: T. Cadell, Jr. and W. Davies, 1802–03), ii. 228–43; Southey, *Thalaba* (1814 edn), 108; see Preface to Henry Thomas Liddell, earl of Ravensworth, 'The Vampire Bride', in *The Wizard of the North; The Vampire Bride; and Other Poems* (Edinburgh: W. Blackwood, and London: T. Cadell, 1833), 29–56, at 30.

79. Liddell, 'The Vampire Bride', 39.

80. Liddell, 'The Vampire Bride', 50.

81. James Clerk Maxwell, 'The Vampyre', in Lewis Campbell and William Garnett, *The Life of James Clerk Maxwell with a Selection from his Correspondence and Occasional Writings and a Sketch of his Contributions to Science* (London: Macmillan and Co., 1882), 585–87, at 586–87.

82. See Sara Hackenberg, 'Vampires and Resurrection Men: The Perils and Pleasures of the Embodied Past in 1840s Sensational Fiction', *Victorian Studies*, 52 (2009), 63–75; for a Gothic overview of the Civil Wars and their aftermath, see my book, *The Gothic: A Very Short Introduction*, 44–53; for a summary of *Varney*'s influence, see Frayling, *Vampyres*, 38–41, and his useful 'Vampire Mosaic' survey, 42–63.

83. James Malcolm Rymer, *Varney the Vampyre or, The Feast of Blood*. ed. Dick Collins (London: Wordsworth Editions, 2010), 8 (chapter 1).

84. Rymer, *Varney the Vampyre*, 28 (chapter 4).

85. Rymer, *Varney the Vampyre*, 95 (chapter 15).

86. His successful suicide closes the book (Rymer, *Varney the Vampyre*, 1166, chapter 220); this follows extraordinary revivals after drownings.

87. Rymer, *Varney the Vampyre*, 370 (chapter 64).

88. Beresford, *From Demons to Dracula*, 123: Beresford goes on to claim 'until the pioneering *Vampire Chronicles* by Anne Rice'.

89. Lawrence, 'Poe', in *Studies in Classic American Literature*, 74, 78.

90. Charlotte Brontë, *Jane Eyre*, ed. Margaret Smith and Sally Shuttleworth (Oxford: Oxford University Press, 2000), 284 (for a discussion of the German influence, see Butler, *Metamorphoses of the Vampire*, 129–76).

91. Phil Robinson, 'Medusa', in Phil Robinson, E. Kay Robinson and H. Perry Robinson, *Tales by Three Brothers* (London: Isbister and Company, 1902), 163–95, at 174.

92. Donovan also wrote a sequel/prequel.

93. Rudyard Kipling, 'The Vampire', in *The Collected Poems*, ed. R.T. Jones (Ware: Wordsworth, 2001), 232; as such, it has attracted highly sexualized readings: see, for example, Anne Morey and Claudia Nelson, 'Phallus and Void in Kipling's "The Vampire" and Its Progeny', *Frame*, 24 (2011), 39–55. The notion of the abject is suggestively and influentially investigated by Julia Kristeva in *The Powers of Horror: An Essay on Abjection*, trans. Leon S. Roudiez (New York: Columbia University Press, 1982).

94. Robert Louis Stevenson, 'Olalla', in *The Merry Men and Other Tales and Fables* (London: Chatto & Windus, 1905), 143–200, at 166, 163, 174.

95. Such as 'vamped up', 'basilisks', 'bewitched' (Stevenson, 'Olalla', 198).

96. Stevenson, 'Olalla', 191.

97. Sara Wasson, 'Olalla's Legacy: Twentieth-Century Vampire Fiction and Genetic Previvorship', *Journal of Stevenson Studies*, 7 (2010), 55–81, at 55, 75; Wasson sees the story inaugurating a tradition that includes Tanith Lee's *Blood Dance* (1991) and Poppy Z. Brite's *Lost Souls* (1992).

98. See Brenda Mann Hammack, 'Florence Marryat's Female Vampire and the Scientizing of Hybridity', *Studies in English Literature, 1500–1900*, 48 (2008), 885–96.

99. Florence Marryat, *Blood of the Vampire* (Leipzig: Bernhard Tauchnitz, 1897), 7; there are also editions ed. Greta Depledge (Brighton: Victorian Secrets, 2010) and ed. Brenda Mann Hammack (Kansas City, KS: Valancourt Books, 2009).

100. Marryat, *Blood of the Vampire*, 115.

101. Marryat, *Blood of the Vampire*, 133.

102. Marryat, *Blood of the Vampire*, 281.

103. Marryat, *Blood of the Vampire*, 261.

104. For criticism, see, primarily, Joseph Sheridan Le Fanu, *Carmilla: A Critical Edition*, ed. Kathleen Costello-Sullivan (New York: Syracuse University Press, 2013), 99–137; see also, for example, Day (ed.), *Vampires: Myths and Metaphors*, 21–38; Ardel Haefele-Thomas, *Queer Others in Victorian Gothic: Transgressing Monstrosity* (Cardiff: University of Wales Press, 2012), 96–119; and Julieann Ulin, 'Sheridan Le Fanu's Vampires and Ireland's Invited Invasion', in George and Hughes (eds), *Open Graves, Open Minds*, 39–55. See also influence on film, notably Carl Dreyer's *Vampyr* (1932), the first vampire film not based explicitly on *Dracula* (Le Fanu, *Carmilla: A Critical Edition*, 138–48).

105. See Willis, 'Le Fanu's "Carmilla"', 111–30.
106. LeFanu, 'Carmilla', 274–339, at 275.
107. LeFanu, 'Carmilla', 277.
108. LeFanu, 'Carmilla', 304, see also 313.
109. LeFanu, 'Carmilla', 291.
110. LeFanu, 'Carmilla', 296.
111. LeFanu, 'Carmilla', 307.
112. LeFanu, 'Carmilla', 337.
113. LeFanu, 'Carmilla', 307–08.
114. LeFanu, 'Carmilla', 313, see also 331.
115. LeFanu, 'Carmilla', 326–27.
116. LeFanu, 'Carmilla', 335.
117. LeFanu, 'Carmilla', 336.
118. LeFanu, 'Carmilla', 337.
119. LeFanu, 'Carmilla', 337.
120. LeFanu, 'Carmilla', 336–37.

Chapter 7

1. Capaneus, in Dante's *Inferno*, canto xiv, 51. See Thacker, 'Blasphemous Life', *In the Dust of This Planet*, 101–02; Thacker suggests that this means 'I am a living contradiction' – '*living dead*'.
2. Virginia Woolf, *The Waves* (London: Hogarth Press, 1931), 92.
3. From the anonymous *Book of a Hundred Chapters*, attributed to 'The Revolutionary of the Upper Rhine', quoted by Norman Cohn, *The Pursuit of Millennium: Revolutionary Millenarians and Mystical Anarchists of the Middle Ages* (London: Paladin, 1970), 121; Cohn describes this apocalyptic treatise as 'the last and most comprehensive expression of the popular eschatology of the Middle Ages' (119).
4. Bynum, *Science and the Practice of Medicine*, 14, 124; more generally, see Thomas L. Hankins, *Biology in the Nineteenth Century: Problems of Form, Function, and Transformation*, 2nd edn (Cambridge: Cambridge University Press, 1977).
5. Immanuel Kant, 'Anthropology from a Pragmatic Point of View' (1798), trans. Robert B. Louden, in Robert B. Louden and Günter Zöller (ed. and trans.), *Anthropology, History, and Education* (Cambridge: Cambridge University Press, 2007), 227–429, at 414; Thomas Hardy, *Jude the Obscure*, ed. Patricia Ingham (Oxford: Oxford University Press, 2002), 70; a comparable theme also runs through *Tess of the D'Urbervilles* (1891).
6. Marion Harry Spielmann, 'The Paris Salons', *The Magazine of Art*, 22 (1898), 489–97, at 495. The French novelist 'Rachilde' (Marguerite Eymery-Vallette, known as 'Mademoiselle Baudelaire') used the painting as inspiration for her short story, 'The Blood Drinker' (1900), a fantasy about the moon living off the blood of women: see Dijkstra, *Idols of Perversity*, 337–40; see also Maria Parsons, 'Vamping the Woman: Menstrual Pathologies in Bram Stoker's *Dracula*', *Irish Journal of Gothic and Horror Studies*, 1 (2006), 66–83.
7. See Masson, *History of Blood Transfusion in Edinburgh*, 7; blood groups were discovered by Karl Landsteiner in 1900. For blood superstitions, see above, Introduction, pp. 6–12; see Strack, *The Jew and Human Sacrifice*, 70–76: taking living blood in this way was practised in Germany throughout the century – for instance in 1823, 1844, 1859 and 1862 (71–73); see also the desecration of graves for body parts throughout nineteenth-century Germany (92–95). In Bavaria, meanwhile, dried pigeon blood mixed with snuff was believed to cure nose-bleeding.
8. See James Ewing, *Clinical Pathology of the Blood* (London: Henry Kimpton, 1904), 44.
9. See Havelock Ellis, *Man and Woman: A Study of Human Secondary Sexual Characters* (London: Walter Scott, 1894), especially 196–202.
10. Arthur Symons, *Lesbia and Other Poems* (New York: E.F. Dutton & Company, 1920), 1; the repetition of the word 'white' drains the lines of richness and vitality. The short poem goes on, echoing Walter Pater's response to *La Gioconda*: 'Whose eyes remember many martyrdoms, / So that their depths, whose depth cannot be found, / Are shadowed pools in which a soul lies drowned' (see below, pp. 190–91).
11. Dijkstra, *Idols of Perversity*, 309; note that the 'bloofer lady' (see below, p. 240) takes children.
12. Dante Gabriel Rossetti, 'Eden Bower', in *Poems* (London: Ellis & White, 1881), 82–91, at 82.
13. Dijkstra, *Idols of Perversity*, 291.

14. Henry Maudsley, *Gulstonian Lectures* (1870), published as *Body and Mind: An Inquiry into their Connection ad Mutual Influence, Specially in Reference to Mental Disorders* (London: Macmillan and Co., 1870), 73, 78, 80 (quoted in Otis (ed.), *Literature and Science*, 364–69).

15. Cæsar Lombroso and William Ferrero, *The Female Offender* (New York: Appleton and Company, 1895), 151; moreover, 'women are big children; . . . their evil tendencies are more numerous and more varied than men's, but generally remain latent. When they are awakened and excited they produce results proportionately greater.' Dracula has a 'child-brain' (Stoker, *Dracula*, ed. Luckhurst, 281, 315): see below, p. 184.

16. Lombroso and Ferrero, *The Female Offender*, 151–52.

17. See Laura Otis, *Organic Memory: History and the Body in the Late Nineteenth & Early Twentieth Centuries* (Lincoln, NE and London: University of Nebraska Press, 1994), 49–50. Morel also pioneered the theory of 'dementia praecox', or 'precocious madness': the catastrophic deterioration of mental states in early life; it has since been replaced by a spectrum of psychiatric disorders.

18. Cesare Lombroso, *Criminal Man*, ed. Gina Lombroso-Ferrero (New York and London: G.P. Putnam's Sons, 1911), 5; revised editions followed in 1878, 1884, 1889 and 1896–97; the text has been comprehensively edited by Mary Gibson and Nicole Hahn Rafter (Durham, NC, and London: Duke University Press, 2006) (see also Otis (ed.), *Literature and Science*, 516–19, at 517); see Otis, *Organic Memory*, 50–52. The following account draws on Paolo Mazzarello, 'Cesare Lombroso: An Anthropologist between Evolution and Degeneration', *Functional Neurology*, 26 (2011), 97–101; see also Frank E. Hagan, *Introduction to Criminology: Theories, Methods, and Criminal Behavior*, 6th edn (Los Angeles, CA, and London: Sage Publications, 2008), 119–121; also interesting is Marvin E. Wolfgang, 'Pioneers in Criminology: Cesare Lombroso (1835–1900)', *Journal of Criminal Law, Criminology, and Police Science*, 52 (1961), 361–91.

19. Lombroso, *Criminal Man*, ed. Lombroso-Ferrero, xv.

20. William Patrick Day, *In the Circles of Fear and Desire: A Study of Gothic Fantasy* (Chicago, IL, and London: University of Chicago Press, 1985), 114.

21. Lombroso's thesis on genius and insanity inspired him to visit Leo Tolstoy, whom he expected to find 'cretinous and degenerate looking', but who was in reality as sharp as a pin and utterly dismissive of Lombroso's theories; Lombroso's reward was to have his theories ridiculed in Tolstoy's final novel, *Resurrection* (1899) (quoted by Mazzarello, 'Cesare Lombroso', 100).

22. Max Nordau, *Degeneration* (London: William Heinemann, 1898), 7.

23. Nordau, *Degeneration*, 34.

24. Nordau, *Degeneration*, 39.

25. Nordau, *Degeneration*, 36 (some of Nordau's material is usefully quoted by Otis (ed.), *Literature and Science*, 525–29).

26. Biale, *Blood and Belief*, xi–xii.

27. See Biale, *Blood and Belief*, 1–2; see also Susanna Buttaroni and Stanisław Musiał (eds), *Ritual Murder: Legend in European History* (Cracow, Nuremberg and Frankfurt: Association for Cultural Initiatives, 2003), particularly Rainer Erb, 'The Ritual Murder Legend: From the Beginning until the 20th Century', 10–19; Alan Dundes, *The Blood Libel Legend: A Casebook of Anti-Semitic Folklore* (Madison, WI: University of Wisconsin Press, 1991); and Uli Linke, *Blood and Nation: The European Aesthetics of Race* (Philadelphia, PA: University of Pennsylvania Press, 1999).

28. 'Haemodynamic discourse' covers the blood of the covenant, God's blood, blood community and, of course, bloodsucking.

29. Biale links Jewish and Christian notions of the circulation of blood through history as 'the control of blood as an index of power' (*Blood and Belief*, 8).

30. See Leviticus 17:10, which prompted a huge commentary by Jacob Milgrom in the *Anchor Bible* (New Haven, CT: Yale University Press, 2007); there are also laws against spilling blood in Genesis, Deuteronomy and Ezekiel (Biale, *Blood and Belief*, 44.).

31. Quoted by Jonathan Frankel, *The Damascus Affair: 'Ritual Murder', Politics, and the Jews in 1840* (Cambridge: Cambridge University Press, 1997), 76.

32. *The Times* (25 June 1840), quoted by Frankel, *The Damascus Affair*, 76.

33. See Biale, *Blood and Belief*, 127.

34. Disraeli himself briefly alluded to vampires in his early novel, *The Voyage of Captain Popanilla* (1828).

35. Biale, *Blood and Belief*, 172.

36. There have been passionate – and finely argued – cases that *Dracula* in particular is an anti-Semitic text; these take some of their inspiration from the theory of 'reverse colonialism' (see Arata, cited

above, pp. 41–42): see, in particular, Judith Halberstam, *Skin Shows: Gothic Horror and the Technology of Monsters* (Durham, NC, and London: Duke University Press, 2006), 86–106; see also Carol Margaret Davison, *Anti-Semitism and British Gothic Literature* (Basingstoke: Palgrave Macmillan, 2004), 120–57; and Ken Gelder, *Reading the Vampire* (London and New York: Routledge, 1994), 13–17, 22–23, 96–97.

37. Moses Hess, 'Das Geldwesen', in *Philosophische und sozialistiche Schriften 1837–1850*, ed. Wolfgang Mönke (Vaduz: Topos, 1980), 335 (translated by Biale, *Blood and Belief*, 177).

38. Robert Burns, 'To Robert Graham of Fintry, Esq.' (1793), in Robert Burns, *The Canongate Burns*, ed. Andrew Noble and Patrick Scott Hogg (Edinburgh: Canongate, 2001), 246–56, at 247; Thomas Moore, 'Corruption, An Epistle, &c. &c.', in *Corruption and Intolerance: Two Poems* (London: J. Carpenter, 1808), 26.

39. Philip H. Bagenal, *The Irish Agitator in Parliament and on the Platform: A Complete History of Irish Politics for the Year 1879; with a Summary of Conclusions and an Appendix, containing Documents of Political Importance published during the Year* (Dublin: Hodges, Foster, and Figgis, 1880), 84; see also Michael J. Winstanley, *Ireland and the Land Question, 1800–1922* (London and New York: Methuen, 1984), 17–18.

40. John Maynard Keynes, *Essays in Biography* (London: Macmillan and Co., 1933), 37.

41. Terry Eagleton, *Ideology of the Aesthetic* (Oxford: Blackwell, 2000), 201; Eagleton is paraphrasing Marx's own comments in his 'Economic and Philosophic Manuscripts': see below, p. 159 (nevertheless, this is obviously suggestive of Oscar Wilde, *The Picture of Dorian Gray*: see below, p. 190); for an account of vampirism, blood and consumption in another sense, see Aspasia Stephanou, *Reading Vampire Gothic Through Blood: Bloodlines* (Basingstoke: Palgrave Macmillan, 2014).

42. For discussion of Marx, see Terrell Carver, 'Making Capital out of Vampires', *Times Higher Education Supplement* (June 1984), 15; Terrell Carver, *The Postmodern Marx* (Manchester: Manchester University Press, 1998), 14; and David McNally, *Monsters of the Market: Zombies, Vampires and Global Capitalism* (Leiden and Boston, MA: Brill, 2011), especially 113–73 and 140–46. Most of the following examples are based on Mark Neocleous's excellent research: see 'The Political Economy of the Dead: Marx's Vampires', *History of Political Thought*, 24(4) (2003), 668–84; and also *The Monstrous and the Dead: Burke, Marx, Fascism* (Cardiff: University of Wales Press, 2005), especially 36–71. See also Matthew MacLellan, 'Marx's Vampires: An Althusserian Critique', *Rethinking Marxism: A Journal of Economics, Culture & Society*, 25 (2013), 549–65. Marx's use of spectral imagery inspired Jacques Derrida's famous notion of hauntology; however, unlike Marx himself, Derrida barely considers the figure of the Marxist vampire: see Derrida, *Specters of Marx*, 155.

43. Karl Marx, *The Class Struggles in France: 1848 to 1850* (1850), in David Fernbach (ed.), *Surveys from Exile* (Harmondsworth: Penguin, 1973), 35–142, at 88; Karl Marx, *The Eighteenth Brumaire of Louis Bonaparte* (1852), in Fernbach, *Surveys from Exile*, 143–249, at 242; there is a possible allusion to Vlad the Impaler in *The Civil War in France* and *The Eighteenth Brumaire* (Frayling, *Vampyres*, 84; Neocleous, 'Political Economy of the Dead', 670). Burke describes the Revolutionaries in supernatural terms and undead imagery: they were intoxicated, for example, by 'the hot spirit drawn out of the alembick of hell', and having hacked their parent (the state) to pieces 'put him into the kettle of magicians, in hopes that by their poisonous weeds, and wild incantations, they may regenerate the paternal constitution, and renovate their father's life' (Edmund Burke, *Reflections on the Revolution in France*, ed. L.G. Mitchell (Oxford: Oxford University Press, 1993), 91, 96); the Jacobins had also of course been described as 'blood drinkers' (*buveurs de sang*) (see Klaniczay, *Uses of Supernatural Power*, 238n.).

44. Karl Marx, *Grundrisse*, trans. Martin Nicolaus ([1857–58] Harmondsworth: Penguin, 1973), 646, 660.

45. Karl Marx, *The Civil War in France* (1871), in *The First International and After*, ed. David Fernbach (Harmondsworth: Penguin, 1974), 215 (see also 249).

46. See Gary Day, 'The State of *Dracula*: Bureaucracy and the Vampire', in Alice Jenkins and Juliet John (eds), *Rereading Victorian Fiction* (New York: St Martin's Press, 2000), 81–95, at 87.

47. Karl Marx, *Capital: A Critique of Political Economy*, Vol. 1 (1867), trans. Ben Fowkes (Harmondsworth: Penguin, 1976), 342.

48. Marx, *Capital*, 367, 416.

49. Frederick Engels, *The Condition of the Working Class in England in 1844*, trans. Florence Kelley Wischnewetzky (New York: Cosimo Books, 2008), 238.

50. Karl Marx, 'Inaugural Address of the International Working Men's Association' (1864), in *The First International and After*, 79.

51. For the werewolf: 'So far, we have observed the drive towards the extension of the working day, and the werewolf-like hunger for surplus labour, in an area where capital's monstrous outrages . . . caused it at last to be bound by the chains of legal regulations' (Marx, *Capital*, 353).

52. Neocleous, 'Political Economy of the Dead', 669 (see also Neocleous, *The Monstrous and the Dead*).

53. Marx, *Capital*, 926.

54. Karl Marx, 'Justification of the Correspondent from the Mosel', in Karl Marx and Friedrich Engels, *Marx–Engels Collected Works*, 50 vols (Moscow: Progress Publishers, 1975–2005), i. 334 (for an oblique perspective, see Andrew Smith, 'Reading Wealth in Nigeria: Occult Capitalism and Marx's Vampires', *Historical Materialism*, 9 (2001), 39–59).

55. Carver, 'Making Capital out of Vampires'; Carver, *Postmodern Marx*, 16–18.

56. See above, pp. 85–86.

57. Karl Marx, 'Economic and Philosophic Manuscripts' (1844), in *Early Writings*, trans. Rodney Livingstone and Gregor Benton (Harmondsworth: Penguin, 1975), 324 (emphasis in original).

58. James Anthony Froude, *Thomas Carlyle: A History of his Life in London, 1834–1888*, 4th edn, 2 vols (London: Longmans, Green and Co., 1885), i. 54.

59. Slavoj Žižek, *For They Know Not What They Do: Enjoyment as a Political Factor* (London and New York: Verso, 1991), 221.

60. Žižek, *For They Know Not What They Do*, 221.

61. See Sarah Kay, *Žižek: A Critical Introduction* (Cambridge, Oxford, and Malden, MA: Polity Press, 2003), 48–72.

62. Franco Moretti, *Signs Taken for Wonders: Essays in the Sociology of Literary Forms*, trans. Susan Fischer, David Forgacs and David Miller (London: Verso, 1983), 94.

63. Marx, 'Economic and Philosophic Manuscripts', in *Early Writings*, 361.

64. My thanks to Roger Luckhurst for this point.

65. Cited in Karl Marx and Friedrich Engels, *The German Ideology*, in *Marx–Engels Collected Works*, vol. v.: *1845–1847* (1976), 104. For Bauer, see Douglas Moggach, *The Philosophy and Politics of Bruno Bauer* (Cambridge: Cambridge University Press, 2002); for Stirner, see Saul Newman (ed.), *Max Stirner* (Basingstoke: Palgrave Macmillan, 2011).

66. The classic study is Friedrich Kittler, *Gramophone Film Typewriter*, trans Geoffrey Winthrop-Young and M. Wurz (Stanford, CA: Stanford University Press, 1999); see also Friedrich Kittler, *Discourse Networks 1800/1900*, trans. Michael Metteer (Stanford, CA: Stanford University Press, 1990), 353; Friedrich Kittler, 'Dracula's Legacy', *Stanford Humanities Review*, 1 (1989), 143–73; Jennifer Wicke, 'Vampiric Typewriting', *English Literary History*, 59 (1992), 467–93; and Geoffrey Winthrop-Young, 'Undead Networks: Information Processing and Media Boundary Conflicts in *Dracula*', in Donald Bruce and Anthony Purdey (eds), *Literature and Science* (Atlanta, GA: Rodopi, 1994), 107–29.

67. See Richard Walker, *Labyrinths of Deceit: Culture, Modernity and Identity in the Nineteenth Century* (Chicago, IL: University of Chicago Press, 2007), 256–60.

68. See Natalia Angeles Vieyra, 'Illuminating Addiction: Morphinomania in Fin-de-Siècle Visual Culture', *Hektoen International: A Journal of Medical Humanities*, 7 (2015) (online).

69. Oscar Wilde described a cigarette as 'the perfect type of a perfect pleasure' because 'It is exquisite, and it leaves one unsatisfied' (Oscar Wilde, *The Picture of Dorian Gray*, ed. Peter Ackroyd (Harmondsworth: Penguin, 1985), 107).

70. Harry Ludlum, *A Biography of Dracula: The Life Story of Bram Stoker* (Slough: W. Foulsham, 1962), 25–31 (reproduced as 'Charlotte Stoker's Account of "The Cholera Horror" in a Letter to Bram Stoker (c. 1875)', Appendix II to Bram Stoker, *Dracula*, ed. Maurice Hindle, 2nd edn (London: Penguin, 2003), 412–18, at 413–17). James Hogg described the same outbreak in 'Some Terrible Letters from Scotland' (published in the *Metropolitan Magazine* in 1832; reprinted in Baldick and Morrison (eds), *The Vampyre and Other Tales*, 99–112). David Hamilton makes the passing observation that in *Frankenstein* 'as a subplot, analogous to the hepatitis epidemic, the monster unintentionally brings death and misfortune to those he encounters' (Hamilton, *History of Organ Transplantation*, 494 n.18).

71. Ian Morley, 'City Chaos, Contagion, Chadwick, and Social Justice', *Yale Journal of Biology and Medicine*, 80 (2007), 61–72, at 67.

72. Richard J. Evans, 'Epidemics and Revolutions: Cholera in Nineteenth-Century Europe', in Ranger and Slack (eds), *Epidemics and Ideas*, 149–73, at 149–150.

73. Evans, 'Epidemics and Revolutions', 159; according to Gilles Deleuze and Félix Guattari, 'Bands, human or animal, proliferate by contagion, epidemics, battlefield, and catastrophes' (Gilles Deleuze and Félix Guattari, '1730: Becoming-Intense, Becoming-Animal, Becoming-Imperceptible', in *A Thousand Plateaus*, 232–309, at 241).

74. See Evans, 'Epidemics and Revolutions', 163–65.

75. See Linebaugh 'The Tyburn Riot against the Surgeons', 65–118.

76. An anonymous short story, 'The Victim' (published in the *New Monthly Magazine* in 1831), was devoted to body-snatching (reprinted in Baldick and Morrison (eds), *The Vampyre and Other Tales*, 87–98).
77. Bynum, *Science and the Practice of Medicine*, 59–60.
78. For the effects on burial practices, see Chris Brooks, *Mortal Remains: The History and Present State of the Victorian and Edwardian Cemetery* (Exeter: Wheaton Publishers in association with the Victorian Society, 1989), especially 32–35.
79. Henry Mayhew, 'Home is Home, be it Never so Homely', in *Meliora: or, Better Times to Come*, ed. Viscount Ingestre (London: John W. Parker and Son, 1852), 258–80, at 276–77: see Judith Flanders, 'Slums' (https://www.bl.uk/romantics-and-victorians/articles/slums (accessed 19 February 2018)) and *The Victorian City: Everyday Life in Dickens' London* (London: Atlantic Books, 2012), chapter 7.
80. *The Times* (5 July 1849), 5: see Flanders, 'Slums'.
81. Walter Thornbury (vols 1–2) and Edward Walford (vols 3–6), *Old and New London: A Narrative of its History, its People, and its Places*, 6 vols (London, Paris and New York: Cassell, Petter & Galpin, 1878), iii. 206.
82. H.R. Haweis, for instance, was an advocate of cremation, and also helpfully provided instances of premature burial that had occurred in the nineteenth century (see *Ashes to Ashes* (London: Dalby, Isbister & Co., 1875), and G.A. Walker, *Gatherings from Graveyards; particularly those of London: with a Concise History of the Modes of Interment among Different Nations, from the Earliest Periods* (London: Longman and Company, 1839), 191, 194–95). Surprisingly, the London Association for the Prevention of Premature Burial was not established until 1896.
83. John V. Pickstone, 'Dearth, Dirt and Fever Epidemics: Rewriting the History of British "Public Health", 1780–1850', in Ranger and Slack (eds), *Epidemics and Ideas*, 125–48, at 137. For other legislation see, for example, Food and Drugs Act 1875, the Public Health Act 1875 and the Contagious Diseases Acts 1864, 1866 and 1868; note, too, the importance of both lawyers and doctors in fiction such as *Strange Case of Dr Jekyll and Mr Hyde* and the Sherlock Holmes stories (i.e. Utterson and Watson), and the popularity of medical fiction (*Blackwood's Magazine* ran a series of 'Passages from the Diary of a Late Physician' from 1830 to 1837). Full reports are at http://navigator.health.org.uk/content/edwin-chadwicks-report-sanitary-conditions-labouring-population-great-britain-was-published (accessed 19 February 2018).
84. Southwood Smith, *A Treatise on Fever* (London: Longman, Rees, Orme, Brown and Green, 1830), 360, 364; Smith was promptly quoted in the *Fourth Annual Report of the Poor Law Commissioners for England and Wales; together with Appendices A. B. & C.* (London: W. Clowes and Sons, 1838), 133 (Appendix A, No. 1).
85. Pickstone. 'Dearth, Dirt and Fever Epidemics', 138.
86. Pickstone. 'Dearth, Dirt and Fever Epidemics', 138.
87. Otis, *Membranes*, 11.
88. Otis, *Membranes*, 94.
89. For excellent cultural histories, see William Hughes, *That Devil's Trick: Hypnotism and the Victorian Popular Imagination* (Manchester: Manchester University Press, 2015); Roger Luckhurst, *The Invention of Telepathy: 1870–1901* (Oxford: Oxford University Press, 2002); and Alison Winter, *Mesmerized: Powers of Mind in Victorian Britain* (Chicago, IL and London: University of Chicago Press, 1998).

Chapter 8

1. Review of *Dracula*, *Punch* (26 June 1897), 3; the review in the *Spectator* noted the book's 'up-to-dateness' (31 July 1897).
2. Spoken by Count Dracula; Stoker, *Dracula*, ed. Luckhurst, 40.
3. From certain versions of Leviticus 17:14 and Deuteronomy 12:23.
4. It is impossible to read everything written about *Dracula*; like Mary Shelley's *Frankenstein* – not to mention the Gothic more generally – the commentary on the text and its influence is growing exponentially; for a guide to Stoker's writings, see Richard Dalby and William Hughes, *Bram Stoker: A Bibliography* (Westcliff-on-Sea: Desert Island Books, 2004).
5. Herbert Mayo, 'Vampyrism', in *On the Truths Contained in Popular Superstitions with an Account of Mesmerism*, 2nd edn (Edinburgh and London: William Blackwood and Sons, 1851), 20–40, at 21 (a version is reprinted in Clive Leatherdale, *The Origins of Dracula: The Background to Bram Stoker's Gothic Masterpiece* (London: William Kimber and Co., 1987)). Mayo is included in Stoker's preliminary list of books for *Dracula* (Robert Eighteen-Bisang and Elizabeth Miller (eds), *Bram Stoker's Notes for* Dracula*: A Facsimile Edition* (Jefferson, NC and London: McFarland & Company, Inc., 2008), 172–75 – probably the single most essential source for those researching the novel); see also Thomas

Joseph Pettigrew, *On Superstitions Connected with the History and Practice of Medicine and Surgery* (London: John Churchill, 1844); and Joseph von Görres, *Die Christliche Mystik*, 4 vols (Regensburg and Landshut: G. Joseph Manz, 1836–42), cited by Keyworth, 'Was the Vampire a Unique Type of Undead-Corpse?', 254. Interestingly, the 'smell of the grave', which characterizes the vampires in *Dracula*, indicates the onset of putrefaction as opposed to incorruptibility.

6. Mayo, 'Vampyrism', 22.
7. Mayo, 'Vampyrism', 25, see also 29.
8. Mayo, 'Vampyrism', 31.
9. 'Mr. Bram Stoker: A Chat with the Author of *Dracula*': the whole interview is helpfully transcribed by Glennis Byron in her edition of *Dracula* (Peterborough, ON: Broadview Press, 1998), 484–88.
10. See McCarthy, ' "Death to Vampires!" ', 189–208, at 195; quoted in Peter Haining (ed.), *The Dracula Scrapbook: Articles, Essays, Letters, Newspaper Cuttings, Anecdotes, Illustrations, Photographs and Memorabilia about the Vampire Legend* (London: New English Library, 1976), 45.
11. Eighteen-Bisang and Miller (eds), *Bram Stoker's Notes*, 186–93; earlier American cases are cited by Keyworth, 'Was the Vampire a Unique Type of Undead-Corpse?', 254–55; see also Paul Grant-Costa, 'A Surprising Account of those Spectres called Vampyres', unpublished paper.
12. Frayling surveys some of this material (*Vampyres*, 71–75), and Luckhurst generously incorporates details in the notes to his edition (Stoker, *Dracula*, ed. Luckhurst, 363–91).
13. Nina Elizabeth Mazuchelli, *'Magyarland;' Being the Narrative of our Travels through the Highlands and Lowlands of Hungary* (London: Sampson, Low, Marston, Searle & Rivington, 1881); Isabella L. Bird, *The Golden Chersonese and the Way Thither* (London: John Murray, 1883); Andrew F. Crosse, *Round About the Carpathians* (Edinburgh and London: William Blackwood and Sons, 1878); E.C. Johnson, *On the Track of the Crescent; Erratic Notes from Piraeus to Pesth* (London: Hurst and Blackett, 1885) – Stoker had prepared a century-by-century chronicle of ethnic conflict and migration (Eighteen-Bisang and Miller (eds), *Bram Stoker's Notes*, 170–71); and Charles Boner, *Transylvania; Its Products and Its People* (London: Longmans, Green, Reader and Dyer, 1865): Stoker made typewritten notes from these volumes (see Eighteen-Bisang and Miller (eds), *Bram Stoker's Notes*, 199–251).
14. William Wilkinson's *An Account of the Principalities of Wallachia and Moldavia: with Various Political Reflections Relating to them* (London: Longman, Hurst, Rees, Orme and Brown, 1820): see Eighteen-Bisang and Miller (eds), *Bram Stoker's Notes*, 244–45, 285; the editors note that the role of Vlad the Impaler in Stoker's conception has been overstated and that Wilkinson does not refer to 'Vlad', or 'Vlad Țepeș', or 'the Impaler'.
15. Emily Gerard, 'Transylvanian Superstitions', first printed in *Nineteenth Century*, 18 (July 1885), 130–50; Gerard had lived in Transylvania for two years, from 1883 to 1885: see Eighteen-Bisang and Miller (eds), *Bram Stoker's Notes*, 21, 29 and 121–28, at 127.
16. Rodd, *The Customs and Lore of Modern Greece*, 188 (see also the various references to Tournefort mentioned above).
17. Details from Baring-Gould's *Book of Werewolves* are in Eighteen-Bisang and Miller (eds), *Bram Stoker's Notes*, 129–31 and 172–73, though the editors reject the Báthory influence (see above, pp. 10, 173); see Butler, *Metamorphoses of the Vampire*, 107–26; McClelland claims that Stoker was the first to connect vampires with Vlad: see Bruce A. McClelland, *Slayers and their Vampires: A Cultural History of Killing the Dead* (Ann Arbor, MI: University of Michigan Press, 2006), 16; see also above, pp. 53, 173, and Artenie's books *Dracula Invades England* and *Dracula: A Study of Editorial Practices*.
18. Despite the fact that the news of Vámbéry's role in intelligence broke on All Fools' Day (1 April 2005: see Richard Norton-Taylor, 'Dracula's Nemesis to Prototype Foreign Spy', *Guardian* online (31 March 2005) (accessed 9 February 2018)), it has since been corroborated elsewhere (see, for example, Hamid Dabashi, 'Introduction to the AldineTransaction [*sic*] Edition: Ignaz Goldziher and the Question Concerning Orientalism', in Ignaz Goldziher, *Muslim Studies*, ed. S.M. Stern, trans. C.R. Barber and S.M. Stern (London and New York: Routledge, 2006), ix–xciii, at xxxv–xxxvii).
19. Eighteen-Bisang and Miller (eds), *Bram Stoker's Notes*, 132–36, 272–73, 154–55, 140–42, 143–49, and 252–71.
20. Eighteen-Bisang and Miller (eds), *Bram Stoker's Notes*, 15, 29: Stoker's first note reveals that he began to write 'Germany', before crossing it out and instead writing 'Styria'.
21. Stoker, *Dracula*, ed. Luckhurst, 222.
22. Stoker, *Dracula*, ed. Luckhurst, 9, 200, 224; see Perkowski, *Vampire Lore*, 450, suggesting that 'bloofer lady' is 'beautiful lady'.
23. Stoker, *Dracula*, ed. Luckhurst, 295.
24. Noted by Arata, 'The Occidental Tourist', 627–31; but see a full treatment by Matthew Gibson, *Dracula and the Eastern Question: British and French Vampire Narratives of the Nineteenth-Century Near East* (Basingstoke: Palgrave Macmillan, 2006), especially 69–95.

25. 'Alexander Smith' [Sydney Dobell], *Sonnets on the War* (London: David Bogue, 1855), 35.

26. John Paul Riquelme points out that 'Helsing' is an anagram of 'English'; this effectively ties together the vampire slayers as versions of Englishness, whether being English, Anglophiles or textual enigmas: see 'Doubling and Repetition/Realism and Closure in Dracula', in Bram Stoker, *Dracula (Case Studies in Contemporary Criticism)*, ed. John Paul Riquelme (Boston, MA and New York: Bedford/St Martin's Press, 2002), 559–72, at 564. Stoker plays with other names in the novel – 'Mina' suggesting '*anima*', Latin for 'soul', for example – and anagrams also play a key role in Le Fanu's 'Carmilla', as Carmilla cannot adopt any random alias but is obliged to anagrammatize her name (Van Helsing's name is also perhaps partly derived from that of Dr Hesselius in Le Fanu's tale); all this could nevertheless be coincidental. 'Defenders of Light' plays on *defensores lucem* (i.e. wordplay on 'defenders of Lucy') and is adapted from Craft's suggestion that the protagonists be known as the 'Crew of Light' (Christopher Craft, '"Kiss Me with those Red Lips": Gender and Inversion in Bram Stoker's *Dracula*', *Representations*, 8 (1984), 107–33, at 130n.).

27. Stoker, *Dracula*, ed. Luckhurst, 24; see Robin L. Murray and Joseph K. Heumann, *Monstrous Nature: Environment and Horror on the Big Screen* (Lincoln, NE and London: University of Nebraska Press, 2016), 43.

28. Stoker, *Dracula*, ed. Luckhurst, 209. Some two dozen books are listed in a bibliography prepared by Stoker, though obviously it is not known whether he read all of these: see Eighteen-Bisang and Miller (eds), *Bram Stoker's Notes*, 172–75, 304–05; *Hamlet*, for example, is quoted directly (Stoker, *Dracula*, ed. Luckhurst, 37, 124).

29. Quoted by Nicholas Rance, '"Jonathan's Great Knife": *Dracula* meets Jack the Ripper', in Alexandra Warwick and Martin Willis (eds), *Jack the Ripper: Media, Culture, History* (Manchester: Manchester University Press, 2007), 124–43, at 126 (reprinted from *Victorian Literature and Culture*, 30 (2002), 439–53).

30. Eighteen-Bisang and Miller (eds), *Bram Stoker's Notes*, 285–86; Stoker's claim that Jack the Ripper contributed to the novel is made in his Preface to the Icelandic edition of *Dracula* (*Makt Myrkranna* ['the power of darkness'], 1901), reprinted in *Dracula and The Lair of the White Worm*, ed. Richard Dalby (London: W. Foulsham & Co. Ltd, 1986), 11–12; Stoker, *Dracula*, ed. Luckhurst, 317.

31. Luckhurst, *The Invention of Telepathy*, 210.

32. Robert Gray, *The Theory of Dreams*, 2 vols (London: F.C. & J. Rivington, 1808): see Eighteen-Bisang and Miller (eds), *Bram Stoker's Notes*, 238–39.

33. See Eighteen-Bisang and Miller (eds), *Bram Stoker's Notes*, 176–77, 236–37 (arrow brackets indicate words deleted); from Browne's *Religio Medici* (B 11 & 12).

34. The Romantic laureate of sleep and death undoubtedly being John Keats.

35. Emmanuel Levinas, *Ethics and Infinity: Conversations with Philippe Nemo*, trans. Richard A. Cohen (Pittsburgh, PA: Duquesne University Press, 1985), 49: quoted by Trigg, *The Thing*, 52.

36. Trigg, *The Thing*, 52.

37. Stoker, *Dracula*, ed. Luckhurst, 199, 202.

38. Dijkstra, *Idols of Perversity*, 32; see Auguste Comte, *System of Positive Polity, or Treatise on Sociology, Instituting the Religion of Humanity*, 4 vols (1851–54), trans. Richard Congreve and Frederick Harrison (London: John Henry Bridges, 1875–77), see esp. ii. 197 and iv. 98; Stoker refers to *Macbeth*'s Weird Sisters in Eighteen-Bisang and Miller (eds), *Bram Stoker's Notes*, 281.

39. Stoker, *Dracula*, ed. Luckhurst, 39.

40. Stoker, *Dracula*, ed. Luckhurst, 268.

41. Stoker also had hints of manducation in early notes to chapter 6, 'Jonathan Harker's Diary Cont.': 'Attempt to get away from castle – Wolves – wehr wolf – old chapel – carting earth – shrieks from grave – sights of terror & falling senseless – found by Count.' Eighteen-Bisang and Miller (eds), *Bram Stoker's Notes*, 43 (in a rare moment, the editors are flummoxed by this information).

42. In Dracula's castle Harker finds 'a great heap of gold . . . Roman, and British, and Austrian, and Hungarian, and Greek and Turkish money, covered with a film of dust, as though it had lain long in the ground', along with jewellery 'old and stained' (Stoker, *Dracula*, ed. Luckhurst, 47); my thanks to Roger Luckhurst for some of the ideas here.

43. Stoker, *Dracula*, ed. Luckhurst, 32, 152.

44. Halberstam, *Skin Shows*, 187: the vampire was called 'Count' before Stoker encountered the name 'Dracula' (Eighteen-Bisang and Miller (eds), *Bram Stoker's Notes*, 15).

45. Moretti, *Signs Taken for Wonders*, 91.

46. William Shakespeare, *The Merchant of Venice*, in *Complete Works*, ed. Wells and Taylor, III. i. 59–60 (p. 438).

47. Stoker, *Dracula*, ed. Luckhurst, 160; there is, however, a Jewish caricature in the novel in the description of Immanuel Hildesheim (Stoker, *Dracula*, ed. Luckhurst, 324).

48. Calmet, *Dissertations*, 185. For the relationship of the novel to earlier beliefs about blood, see above pp. 6–12, and *passim*, and Anthony Bale, '*Dracula's* Blood', in Roger Luckhurst (ed.), *The Cambridge Companion to Dracula* (Cambridge: Cambridge University Press, 2018), 104–13.

49. Harker records that his clothes were taken on 31 May, and he sees that Dracula is wearing them over three weeks later (Stoker, *Dracula*, ed. Luckhurst, 43, 44).

50. Laura Otis, *Networking: Communicating with Bodies and Machines in the Nineteenth Century* (Ann Arbor, MI: University of Michigan Press, 2001), 215; Otis, however, argues that this is not really circulation: 'Like information, blood and energy flow one way: toward the parasites, toward those in positions of power' (216); but surely the flow is circulatory. Georges Canguilhem points out that in 1859 Claude Bernard published his *Lectures on the Physiological Properties and Pathological Alterations to the Liquids of the Organism*, in which blood is conceived as an 'intraorganic environment' – what would later be described as an 'internal environment' or homeostasis (Georges Canguilhem, *Ideology and Rationality in the History of the Life Sciences*, trans. Arthur Goldhammer (Cambridge, MA, and London: MIT Press, 1988), 106).

51. See, for example, Stoker, *Dracula*, ed. Luckhurst, 143, 149.

52. Otis, *Networking*, 218.

53. Otis, *Networking*, 219; see Regenia Gagnier, 'Evolution and Information, or Eroticism and Everyday Life, in *Dracula* and Late Victorian Aestheticism', in Regina Barreca (ed.), *Sex and Death in Victorian Literature* (Bloomington, IN: Indiana University Press, 1990), 140–57.

54. For example, in Mina transcribing Harker's shorthand for Van Helsing (Stoker, *Dracula*, ed. Luckhurst, 173).

55. Stoker, *Dracula*, ed. Luckhurst, 210. Butler (*Metamorphoses of the Vampire*, 130–43) has an account of Daniel Paul Schreber (a real-life Renfield). Renfield is not only an epileptic-criminal type derived from Lombroso (see Eighteen-Bisang and Miller (eds), *Bram Stoker's Notes*, 45), he is also bestial in his behaviour and eating habits, sniffing 'as a dog does when setting' (Stoker, *Dracula*, ed. Luckhurst, 95, 132).

56. Stoker, *Dracula*, ed. Luckhurst, 246; Luckhurst, *The Invention of Telepathy*, 211–13.

57. Bynum, *Science and the Practice of Medicine*, 173–74.

58. Bynum, *Science and the Practice of Medicine*, 175.

59. 'Men sneered at vivisection, and yet look at its results today!' The novel also includes mention of the Society for the Prevention of Cruelty to Animals, which ironically would have protected Dracula when he escapes from Whitby as a dog (Stoker, *Dracula*, ed. Luckhurst, 69, 78; see also 69 and note).

60. Stoker, *Dracula*, ed. Luckhurst, 134–35, 221, 223; Perkowski, *Vampire Lore*, 450.

61. Otis, *Networking*, 10.

62. Stoker, *Dracula*, ed. Luckhurst, 133.

63. There are psychic vampires: 'The Winning Shot' (*Bow Bells*, 11 July 1883); 'John Barrington Cowles' (*Cassell's Saturday Journal*, April 1884); 'The Parasite' (*Lloyds Weekly Newspaper*, 11 November– 2 December 1894).

64. See Luckhurst, *The Invention of Telepathy*.

65. Eliphas Lévi, *The Key of the Mysteries*, trans. Aleister Crowley (1861), quoted by Antoine Faivre, *Theosophy, Imagination, Tradition: Studies in Western Esotericism*, trans. Christine Rhone (Albany, NY: State University of New York Press, 2000), 123.

66. See Joseph Laycock, *Vampires Today: The Truth about Modern Vampirism* (Westport, CT, and London: Praeger, 2009); there were over a dozen articles on vampires in the *Occult Review* in the first years of the twentieth century.

67. H.P. Blavatsky, *Isis Unveiled: A Master-Key to the Mysteries of Ancient and Modern*, 2 vols (New York: J. Bouton, 1877), i. 319.

68. Blavatsky, *Isis Unveiled*, ii. 567.

69. Blavatsky, *Isis Unveiled*, i. 449–56, at 452–53, 449 (reiterated ii. 564); Blavatsky's source was probably the comparative account of the vampire ('Katakhanás' or 'Vurvúlakas') in Robert Pashley, *Travels in Crete*, 2 vols (Cambridge: Pitt Press, and London: John Murray, 1837), ii. 196–214, 221–22, 230–31; see also Adolphe D'Assier, who in *Posthumous Humanity* (1887) notes of 'posthumous vampirism' that, in astral terms, 'the post-sepulchral phantom is the continuation of the living phantom'; consequently, 'All the blood swallowed by the spectre passes instantly into the organs of the corpse which it has just left, and to which it returns as soon as its poaching work is finished. The constant arrival of this vivifying liquid, which at once disseminates itself through the circulation, prevents putrefaction, preserves in the limbs their natural suppleness and in the flesh its fresh and reddish tint.' (Adolphe D'Assier, *Posthumous Humanity: A Study of Phantoms* (London: George Redway, 1887), 280.)

70. See Christine Ferguson, '*Dracula* and the Occult', in Luckhurst (ed.), *Companion*, 57–66.

71. Blavatsky, *Isis Unveiled*, i. 463.
72. Perkowski, *Vampire Lore*, 177–90.
73. Warwick Gould, 'Althea Gyles', *ODNB*. For the accommodation of psychic vampirism within Golden Dawn thinking, see 'V.H. Fra. Resurgam' [Edward William Berridge], 'Flying Roll No. V: Some Thoughts on the Imagination', in S.L. MacGregor Mathers, et al., *Astral Projection, Ritual Magic, and Alchemy: Golden Dawn Material*, ed. Francis King (Rochester, VT: Destiny Books, 1987), 47–52, at 48; see also Kathleen Raine, 'Yeats, The Tarot and the Golden Dawn', in *Yeats the Initiate: Essays on Certain Themes in the Work of W.B. Yeats* (Savage, MD: Barnes & Noble Books, 1990), 177–246.
74. Strack, *The Jew and Human Sacrifice*, 97.
75. For Thacker 'ooze begins to take on the qualities of thought itself' (Thacker, *In the Dust of This Planet*, 91; see also 81–83).
76. Woodard, *Slime Dynamics*, 11; Woodard takes this further, claiming that ooze can arouse 'the sickening realization of an inhospitable universe, . . . the production of life as an accidental event in time'.
77. Stoker, *Dracula*, ed. Luckhurst, 213. This comment moves Dracula to the realm of the 'wholly other': 'The truly "mysterious" object is beyond our apprehension and comprehension, not only because our knowledge has certain irremovable limits, but because in it we come upon something inherently "wholly other", whose kind and character are incommensurable with our own, and before which we therefore recoil in a wonder that strikes us chill and numb' (Rudolf Otto, *The Idea of the Holy: An Inquiry into the Non-Rational Factor in the Idea of the Divine and its Relation to the Rational*, trans. John W. Harvey (London, Oxford and New York: Oxford University Press, 1958), 28; Otto goes on to discuss ghosts).
78. An influential starting point for this – irresistible to some – being Craft, '"Kiss Me with those Red Lips"', 107–33; Craft considers same-sex sexuality at 111–16; Frayling wittily labels this tendency to sexualize vampires as 'Haemosexuality' (*Vampyres*, 385).
79. Maurice Richardson's early psychoanalytic account infamously (and cheekily) describes *Dracula* as 'a kind of incestuous necrophilous, oral-anal-sadistic all-in wrestling match' ('The Psychoanalysis of Ghost Stories', *Twentieth Century*, 16 (1959), 419–31, at 427).
80. Eighteen-Bisang and Miller, *Bram Stoker's Notes*, 178–85, at 183: see Stoker, *Dracula*, ed. Luckhurst, 257. Stoker's brother George had also practised medicine as a military doctor in Bulgaria.
81. Stephen Blankaart, *The Physical Dictionary* (London, 1708), 23 (*Aphrodisia Phrenitis*).
82. See Franz Hartmann, 'Vampires', in the quarterly review *Borderland* (London), 3 (July 1896).
83. William Acton, *The Functions and Disorders of the Reproductive Organs in Childhood, Youth, Adult Age, and Advanced Life considered in their Physiological, Social, and Moral Relations*, 8th edn (Philadelphia, PA: P. Blakiston, Son & Co., 1894), 209.
84. Maudsley, *Body and Mind*, 82.
85. D.H. Tuke (ed.), *A Dictionary of Psychological Medicine giving the Definition, Etymology, and Synonyms of the Terms used in Medical Psychology . . .*, 2 vols (Philadelphia, PA: P. Blakiston, Son & Co., 1892), ii. 863–66, at 863, 864.
86. August Forel, *The Sexual Question: A Scientific, Psychological, Hygienic and Sociological Study*, 2nd English edn, trans. C.F. Marshall (New York: Medical Art Agency, 1906), 227.
87. Nicholas Francis Cooke, *Satan in Society* (Cincinnati, OH, and New York: C.F. Vent, 1871), 281.
88. See Dijkstra, *Idols of Perversity*, 310–80: for Dijkstra on vampires, see 333–51.
89. LeFanu, 'Carmilla', 290.
90. Stoker, *Dracula*, ed. Luckhurst, 58.
91. Stoker, *Dracula*, ed. Luckhurst, 164.
92. See Stoker, *Dracula*, ed. Luckhurst, 85.
93. Cooke, *Satan in Society*, 111.
94. Bernard Talmey, *Woman; A Treatise on the Normal and Pathological Emotions of Feminine Love*, 2nd edn (New York: Practitioners Publishing Co., 1908), 166; the theory that a wandering womb caused hysteria is proposed by Plato in the *Timaeus* (see Niel Micklem, *The Nature of Hysteria* (London and New York: Routledge, 1996), 42).
95. Lombroso and Ferrero, *The Female Offender*, 150.
96. Stoker, *Dracula*, ed. Luckhurst, 90, 202 (also 186; see Žižek, *For They Know Not What They Do*, 220).
97. William J. Robinson, *Married Life and Happiness* (New York: Eugenics Publishing Company, 1922), 90; Robinson generously conceded a normal wife was 'satisfied with occasional relations – not more than once in two weeks or ten days'.
98. Richard von Krafft-Ebing, *Psychopathia Sexualis, with Especial Reference to Contrary Sexual Instinct: A Medico-Legal Study*, 7th edn, trans. Charles Gilbert Chaddock (Philadelphia, PA: F.A. Davis Company, 1894), 59–71 (Frayling's account of these citations is unfortunately anachronistic).

99. This figure has been extensively analysed by, for example, Nina Auerbach *Woman and the Demon: The Life of a Victorian Myth* (Cambridge, MA, and London: Harvard University Press, 1982); Elisabeth Bronfen, *Over Her Dead Body: Death, Femininity and the Aesthetic* (Manchester: Manchester University Press, 1992); and Rebecca Stott, *The Fabrication of the Late Victorian Femme Fatale: The Kiss of Death* (Basingstoke: Macmillan, 1996).

100. Quoted and trans. Dijkstra, *Idols of Perversity*, 63.

101. John Berger, *Ways of Seeing* (Harmondsworth: Penguin, 1972), 45–64.

102. John Milton, *Paradise Lost*, ed. Alastair Fowler (London and New York: Longman, 1971), 221–22 (Bk IV. ll. 456–76).

103. Eighteen-Bisang and Miller (eds), *Bram Stoker's Notes*, 19; he also recorded that he 'never eats nor drinks', has to be 'carried or led over threshold', and has 'enormous strength' and the 'power of getting small or large': there are sources for these characteristics in both folklore and preceding vampire literature.

104. Eighteen-Bisang and Miller (eds), *Bram Stoker's Notes*, 21; see also 25; in addition, he 'goes through fog by instinct', has 'white teeth', can only cross 'river & running water at exact slack or flood of tide', possesses 'influence over rats' and is insensible to music. George claims that the mirror motif is not in Stoker's sources (Sam George, '"He Make in the Mirror No Reflect [Van Helsing]": Undead Aesthetics and Mechanical Reproduction – *Dorian Gray*, *Dracula* and David Reed's "Vampire Painting"', in George and Hughes (eds), *Open Graves, Open Minds*, 56–78, at 58); however, folklore concerning mirrors does go back centuries, and in 1814 Adelbert von Chamisso published the fable of Peter Schlemihl, who sold his shadow to the Devil (see Victor I. Stoichita, *A Short History of the Shadow* (London: Reaktion Books, 1997), 172–85).

105. This sentence adapts Walter Benjamin's notion of 'aura': the apparently authentic 'aura' of a work of art is actually an effect of the multiple reproductions that derive from it and thereby verify its status (Walter Benjamin, 'The Work of Art in the Age of Mechanical Reproduction', in Hannah Arendt (ed.), *Illuminations*, trans. Harry Zohn (New York: Schocken Books, 1968), 217–51). As to great works of Gothic fiction being simultaneously love stories, one need look no further than Mark Danielewski's contemporary masterpiece, 'Zampanò', ed. Johnny Truant, *House of Leaves*, '2nd edn' (New York: Pantheon Books, 2000).

106. For a thought-provoking reading of *Dorian Gray*, see George, '"He Make in the Mirror No Reflect"', 64; Twitchell, *The Living Dead*, also argues that Dorian Gray is vampiric and that Dorian effectively – if inadvertently – stakes himself (177).

107. Basil repeats the word, and once murdered becomes a 'thing' himself: see Wilde, *Dorian Gray*, 190, 192.

108. Walter Pater, *The Renaissance: Studies in Art and Poetry* (London: Macmillan and Co., 1925), 124–26.

Conclusion

1. Deleuze and Guattari, *A Thousand Plateaus*, 237.

2. Francis Ford Coppola on his film *Bram Stoker's Dracula*: quoted by Mick Mercer, *Hex Files: The Goth Bible* (London: B.T. Batsford, 1996), 226.

3. D.J. Haraway, *Modest_Witness@Second_Millennium.FemaleMan©_Meets_OncoMouse™: Feminism and Technoscience* (New York and London: Routledge, 1997), 215.

4. See Alan Dundes, 'The Vampire as Bloodthirsty Revenant: A Psychoanalytic Post Mortem', in Alan Dundes (ed.), *The Vampire: A Casebook* (Madison, WI: University of Wisconsin Press, 1998), 159–75, at 168.

5. See Reynold Humphries, *The Hollywood Horror Film, 1931–41: Madness in a Social Landscape* (Lanham, MD, Toronto and Oxford: Scarecrow Press, 2006); Melvin E. Matthews Jr, *Fear Itself: Horror on Screen and in Reality during the Depression and World War II* (Jefferson, NC, and London: McFarland & Company, 2009); Murray and Heumann, *Monstrous Nature*; Alain Silver and James Ursini, *The Vampire Film: From Nosferatu to True Blood*, 4th updated edn (New York: Limelight Editions, 2011); and Waller, *The Living and the Undead*.

6. See Cristina Massaccesi, *Nosferatu: A Symphony of Horror* (New York: Columbia University Press, 2016).

7. Jeffrey Andrew Weinstock, 'American Vampires', in Joel Faflak and Jason Haslam (eds), *American Gothic Culture: An Edinburgh Companion* (Edinburgh: Edinburgh University Press, 2016), 203–21, at 208.

8. See John Harvey, *Men in Black* (London: Reaktion Books, 1995), 252–53.

9. See Natasha Scharf, *The Art of Gothic: Music † Fashion † Alt Culture* (London: Omnibus Press, 2014), 130–35.

10. T.S. Eliot, *The Waste Land*, in *The Complete Poems and Plays* ([1922] London and Boston, MA: Faber and Faber, 1969), ll. 387–84 (pp. 59–80, at 73).

11. Taking academic research as an example, following a handful books and articles work on vampires really began in earnest in the 1980s, inspired by David Punter's classic *The Literature of Terror: A History of Gothic Fictions from 1765 to the Present Day* (London and New York: Longman, 1980) and rapidly followed by detailed studies such as James Twitchell's *The Living Dead* (1981) and A.N. Wilson's unfortunately patchy edition of *Dracula* for Oxford World's Classics (Oxford and New York: Oxford University Press, 1983); since then vampire studies have exploded into a substantial scholarly industry: the current edition of J. Gordon Melton's extensive reference work *The Vampire Book: The Encyclopedia of the Undead* (Detroit, MI, and London: Visible Ink Press, 2011) runs to over 900 pages.

12. Jonathan Rigby has provided the most comprehensive account in the richly illustrated *English Gothic: A Century of Horror Cinema*, 3rd edn (London: Reynolds & Hearn, 2004).

13. Titles include *Dracula* (1931, 1933), *The Vampire Returns* (1944), *The Horror of Dracula* (1958), *Dracula Has Risen from the Grave* (1967), *Blacula* (1972), *Scream Blacula Scream* (1973), *Rabid* (1976), *Love at First Bite* (1979), *Red-Blooded American Girl* (1990), *Bram Stoker's Dracula* (1992), *Dracula: Dead and Loving It* (1995), *Van Helsing* (2004, 2012), *Underworld* (2003, 2006, 2009, 2012), *Let the Right One In* (2007) and *Vamps* (2012) – the list goes on. Such films also stimulated a longstanding market for books of these films, from Michael Parry's *Countess Dracula* (1971) to Jean Rollin's *Little Orphan Vampires* (1995). For vampires with a conscience, see George and Hughes (eds), *Open Graves, Open Minds*, 1–2.

14. See Stacey Abbott, 'Dracula on Film and TV from 1960 to the Present', in Luckhurst (ed.), *Companion*, 192–206; and Ken Gelder, *Vampire Cinema* (London: British Film Institute, 2012); see also Margaret L. Carter, 'The Vampire', in S.T. Joshi (ed.), *Icons of Horror and the Supernatural: An Encyclopedia of Our Worst Nightmares*, 2 vols (Westport, CT, and London: Greenwood Press, 2007), ii. 619–52, especially 627ff; and see also Alyssa Rosenberg, 'A Condemnation of Sparkly Vampires', *The Atlantic* (November 2009), online edn; the phenomenon is explored in detail in Joseph Crawford's *The Twilight of the Gothic? Vampires and the Rise of the Paranormal Romance, 1991–2012* (Cardiff: University of Wales Press, 2014).

15. Angela Carter, 'The Lady of the House of Love', in *The Bloody Chamber* (London: Vintage, 1979), 107–25; see Veronica Hollinger 'Fantasies of Absence: The Postmodern Vampire', in Joan Gordon and Veronica Hollinger (eds), *Blood Read: The Vampire as Metaphor in Contemporary Culture* (Philadelphia, PA: University of Pennsylvania Press, 1997), 199–212, at 205–12.

16. Natasha Scharf, *Worldwide Gothic: A Chronicle of a Tribe* (Church Stretton: Independent Music Press, 2011), 54–62. Among the albums released by Inkubus Sukkubus are *Vampyre Erotica* (1997) and *Vampire Queen* (2018).

17. See Phil Hodkinson, *Goth: Identity, Style and Subculture* (Oxford and New York: Berg, 2002), 44–46; and Catherine Spooner, 'Twenty-First-Century Gothic', in Dale Townshend (ed.), *Terror and Wonder: The Gothic Imagination* (London: British Library, 2014), 180–205, at 204–05. Vamp style has since moved into the mainstream via the burlesque revival: see Dunja Brill, *Goth Culture: Gender, Sexuality and Style* (Oxford and New York: Berg, 2008), 170–71.

18. See Philomena Keet and Yuri Manabe, entries on 'h.NAOTO'[*sic*] and 'Mana Moi-Meme-Moitie', *The Tokyo Look Book: Stylish to Spectacular, Goth to Gyaru, Sidewalk to Catwalk* (Tokyo, New York, and London: Kodansha International, 2007) 74–97; and Masayuki Yoshinaga and Katsuhiko Ishikawa, *Gothic & Lolita* (New York and London: Phaidon, 2007), *passim*.

19. See Nicola Henderson, *Gothic Art: Vampires, Witches, Demons, Dragons, Werewolves & Goths* (London: Flame Tree Publishing, 2013), 37–55; and the website www.deviantart.com

20. For sanguinarians and vampire subcultures, see David Keyworth, 'The Socio-Religious Beliefs and Nature of the Contemporary Vampire Subculture', *Journal of Contemporary Religion*, 17 (2002), 355–70; and Joseph Laycock, 'Real Vampires as an Identity Group: Analyzing Causes and Effects of an Introspective Survey by the Vampire Community', *Nova Religio: The Journal of Alternative and Emergent Religions*, 14 (2010), 4–23. For Temple of the Vampire see http://templeofthevampire.com/ mission (accessed 19 February 2018); although ToV does not condone drinking blood, there is nevertheless considerable suspicion of the teachings of ToV in online forums.

21. Nancy Kilpatrick, *The Goth Bible: A Compendium for the Darkly Inclined* (London: Plexus, 2005), 49–50.

22. The principal characters Buffy Summers and Edward Cullen have also been appropriated and sexualized in other areas: Buffy, for example, in Laurell K. Hamilton's novel *Narcissus in Chains* (2002; see Carol Siegel, *Goth's Dark Empire* (Bloomington, IN: Indiana University Press, 2005), 93), and Cullen through the Tantus Vamp: a sparkly sex toy designed to be chilled in the freezer(!).

23. *House of Frankenstein* was a sequel to the first 'monster rally' movie, *Frankenstein Meets the Wolf Man* (1943), in which Béla Lugosi played the Being.

24. For a comparison of vampires with zombies, see Marina Warner, *Phantasmagoria: Spirit Visions, Metaphors, and Media into the Twenty-First Century* (Oxford: Oxford University Press, 2006), 357–60.

25. *The Tomb of Dracula*, for instance, was reprinted in facsimile in 1979; for later graphic novels, see primarily Jai Nitz and Jack Jadson, *The Ravening* (Rantoul, IL: Boundless, 2016); typical of this subgenre is Frans Mensink's sexually voracious anti-heroine *Kristina, Queen of Vampires* (New York: Eurotica, 2005), and the hentai stylization of *Vampires of the Night* (n.p.: Locofuria, 2014); see also the sardonic scrapbook by Charles S. Anderson Design Co. and Michael J. Nelson (ed.), *Goth-Icky* (New York: Harry N. Abrams, Inc., 2005), especially 64–85.

26. Andi Harriman and Marloes Bontje, *Some Wear Leather Some Wear Lace: The Worldwide Compendium of Punk and Goth in the 1980s* (Bristol and Chicago, IL: Intellect, 2014), 56.

27. Mark Fisher, *The Weird and the Eerie* (London: Repeater Books, 2016), 15.

28. Butler, *Metamorphoses of the Vampire*, 5.

29. Nina Auerbach, *Our Vampires, Ourselves* (Chicago, IL, and London: University of Chicago Press, 1995), 145.

30. Michael Hardt and Antonio Negri confirm that, 'The vampire is one figure that expresses the monstrous, excessive, and unruly character of the flesh of the multitude' (Michael Hardt and Antonio Negri, *Multitude: War and Democracy in the Age of Empire* (New York: Penguin Press, 2004), 193).

31. Stephen Adams, 'Vampires "Over-Farmed" says Neil Gaiman', *Telegraph* (3 July 2010), online edn (interestingly, Gaiman himself has written very little on vampires: see 'Vampire Sestina', in *Smoke and Mirrors: Short Fictions and Illusions* (New York, London, Toronto and Sydney: Harper Perennial, 2001)); in his groundbreaking book *The Living Dead*, James Twitchell was highly dismissive of what he called the 'adolescent' vampire vogue, declaring 'I couldn't care less' (ix).

32. The most forthright claim here is made by Auerbach, *Our Vampires, Ourselves*, 192; for a more considered response, see Catherine Spooner's post-9/11 reflections in *Contemporary Gothic* (London: Reaktion Books, 2006), 154–65.

33. The anthropocene already has a challenging bibliography, but for a thought-provoking series of essays see Timothy Morton, *Dark Ecology: For a Logic of Future Coexistence* (New York: Columbia University Press, 2016).

34. The speculative realist turn has provided some food for thought.

35. See, for example, Gina Wisker, 'Celebrating Difference and Community: The Vampire in African-American and Caribbean Women's Writing', in Tabish Khair and Johan Höglund (eds), *Transnational and Postcolonial Vampires: Dark Blood* (Basingstoke: Palgrave Macmillan, 2013), 46–66; Leo Braudy comments that 'The vampire may be the most prominent standard bearer of the sexual theme in horror . . . involving . . . everything to do with gender, male-female difference, the sense of bodily integrity, [and] sexual norms and their constraints' (Leo Braudy, *Haunted: On Ghosts, Witches, Vampires, Zombies, and Other Monsters of the Natural and Supernatural Worlds* (New Haven, CT, and London: Yale University Press, 2016), 230); see also Marie Mulvey-Roberts, *Dangerous Bodies: Historicising the Gothic Corporeal* (Manchester: Manchester University Press, 2016), 92–128.

36. Perkowski, *Vampire Lore*, 346.

37. Hilary Mantel, 'Harley Street', in *The Assassination of Margaret Thatcher and Other Stories* (London: Fourth Estate, 2014), 85–111, at 104.

38. Both Stevenson's 'Olalla' and Baring-Gould's 'Margery of Quether' also end on artful puns – which in Baring-Gould's case is particularly dreadful.

39. See Luis White, *Speaking with Vampires: Rumor and History in Colonial Africa* (Berkeley, Los Angeles and London: University of California Press, 2000), especially 27–30, and (on the Christian Eucharist) 188–98.

40. See Gordon and Hollinger (eds), *Blood Read* for these essays.

41. Mentioned in passing by Frayling, *Vampyres*, 78; for more detail, see Duncan Light, *The Dracula Dilemma: Tourism, Identity and the State in Romania* (London and New York: Routledge, 2012), 41–56.

42. BBC news (25 June 2001), online: quoted by Beresford, *From Demons to Dracula*, 168.

43. See Faye Ringel, 'Vampires in World Folklore', in Joshi (ed.), *Encyclopedia of the Vampire*, 366–75, at 373 and quoting the Scottish *Herald* headline, 'Vampire Slayer Impales Milosevic to Stop Return' (10 March 2007).

44. Aislinn Laing, '"Vampire" Attacks Spark Witchhunt', *The Times* (6 December 2017), 1 GM.

45. Thacker, 'Quæstio II – On Whether There are Demons, and How to Know Them', *In the Dust of This Planet*, 22–36, at 25; see also Nick Land, 'Making it with Death: Remarks on Thanatos and Desiring-

Production', in *Fanged Noumena: Collected Writings, 1987–2007*, ed. Robin MacKay and Ray Brassier (Falmouth: Urbanomic, and New York: Sequence Press, n.d.), 261–87, at 267.

46. *Cuadecuc, vampi* is a recasting of Jess Franco's *Nachts, wenn Dracula erwacht* (*Count Dracula*, 1970; see also *Umbracle*, dir. Pere Portabella, 1970). Later instalments of *The Strain* are *The Fall* in 2010 and *The Night Eternal* in 2011; it was subsequently reworked as a series of graphic novels (2011), and televised from 2014.

47. Adolf Hitler, 'Speech at the NSDAP Congress on Culture (1933)', in Anson Rabinbach and Sander L. Gilman (eds), *The Third Reich Sourcebook* (Berkeley, Los Angeles and London: University of California Press, 2013), 113. During the Second World War, US troops were given free copies of *Dracula*, as it was considered to be anti-German; it was later also used symbolically in the Cold War: see Butler, *Metamorphoses of the Vampire*, 77–78 n.17; and D.J. Enright, *The Oxford Book of the Supernatural* (Oxford: Oxford University Press, 1994), 206. The Nazi relationship with vampires was promulgated early in the Marvel story 'The Terror – That Stalked Castle Dracula', in *The Tomb of Dracula: The Complete Collection*, 1 vol. currently published (New York: Marvel Worldwide, 2017), i. 384–94, first published in 1973.

48. Quoted in Margaret L. Carter, 'The Vampire as Alien in Contemporary Fiction', in Gordon and Hollinger (eds), *Blood Read*, 27–44, at 33–34; see also Suzy McKee Charnas, 'Meditation in Red: On Writing *The Vampire Tapestry* (1981)' in the same volume, 59–67.

49. Murray and Heumann, *Monstrous Nature*, 42.

50. See Catherine Gallagher, 'The Potato in the Materialist Imagination', in Catherine Gallagher and Stephen Greenblatt (eds), *Practicing New Historicism* (Chicago, IL, and London: University of Chicago Press, 2000), 110–35, at 112–14; Nick Groom, 'William Henry Ireland: From Forgery to Fish 'n' Chips', in Timothy Morton (ed.), *Cultures of Taste/Theories of Appetite: Eating Romanticism* (Basingstoke and New York: Palgrave, 2004), 21–40, especially 28; and Redcliffe N. Salaman, *The History and Social Influence of the Potato*, rev. J.G. Hawkes (Cambridge: Cambridge University Press, 1985), 112–16, 453–56, 481–86.

51. See Timothy Morton, *Hyperobjects: Philosophy and Ecology after the End of the World* (Minneapolis and London: University of Minnesota Press, 2013).

52. See Peter Redgrove, *The Black Goddess and the Unseen Real: Our Unconscious Senses and Their Uncommon Sense* (New York: Grove Press, 1987).

BIBLIOGRAPHY

NB Passing references made in the Endnotes are not included here.

Reference works

Anchor Bible (New Haven, CT: Yale University Press, 2007)
The Bible: A New Translation, trans. James A.R. Moffat (London: Hodder & Stoughton, 1922)
The Bible: King James Version, ed. Robert Carroll and Stephen Prickett ([1611] Oxford and New York: Oxford University Press, 1998)
Encyclopædia Britannica online
Oxford Dictionary of National Biography (ODNB) online
Oxford English Dictionary online
Johnson, Samuel, *A Dictionary of the English Language . . .*, 2 vols (London, 1755–56)
The Old Testament newly translated from the Latin Vulgate, trans. Ronald Knox, 2 vols (London: Burns Oates & Washbourne, 1949)
Tyndale's New Testament, trans. William Tyndale, ed. David Daniell ([1534] New Haven, CT, and London: Yale University Press, 1989)

Periodicals

The Athenæum, A Magazine of Literary and Miscellaneous Information
The Atlantic
Borderland
Cassell's Saturday Journal
Commercium Literarium ad rei Medicae et Scientiae Naturalis Incrementum Instit
La Gazette de France
The Gentleman's Magazine
Guardian
The Imperial Magazine; or, Compendium of Religious, Moral, & Philosophical Knowledge
Lloyd's Weekly Newspaper
Morning Chronicle
New Monthly Magazine
The Occult Review
The Political State of Great Britain
Paul Pry

Public Ledger
Punch
Spirit of the English Magazines
Telegraph
The Times

Online resources

BBC News: www.bbc.co.uk/news
Chadwick, Edwin, *Reports on the Sanitary Conditions of the Labouring Population of Great Britain*: http://navigator.health.org.uk/content/edwin-chadwicks-report-sanitary-conditions-labouring-population-great-britain-was-published
Deviant Art: www.deviantart.com
Dictionary of Spiritual Terms: www.dictionaryofspiritualterms.com/public/home.aspx
Equiamicus, Nicolaus: http://equiamicus.blogspot.co.uk
John Foxe's *The Acts and Monuments* Online: https://www.johnfoxe.org/
Macinnis, Peter: https://oldblockwriter.blogspot.co.uk/
Magia Posthuma: http://magiaposthuma.blogspot.co.uk/
OGOM: www.opengravesopenminds.com
Shroudeater: https://www.shroudeater.com
Temple of the Vampire: http://templeofthevampire.com
Vampiri Europeana: http://archive.is/2PTJ

Primary sources

Aarhus, Bishop of [Lange, Jens Iversen], *A Litil Boke the whiche Traytied and Reherced Many Gode Things necessaries for the . . . Pestilence . . . made by the . . . Bisshop of Arusiens . . .* [London, 1485?], facsimile ed. Guthrie Vine (Manchester: Manchester University Press and London: Bernard Quaritch, and Sherratt and Hughes, 1910)
Abbott, G.F., *Macedonian Folklore* ([1903] Cambridge: Cambridge University Press, 2011)
Acton, William, *The Functions and Disorders of the Reproductive Organs in Childhood, Youth, Adult Age, and Advanced Life considered in their Physiological, Social, and Moral Relations*, 8th edn ([1857] Philadelphia, PA: P. Blakiston, Son & Co., 1894)
Addison, Joseph, Richard Steele, et al., *The Spectator*, 8 vols (London, 1712–15)
Amherst, Nicholas, *see* 'D'Anvers, Caleb'
[Anon.,] *Here is a True and Perfect Relation from the Faulcon at the Banke-Side; of the Strange and Wonderful Aperition* [sic] *of one Mr. Powel, a Baker lately deceased, and of his Appearing in Several Shapes, both at Noon-Day and at Night, with the Several Speeches which past between the Spirit of Mr. Powel and his Maid Jone and Divers Learned Men . . .* (London, 1661)
[Anon.,] *A Strange and Wonderfull Discovery of a Horrid and Cruel Murther committed Fourteen Years Since, upon the Person of Robert Eliot of London, at Great Driffield in the East-Riding of the County of York* (London, 1662)
[Anon.,] *A New Apparition of S. Edmund-Bery Godfrey's Ghost to the E. of D—* [Earl of Danby] *in the Tower* (London, 1681)
[Anon.,] *Sir Edmundbury Godfreys Ghost: or, An Answer to Nat. Thompsons Scandalous Letter from Cambridge to Mr. Miles Prance, in Relation to the Murder of Sir Edmundbury Godfrey* (London, 1682).
[Anon., attributed to Defoe, Daniel] *Reasons humbly offer'd for a Law to Enact the Castration of Popish Ecclesiastics, as the Best Way to Prevent the Growth of Popery in England* (London, 1700; Dublin, 1710)
[Anon.,] *James Hall Footman to John Penny of Clement's Inn* (1741): British Library 1953, 0411
[Anon.,] 'The Travels of Three English Gentlemen, from Venice to Hamburgh, being the Grand Tour of Germany, in the Year 1734', in *The Harleian Miscellany or, A Collection of Rare, Curious, and Entertaining Pamphlets and Tracts, as well in Manuscript as in Print, found in the late Earl of Oxford's Library*, 8 vols (London, 1744–46), iv. 348–59, v. 321–45
[Anon.,] *Anti-Canidia: or, Superstition Detected and Exposed. In a Confutation of the Vulgar Opinion concerning Witches, Spirits, Demons, Magick, Divination, Omens, Prognostications, Dreams, Augurys, Charms, Amulets, Incantations, Astrology, Oracles, &c.* (London, 1762)
[Anon.,] *The Compleat Wizzard; Being a Collection of Authentic and Entertaining Narratives of the Real Existence and Appearance of Ghosts, Demons, and Spectres: Together with Several Wonderful Instances of the Effects of Witchcraft* (London, 1770)

[Anon.,] *The Atheist's Reward: or, A Call from Heaven, on July the 24th, 1786* (London, 1788)

[Anon.,] *Fantasmagoriana, ou Recueil d'Histoires d'Apparitions de Spectres, Revenans, Fantômes, etc.; Traduit de l'Allemand, par un Amateur*, trans. Jean Baptiste Benoit Eyriès, 2 vols. (F. Schoell: Paris, 1812)

[Anon.,] *Der Vampyr oder die Blutige Hochzeit mit der Schönen Kroatin* (Müller, 1812)

Arbuthnot, John, *An Essay Concerning the Effects of Air on Human Bodies* (London, 1733)

Aristotle, *De Generatione et Corruptione*, ed. and trans. C.F.J. Williams (Oxford: Clarendon Press, 1982)

'Arminius', 'The Dead Men of Pest, A Hungarian Legend', *The Athenæum*, 1 (April 1807), 362–66

'Arminius' [John Herman Merivale], 'On Some Popular Superstitions, more particularly on that relating to Vampyres or Blood-Suckers', *The Athenæum*, 2 (July 1807), 19–26

Assheton, William, *The Possibility of Apparitions* (London, 1706)

Aubrey, John, *Remaines of Gentilisme and Judaisme*, ed. James Britten ([1686–87] London: Folk-Lore Society, 1881)

Averroes, *On Aristotle's De Generatione et Corruptione: Middle Commentary and Epitome*, ed. and trans. Samuel Kurland (Cambridge, MA: Medieval Academy of America, 1958)

Back, James de, *see* Harvey, William

Bagenal, Philip H., *The Irish Agitator in Parliament and on the Platform: A Complete History of Irish Politics for the Year 1879; with a Summary of Conclusions and an Appendix, containing Documents of Political Importance published during the Year* (Dublin: Hodges, Foster and Figgis, 1880)

Baldick, Chris and Robert Morrison (eds), *The Vampyre and Other Tales of the Macabre* (Oxford: Oxford University Press, 1997)

Baring-Gould, Sabine, *The Book of Werewolves* ([1865] Stroud: Nonsuch, 2007)

Baxter, Richard, *Of the Immortality of Mans [sic] Soul, and the Nature of it and Other Spirits* (London, 1682)

Beddoes, Thomas Lovell, *The Letters of Thomas Lovell Beddoes*, ed. Edmund Gosse (London: Elkin Mathews & John Lane; and New York: Macmillan & Co., 1894)

Benedicto XIV, Pope [Prospero Lambertini], *Doctrinum De Servorum Dei Beatificatione et Beatorum Canonizatione Redactum in Synopsim* (Rome, 1757)

Bernard, Claude, *An Introduction to the Study of Experimental Medicine*, trans. Henry Copley Greene ([1865] New York: Henry Schuman, Inc., 1949)

Bernhardt, Sarah, *Memories of My Life: Being my Personal, Professional, and Social Recollections as a Woman and Artist* (New York: D. Appleton and Company, 1907)

Beverley, Robert, *The History of Virginia, in Four Parts*, 2nd edn (London, 1722)

'Bickerstaffe, Isaac' [Steele, Richard, Joseph Addison, et al.], *The Lucubrations of Isaac Bickerstaff Esq; Revised and Corrected by the Author* [*The Tatler*], 5 vols (London, 1712)

Birch, Thomas, *The History of the Royal Society of London for Improving of Natural Knowledge, from its First Rise*, 4 vols (London, 1756–57)

Bird, Isabella L., *The Golden Chersonese and the Way Thither* (London: John Murray, 1883)

Blair, Robert, *The Grave. A Poem* (London, 1743)

Blandin, Philippe Frédéric, *Anatomy of the Dental System, Human and Comparative*, trans. Robert Arthur (Baltimore, MD: American Society of Dental Surgeons, 1845)

Blankaart, Stephen, *The Physical Dictionary* (London, 1708)

Blavatsky, H.P., *Isis Unveiled: A Master-Key to the Mysteries of Ancient and Modern*, 2 vols (New York: J. Bouton, 1877)

Blyth, Edward, 'Notice of the Predatory and Sanguivorous Habits of Bats of the Genus Megaderma, with some Remarks on the Blood-Sucking Propensities of other Vespertilionide', *Journal of the Asiatic Society of Bengal*, 123 (1842), 255–62

Bond, John, *Essay on the Incubus, or Night-Mare* (London, 1753)

Boner, Charles, *Transylvania; Its Products and Its People* (London: Longmans, Green, Reader and Dyer, 1865)

Born, Inigo, *Travels through the Bannat of Temeswar, Transylvania, and Hungary, in the Year 1770*, trans. R.E. Raspe (London, 1777)

Boswell, James, *Boswell's Life of Johnson*, ed. George Birkbeck Hill, rev. L.F. Powell, 6 vols ([1791] Oxford: Clarendon Press, 1979)

Boyer, Jean Baptiste de, marquis d'Argens, *The Jewish Spy: being A Philosophical, Historical and Critical Correspondence, by Letters which Lately Pass'd between certain Jews in Turkey, Italy, France, &c. Translated from the Originals into French, by the Marquis D'Argens; and now done into English*, 5 vols ([1737: *Lettres Juives*] London, 1739–40)

Boyer, Jean Baptiste de, marquis d'Argens, *Jewish Letters: or, A Correspondence Philosophical, Historical and Critical, betwixt a Jew and his Correspondents, in Different Parts*, 4 vols (Newcastle, 1739–44)

Boyle, Robert, *The Works of the Honourable Robert Boyle*, new edn, 6 vols (London, 1772)

Bromhall, Thomas, *A Treatise of Specters, or, A History of Apparitions, Oracles, Prophecies, and Predictions* (London, 1658)

Brontë, Charlotte, *Jane Eyre*, ed. Margaret Smith and Sally Shuttleworth ([1847] Oxford: Oxford University Press, 2000)

Buffon, comte de [Georges-Louis Leclerc], *Natural History, General and Particular, by the Count de Buffon, Translated into English*, trans. William Smellie, 9 vols ([1749–1804: *Histoire Naturelle*] London, 1785)

Burke, Edmund, *Reflections on the Revolution in France*, ed. L.G. Mitchell ([1790] Oxford: Oxford University Press, 1993)

Burnet, Thomas, *The Theory of the Earth containing an Account of the Original of the Earth, and of all the General Changes which it hath Already Undergone, or is to Undergo, till the Consummation of All Things* (London, 1684)

Burns, Robert, *The Canongate Burns*, ed. Andrew Noble and Patrick Scott Hogg (Edinburgh: Canongate, 2001)

Burton, Robert, *The Anatomy of Melancholy*, ed. Thomas C. Faulkner, Nicolas K. Kiessling and Rhonda L. Blair, 3 vols ([1621–51] Oxford: Clarendon Press, 1989–94)

Byron, Lord [George Gordon], *The Giaour, A Fragment of a Turkish Tale* (London: John Murray, 1813)

Byron, Lord [George Gordon], *The Giaour, A Fragment of a Turkish Tale*, 10th edn (London: John Murray, 1814)

Byron, Lord [George Gordon], *Lord Byron: The Complete Miscellaneous Prose*, ed. Andrew Nicholson (Oxford: Oxford University Press, 1991)

Calmet, Dom Augustin, *Commentaire Litteral sur Tous les Livres de l'Ancien et du Nouveau Testament*, 26 vols (Paris, 1707–17)

Calmet, Dom Augustin, *Dissertations upon the Apparitions of Angels, Dæmons, and Ghosts, and Concerning the Vampires of Hungary, Bohemia, Moravia, and Silesia* ([1746: *Dissertation sur . . . les oupires ou vampires*] London, 1759)

Calmet, Dom Augustin, *The Phantom World: Concerning Apparitions and Vampires* ([1759] London: Wordsworth Editions, 2001)

Calmet, Dom Augustin, *Dissertation sur les revenants en corps, les excommuniés, les oupires ou vampires, brucolaques etc.*, ed. Roland Villeneuve, 2nd edn ([1986] Grenoble: Editions Jérôme Millon, 1998)

Camfield, Benjamin, *A Theological Discourse of Angels and their Ministries wherein their Existence, Nature, Number, Order and Offices are Modestly Treated of: with the Character of those for whose Benefit especially they are Commissioned, and such Practical Inferences deduced as are Most Proper to the Premise* (London, 1678)

Camm, Dom Bede (ed.), *Lives of the English Martyrs Declared Blessed by Pope Leo XIII in 1886 and 1895*, 2 vols (London: Burns and Oates; New York, Cincinnati and Chicago: Benziger Brothers, 1904–05)

Campbell, Lewis and William Garnett, *The Life of James Clerk Maxwell with a Selection from his Correspondence and Occasional Writings and a Sketch of his Contributions to Science* (London: Macmillan and Co., 1882)

Carter, Angela, *The Bloody Chamber* (London: Vintage, 1979)

Cave, William, *Primitive Christianity: or, The Religion of the Ancient Christians in the First Ages of the Gospel*, 2 vols (London, 1763)

Charles S. Anderson Design Co. and Michael J. Nelson (eds), *Goth-Icky* (New York: Harry N. Abrams, Inc., 2005)

Chémant, Nicolas Dubois de, *A Dissertation on Artificial Teeth in General*, 1st edn (London: J. Barker, 1797)

Chémant, Nicolas Dubois de, *A Dissertation on Artificial Teeth*, 4th edn (London: T. Bensley, 1804)

Clarke, Samuel, *A Demonstration of the Being and Attributes of God: more particularly in Answer to Mr. Hobbs, Spinoza, and their Followers* (London, 1705)

Claudian, *De Bello Gothico: The Gothic War*, trans. Maurice Platnauer, 2 vols, Loeb Classical Library (Cambridge, MA, and London: Harvard University Press, 1963)

Cobbe, Frances Power, *The Janus of Science* (London: Office of the Society for Protection of Animals from Vivisection, 1882)

[*Cobbett's Complete Collection . . .*] T.B. Howell, *A Complete Collection of State Trials and Proceedings for High Treason and Other Crimes and Misdemeanors from the Earliest Period to the Present Time*, 21 vols (London: T.C. Hansard, 1816)

Cockburn, Archibald, *A Philosophical Essay concerning the Intermediate State of Blessed Souls* (London, 1722)

Coleridge, Samuel Taylor, *Poems*, ed. John Beer (Everyman: London and Melbourne, 1983)

A Compendious Abstract of the Public General Acts of the United Kingdom of Great Britain and Ireland: 4 Geo. IV. 1823 (London: J.W. Paget, 1823)

Comte, Auguste, *System of Positive Polity, or Treatise on Sociology, Instituting the Religion of Humanity*, 4 vols, trans. Richard Congreve and Frederick Harrison ([1851–54] London: John Henry Bridges, 1875–77)

Cooke, Nicholas Francis, *Satan in Society* (Cincinnati, OH, and New York: C.F. Vent, 1871)

Cooper, Anthony Ashley, earl of Shaftesbury, *Characteristicks of Men, Manners, Opinions, Times*, 5th edn, 3 vols ([1711] London, 1732)

Cox's Fragmenta: An Historical Miscellany, ed. Simon Murphy (Stroud: The History Press, 2010)

Crawford, Francis Marion, *Wandering Ghosts* (New York: Macmillan, 1911)

Crosse, Andrew F., *Round About the Carpathians* (Edinburgh and London: William Blackwood and Sons, 1878)

Cudworth, Ralph, *The True Intellectual System of the Universe: The First Part; wherein, All the Reason and Philosophy of Atheism is Confuted; and Its Impossibility Demonstrated* (London, 1678)

Danielewski, Mark, *House of Leaves*, '2nd edn' (New York: Pantheon Books, 2000)

'D'Anvers, Caleb', *The Craftsman*, 14 vols (London, 1731–37)

Darwin, Charles, *Works of Charles Darwin*, 29 vols, ed. Paul H. Barrett and R.B. Freeman (London: Routledge, 2016)

Darwin, Erasmus, *The Botanic Garden*, ed. Adam Komisaruk and Allison Dushane, 2 vols ([1791] London and New York: Routledge, 2017)

D'Assier, Adolphe, *Posthumous Humanity: A Study of Phantoms* (London: George Redway, 1887)

Davanzati, Giuseppe, *Dissertazione sopra i Vampiri* (Naples, 1774)

Davanzati, Giuseppe, *Dissertazione sopra i Vampiri*, ed. Giacomo Annibaldis ([1774] Bari: Besa, 1998)

Davenant, Charles, *A Postscript to a Discourse of Credit, and the Means and Methods of Restoring it* (London, 1701)

Davy, Humphry, *The Collected Works of Sir Humphry Davy, Bart. LL.D., F.R.S.*, ed. John Davy, 9 vols (London: Smith, Elder and Co., 1839–40)

De Quincey, Thomas, *On Murder*, ed. Robert Morrison (Oxford: Oxford University Press, 2006)

Defoe, Daniel, *An Essay on the History and Reality of Apparitions* (London, 1727)

Defoe, Daniel, *see* Anon.

Derham, William, *Physico-Theology: or, A Demonstration of the Being and Attributes of God, from his Works of Creation* (London, 1713)

Derham, William, *Astro-Theology: or A Demonstration of the Being and Attributes of God, from a Survey of the Heavens* (London, 1715)

Descartes, René, *The Philosophical Writings of Descartes*, ed. John Cottingham, Robert Stoothoff and Dugald Murdoch, 3 vols (Cambridge: Cambridge University Press, 1985–91)

Dickens, Charles, *The Old Curiosity Shop*, ed. Elizabeth M. Brennan ([1840–41] Oxford: Clarendon Press, 1997)

Disraeli, Benjamin, *The Voyage of Captain Popanilla* (London: Henry Colburn, 1828)

Dobell, Sydney, *see* 'Smith, Alexander'

Dodsley, Robert, *The Correspondence of Robert Dodsley, 1733–1764*, ed. James E. Tierney (Cambridge: Cambridge University Press, 1988)

Donne, John, *Selected Poetry*, ed. John Carey (Oxford: Oxford University Press, 1998)

Dunton, John, et al., *The Athenian Oracle: Being an Entire Collection of all the Valuable Questions and Answers in the Old Athenian Mercuries*, 3 vols (1703–04)

Durham, Mary Edith, 'Of Magic, Witches, and Vampires in the Balkans', *Man*, 23 (1923), 189–90

Eliot, T.S., *The Waste Land* in *The Complete Poems and Plays* ([1922] London and Boston, MA: Faber and Faber, 1969), 59–80

Elliott, C.B., *Travels in the Three Great Empires of Austria, Russia, and Turkey*, 2 vols (London: Richard Bentley, 1838)

Ellis, Havelock, *Man and Woman: A Study of Human Secondary Sexual Characters* (London: Walter Scott, 1894)

Emes, Thomas, *Vindiciæ Mentis. An Essay of the Being and Nature of Mind: Wherein the Distinction of Mind and Body, the Substantiality, Personality, and Perfection of Mind is Asserted; and the Original of our Minds, their Present, Separate, and Future State, is Freely Enquir'd into, in order to a more Certain Foundation for the Knowledge of God, and Our Selves, and the Clearing all Doubts and Objections that have been, or may be made concerning The Life and Immortality of Our Souls* (London, 1702)

Engels, Frederick, *The Condition of the Working Class in England in 1844*, trans. Florence Kelley Wischnewetzky ([1892] New York: Cosimo Books, 2008)

Erasmus, Desiderius, *Collected Works*, 89 vols (Toronto, Buffalo, London: University of Toronto Press, 1974–2018), vol. 35: *Adages III iv 1 to IV ii 100*, trans. Denis L. Drysdall, ed. John N. Grant (Toronto, Buffalo, London: University of Toronto Press, 2005)

'Erinensis' [Green, Peter Hennis], 'On the Exportation of Dead Bodies from Ireland to England and Scotland', *The Lancet*, 21 March 1829 (1828–29), i. 774–78

Ewing, James, *Clinical Pathology of the Blood* (London: Henry Kimpton, 1904)

Eyrbyggja Saga, ed. and trans. Hermann Pálsson and Paul Edwards (London: Penguin, 1989)

Feijóo y Montenegro, Benito Jerónimo, *Cartas Eruditas, y Curiosas, en que, por la mayor parte, se continua el designio Del Teatro Critico Universal . . .*, new edn, 5 vols (Madrid, 1774)

Ferriar, John, 'Of POPULAR ILLUSIONS, and Particularly of MEDICAL DEMONOLOGY', in *Memoirs of the Literary and Philosophical Society of Manchester*, 5 vols (1785–87), iii. 31–105 (12 May 1786)

Ficino, Marsilio, *Della Religione Christiane* (Florence, 1568)

Fielding, Henry, *The Debauchees: or, The Jesuit Caught* (London, 1750)

Forel, August, *The Sexual Question: A Scientific, Psychological, Hygienic and Sociological Study*, 2nd English edn, trans. C.F. Marshall (New York: Medical Art Agency, 1906)

Forman, Charles, *A Second Letter to the Right Honourable Sir Robert Walpole* (London, 1733)

Forman, Charles, *Some Queries and Observations upon the Revolution in 1688, and its Consequences: also a Short View of the Rise and Progress of the Dutch East India Company; with Critical Remarks* (London: Olive Payne, 1741)

Fortis, Alberto, *Travels into Dalmatia; containing General Observations on the Natural History of that Country and the Neighbouring Islands; the Natural Productions, Arts, Manners and Customs of the Inhabitants: in a Series of Letters from Abbe Alberto Fortis, to the Earl of Bute, the Bishop of Londonderry, John Strange, Esq. &c. &c* (London, 1774)

Fourth Annual Report of the Poor Law Commissioners for England and Wales; together with Appendices A. B. & C. (London: W. Clowes and Sons, 1838)

Foxe, John, *Actes and Monuments of these Latter and Perillous Dayes . . .* (London, 1563 and subsequent editions)

Franklin, Caroline (ed.), *The Longman Anthology of Gothic Verse* (Harlow: Longman, 2011)

Froude, James Anthony, *Thomas Carlyle: A History of his Life in London, 1834–1881*, 4th edn, 2 vols (London: Longmans, Green and Co., 1885)

Fulford, Tim (ed.), *Romanticism and Science, 1773–1833*, 5 vols (London and New York: Routledge, 2002)

Furetière, Antoine, *Dictionnaire Universel François et Latin, vulgairement appelé Dictionnaire de Trévoux*, 6th edn, 8 vols (Paris, 1771)

Gaiman, Neil, *Smoke and Mirrors: Short Fictions and Illusions* (New York, London, Toronto and Sydney: Harper Perennial, 2001)

Garmann, Christian Friedrich, *De Miraculis Mortuorum* (Leipzig, 1709)

Geoffrey of Burton, *Life and Miracles of St Modwenna*, ed. Robert Bartlett (Oxford: Oxford University Press, 2002)

Gerard, Emily, 'Transylvanian Superstitions', *Nineteenth Century*, 18 (July 1885), 130–50

Glanvill, Joseph, *A Philosophical Endeavour towards the Defense of the being of Witches and Apparitions* (London, 1666)

Glanvill, Joseph, *Some Philosophical Considerations Touching the Being of Witches and Witchcraft* (London, 1667)

Glanvill, Joseph, *A Blow at Modern Sadducism in some Philosophical Considerations about Witchcraft* (London, 1668)

Glanvill, Joseph, *Saducismus Triumphatus: or, Full and Plain Evidence concerning Witches and Apparitions* (London, 1681)

Goethe, Johann Wolfgang von, *Faustus, A Dramatic Mystery; The Bride of Corinth; The First Walpurgis Night*, trans. John Anster (London: Longman, Rees, Orme, Brown, Green & Longman, 1835)

Goldsmith, Oliver, *The Citizen of the World; or Letters from a Chinese Philosopher, residing in London, to his Friends in the East*, 2 vols (London, 1762)

Görres, Joseph von, *Die Christliche Mystik*, 4 vols (Regensburg and Landshut: G. Joseph Manz, 1836–42)

Gough, Richard, *Sepulchral Monuments in Great Britain applied to illustrate the History of Families, Manners, Habits, and Arts, at the Different Periods from the Norman Conquest to the Seventeenth Century*, 2 vols (London, 1786–96)

Grady, Thomas, *An Impartial View, of the Causes leading this Country to the Necessity of an Union; in which the Two Leading Characters of the State are Contrasted; and in which is contained, a History of the Rise and Progress of Orange Men; A Reply to Cease your Funning, and Mr. Jebb*, 3rd edn (Dublin, 1799)

Grässe, Johann Georg Theodor, *Bibliotheca Magica et Pneumatica oder Wissenschaftlich Geordnete Bibliographie der wichtigsten in das Gebiet der Zauber-, Wunder-, Geister- und Sonstigen Aberglaubens vorzüglich älterer*

Zeit einschlagenden Werke: mit Angabe der aus diesen Wissenschaften auf der Königl. Sächs. Oeff. Bibliothek zu Dresden befindlichen Schriften; ein Beitrag zur Sittengeschichtlichen Literatur (Leipzig: Engelmann, 1843)

Gray, Robert, *The Theory of Dreams*, 2 vols (London: F.C. & J. Rivington, 1808)

Green, Peter Hennis, *see* 'Erinensis'

Grettir's Saga, ed. and trans. Jesse Byock (Oxford: Oxford University Press, 2009)

Grimaldi, Costantino, *Dissertazione in cui si Investiga . . . Magia Diabolica . . . Magia Artificiale e Naturale* (Rome, 1751)

Groom, Nick (ed.), *The Bloody Register*, 4 vols ([1764] London: Routledge/Thoemmes Press, 1999)

Haining, Peter (ed.), *The Dracula Scrapbook: Articles, Essays, Letters, Newspaper Cuttings, Anecdotes, Illustrations, Photographs and Memorabilia about the Vampire Legend* (London: New English Library, 1976)

Hamberger, Klaus, *Mortuus Non Mordet: Dokumente zum Vampirismus 1689–1791* (Vienna: Turia & Kant, 1992)

Hamilton, Laurell K., *Narcissus in Chains* ([2002] London: Headline, 2010)

[*Hansard*] Hansard, T.C. (ed.), *The Parliamentary Debates from the Year 1803 to the Present Time*, 1st ser., 41 vols (London: Longman, Hurst, Rees, Orme and Brown, etc., 1812–20).

Hardy, Thomas, *Jude the Obscure*, ed. Patricia Ingham ([1894–95] Oxford: Oxford University Press, 2002)

Hardy, Thomas, *Late Lyrics and Earlier*, in *The Collected Poems of Thomas Hardy*, 4th edn (London: Macmillan and Company, 1930)

Harenberg, Johann Christoph, *Vernünftige und Christliche Gedanken über die Vampirs Oder Blutsaugende Todten* (Wolffenbüttel, 1733)

Harvey, Gideon, *A Discourse of the Plague* (London, 1665)

Harvey, William, *The Anatomical Exercises of Dr. William Harvey Professor of Physick, and Physician to the Kings Majesty, concerning the Motion of the Heart and Blood. . . . To which is added Dr. James De Back his Discourse of the Heart, Physician in Ordinary to the Town of Roterdam* (London, 1653)

Harvey, William, *Exercitatio Anatomica de Motu Cordis et Sanguinis in Animalibus* (Frankfurt, 1628)

Haweis, H.R., *Ashes to Ashes* (London: Dalby, Isbister & Co., 1875)

Heber, Reginald, *An Historical List of Horse-Matches Run* (London, 1752)

Hervey, James, *Meditations among the Tombs* (London and Bath, 1746)

Hess, Moses, *Philosophische und Sozialistische Schriften 1837–1850*, ed. Wolfgang Mönke (Vaduz: Topos, 1980)

Hobbes, Thomas, *Leviathan*, ed. C.B. Macpherson ([1651] Harmondsworth: Penguin, 1985)

Hornby, Charles, *Three Letters, containing Remarks on Some of the Numberless Errors and Defects in Dugdale's Baronage: and Occasionally on Some Other Authors* (London, 1738)

Hornby, Charles, *A Third Letter, containing some further Remarks on a Few More of the Numberless Errors and Defects in Dugdale's Baronage: with Occasional Observations on Some Other Authors* (London, 1738)

Horrox, Rosemary (ed. and trans.), *The Black Death* (Manchester: Manchester University Press, 1994)

Hume, David, *Philosophical Essays Concerning Human Understanding* (London, 1748)

Hunter, John, *The Natural History of the Human Teeth: Explaining their Structure, Use, Formation, Growth, and Diseases* (London, 1771)

St Ignatius of Loyola, *The Spiritual Exercises of St Ignatius of Loyola*, new edition, ed. Thomas Corbishley ([1522–24] Wheathamstead: Anthony Clarke Books, 1973)

Jago, Richard, *The Causes of Impenitence Consider'd: as well in the Case of Extraordinary Warnings, as under the General Laws of Providence, and Grace* (Oxford, 1755)

Jenner, Edward, *An Inquiry into the Causes and Effects of the Variolæ Vaccinæ, a Disease discovered in some of the Western Counties of England, particularly Gloucestershire, and known by the Name of the Cow Pox* (London, 1798)

Johnson, E.C., *On the Track of the Crescent; Erratic Notes from Piraeus to Pesth* (London: Hurst and Blackett, 1885)

Jordanes, *The Gothic History*, trans. Charles Christopher Mierow (Princeton, NJ: Princeton University Press, and London: Oxford University Press, 1915)

Kant, Immanuel, 'Anthropology from a Pragmatic Point of View', trans. Robert B. Louden, in Robert B. Louden and Günter Zöller (ed. and trans.), *Anthropology, History, and Education* ([1798] Cambridge: Cambridge University Press, 2007), 227–429

Keats, John, *Poetical Works*, ed. H.W. Garrod (Oxford and New York: Oxford University Press, 1982)

Keet, Philomena and Yuri Manabe, *The Tokyo Look Book: Stylish to Spectacular, Goth to Gyaru, Sidewalk to Catwalk* (Tokyo, New York and London: Kodansha International, 2007)

Keynes, John Maynard, *Essays in Biography* (London: Macmillan and Co., 1933)

King, Edmund, 'An Account of the Experiment of *Transfusion*, Practised upon a *Man* in *London*', *Philosophical Transactions*, 30 (1667), 557–59

Kipling, Rudyard, *The Collected Poems*, ed. R.T. Jones (Ware: Wordsworth, 2001)

Krafft-Ebing, Richard von, *Psychopathia Sexualis, with Especial Reference to Contrary Sexual Instinct: A Medico-Legal Study*, 7th edn, trans. Charles Gilbert Chaddock ([1886] Philadelphia, PA: F.A. Davis Company, 1894)

Kramer, Heinrich (alias 'Henricus Institoris') and Jacob Sprenger, *The Malleus Maleficarum*, ed. and trans. P.G. Maxwell-Stuart ([1486?, 1588] Manchester and New York: Manchester University Press, 2007)

Lange, Jens Iversen, *see* Aarhus, Bishop of

Lavallée, Joseph, *Travels in Istria and Dalmatia; Drawn Up from the Itinerary of L.F. Cassas* (London: Richard Phillips, 1805)

Lavater, Ludwig, *Of Ghosts and Spirits Walking by Nyght*, ed. M. Yardley ([1572] Oxford: Oxford University Press, 1929)

Lawrence, D.H., *Studies in Classic American Literature*, ed. Ezra Greenspan, Lindeth Vasey and John Worthen ([1923] Cambridge: Cambridge University Press, 2003)

Leake, William Martin, *Travels in Northern Greece*, 4 vols (London: J. Rodwell, 1835)

Le Fanu, Joseph Sheridan, *Carmilla: A Critical Edition*, ed. Kathleen Costello-Sullivan (New York: Syracuse University Press, 2013)

LeFanu [*sic*], J.S., *Best Ghost Stories*, ed. E.F. Bleiler (New York: Dover Publications, 1964)

Levack, Brian P. (ed.), *The Witchcraft Sourcebook*, 2nd edn (London and New York: Routledge, 2015)

Lévi, Eliphas, *The Key of the Mysteries*, trans. Aleister Crowley ([1861: *La Clef des Grands Mystères*] London: Rider & Co., 1959)

Lewis, Matthew, *The Monk*, ed. Nick Groom ([1796] Oxford: Oxford University Press, 2016)

L'Homond, C.F., *Pious Lectures, explanatory of the Principles, Obligations and Resources, of the Catholic Religion*, trans. the Revd Appleton (London, 1794)

L'Homond, C.F., *Theophilus, or The Pupil Instructed in the Principles, the Obligations, and the Resources of the Roman Catholic Religion*, trans. the Rev. Appleton (Wolverhampton, 1794)

Liepopili, Ante, 'Vukodlaci' in *Zbornik za Narodni Život i Običaje Južnih Slavena*, 13 (Zagreb: Knižarnica Jugoslavenske Akademije, 1918), 277–90

Locke, John, *An Essay Concerning Human Understanding*, ed. Peter H. Nidditch ([1689] Oxford: Oxford University Press, 1979)

Locke, John, *An Essay Concerning Human Understanding*, ed. Pauline Phemister ([1689] Oxford: Oxford University Press, 2008)

Locke, John, *Some Thoughts Concerning Education*, ed. John W. Yolton and Jean S. Yolton ([1693] Oxford: Oxford University Press, 2000)

Lombroso, Cesare, *Criminal Man*, ed. Mary Gibson and Nicole Hahn Rafter ([1876] Durham, NC, and London: Duke University Press, 2006)

Lombroso, Cesare, *Criminal Man*, ed. Gina Lombroso-Ferrero ([1876] New York and London: G.P. Putnam's Sons, 1911)

Lombroso, Cæsar and William Ferrero, *The Female Offender* (New York: Appleton and Company, 1895)

Mallet, David, *Poems on Several Occasions* (London, 1762)

Mantel, Hilary, *The Assassination of Margaret Thatcher and Other Stories* (London: Fourth Estate, 2014)

Marryat, Florence, *Blood of the Vampire* (Leipzig: Bernhard Tauchnitz, 1897)

Marryat, Florence, *Blood of the Vampire*, ed. Greta Depledge ([1897] Brighton: Victorian Secrets, 2010)

Marryat, Florence, *Blood of the Vampire*, ed. Brenda Mann Hammack ([1897] Kansas City, KS: Valancourt Books, 2009)

Marx, Karl, *The Class Struggles in France: 1848 to 1850*, in David Fernbach (ed.), *Surveys from Exile* ([1850] Harmondsworth: Penguin, 1973), 35–142

Marx, Karl, *The Eighteenth Brumaire of Louis Bonaparte* [1852], in David Fernbach (ed.), *Surveys from Exile*, 143–249

Marx, Karl, *Grundrisse*, trans. Martin Nicolaus ([1857–58] Harmondsworth: Penguin, 1973)

Marx, Karl, *The First International and After*, ed. David Fernbach ([1864] Harmondsworth: Penguin, 1974)

Marx, Karl, *Capital: A Critique of Political Economy*, Vol. 1, trans. Ben Fowkes ([1867] Harmondsworth: Penguin, 1975)

Marx, Karl, *Early Writings*, trans. Rodney Livingstone and Gregor Benton (Harmondsworth: Penguin, 1975)

Marx, Karl and Friedrich Engels, *The German Ideology*, in *Marx–Engels Collected Works*, 50 vols ([1845–46] Moscow: Progress Publishers, 1975–2005)

Maubray, John, *The Female Physician, containing all the Diseases incident to that Sex, in Virgins, Wives, and Widows; together with their Causes and Symptoms, their Degrees of Danger, and Respective Methods of Prevention and Cure* (London, 1730)

Maudsley, Henry, *Body and Mind: An Inquiry into their Connection and Mutual Influence, Specially in Reference to Mental Disorders* (London: Macmillan and Co., 1870)

Mayhew, Henry, *London Labour and the London Poor*, ed. Robert Douglas-Fairhurst ([1850–52] Oxford: Oxford University Press, 2010)

Mayhew, Henry, 'Home is Home, be it Never so Homely', in *Meliora: or, Better Times to Come*, ed. Viscount Ingestre (London: John W. Parker and Son, 1852), 258–80

Mayo, Herbert, *On the Truths Contained in Popular Superstitions with an Account of Mesmerism*, 2nd edn (Edinburgh and London: William Blackwood and Sons, 1851)

Mazuchelli, Nina Elizabeth, *'Magyarland;' Being the Narrative of our Travels through the Highlands and Lowlands of Hungary* (London: Sampson, Low, Marston, Searle & Rivington, 1881)

Mensink, Frans, *Kristina, Queen of Vampires* (New York: Eurotica, 2005)

Mercer, Mick, *Hex Files: The Goth Bible* (London: B.T. Batsford, 1996)

Merivale, John Herman, *see* 'Arminius'

Middleton, Thomas, *A Tragi-Coomodie [sic], called The Witch; long since acted by His Maties Servants at the Black-Friers* (London, 1778)

Miles, Robert, *Gothic Writing, 1750–1820: A Genealogy* (London and New York: Routledge, 1993)

Milton, John, *Paradise Lost*, ed. Alastair Fowler (London and New York: Longman, 1971)

Monboddo, Lord [James Burnet[t]], *Of the Origin and Progress of Language*, 6 vols (Edinburgh, 1773–92)

Moore, Thomas, *Corruption and Intolerance: Two Poems* (London: J. Carpenter, 1808)

More, Henry, *An Antidote Against Atheism or, An Appeal to the Naturall Faculties of the Minde of Man, Whether there be not a God*, 2nd edn (London, 1655)

More, Henry, *An Antidote Against Atheism: or, An Appeal to the Natural Faculties of the Mind of Man, Whether there be not a God*, 3rd edn [1662], in *A Collection of Several Philosophical Writings of Dr. Henry More [,] Fellow of Christ's Colledge [sic] in Cambridge*, 2nd edn (London, 1662)

Morris, William, *The Collected Works of William Morris*, ed. May Morris, 24 vols (London: Longmans Green and Company, 1911 [1910–15])

Murgoçi, Agnes, 'The Vampire in Roumania', *Folklore*, 37 (1926), 320–49

Newbery, John, rev. Oliver Goldsmith, *The Art of Poetry on a New Plan: Illustrated with a Great Variety of Examples from the Best English Poets; and of Translations from the Ancients: Together with Such Reflections and Critical Remarks as may tend to form in our Youth an Elegant Taste, and render the Study of this Part of the Belles Lettres more Rational and Pleasing*, 2 vols (London, 1762)

Nietzsche, Friedrich, *The Gay Science with a Prelude in Rhymes and an Appendix of Songs*, trans. Walter Kaufman ([1882] New York: Vintage, 1974)

Nitz, Jai and Jack Jadson, *The Ravening* (Rantoul, IL: Boundless, 2016)

Nordau, Max, *Degeneration* ([1892] London: William Heinemann, 1898)

North, Roger, *The Life of the Honourable Sir Dudley North, Knt . . . . and of the Honourable and Reverend Dr. John North . . .* (London, 1744)

Oldham, John, *Garnets Ghost, Addressing to the Jesuits, met in Private Caball, just after the Murther of Sir Edmund-Bury Godfrey* (London, 1679)

Otis, Laura (ed.), *Literature and Science in the Nineteenth Century: An Anthology* (Oxford: Oxford University Press, 2002)

Parry, Michael, *Countess Dracula* ([1971] London: Redemption Press, 1995)

Pashley, Robert, *Travels in Crete*, 2 vols (Cambridge: Pitt Press, and London: John Murray, 1837)

Pater, Walter, *The Renaissance: Studies in Art and Poetry* ([1873] London: Macmillan and Co., 1925)

Pegge, Samuel, *Anonymiana; or, Ten Centuries of Observations on Various Authors and Subjects* ([1766] London: John Nichols and Son, 1809)

Pepys, Samuel, *The Diary of Samuel Pepys*, ed. John Warrington, 3 vols ([1906] London, Melbourne and Toronto: J.M. Dent and Sons, 1978)

Percy, Thomas (ed.), *Reliques of Ancient English Poetry*, 3 vols (London, 1765)

Pettigrew, Thomas Joseph, *On Superstitions Connected with the History and Practice of Medicine and Surgery* (London: John Churchill, 1844)

Piozzi, Hesther Lynch, *Anecdotes of the Late Samuel Johnson LLD.*, in George Birkbeck Hill (ed.), *Johnsonian Miscellanies*, 2 vols ([1786] London: Constable & Co. Ltd, 1966)

Pliny, *Natural History*, trans. W.H.S. Jones, 10 vols, Loeb Classical Library (Cambridge, MA: Harvard University Press, and London: William Heinemann, 1963)

Poe, Edgar Allan, *Tales of Mystery and Imagination*, illustrated by Arthur Rackham (London: George G. Harrap and Co., 1935)

Poe, Edgar Allan, *The Complete Tales* (New York: Avenel Books, 1981)

Polidori, John William, *The Vampyre and Ernestus Berchtold; or, the Modern Oedipus: Collected Fiction of John William Polidori*, ed. D.L. Macdonald and Kathleen Scherf ([1819] Toronto, Buffalo and London: University of Toronto Press, 1994)

Polidori, John William, *The Diary of Dr. John William Polidori, 1816: Relating to Byron, Shelley, etc.*, ed. William Michael Rossetti (London: Elkin Mathews, 1911)

Pond, John, *The Sporting Calendar* (London, 1751)

Pope, Alexander (ed.), *Poems on Several Occasions* (Dublin, 1722)

Pope, Alexander, *The Works of Alexander Pope*, ed. Whitwell Elwin and William John Courthope, with John Wilson Croker, new edn, 10 vols (London: John Murray, 1871–89)

Priestley, Joseph, *An History of the Corruptions of Christianity*, 2 vols (Birmingham, 1782)

'Putoneo' [Meinig, J.C.], *Besondere Nachricht von denen Vampyren oder so genannten Blut-Saugern* (Leipzig, 1732)

Rabinbach, Anson and Sander L. Gilman (eds), *The Third Reich Sourcebook* (Berkeley, Los Angeles and London: University of California Press, 2013)

Ranft, Michael, *De Masticatione Mortuorum in Tumulis (oder von dem Kauen und Schmatzen der Todten in Gräbern,) liber singularis: Duas Exhibens Exceritationes, quarum Prior Historico-Critica Posterior Philosophica* (Leipzig, 1725).

Ranft, Michael, *Tractat von dem Kauen und Schmatzen der Todten in Gräbern, worin die wahre Beschaffenheit derer Hungarischen Vampyrs und Blut-Sauger gezeiget, Auch alle von dieser Materie bißher zum Vorschein gekommene Schrifften recensiret werden* (Leipzig, 1734)

Ravensworth, earl of [Henry Thomas Liddell], *The Wizard of the North; The Vampire Bride; and Other Poems* (Edinburgh: W. Blackwood, and London: T. Cadell, 1833)

Ray, John, *The Wisdom of God manifested in the Works of the Creation being the Substance of Some Common Places Delivered in the Chappel [sic] of Trinity-College, in Cambridge* (London, 1691)

'R.B.', *The Kingdom of Darkness: or The History of Dæmons, Specters, Witches, Apparitions, Possessions, Disturbances, and other Wonderful and Supernatural Delusions, Mischievous Feats, and Malicious Impostures of the Devil* (London, 1688)

Reeve, Clara, *The Old English Baron*, ed. James Trainer and James Watt ([1778; *The Champion of Virtue*, 1777] Oxford: Oxford University Press, 2008)

Ricaut, Paul, *The Present State of the Greek and Armenian Churches* (London, 1679)

Robinson, Phil, E. Kay Robinson and H. Perry Robinson, *Tales by Three Brothers* (London: Isbister and Company, 1902)

Robinson, William J., *Married Life and Happiness* (New York: Eugenics Publishing Company, 1922)

Rodd, Rennell, *The Customs and Lore of Modern Greece* (London: David Stott, 1892)

Rohr, Phillip, *Dissertatio De Masticatione Mortuorum* (University of Leipzig, 16 August 1679)

Rollin, Jean, *Little Orphan Vampires*, trans. Peter Tombs (London: Redemption Books, 1995)

Rossetti, Dante Gabriel, *Poems* (London: Ellis & White, 1881)

Rousseau, Jean-Jacques, *An Expostulatory Letter from J.J. Rousseau, Citizen of Geneva, to Christopher de Beaumont, Archbishop of Paris* (London, 1763)

Rousseau, John James [*sic*: for Jean-Jacques], *Emilius; or, An Essay on Education*, trans. Thomas Nugent, 2 vols ([1762] London, 1763)

Rymer, James Malcolm, *Varney the Vampyre or, The Feast of Blood*, ed. Dick Collins ([1845–47] London: Wordsworth Editions, 2010)

Rzączyński, Fr Gabriel, SJ, *Historia Naturalis Curiosa Regni Poloniæ, Magni Ducatus Litvaniæ, Annexarum; Provinciarum, in Tractatus XX Divisa . . .* (Sandomir, 1721)

Sacheverell, Henry, *The Political Union. A Discourse shewing the Dependance [sic] of Government on Religion in General: and of the English Monarchy on the Church of England in Particular* (Oxford, 1702)

'Sagann af Kyrielax Keysara', British Library, Add MS 4859

Scharf, Natasha, *The Art of Gothic: Music † Fashion † Alt Culture* (London: Omnibus Press, 2014)

Schelling, Friedrich Wilhelm, Joseph von, *Philosophical Investigations into the Essence of Human Freedom*, trans. and ed. Jeff Love and Johannes Schmidt ([1809] Albany, NY: State University of New York Press, 2006)

Schertz, Karl Ferdinand, *Magia Posthuma per Juridicum Illud Pro & Contra Suspenso Non Nullibi Judicio Investigata* (Olmütz, 1704)

Schonhorn, Manuel (ed.), *Accounts of the Apparition of Mrs Veal*, Augustan Reprint Society No. 115 (Los Angeles, CA: William Andrews Clark Memorial Library, 1965)

Scott, Walter, *The Chase, and William and Helen* (Edinburgh, 1796)

Scott, Walter, *Minstrelsy of the Scottish Border*, 3 vols (London: T. Cadell, Jr. and W. Davies, 1802–03)

Scott, Walter, *Rokeby, A Poem*, 5th edn (Edinburgh: A. Constable and Co., and John Ballantyne and Co.; and London: Longman, Hurst, Rees, Orme and Brown, 1813)

Shakespeare, William, *The Oxford Shakespeare: The Complete Works*, gen. eds Stanley Wells and Gary Taylor (Oxford: Clarendon Press, 1988)

Shelley, Mary, *Frankenstein; or, The Modern Prometheus*, ed. Nick Groom (Oxford: Oxford University Press, 2018)

Shelley, Percy Bysshe, *The Letters of Percy Bysshe Shelley*, ed. Frederick L. Jones, 2 vols (Oxford: Clarendon Press, 1964)

Shelley, Percy Bysshe, *Shelley's Poetry and Prose*, ed. Donald H. Reiman and Sharon B. Powers (New York and London: W.W. Norton & Company, 1977)

Sinclar [Sinclair], George, *Satans Invisible World Discovered; or, A Choice Collection of Modern Relations, proving evidently against the Saducees and Atheists of this Present Age, that there are Devils, Spirits, Witches, and Apparitions, from Authentick Records, Attestations of Witnesses, and [sic] Undoubted Verity* (Edinburgh, 1685)

'Smith, Alexander' [Sydney Dobell], *Sonnets on the War* (London: David Bogue, 1855)

Smith, Southwood, *A Treatise on Fever* (London: Longman, Rees, Orme, Brown and Green, 1830)

Southey, Robert, *Thalaba the Destroyer*, 2nd edn, 2 vols (London: Longman, Hurst, Rees and Orme, 1809)

Spielmann, Marion Harry, 'The Paris Salons', *The Magazine of Art*, 22 (1898), 489–97

Stagg, John, *The Minstrel of the North; or, Cumbrian Legends. Being a Poetical Miscellany of Legendary, Gothic, and Romantic Tales* (Manchester: Mark Wardle, 1816)

Steele, Richard, Joseph Addison, et al., *The Tatler*, see 'Bickerstaffe, Isaac'

Stevenson, Robert Louis, *The Merry Men and Other Tales and Fables* ([1885] London: Chatto & Windus, 1905)

Stoker, Bram, *Dracula*, ed. A.N. Wilson ([1897] Oxford and New York: Oxford University Press, 1983)

Stoker, Bram, *Dracula*, ed. Glennis Byron ([1897] Peterborough, ON: Broadview Press, 1998)

Stoker, Bram, *Dracula*, ed. Maurice Hindle, 2nd edn ([1897] London: Penguin, 2003)

Stoker, Bram, *Dracula*, ed. Roger Luckhurst ([1897] Oxford: Oxford University Press, 2011)

Stoker, Bram, *Dracula (Case Studies in Contemporary Criticism)*, ed. John Paul Riquelme ([1897] Boston, MA and New York: Bedford/St Martin's Press, 2002)

Stoker, Bram, *Dracula and The Lair of the White Worm*, ed. Richard Dalby ([1911] London: W. Foulsham & Co. Ltd, 1986)

Strype, John, *Annals of the Reformation and Establishment of Religion, and Other Various Occurrences in the Church of England, during Queen Elizabeth's Happy Reign*, new edn, 4 vols in 7 (Oxford: Clarendon Press, 1824)

Stubbes, Phillip [*sic*], *Anatomy of the Abuses in England in Shakspere's Youth, A.D. 1583*, 2 vols in 3, ed. Frederick J. Furnivall (London: New Shakspere Society, 1877–82)

Swieten, Gerhard van, *Vampyrismus*, ed. Piero Violante ([1768] Palermo: Flaccovio, 1988)

Swinburne, Algernon Charles, *The Poems of Algernon Charles Swinburne*, 6 vols (London: Chatto and Windus, 1912)

Symons, Arthur, *Lesbia and Other Poems* (New York: E.F. Dutton & Company, 1920)

Tallar, Georg, *Visum Repertum Anatomico-Chirurgicum von den Sogenannten Vampier, oder Moroi in der Wallachei, Siebenbürgen und Banat, welche eine Eigens dahin Abgeordnete Untersuchungskommission der Löbl. K. K. Administration in Jahre 1756 erstattet hat* (Vienna/Leipzig, 1784)

Talmey, Bernard, *Woman; A Treatise on the Normal and Pathological Emotions of Feminine Love*, 2nd edn ([1904], New York: Practitioners Publishing Co., 1908)

Thornbury, Walter (vols 1–2) and Edward Walfourd (vols 3–6), *Old and New London: A Narrative of its History, its People, and its Places*, 6 vols (London, Paris and New York: Cassell, Petter & Galpin, 1878)

The Tomb of Dracula: The Complete Collection, 1 vol. currently published ([1973] New York: Marvel Worldwide, 2017)

Tournefort, Joseph Pitton de, *A Voyage into the Levant: perform'd by Command of the late French King*, 2 vols (London, 1718; reprinted in 3 vols London, 1741)

Tuke, D.H., *A Dictionary of Psychological Medicine giving the Definition, Etymology, and Synonyms of the Terms used in Medical Psychology . . .*, 2 vols (Philadelphia, PA: P. Blakiston, Son & Co., 1892)

Valvasor, Johann Weikhard von, *Die Ehre Deß Hertzogthums Crain: Das ist Wahre Gründliche und Recht eigendliche Gelegen- und Beschaffenheit dieses in manchen Alten und Neuen Geschicht-Büchern zwar rühmlich berührten doch bishero nie annoch recht beschriebenen Römisch-Keyserlichen herrlichen Erblandes:*

258

Anjetzo Vermittelst einer Vollkommenen und Ausführlichen Erzehlung aller seiner Landschafften . . . deß Welt-Berühmten Cirknitzer Wunder-Sees . . . ungemeiner Natur-Wunder imgleichen der Gewächse Mineralien Bergwercke Edelgesteine alter Müntz-Stücken Thiere . . . auch der Gebiete Herrschafften Schlösser Städte Märckten . . . Einwohner Sprachen Sitten Trachten Gewerben Handthierungen Religion . . . wie auch der Lands-Fürsten Jahr-Geschichte alter und neuer Denckwürdigkeiten, 15 vols (Laybach and Nuremberg, 1689)

Vampires of the Night (n.p.: Locofuria, 2014)

Vernous, Marc, *A Preservative against the False Prophets of the Times: or, A Treatise concerning True and False Prophets, with their Characters: likewise a Letter to Mr. Maximilian Misson, upon the Subject of the Miracles, pretended to be wrought by the French Prophets, and their Adherents; particularly that of the Fiery Tryal, pretended to be wrought by Clary, in the Cevennes* (London, 1708)

Virgil, *The Works of Virgil: containing his Pastorals, Georgics and Æneis*, trans. John Dryden, 4th edn, 3 vols ([1697] London, 1716)

Voltaire, *A Philosophical Dictionary*, 6 vols ([1764] London: John and Henry Hunt, 1824)

Voltaire, *A Philosophical Dictionary*, 2 vols ([1764] London: W. Dugdale, 1843)

Voltaire, *Dictionnaire Philosophique* (London [Geneva], 1764)

Voltaire, *Questions sur L'Encyclopédie, distribuées en Forme de Dictionnaire*, 2nd edn, 9 vols (London, 1772)

Wale, Samuel, 'James Hall Murdering Mr Penny in Clement's Inn [?], 1741' (n.p., *c.*1730–86): British Library 1953, 0411.37

Walfourd, Edward, *see* Thornbury, Walter

Walker, G.A., *Gatherings from Graveyards; particularly those of London: with a Concise History of the Modes of Interment among Different Nations, from the Earliest Periods* (London: Longman and Company, 1839)

Walpole, Horace, *The Castle of Otranto*, ed. Nick Groom ([1764] Oxford: Oxford University Press, 2014)

Walpole, Horace, *Correspondence*, ed. W.S. Lewis et al., 48 vols (New Haven, CT: Yale University Press; and London: Oxford University Press, 1937–83)

Ward, Edward, *The London-Spy Compleat* (London, 1700)

Waterton, Charles, *Wanderings in South America, the North-West of the United States, and the Antilles, in the Years 1812, 1816, 1820, and 1824* (London: J. Mawman, 1825)

Watson, William, 'An Account of a Disease Occasioned by Transplanting a Tooth', in *Medical Commentaries*, 12 (1787), 209–17

Webster, John [and Thomas Heywood], *Appius and Virginia. A Tragedy* (London, 1659)

Webster, John, *The Duchess of Malfi and Other Plays*, ed. René Weiss (Oxford: Oxford University Press, 2009)

Weld, Charles Richard, *A History of the Royal Society, with Memoirs of the Presidents*, 2 vols (London: John W. Parker, 1848)

Wilde, Oscar, *The Picture of Dorian Gray*, ed. Peter Ackroyd ([1891] Harmondsworth: Penguin, 1985)

Wilkinson, William, *An Account of the Principalities of Wallachia and Moldavia: with Various Political Reflections Relating to them* (London: Longman, Hurst, Rees, Orme and Brown, 1820)

[William of Newburgh] Willelmi Parvi de Newburgh, *Historia Rerum Anglicarum*, ed. Hans Claude Hamilton, 2 vols (London: Sumptibus Societatis, 1856)

Willis, Thomas, *The Remaining Medical Works of that Famous and Renowned Physician Dr Thomas Willis . . .*, trans. Samuel Pordage (London, 1681)

Woodward, Josiah, *Fair Warnings to a Careless World, or, The Serious Practice of Religion recommended by the Admonitions of Dying Men, and the Sentiments of All People in their Most Serious Hours: and Other Testimonies of an Extraordinary Nature* (London, 1707)

Woolf, Virginia, *The Waves* (London: Hogarth Press, 1931)

Yoshinaga, Masayuki and Katsuhiko Ishikawa, *Gothic & Lolita* (New York and London: Phaidon, 2007)

Zopf, Johann Heinrich (and Christian Friedrich van Dalen), *Dissertatio de Vampyris Serviensibus* (Duisburg, 1733)

Zopf, Johann Heinrich, *Dissertatio Physico-Theologica de eo quod Iustum est circa Cruentationem Cadaverum* (Duisburg, 1737)

Secondary sources

Abbott, Stacey, 'Dracula on Film and TV from 1960 to the Present', in Roger Luckhurst (ed.), *The Cambridge Companion to Dracula* (Cambridge: Cambridge University Press, 2018), 192–206

Adams, Stephen, 'Vampires "Over-Farmed" says Neil Gaiman', *Telegraph* (3 July 2010), online edn

Afanasev, Aleksandr N., 'Poetic Views of the Slavs Regarding Nature', trans. Jan Louis Perkowski, in Jan Louis Perkowski, *Vampire Lore: From the Writings of Jan Louis Perkowski* (Bloomington, IN: Slavica Publishers, 2006), 195–211

Aldridge, Alfred Owen, *Voltaire and the Century of Light* (Princeton, NJ: Princeton University Press, 1975)

Allen, Nicholas, Nick Groom and Jos Smith (eds), *Coastal Works: Cultures of the Atlantic Edge* (Oxford: Oxford University Press, 2017)

Almási, Gábor and Lav Šubarić (eds), *Latin at the Crossroads of Identity: The Evolution of Linguistic Nationalism in the Kingdom of Hungary* (Leiden: Brill, 2015)

Ankarloo, Bengt and Gustav Henningsen (eds), *Early Modern European Witchcraft: Centres and Peripheries* (Oxford: Oxford University Press, 2001)

Aquilina, Conrad, 'The Deformed Transformed; or, From Bloodsucker to Byronic Hero – Polidori and the Literary Vampire', in Sam George and Bill Hughes (eds), *Open Graves, Open Minds: Representations of Vampires and the Undead from the Enlightenment to the Present Day* (Manchester and New York: Manchester University Press, 2013), 24–38

Arata, Stephen, 'The Occidental Tourist; *Dracula* and the Anxiety of Reverse Colonization', *Victorian Studies*, 33 (1990), 621–45

Arikha, Noga, *Passions and Tempers: A History of the Humours* (New York: HarperCollins, 2007)

Artenie, Cristina, *Dracula: A Study of Editorial Practices* (Montreal: Universitas Press, 2016)

Artenie, Cristina, *Dracula Invades England: The Text, the Context, and the Readers* (Montreal: Universitas Press, 2015)

Atalić, Bruno and Stella Fatović-Ferenčić, 'Emanuel Edward Klein – The Father of British Microbiology and the Case of the Animal Vivisection Controversy of 1875', *Toxicologic Pathology*, 37 (2009), 708–13

Auerbach, Nina, *Our Vampires, Ourselves* (Chicago, IL, and London: University of Chicago Press, 1995)

Auerbach, Nina, *Woman and the Demon: The Life of a Victorian Myth* (Cambridge, MA, and London: Harvard University Press, 1982)

Bale, Anthony, 'Dracula's Blood', in Roger Luckhurst (ed.), *The Cambridge Companion to Dracula* (Cambridge: Cambridge University Press, 2018), 104–13

Barber, Paul, *Vampires, Burial, and Death: Folklore and Reality*, 2nd edn ([1988] New Haven, CT, and London: Yale University Press, 2010)

Barreca, Regina (ed.), *Sex and Death in Victorian Literature* (Bloomington, IN: Indiana University Press, 1990)

Barry, Jonathan, 'News from the Invisible World: The Publishing History of Tales of the Supernatural c.1660–1832', in Jonathan Barry, Owen Davies and Cornelie Usborne (eds), *Cultures of Witchcraft in Europe from the Middle Ages to the Present* (Basingstoke: Palgrave Macmillan, 2017), 179–213

Barry, Jonathan, Owen Davies and Cornelie Usborne (eds), *Cultures of Witchcraft in Europe from the Middle Ages to the Present* (Basingstoke: Palgrave Macmillan, 2017)

Bartlett, Wayne and Flavia Idriceanu, *Legends of Blood: The Vampire in History and Myth* (Stroud: Sutton, 2005)

Bather, Philippa and Claire Stocks (eds), *Horace's Epodes: Contexts, Intertexts, and Reception* (Oxford: Oxford University Press, 2016)

Beatty, Bernard and Jonathan Shears (eds), *Byron's Temperament: Essays in Body and Mind* (Newcastle upon Tyne: Cambridge Scholars Publishing, 2016)

Bekoff, Marc, with Carron A. Meaney (eds), *Encyclopedia of Animal Rights and Animal Welfare* (London and New York: Routledge, 2013)

Benjamin, Walter, *Illuminations*, trans. Harry Zohn, ed. Hannah Arendt (New York: Schocken Books, 1968)

Benjamin, Walter, 'The Work of Art in the Age of Mechanical Reproduction', in Benjamin, *Illuminations*, ed. Arendt, 217–51

Bennett, Gillian, 'Ghost and Witch in the Sixteenth and Seventeenth Centuries', *Folklore*, 97 (1986), 3–14

Beresford, Matthew, *From Demons to Dracula: The Creation of the Modern Vampire Myth* (London: Reaktion Books, 2008)

Berger, John, *Ways of Seeing* (Harmondsworth: Penguin, 1972)

Berridge, Edward William, *see* 'Resurgam V.H., Fra.'

Biale, David, *Blood and Belief: The Circulation of a Symbol between Jews and Christians* (Berkeley, Los Angeles, London: University of California Press, 2007)

Black, Winston, 'Animated Corpses and Bodies with Power in the Scholastic Age', in Joëlle Rollo-Koster (ed.), *Death in Medieval Europe: Death Scripted and Death Choreographed* (London: Routledge, 2017), 71–92

Blécourt, Willem de (ed.), *Werewolf Histories* (Basingstoke: Palgrave Macmillan, 2015)

Bloom, Harold, *The Anxiety of Influence: A Theory of Poetry*, 2nd edn ([1973] New York: Oxford University Press, 1997)

Boddice, Rob, *The Science of Sympathy: Morality, Evolution, and Victorian Civilization* (Urbana, Chicago and Springfield: University of Illinois Press, 2016)

Bostridge, Ian, *Witchcraft and its Transformations c. 1650 – c. 1700* (Oxford and New York: Clarendon Press, 1997)

Bracher, Mark, et al. (eds), *Lacan's Theory of Discourse: Subject, Structure and Society* (Albany, NY: Suny Press, 1994)

Braudy, Leo, *Haunted: On Ghosts, Witches, Vampires, Zombies, and Other Monsters of the Natural and Supernatural Worlds* (New Haven, CT, and London: Yale University Press, 2016)

Bräunlein, Peter J., 'The Frightening Borderlands of Enlightenment: The Vampire Problem', *Studies in History and Philosophy of Biological and Biomedical Sciences*, 43(3) (2012), 710–19

Brechka, Frank T., *Gerard van Swieten and His World: 1700–1772* (The Hague: Martinus Nijhof, 1970)

Brill, Dunja, *Goth Culture: Gender, Sexuality and Style* (Oxford and New York: Berg, 2008)

Brockbank, William, 'Sovereign Remedies: A Critical Depreciation of the 17th-Century London Pharmacopoeia', *Medical History*, 8 (1964), 1–14

Bronfen, Elisabeth, *Over Her Dead Body: Death, Femininity and the Aesthetic* (Manchester: Manchester University Press, 1992)

Brooks, Chris, *Mortal Remains: The History and Present State of the Victorian and Edwardian Cemetery* (Exeter: Wheaton Publishers in association with the Victorian Society, 1989)

Brittain, Robert P., 'Cruentation in Legal Medicine and in Literature', *Medical History*, 9 (1965), 82–88

Bruce, Donald and Anthony Purdey (eds), *Literature and Science* (Atlanta, GA: Rodopi, 1994)

Bulfin, Ailise, *Gothic Invasions: Imperialism, War and Fin-de-Siècle Popular Fiction* (Cardiff: University of Wales Press, 2018)

Burns, R.M., *The Great Debate on Miracles: From Joseph Glanvill to David Hume* (Lewisburg, PA: Bucknell University Press; London and Toronto: Associated University Presses, 1983)

Butler, Erik, 'The Counter-Reformation in Stone and Metal: Spiritual Substances', in Nicola Masciandaro (ed.), *Hideous Gnosis: Black Metal Theory Symposium I* (no place, no date; open access), 23–31

Butler, Erik, *Metamorphoses of the Vampire in Literature and Film: Cultural Transformations in Europe, 1732–1933* (Rochester, NY: Camden House, 2010)

Butler, Todd, 'The Haunting of Isabell Binnington: Ghosts of Murder, Texts, and Law in Restoration England', *Journal of British Studies*, 50 (2011), 248–76

Buttaroni, Susanna and Stanisław Musiał (eds), *Ritual Murder: Legend in European History* (Cracow, Nuremberg and Frankfurt: Association for Cultural Initiatives, 2003)

Bynum, W.F., *Science and the Practice of Medicine in the Nineteenth Century* (Cambridge: Cambridge University Press, 1994)

Caciola, Nancy Mandeville, *Afterlives: The Return of the Dead in the Middle Ages* (Ithaca, NY: Cornell University Press, 2016)

Calzoni, Raul, 'Liminal Figurations of the Vampire in the German Enlightenment, *Sturm und Drang* and Romanticism', in Raul Calzoni and Greta Perletti (eds), *Monstrous Anatomies: Literary and Scientific Imagination in Britain and Germany during the Long Nineteenth Century* (Göttingen: V&R Unipress, 2015), 41–60

Calzoni, Raul and Greta Perletti (eds), *Monstrous Anatomies: Literary and Scientific Imagination in Britain and Germany during the Long Nineteenth Century* (Göttingen: V&R Unipress, 2015)

Camille, Michael, *The Gargoyles of Notre-Dame: Medievalism and the Monsters of Modernity* (Chicago, IL, and London: University of Chicago Press, 2009)

Camporesi, Piero, *Juice of Life: The Symbolic and Magic Significance of Blood*, trans. Robert R. Barr (New York: Continuum, 1995)

Canguilhem, Georges, *Ideology and Rationality in the History of the Life Sciences*, trans. Arthur Goldhammer (Cambridge, MA, and London: MIT Press, 1988)

Carter, Margaret L., 'The Vampire', in S.T. Joshi (ed.), *Icons of Horror and the Supernatural: An Encyclopedia of Our Worst Nightmares*, 2 vols (Westport, CT, and London: Greenwood Press, 2007), ii. 619–52

Carter, Margaret L., 'The Vampire as Alien in Contemporary Fiction', in Joan Gordon and Veronica Hollinger (eds), *Blood Read: The Vampire as Metaphor in Contemporary Culture* (Philadelphia, PA: University of Pennsylvania Press, 1997), 27–44

Carver, Terrell, 'Making Capital out of Vampires', *Times Higher Education Supplement* (June 1984), 15

Carver, Terrell, *The Postmodern Marx* (Manchester: Manchester University Press, 1998)

Cazacu, Matei, *Dracula*, ed. Stephen W. Reinert, trans. Nicole Mordarski, Stephen W. Reinert, Alice Brinton and Catherine Healey (Leiden and Boston, MA: Brill, 2017)

Ceglia, Francesco Paolo de, 'The Archbishop's Vampires: Giuseppe Davanzati's *Dissertation* and the Reaction of "Scientific" Italian Catholicism to the "Moravian Events"', *Archives Internationales d'Histoire des Sciences*, 61 (2011), 487–510

Charnas, Suzy McKee, 'Meditation in Red: On Writing *The Vampire Tapestry* (1981)', in Joan Gordon and Veronica Hollinger (eds), *Blood Read: The Vampire as Metaphor in Contemporary Culture* (Philadelphia, PA: University of Pennsylvania Press, 1997), 59–67

Christie, John and Sally Shuttleworth (eds), *Nature Transfigured: Science and Literature, 1700–1900* (Manchester: Manchester University Press, 1989)

Clark, Stuart, 'Protestant Demonology: Sin, Superstition, and Society (c.1520–c.1630)', in Ankarloo and Henningsen (eds), *Early Modern European Witchcraft*, 45–81

Clark, Stuart, *Thinking with Demons: The Idea of Witchcraft in Early Modern Europe* (Oxford: Clarendon Press, 1997)

Clery, E.J., *The Rise of Supernatural Fiction, 1762–1800* (Cambridge: Cambridge University Press, 1995)

Cohen, Ed, *A Body Worth Defending: Immunity, Biopolitics, and the Apotheosis of the Modern Body* (Durham, NC: Duke University Press, 2009)

Cohen, Jeffrey Jerome (ed.), *Monster Theory: Reading Culture* (Minneapolis, MN and London: University of Minnesota Press, 1996)

Cohn, Norman, *The Pursuit of Millennium: Revolutionary Millenarians and Mystical Anarchists of the Middle Ages* (London: Paladin, 1970)

Coleman, William, *Biology in the Nineteenth Century: Problems of Form, Function, and Transformation* (Cambridge: Cambridge University Press, 1977)

Connole, Edia and Gary J. Shipley (eds), *Serial Killing: A Philosophical Anthology* (no place: Schism Press, 2015)

Cooper, Brian, 'The Word *Vampire*: Its Slavonic Form and Origin', *Journal of Slavic Linguistics*, 13 (2005), 251–70

Cooper, Chris, *Blood: A Very Short Introduction* (Oxford: Oxford University Press, 2016)

Cornis-Pope, Marcel and John Neubauer (eds), *History of the Literary Cultures of East-Central Europe: Junctures and Disjunctures in the 19th and 20th Centuries*, vol. iv: *Types and Stereotypes* (Amsterdam and Philadelphia, PA: John Benjamins Publishing Company, 2004)

Coster, Will and Andrew Spicer (eds), *Sacred Space in Early Modern Europe* (Cambridge: Cambridge University Press, 2005)

Cox, Ann M., 'Porphyria and Vampirism: Another Myth in the Making', *Postgraduate Medical Journal*, 71(841) (1995), 643–44

Craft, Christopher, '"Kiss Me with those Red Lips": Gender and Inversion in Bram Stoker's *Dracula*', *Representations*, 8 (1984), 107–33

Crawford, Heide, *The Origins of the Literary Vampire* (Lanham, MD: Rowman & Littlefield, 2016)

Crawford, Joseph, *The Twilight of the Gothic? Vampires and the Rise of the Paranormal Romance, 1991–2012* (Cardiff: University of Wales Press, 2014)

Crowder, John, *The Ecstasy of Loving God: Trances, Raptures, and the Supernatural Pleasures of Jesus Christ* (Shippensburg, PA: Destiny Image, 2009)

Cruz, Joan Carroll, *The Incorruptibles: A Study of the Incorruption of the Bodies of Various Catholic Saints and Beati* ([1977] Charlotte: TAN Books, 2012)

Cunningham, Andrew, *The Anatomist Anatomis'd: An Experimental Discipline in Enlightenment Europe* (Farnham: Ashgate, 2010)

Dabashi, Hamid, 'Introduction to the AldineTransaction [*sic*] Edition: Ignaz Goldziher and the Question Concerning Orientalism', in Ignaz Goldziher, *Muslim Studies*, ed. S.M. Stern, trans. C.R. Barber and S.M. Stern (London and New York: Routledge, 2006), ix–xciii

Dalby, Richard and William Hughes, *Bram Stoker: A Bibliography* (Westcliff-on-Sea: Desert Island Books, 2004)

D'Arcy, Julian and Kirsten Wolf, 'Sir Walter Scott and *Eyrbyggja Saga*', *Studies in Scottish Literature*, 22 (1987), 30–43

Daston, Lorraine and Katherine Park, *Wonders and the Order of Nature, 1150–1750* (New York: Zone Books, 1998)

Daston, Lorraine and Gianna Pomata (eds), *The Faces of Nature in Enlightenment Europe* (Berlin: Berliner Wissenschafts-Verlag, 2003)

Davies, Owen, *The Haunted: A Social History of Ghosts* (Basingstoke: Palgrave Macmillan, 2007)

Davies, Owen, 'Methodism, the Clergy, and the Popular Belief in Witchcraft and Magic', *History*, 82 (1997), 252–65

Davies, Owen, *Witchcraft, Magic and Culture, 1736–1951* (Manchester: Manchester University Press, 1999)

Davies, Owen and Francesca Matteoni, *Executing Magic in the Modern Era: Criminal Bodies and the Gallows in Popular Medicine* (Basingstoke: Palgrave Macmillan, 2017)

Davison, Carol Margaret, *Anti-Semitism and British Gothic Literature* (Basingstoke: Palgrave Macmillan, 2004)

Day, Gary, 'The State of *Dracula*: Bureaucracy and the Vampire', in Alice Jenkins and Juliet John (eds), *Rereading Victorian Fiction* (New York: St Martin's Press, 2000), 81–95

Day, Peter (ed.), *Vampires: Myths and Metaphors of Enduring Evil* (Amsterdam and New York: Rodopi, 2006)

Day, William Patrick, *In the Circles of Fear and Desire: A Study of Gothic Fantasy* (Chicago, IL, and London: University of Chicago Press, 1985)

Deleuze, Gilles and Félix Guattari, *A Thousand Plateaus: Capitalism and Schizophrenia*, trans. Brian Massumi (Minneapolis, MN and London: University of Minnesota Press, 1987)

Derrida, Jacques, 'The Law of Genre', *Acts of Literature*, ed. Derek Attridge (New York and London: Routledge, 1992), 221–53

Derrida, Jacques, *Specters of Marx: The State of the Debt, the Work of Mourning and the New International*, trans. Peggy Kamuf (New York and London: Routledge, 1994)

Dijkstra, Bram, *Idols of Perversity: Fantasies of Feminine Evil in Fin-de-Siècle Culture* (New York and Oxford: Oxford University Press, 1986)

Dimić, Milan V., 'Vampiromania in the Eighteenth Century: The Other Side of Enlightenment', *Man and Nature / L'Homme et la Nature*, 3 (1984), 1–22

Ditmars, Raymond L. and Arthur M. Greenhall, 'The Vampire Bat: A Presentation of Undescribed Habits and a Review of its History' (1933–34), in Jan Louis Perkowski, *Vampire Lore: From the Writings of Jan Louis Perkowski* (Bloomington, IN: Slavica Publishers, 2006), 294–310

Douglas, Mary, *Purity and Danger: An Analysis of Concepts of Pollution and Taboo* (New York: Frederick A. Praeger, 1966)

Duff, David (ed.), *The Oxford Handbook of British Romanticism* (Oxford: Oxford University Press, 2018)

Dundes, Alan, *The Blood Libel Legend: A Casebook of Anti-Semitic Folklore* (Madison, WI: University of Wisconsin Press, 1991)

Dundes, Alan, 'The Vampire as Bloodthirsty Revenant: A Psychoanalytic Post Mortem', in Alan Dundes (ed.), *The Vampire: A Casebook* (Madison, WI: University of Wisconsin Press, 1998), 159–75

Dundes, Alan (ed.), *The Vampire: A Casebook* (Madison, WI: University of Wisconsin Press, 1998)

Eagleton, Terry, *Ideology of the Aesthetic* (Oxford: Blackwell, 2000)

Eighteen-Bisang, Robert and Elizabeth Miller (eds), *Bram Stoker's Notes for* Dracula*: A Facsimile Edition* (Jefferson, NC, and London: McFarland & Company, Inc., 2008)

Ellis, Markman, *The History of Gothic Fiction* (Edinburgh: Edinburgh University Press, 2000)

Emerson, Oliver Farrar, *The Earliest English Translations of Burger's* Lenore*: A Study in English and German Romanticism* (Cleveland, OH: Western Reserve University Press, 1916) [*Western Reserve University Bulletins*, new series, 18 (May 1916), *Literary Section Supplement, Western Reserve Studies*, 1]

Enright, D.J., *The Oxford Book of the Supernatural* (Oxford: Oxford University Press, 1994)

Erb, Rainer, 'The Ritual Murder Legend: From the Beginning until the 20th Century', in Susanna Buttaroni and Stanisław Musiał (eds), *Ritual Murder: Legend in European History* (Cracow, Nuremberg and Frankfurt: Association for Cultural Initiatives, 2003), 10–19

Evans, Richard J., 'Epidemics and Revolutions: Cholera in Nineteenth-Century Europe', in Terence Ranger and Paul Slack (eds), *Epidemics and Ideas: Essays on the Historical Perception of Pestilence* (Cambridge: Cambridge University Press, 1992), 149–73

Faflak, Joel and Jason Haslam (eds), *American Gothic Culture: An Edinburgh Companion* (Edinburgh: Edinburgh University Press, 2016)

Faivre, Antoine, *Theosophy, Imagination, Tradition: Studies in Western Esotericism*, trans. Christine Rhone (Albany, NY: State University of New York Press, 2000)

Faivre, Antoine, 'Du Vampire Villageois aux Discours des Clercs', in [collective work] *Les Vampires* (Paris: Albin Michel, 1993), 45–74

Farge, Arlette and Jacques Revel, *The Vanishing Children of Paris: Rumour and Politics before the French Revolution*, trans. Claudia Miéville (Cambridge, MA: Harvard University Press, 1991)

Feder, Helena, *Ecocriticism and the Idea of Culture: Biology and the Bildungsroman* (London and New York: Routledge, 2016)

Fejes, Nárcisz, 'Lasting Legacies: Vlad Țepeș and Dracula in Romanian National Discourse', in Marcel Cornis-Pope and John Neubauer (eds), *History of the Literary Cultures of East-Central Europe: Junctures and Disjunctures in the 19th and 20th Centuries*, vol. iv: *Types and Stereotypes* (Amsterdam and Philadelphia, PA: John Benjamins Publishing Company, 2004), 333–42

Ferguson, Christine, '*Dracula* and the Occult', in Roger Luckhurst (ed.), *The Cambridge Companion to Dracula* (Cambridge: Cambridge University Press, 2018), 57–66

Fisher, Mark, *The Weird and the Eerie* (London: Repeater Books, 2016)

Flanders, Judith, 'Slums', www.bl.uk/romantics-and-victorians/articles/slums

Flanders, Judith, *The Victorian City: Everyday Life in Dickens' London* (London: Atlantic Books, 2012)

Florescu, Radu and Raymond T. McNally, *In Search of Dracula: A True History of Dracula and Vampire Legends* (Greenwich, CT: New York Graphic Society, 1972)

Foucault, Michel, *Abnormal: Lectures at the Collège de France, 1974–1975*, ed. Valerio Marchetti and Antonella Salomoni, trans. Graham Burchell (London and New York: Verso, 2003)

Frankel, Jonathan, *The Damascus Affair: 'Ritual Murder', Politics, and the Jews in 1840* (Cambridge: Cambridge University Press, 1997)

Franklin, J. Jeffrey, 'The Economics of Immortality: The Demi-Immortal Oriental, Enlightenment Vitalism, and Political Economy in *Dracula*', *Cahiers Victoriens et Édouardiens*, 76 (2012), 127–48

Frankowski, Stanislaw, 'Post-Communist Europe', in Peter Hodgkinson and Andrew Rutherford (eds), *Capital Punishment: Global Issues and Prospects* (Winchester: Waterside Press, 1996), 215–41

Frayling, Christopher, *Vampyres: Lord Byron to Count Dracula* (London: Faber and Faber, 1991)

Frayling, Christopher and Robert Wokler, 'From the Orang-Utan to the Vampire: Towards an Anthropology of Rousseau', in R.A. Leigh (ed.), *Rousseau after 200 Years: Proceedings of the Cambridge Bicentennial Colloquium* ([1982] Cambridge: Cambridge University Press, 2010), 109–24

French, Barbara, 'False Vampires and Other Carnivores: A Glimpse at this Select Group of Bats Reveals Efficient Predators with a Surprisingly Gentle Side . . .', *Bats Magazine*, 15 (1997), online edn

Gagnier, Regenia, 'Evolution and Information, or Eroticism and Everyday Life, in *Dracula* and Late Victorian Aestheticism', in Regina Barreca (ed.), *Sex and Death in Victorian Literature* (Bloomington, IN: Indiana University Press, 1990), 140–57

Gallagher, Catherine, 'The Potato in the Materialist Imagination', in Catherine Gallagher and Stephen Greenblatt (eds), *Practicing New Historicism* (Chicago, IL, and London: University of Chicago Press, 2000), 110–35

Gallagher, Catherine and Stephen Greenblatt (eds), *Practicing New Historicism* (Chicago, IL, and London: University of Chicago Press, 2000)

Gaskill, Malcolm, *Crime and Mentalities in Early Modern England* (Cambridge: Cambridge University Press, 2000)

Gaston, Sean, 'An Event Without an Object: The Cock Lane Ghost, London 1762–1763', *The Literary London Journal*, 12 (2015), 3–21

Gelder, Ken, *Reading the Vampire* (London and New York: Routledge, 1994)

Gelder, Ken, *Vampire Cinema* (London: British Film Institute, 2012)

George, Sam, '"He Make in the Mirror No Reflect [Van Helsing]": Undead Aesthetics and Mechanical Reproduction – *Dorian Gray, Dracula* and David Reed's "Vampire Painting"', in Sam George and Bill Hughes (eds), *Open Graves, Open Minds: Representations of Vampires and the Undead from the Enlightenment to the Present Day* (Manchester and New York: Manchester University Press, 2013), 56–78

George, Sam and Bill Hughes (eds), *Open Graves, Open Minds: Representations of Vampires and the Undead from the Enlightenment to the Present Day* (Manchester and New York: Manchester University Press, 2013)

Gibbons, Michael T. et al. (eds), *The Encyclopedia of Political Thought*, 8 vols [continuously paginated] (New York: Wiley-Blackwell, 2015)

Gibson, Marion and Jo Ann Esra, *Shakespeare's Demonology: A Dictionary* (London: Bloomsbury, 2014)

Gibson, Matthew, *Dracula and the Eastern Question: British and French Vampire Narratives of the Nineteenth-Century Near East* (Basingstoke: Palgrave Macmillan, 2006)

Gittings, Clare, *Death, Burial and the Individual in Early Modern England* (London: Croom Helm, 1984)

Gordon, Joan and Veronica Hollinger (eds), *Blood Read: The Vampire as Metaphor in Contemporary Culture* (Philadelphia, PA: University of Pennsylvania Press, 1997)

Gordon, Stephen, 'Emotional Practice and Bodily Performance in Early Modern Vampire Literature', *Preternature: Critical and Historical Studies on the Preternatural*, 6 (2017), 93–124

Grant-Costa, Paul, 'A Surprising Account of those Spectres called Vampyres', unpublished paper

Grayling, A.C., *Descartes: The Life of René Descartes and Its Place in His Times* (London: Pocket Books, 2006)

Greenblatt, Stephen, *Hamlet in Purgatory* (Princeton, NJ: Princeton University Press, 2001)

Gregory, Jeremy, *Restoration, Reformation and Reform, 1660–1828* (Oxford and New York: Oxford University Press, 2000)

Groom, Nick, 'Draining the Irish Sea: The Colonial Politics of Water', in Allen, Groom and Smith (eds), *Coastal Works*, 20–39

Groom, Nick, *The Forger's Shadow: How Forgery Changed the Course of Literature* (London: Picador, 2003)

Groom, Nick, *The Gothic: A Very Short Introduction* (Oxford: Oxford University Press, 2012)

Groom, Nick, 'Romanticism and Forgery', *Literature Compass Online*, 4 (2007), online edn

Groom, Nick, *The Seasons: A Celebration of the English Year* (London: Atlantic, 2014)

Groom, Nick, 'William Henry Ireland: From Forgery to Fish 'n' Chips', in Timothy Morton (ed.), *Cultures of Taste/Theories of Appetite: Eating Romanticism* (Basingstoke and New York: Palgrave, 2004), 21–40

Gurr, Andrew, '*Coriolanus* and the Body Politic', *Shakespeare Survey*, 28 (1975), 63–70

Hackenberg, Sara, 'Vampires and Resurrection Men: The Perils and Pleasures of the Embodied Past in 1840s Sensational Fiction', *Victorian Studies*, 52 (2009), 63–75

Haefele-Thomas, Ardel, *Queer Others in Victorian Gothic: Transgressing Monstrosity* (Cardiff: University of Wales Press, 2012)

Hagan, Frank E., *Introduction to Criminology: Theories, Methods, and Criminal Behavior*, 6th edn (Los Angeles, CA, and London: Sage Publications, 2008)

Halberstam, Judith, *Skin Shows: Gothic Horror and the Technology of Monsters* (Durham, NC, and London: Duke University Press, 2006)

Hamilton, David, *A History of Organ Transplantation: Ancient Legends to Modern Practice* (Philadelphia, PA: University of Pittsburgh Press, 2012)

Hammack, Brenda Mann, 'Florence Marryat's Female Vampire and the Scientizing of Hybridity', *Studies in English Literature, 1500–1900*, 48 (2008), 885–96

Handley, Sasha, *Visions of an Unseen World: Ghost Beliefs and Ghost Stories in Eighteenth-Century England* (London: Pickering and Chatto, 2007)

Hankins, Thomas L., *Biology in the Nineteenth Century: Problems of Form, Function, and Transformation*, 2nd edn (Cambridge: Cambridge University Press, 1977)

Haraway, D.J., *Modest_Witness@Second_Millennium.FemaleMan©_Meets_OncoMouse™: Feminism and Technoscience* (New York and London: Routledge, 1997)

Hardt, Michael and Antonio Negri, *Multitude: War and Democracy in the Age of Empire* (New York: Penguin Press, 2004)

Harriman, Andi and Marloes Bontje, *Some Wear Leather Some Wear Lace: The Worldwide Compendium of Punk and Goth in the 1980s* (Bristol and Chicago, IL: Intellect, 2014)

Harvey, John, *Men in Black* (London: Reaktion Books, 1995)

Haskell, Yasmin (ed.), *Diseases of the Imagination and Imaginary Diseases in the Early Modern Period* (Turnhout: Brepols Publishers, 2011)

Hay, Douglas, Peter Linebaugh, John G. Rule, E.P. Thompson and Cal Winslow, *Albion's Fatal Tree: Crime and Society in Eighteenth-Century England* (New York: Pantheon Books, 1975)

Heldreth, Leonard G. and Mary Pharr (eds), *The Blood is the Life: Vampires in Literature* (Bowling Green, OH: Bowling Green State University Press, 1999)

Henderson, Nicola, *Gothic Art: Vampires, Witches, Demons, Dragons, Werewolves & Goths* (London: Flame Tree Publishing, 2013)

Herbrechter, Stefan and Ivan Callus (eds), *Posthumanist Shakespeares* (Basingstoke: Palgrave Macmillan, 2012)

Hill, Christopher, 'The Religion of Gerrard Winstanley', *Past and Present Supplement*, 5 (1978)

Hirsch, Brett D., 'Lycanthropy in Early Modern England: The Case of John Webster's *The Duchess of Malfi*', in Yasmin Haskell (ed.), *Diseases of the Imagination and Imaginary Diseases in the Early Modern Period* (Turnhout: Brepols Publishers, 2011), 301–40

Hodgkinson, Peter and Andrew Rutherford (eds), *Capital Punishment: Global Issues and Prospects* (Winchester: Waterside Press, 1996)

Hodkinson, Phil, *Goth: Identity, Style and Subculture* (Oxford and New York: Berg, 2002)

Hoeveler, Diane Long, *Gothic Riffs: Secularizing the Uncanny in the European Imaginary, 1780–1820* (Columbus, OH: Ohio State University Press, 2010)

Hollinger, Veronica, 'Fantasies of Absence: The Postmodern Vampire', in Joan Gordon and Veronica Hollinger (eds), *Blood Read: The Vampire as Metaphor in Contemporary Culture* (Philadelphia, PA: University of Pennsylvania Press, 1997), 199–212

Houlbrooke, Ralph, *Death, Religion, and the Family in England, 1480–1750* (Oxford: Clarendon Press, 1988)

Huet, Marie-Hélène, 'Deadly Fears: Dom Augustin Calmet's Vampires and the Rule over Death', *Eighteenth-Century Life*, 21(2) (1997), 222–32

Hughes, William, *That Devil's Trick: Hypnotism and the Victorian Popular Imagination* (Manchester: Manchester University Press, 2015)

Humphries, Reynold, *The Hollywood Horror Film, 1931–41: Madness in a Social Landscape* (Lanham, MD, Toronto and Oxford: Scarecrow Press, 2006)

Hurren, Elizabeth T., *Dissecting the Criminal Corpse: Staging Post-Execution Punishment in Early Modern England* (Basingstoke: Palgrave Macmillan, 2016)

Hutton, Ronald, 'The English Reformation and the Evidence of Folklore', *Past and Present*, 148 (1995), 89–116

Hutton, Ronald, *The Witch: A History of Fear from Ancient Times to the Present* (New Haven, CT, and London: Yale University Press, 2017)

Ingram, Margaret, 'Bodies That Speak: Early Modern European Gender Distinctions in Bleeding Corpses and Demoniacs' (MA Thesis: University of Oregon, 2017)

Jackson, MacD.P., 'John Webster and Thomas Heywood in *Appius and Virginia*: A Bibliographical Approach to the Problem of Authorship', *Studies in Bibliography*, 38 (1985), 217–35

Jenkins, Alice and Juliet John (eds), *Rereading Victorian Fiction* (New York: St Martin's Press, 2000)

Jones, Colin, *The Smile Revolution in Eighteenth-Century Paris* (Oxford: Oxford University Press, 2014)

Jones, Richard, *Walking Haunted London* (London: New Holland Publishers, 1999)

Joshi, S.T. (ed.), *Encyclopedia of the Vampire: The Living Dead in Myth, Legend, and Popular Culture* (Santa Barbara, CA, Denver, CO, and Oxford: Greenwood, 2011)

Joshi, S.T. (ed.), *Icons of Horror and the Supernatural: An Encyclopedia of Our Worst Nightmares*, 2 vols (Westport, CT, and London: Greenwood Press, 2007)

Kay, Sarah, *Žižek: A Critical Introduction* (Cambridge, Oxford and Malden, MA: Polity Press, 2003)

Kelly, J. Robert and Paula Benetti, 'Ceramic Materials in Dentistry: Historical Evolution and Current Practice', *Australian Dental Journal*, 56 (2011), 84–96

Keyworth, David, 'The Socio-Religious Beliefs and Nature of the Contemporary Vampire Subculture', *Journal of Contemporary Religion*, 17 (2002), 355–70

Keyworth, G. David, 'Was the Vampire of the Eighteenth Century a Unique Type of Undead-Corpse?', *Folklore*, 117 (2006), 241–60

Khair, Tabish and Johan Höglund (eds), *Transnational and Postcolonial Vampires: Dark Blood* (Basingstoke: Palgrave Macmillan, 2013)

Kilpatrick, Nancy, *The Goth Bible: A Compendium for the Darkly Inclined* (London: Plexus, 2005)

King, Peter, *Punishing the Criminal Corpse, 1700–1840: Aggravated Forms of the Death Penalty in England* (Basingstoke: Palgrave Macmillan, 2017)

Kittler, Friedrich, *Discourse Networks 1800/1900*, trans. Michael Metteer (Stanford, CA: Stanford University Press, 1990)

Kittler, Friedrich, 'Dracula's Legacy', *Stanford Humanities Review*, 1 (1989), 143–73

Kittler, Friedrich, *Gramophone Film Typewriter*, trans. Geoffrey Winthrop-Young and M. Wurz (Stanford, CA: Stanford University Press, 1999)

Klaniczay, Gábor, 'The Decline of Witches and the Rise of Vampires under the Eighteenth-Century Habsburg Monarchy', *Ethnologia Europaea*, 17 (1987), 165–80

Klaniczay, Gábor, *The Uses of Supernatural Power: The Transformation of Popular Religion in Medieval and Early-Modern Europe* (Cambridge and Oxford: Polity Press, 1990)

Klaniczay, Gábor, 'Witch-Trials in Hungary (1520–1777): The Accusations and the Popular Universe of Magic', in Bengt Ankarloo and Gustav Henningsen (eds), *Early Modern European Witchcraft: Centres and Peripheries* (Oxford: Oxford University Press, 2001), 219–55

Klaniczay, Gábor and Éva Pócs (eds), *Christian Demonology and Popular Mythology: Demons, Spirits, Witches*, vol. ii (Budapest and New York: Central European University Press, 2006)

Kreuter, Peter Mario, 'The Name of the Vampire: Some Reflections on Current Linguistic Theories on the Etymology of the Word *Vampire*', in Peter Day (ed.), *Vampires: Myths and Metaphors of Enduring Evil* (Amsterdam and New York: Rodopi, 2006), 57–63

Kristeva, Julia, *The Powers of Horror: An Essay on Abjection*, trans. Leon S. Roudiez (New York: Columbia University Press, 1982)

Laing, Aislinn, ' "Vampire" Attacks Spark Witchhunt', *The Times* (6 December 2017), 1 GM

Lake, Bernard, '*A Discourse of the Heart* by James de Back', *Medical History*, 10 (1966), 60–69

Land, Nick, *Fanged Noumena: Collected Writings, 1987–2007*, ed. Robin MacKay and Ray Brassier (Falmouth: Urbanomic; and New York: Sequence Press, n.d.)

Lassek, A.M., *Human Dissection: Its Drama and Struggle* (Springfield, IL: Charles C. Thomas, 1958)

Laycock, Joseph, 'Real Vampires as an Identity Group: Analyzing Causes and Effects of an Introspective Survey by the Vampire Community', *Nova Religio: The Journal of Alternative and Emergent Religions*, 14 (2010), 4–23

Laycock, Joseph, *Vampires Today: The Truth about Modern Vampirism* (Westport, CT, and London: Praeger, 2009)

Leatherdale, Clive, *The Origins of Dracula: The Background to Bram Stoker's Gothic Masterpiece* (London: William Kimber and Co., 1987)

Leigh, R.A. (ed.), *Rousseau after 200 Years: Proceedings of the Cambridge Bicentennial Colloquium* ([1982] Cambridge: Cambridge University Press, 2010)

Levinas, Emmanuel, *Ethics and Infinity: Conversations with Philippe Nemo*, trans. Richard A. Cohen (Pittsburgh, PA: Duquesne University Press, 1985)

Light, Duncan, *The Dracula Dilemma: Tourism, Identity and the State in Romania* (London and New York: Routledge, 2012)

Linebaugh, Peter, 'The Tyburn Riot against the Surgeons', in Douglas Hay, Peter Linebaugh, John G. Rule, E.P. Thompson and Cal Winslow, *Albion's Fatal Tree: Crime and Society in Eighteenth-Century England* (New York: Pantheon Books, 1975), 65–118

Linke, Uli, *Blood and Nation: The European Aesthetics of Race* (Philadelphia, PA: University of Pennsylvania Press, 1999)

Lipka, Jennifer, 'Joseph Conrad's *Heart of Darkness* as a Gothic Novel', *Conradiana*, 40 (2008), 25–37

Lubac, Henri Cardinal de, SJ [Henri-Marie Joseph Sonier de Lubac], *Corpus Mysticum: The Eucharist and the Church in the Middle Ages*, trans. Gemma Simmons, CJ, with Richard Price and Christopher Stephens, ed. Laurence Paul Hemming and Susan Frank Parsons ([1949] London: SCM Press, 2006)

Luckhurst, Roger (ed.), *The Cambridge Companion to Dracula* (Cambridge: Cambridge University Press, 2018)

Luckhurst, Roger, *The Invention of Telepathy: 1870–1901* (Oxford: Oxford University Press, 2002)

Ludlum, Harry, *A Biography of Dracula: The Life Story of Bram Stoker* (Slough: W. Foulsham, 1962)

Lüthy, Christoph H., 'Historical and Philosophical Reflections on Natural, Enhanced and Artificial Men and Women', in Bert-Jap Koops, Christoph H. Lüthy, Annemiek Nelis, Carla Sieburgh, J.P.M. Jansen and Monika S. Schmid (eds), *Engineering the Human: Human Enhancement Between Fiction and Fascination* (Springer-Verlag: Berlin and Heidelberg, 2013), 11–28

Koops, Bert-Jap, Christoph H. Lüthy, Annemiek Nelis, Carla Sieburgh, J.P.M. Jansen and Monika S. Schmid (eds), *Engineering the Human: Human Enhancement Between Fiction and Fascination* (Springer-Verlag: Berlin and Heidelberg, 2013)

McCarthy, Elizabeth, '"Death to Vampires!": The Vampire Body and the Meaning of Mutilation', in Peter Day (ed.), *Vampires: Myths and Metaphors of Enduring Evil* (Amsterdam and New York: Rodopi, 2006), 189–208

McClelland, Bruce A., *Slayers and their Vampires: A Cultural History of Killing the Dead* (Ann Arbor, MI: University of Michigan Press, 2006)

MacLellan, Matthew, 'Marx's Vampires; An Althusserian Critique', *Rethinking Marxism: A Journal of Economics, Culture & Society*, 25 (2013), 549–65

McManners, John, *Death and the Enlightenment: Changing Attitudes to Death among Christians and Unbelievers in Eighteenth-Century France* (Oxford: Oxford University Press, 1981)

McNally, David, *Monsters of the Market: Zombies, Vampires and Global Capitalism* (Leiden and Boston, MA: Brill, 2011)

McNally, Raymond, *Dracula was a Woman: In Search of the Blood Countess of Transylvania* (New York: McGraw-Hill, 1983)

Maiello, Giuseppe, 'Racionalismus Karla Ferdinanda Schertze a *Magia Posthuma*', *Slavica Litteraria*, 5 (2012), 215–22

Maiello, Giuseppe, *Vampyrismus & Magia Posthuma: Vampyrismus v Kulturních Dějinách Evropy* (Prague: Nakladatelství Epocha, 2014)

Maluf, N.S.R., 'History of Blood Transfusion', *Journal of the History of Medicine*, 9 (1954), 59–107

Man, John, *Attila the Hun: A Barbarian King and the Fall of Rome* (London: Bantam, 2006)

Marshall, Peter, *Beliefs and the Dead in Reformation England* (Oxford: Oxford University Press, 2002)

Marshall, Peter and Alexandra Walsham (eds), *Angels in the Early Modern World* (Cambridge: Cambridge University Press, 2006)

Martin, Emily, *Flexible Bodies: Tracking Immunity in American Culture from the Days of Polio to the Age of AIDS* (Boston, MA: Beacon, 1994)

Masciandaro, Nicola (ed.), *Hideous Gnosis: Black Metal Theory Symposium I* (no place, no date; open access)

Masciandaro, Nicola, '*Non potest hoc Corpus Decollari*: Beheading and the Impossible', in Larissa Tracy and Jeff Massey (eds), *Heads Will Roll: Decapitation in the Medieval and Early Modern Imagination* (Leiden and Boston, MA: Brill, 2012), 15–36

Massaccesi, Cristina, *Nosferatu: A Symphony of Horror* (New York: Columbia University Press, 2016)

Masson, Alastair H.B., *A History of Blood Transfusion in Edinburgh* (Edinburgh: Blood Transfusion Service, n.d.)

Mathers, S.L. MacGregor, et al., *Astral Projection, Ritual Magic, and Alchemy: Golden Dawn Material*, ed. Francis King (Rochester, VT: Destiny Books, 1987)

Matteoni, Francesca, 'The Criminal Corpse in Pieces', *Mortality*, 21 (2016), 198–209

Matthews, Melvin E., Jr, *Fear Itself: Horror on Screen and in Reality during the Depression and World War II* (Jefferson, NC, and London: McFarland & Company, 2009)

Mazzarello, Paolo, 'Cesare Lombroso: An Anthropologist between Evolution and Degeneration', *Functional Neurology*, 26 (2011), 97–101

Melton, J. Gordon, *The Vampire Book: The Encyclopedia of the Undead* (Detroit, MI, and London: Visible Ink Press, 2011)

Micklem, Niel, *The Nature of Hysteria* (London and New York: Routledge, 1996)

Midelfort, H.C. Erik, *Exorcism and Enlightenment: Johann Joseph Gassner and the Demons of Eighteenth-Century Germany* (New Haven, CT, and London: Yale University Press, 2005)

Moggach, Douglas, *The Philosophy and Politics of Bruno Bauer* (Cambridge: Cambridge University Press, 2002)

Moore, Pete, *Blood and Justice: The Seventeenth-Century Parisian Doctor who Made Blood Transfusion History* (Chichester: John Wiley & Sons, 2003)

Moran III, Francis, 'Between Primates and Primitives: Natural Man as the Missing Link in Rousseau's *Second Discourse*', in Julie K. Ward and Tommy L. Lott, *Philosophers on Race: Critical Essays* (Oxford and Malden, MA: Blackwell Publishing, 2002), 125–44

Moretti, Franco, *Signs Taken for Wonders: Essays in the Sociology of Literary Forms*, trans. Susan Fischer, David Forgacs and David Miller (London: Verso, 1983)

Morey, Anne and Claudia Nelson, 'Phallus and Void in Kipling's "The Vampire" and Its Progeny', *Frame*, 24 (2011), 39–55

Morley, Ian, 'City Chaos, Contagion, Chadwick, and Social Justice', *Yale Journal of Biology and Medicine*, 80 (2007), 61–72

Morton, Timothy (ed.), *Cultures of Taste/Theories of Appetite: Eating Romanticism* (Basingstoke and New York: Palgrave, 2004)

Morton, Timothy, *Dark Ecology: For a Logic of Future Coexistence* (New York: Columbia University Press, 2016)

Morton, Timothy, *Hyperobjects: Philosophy and Ecology after the End of the World* (Minneapolis and London: University of Minnesota Press, 2013)

Moszyński, Kazimierz, 'Slavic Folk Culture', trans. Perkowski, in Jan Louis Perkowski, *Vampire Lore: From the Writings of Jan Louis Perkowski* (Bloomington, IN: Slavica Publishers, 2006), 213–17

Mulvey-Roberts, Marie, *Dangerous Bodies: Historicising the Gothic Corporeal* (Manchester: Manchester University Press, 2016)

Murray, Robin L. and Joseph K. Heumann, *Monstrous Nature: Environment and Horror on the Big Screen* (Lincoln, NE and London: University of Nebraska Press, 2016)

Negarestani, Rega, 'The Corpse Bride: Thinking with Nigredo', *Collapse*, 4 (2009), 129–60

Neocleous, Mark, *The Monstrous and the Dead: Burke, Marx, Fascism* (Cardiff: University of Wales Press, 2005)

Neocleous, Mark, 'The Political Economy of the Dead: Marx's Vampires', *History of Political Thought*, 24(4) (2003), 668–84

Newman, Saul (ed.), *Max Stirner* (Basingstoke: Palgrave Macmillan, 2011)

Norton-Taylor, Richard, 'Dracula's Nemesis to Prototype Foreign Spy', *Guardian* (31 March 2005) online edn

Nowosadtko, Jutta, 'Der "Vampyrus Serviensis" und sein Habitat: Impressionen von der Österreichischen Militärgrenze', *Arbeitskreis Militär und Gesellschaft in der frühen Neuzeit e.V.*, 8 (2004), 151–67

O'Brien, Elizabeth, *Post-Roman Britain to Anglo-Saxon England: Burial Practices Reviewed* in *British Archaeological Reports*, British Series 289 (1999)

Oesterdiekhoff, Georg, *Traditionales Denken und Modernisierung: Jean Piaget und die Theorie der Sozialen Evolution* (1992) and *Kulturelle Evolution des Geistes. Die Historische Wechselwirkung von Psyche und Gesellschaft*, 2nd edn (2006), translated as *Mental Growth of Humankind in History* (n.p., n.d.; open access)

Oliensis, Ellen, 'Scenes from the Afterlife of Horace's *Epodes* (c.1600–1900)', in Philippa Bather and Claire Stocks (eds), *Horace's Epodes: Contexts, Intertexts, and Reception* (Oxford: Oxford University Press, 2016), 219–39

O'Mahoney, Elizabeth, 'Representations of Gender in Seventeenth-Century Netherlandish Alchemical Genre Painting', 2 vols (PhD thesis: University of York, 2005)

Oschema, Klaus, 'Blood-Brothers: A Ritual of Friendship and the Construction of the Imagined Barbarian in the Middle Ages', *Journal of Medieval History*, 32 (2006), 275–301

Otis, Laura, *Membranes: Metaphors of Invasion in Nineteenth-Century Literature, Science, and Politics* (Baltimore, MD: Johns Hopkins University Press, 1999)

Otis, Laura, *Networking: Communicating with Bodies and Machines in the Nineteenth Century* (Ann Arbor, MI: University of Michigan Press, 2001)

Otis, Laura, *Organic Memory: History and the Body in the Late Nineteenth & Early Twentieth Centuries* (Lincoln, NE and London: University of Nebraska Press, 1994)

Otto, Rudolf, *The Idea of the Holy: An Inquiry into the Non-Rational Factor in the Idea of the Divine and its Relation to the Rational*, trans. John W. Harvey (London, Oxford and New York: Oxford University Press, 1958)

Packham, Catherine, *Eighteenth-Century Vitalism: Bodies, Culture, Politics* (Basingstoke: Palgrave Macmillan, 2012)

Parker, Joanne, 'Sensation and Superstition in *The Book of Werewolves*', *Transactions of the Sabine Baring-Gould Appreciation Society*, 10 (2010), 66–77

Parsons, Maria, 'Vamping the Woman: Menstrual Pathologies in Bram Stoker's *Dracula*', *Irish Journal of Gothic and Horror Studies*, 1 (2006), 66–83

Paule, Maxwell Teitel, *Canidia, Rome's First Witch* (London and New York: Bloomsbury, 2017)

Perkowski, Jan Louis, *Vampire Lore: From the Writings of Jan Louis Perkowski* (Bloomington, IN: Slavica Publishers, 2006)

Perkowski, Jan Louis, 'Vampires, Dwarves, and Witches among the Ontario Kashubs' (1972), reprinted in Jan Louis Perkowski, *Vampire Lore: From the Writings of Jan Louis Perkowski* (Bloomington, IN: Slavica Publishers, 2006), 1–54

Perkowski, Jan Louis, *The Darkling: A Treatise on Slavic Vampirism* (1989), reprinted in Jan Louis Perkowski, *Vampire Lore: From the Writings of Jan Louis Perkowski* (Bloomington, IN: Slavica Publishers, 2006), 317–488

Pfannebaker, Mareile, 'Cyborg Coriolanus/Monster Body Politic', in Stefan Herbrechter and Ivan Callus (eds), *Posthumanist Shakespeares* (Basingstoke: Palgrave Macmillan, 2012), 114–32

Phelps, Norm, *The Longest Struggle: Animal Advocacy from Pythagoras to PETA* (New York: Lantern Books, 2007)

Phillips, John, 'Circles of Influence: Lewis, Sade, Artaud', *Comparative Critical Studies*, 9 (2012), 61–82

Pickstone, John V., 'Dearth, Dirt and Fever Epidemics: Rewriting the History of British "Public Health", 1780–1850', in Terence Ranger and Paul Slack (eds), *Epidemics and Ideas: Essays on the Historical Perception of Pestilence* (Cambridge: Cambridge University Press, 1992), 125–148

Poo, Mu-Chou (ed.), *Rethinking Ghosts in World Religions* (Leiden and Boston, MA: Brill, 2009)

Punter, David, *The Literature of Terror: A History of Gothic Fictions from 1765 to the Present Day* (London and New York: Longman, 1980)

Rack, Henry D., *Reasonable Enthusiast: John Wesley and the Rise of Methodism*, 3rd edn ([1989] London: Epworth Press, 2002)

Raine, Kathleen, 'Yeats, the Tarot and the Golden Dawn', in *Yeats the Initiate: Essays on Certain Themes in the Work of W.B. Yeats* (Savage, MD: Barnes & Noble Books, 1990), 177–246

Ramšak, Mojca, 'Folk Explanations of Blood-Lands: The Map of Massacres and Bestial Cruelties', *Slovenský Národopis / Slovak Ethnology*, 64 (2016), 423–46

Rance, Nicholas, ' "Jonathan's Great Knife": *Dracula* meets Jack the Ripper', in Alexandra Warwick and Martin Willis (eds), *Jack the Ripper: Media, Culture, History* (Manchester: Manchester University Press, 2007), 124–43

Ranger, Terence and Paul Slack (eds), *Epidemics and Ideas: Essays on the Historical Perception of Pestilence* (Cambridge: Cambridge University Press, 1992)

Redgrove, Peter, *The Black Goddess and the Unseen Real: Our Unconscious Senses and Their Uncommon Sense* (New York: Grove Press, 1987)

'Resurgam V.H., Fra.' [Berridge, Edward William], 'Flying Roll No. V: Some Thoughts on the Imagination', in S.L. MacGregor Mathers, et al., *Astral Projection, Ritual Magic, and Alchemy: Golden Dawn Material*, ed. Francis King (Rochester, VT: Destiny Books, 1987), 47–52

Richardson, Maurice, 'The Psychoanalysis of Ghost Stories', *Twentieth Century*, 16 (1959), 419–31

Richardson, Ruth, *Death, Dissection and the Destitute* (London: Routledge & Kegan Paul, 2001)

Rigby, Jonathan, *English Gothic: A Century of Horror Cinema*, 3rd edn ([2000] London: Reynolds & Hearn, 2004)

Riley, James C., *The Eighteenth-Century Campaign to Avoid Disease* (Basingstoke: Macmillan, 1987)

Riquelme, John Paul, 'Doubling and Repetition/Realism and Closure in *Dracula*', in Bram Stoker, *Dracula (Case Studies in Contemporary Criticism)*, ed. John Paul Riquelme ([1897] Boston, MA and New York: Bedford/St Martin's Press, 2002), 559–72

Risteski, L'upcho S., 'Categories of the "Evil Dead" in Macedonian Folk Religion', in Gábor Klaniczay and Éva Pócs (eds), *Christian Demonology and Popular Mythology: Demons, Spirits, Witches*, ii (Budapest and New York: Central European University Press, 2006), 202–12

Ristović, Nenad, 'Latin and Vernacular Relations in the Eighteenth and Nineteenth Centuries: The Serbian Case', in Gábor Almási and Lav Šubarić (eds), *Latin at the Crossroads of Identity: The Evolution of Linguistic Nationalism in the Kingdom of Hungary* (Leiden: Brill, 2015), 256–77

Roberts, Gareth, *The Mirror of Alchemy: Alchemical Ideas and Images in Manuscripts and Books* (London: British Library, 1994)

Roden, David, 'Aliens Under the Skin: Serial Killing and the Seduction of our Common Inhumanity', in Edia Connole and Gary J. Shipley (eds), *Serial Killing: A Philosophical Anthology* (no place: Schism Press, 2015), 9–20

Roden, David, 'Nature's Dark Domain: An Argument for a Naturalised Phenomenology', *Royal Institute of Philosophy Supplement*, 72 (2013), 169–88

Rollo-Koster, Joëlle (ed.), *Death in Medieval Europe: Death Scripted and Death Choreographed* (London: Routledge, 2017)

Rosenberg, Alyssa, 'A Condemnation of Sparkly Vampires', *The Atlantic* (November 2009), online edn

Rudacille, Deborah, *The Scalpel and the Butterfly: The Conflict between Animal Research and Animal Protection* (Berkeley, Los Angeles and London: University of California Press, 2000)

Russo, Joseph, 'Perpetue Putesco: Perpetually I Putrefy', in Masciandaro (ed.), *Hideous Gnosis*, 93–103

Ruston, Sharon, 'Has Man "Paid Too Dear a Price for his Empire"? Monsters in Romantic-Era Literature', in Calzoni and Perletti (eds), *Monstrous Anatomies*, 133–48

Ruston, Sharon (ed.), *Literature and Science* (Cambridge: Boydell and Brewer, 2008)

St Clair, William, *The Reading Nation in the Romantic Period* (Cambridge: Cambridge University Press, 2004)

Salaman, Redcliffe N., *The History and Social Influence of the Potato*, rev. J.G. Hawkes ([1949] Cambridge: Cambridge University Press, 1985)

Sayers, William, 'The Alien and Alienated as Unquiet Dead in the Sagas of the Icelanders', in Jeffrey Jerome Cohen (ed.), *Monster Theory: Reading Culture* (Minneapolis, MN and London: University of Minnesota Press, 1996), 242–63

Schaffner, Anna Katharina and Shane Weller, *Modernist Eroticisms: European Literature after Sexology* (Basingstoke: Palgrave Macmillan, 2012)

Scharf, Natasha, *Worldwide Gothic: A Chronicle of a Tribe* (Church Stretton: Independent Music Press, 2011)

Schechter, D.C., 'Transplantation of Teeth', *Surgery, Gynecology & Obstetrics*, 132 (1971), 309–19

Schneck, Stephen F., 'Body Politic', in Michael T. Gibbons et al. (eds), *The Encyclopedia of Political Thought*, 8 vols [continuously paginated] (New York: Wiley-Blackwell, 2015), i. 362

Senf, Carol A., 'Daughters of Lilith: Women Vampires in Popular Literature', in Leonard G. Heldreth and Mary Pharr (eds), *The Blood is the Life: Vampires in Literature* (Bowling Green, OH: Bowling Green State University Press, 1999), 199–216

Shakespeare, Steven, 'The Light that Illuminates Itself, the Dark that Soils Itself: Blackened Notes from Schelling's Underground', in Masciandaro (ed.), *Hideous Gnosis*, 5–22

Shapin, Stephen and Simon Schama, *Leviathan and the Air-Pump: Hobbes, Boyle, and the Experimental Life* (Princeton, NJ: Princeton University Press, 1989)

Shears, Jonathan, 'Byron's Hypochondria', in Bernard Beatty and Jonathan Shears (eds), *Byron's Temperament: Essays in Body and Mind* (Newcastle upon Tyne: Cambridge Scholars Publishing, 2016), 100–17

Siegel, Carol, *Goth's Dark Empire* (Bloomington, IN: Indiana University Press, 2005)

Silver, Alain and James Ursini, *The Vampire Film: From Nosferatu to True Blood*, 4th updated edn ([1993] New York: Limelight Editions, 2011)

Smith, Andrew, 'Reading Wealth in Nigeria: Occult Capitalism and Marx's Vampires', *Historical Materialism*, 9 (2001), 39–59

Spaeth, Donald, *The Church in an Age of Danger: Parsons and Parishioners, 1660–1740* (Cambridge: Cambridge University Press, 2000)

Spooner, Catherine, *Contemporary Gothic* (London: Reaktion Books, 2006)

Spooner, Catherine, 'Twenty-First-Century Gothic', in Dale Townshend (ed.), *Terror and Wonder: The Gothic Imagination* (London: British Library, 2014), 180–205

Spooner, Catherine, Dale Townshend and Angela Wright (eds), *The Cambridge History of the Gothic*, 3 vols (Cambridge: Cambridge University Press, forthcoming)

Stephanou, Aspasia, 'Exquisite Corpse: Serial Killing and the Horripilation of Writing', in Edia Connole and Gary J. Shipley (eds), *Serial Killing: A Philosophical Anthology* (no place: Schism Press, 2015), 147–62

Stephanou, Aspasia, *Reading Vampire Gothic Through Blood: Bloodlines* (Basingstoke: Palgrave Macmillan, 2014)

Stoichita, Victor I., *A Short History of the Shadow* (London: Reaktion Books, 1997)

Stokoe, F.W., *German Influence in the English Romantic Period, 1788–1818* (Cambridge: Cambridge University Press, 1926)

Stott, Rebecca, *The Fabrication of the Late Victorian Femme Fatale: The Kiss of Death* (Basingstoke: Macmillan, 1996)

Strack, Hermann L., *The Jew and Human Sacrifice (Human Blood and Jewish Ritual): An Historical and Sociological Inquiry*, trans. Henry Blanchamp ([1891; first translation of rev. 8th edn] London: Cope and Fenwick, 1909)

Stuart, Kathy, *Defiled Trades and Social Outcasts: Honor and Ritual Pollution in Early Modern Germany* (Cambridge: Cambridge University Press, 1999)

Stuart, Roxana, *Stage Blood: Vampires of the 19th-Century Stage* (Bowling Green, OH: Bowling Green State University Popular Press, 1994)

Sugg, Richard, *Mummies, Cannibals, and Vampires: The History of Corpse Medicine from the Renaissance to the Victorians* (London and New York: Routledge, 2011)

Summers, Montague, *The Vampire, His Kith and Kin* (London: Kegan, Paul, Trench, Trubner & Co., 1928)

Summers, Montague, *The Vampire in Europe* ([1929] New York: University Books, 1968)

Tannahill, Reay, *Flesh and Blood: A History of the Cannibal Complex*, rev. edn ([1975] London: Abacus, 1996)

Thacker, Eugene, 'Biological Sovereignty', *Pli: The Warwick Journal of Philosophy*, 17 (2006), 1–17

Thacker, Eugene, *In the Dust of This Planet* [*Horror of Philosophy*, vol. 1] (Winchester and Washington, DC: Zero Books, 2011)

Thacker, Eugene, *Starry Speculative Corpse* [*Horror of Philosophy*, vol. 2] (Winchester and Washington, DC: Zero Books, 2014)

Thacker, Eugene, *Tentacles Longer Than Night* [*Horror of Philosophy*, vol. 3] (Winchester and Washington, DC: Zero Books, 2015)

Thomas, Keith, *Religion and the Decline of Magic: Studies in Popular Beliefs in Sixteenth and Seventeenth Century England* (Oxford: Oxford University Press, 1971)

Thompson, E.A., *The Goths in Spain* (Oxford: Clarendon Press, 1969)

Thorne, Tony, *Children of the Night: Of Vampires and Vampirism* (London: Victor Gollancz, 1999)

Tille, Rebecca, *Der Vampir als Element der Literaturgeschichte: Literaturwissenschaftliche Untersuchung zur Schwarzromantischen Vampirmotivik* (Hamburg: Diplomica Verlag, 2013)

Titmuss, Richard M., *The Gift Relationship: From Human Blood to Social Policy* ([1970] London: George Allen & Unwin, 2002)

Townshend, Dale (ed.), *Terror and Wonder: The Gothic Imagination* (London: British Library, 2014)

Tracy, Larissa and Jeff Massey (eds), *Heads Will Roll: Decapitation in the Medieval and Early Modern Imagination* (Leiden and Boston, MA: Brill, 2012)

Trigg, Dylan, *The Thing: A Phenomenology of Horror* (Winchester and Washington, DC: Zero Books, 2014)

Turner, Denys, 'Christianity and Politics: The Case of Gerrard Winstanley', *New Blackfriars*, 62 (1981), 500–09

Twitchell, James B., *The Living Dead: A Study of the Vampire in Romantic Literature* (Durham, NC: Duke University Press, 1981)

Ulin, Julieann, 'Sheridan Le Fanu's Vampires and Ireland's Invited Invasion', in George and Hughes (eds), *Open Graves, Open Minds*, 39–55

[Collective work,] *Les Vampires* (Paris: Albin Michel, 1993)

Vidal, Fernando, 'Extraordinary Bodies and the Physicotheological Imagination', in Daston and Pomata (eds), *The Faces of Nature in Enlightenment Europe*, 61–96

Vidal, Fernando, 'Ghosts of the European Enlightenment', in Poo (ed.), *Rethinking Ghosts in World Religions*, 163–82

Vieyra, Natalia Angeles, 'Illuminating Addiction: Morphinomania in Fin-de-Siècle Visual Culture', *Hektoen International: A Journal of Medical Humanities*, 7 (2015), online edn

Vrazhinovski, Tanas, Vladimir Karadzhoski, L'upcho S. Risteski and Lola Shimoska, *Narodna Demonologia na Makedonskite* (Skopje – Prilep: Knigoizdatelstvo 'Matitsa Makedonska' – Institut za Staroslovenska Kultura, 1995)

Vukanović, T.P., 'The Vampire', trans. Perkowski, in Perkowski, *Vampire Lore*, 230–59

Walker, Richard, *Labyrinths of Deceit: Culture, Modernity and Identity in the Nineteenth Century* (Chicago, IL: University of Chicago Press, 2007)

Waller, Gregory A., *The Living and the Undead: Slaying Vampires, Exterminating Zombies* (Urbana, IL: University of Illinois Press, 2010)

Ward, Julie K. and Tommy L. Lott, *Philosophers on Race: Critical Essays* (Oxford and Malden, MA: Blackwell Publishing, 2002)

Ward, Maryanne C., 'A Painting of the Unspeakable: Henry Fuseli's *The Nightmare* and the Creation of Mary Shelley's *Frankenstein*', *Journal of the Midwest Modern Language Association*, 33 (2000), 20–31

Ward, Richard (ed.), *A Global History of Execution and the Criminal Corpse* (Basingstoke: Palgrave Macmillan, 2015)

Warner, Marina, *Phantasmagoria: Spirit Visions, Metaphors, and Media into the Twenty-First Century* (Oxford: Oxford University Press, 2006)

Warwick, Alexandra and Martin Willis (eds), *Jack the Ripper: Media, Culture, History* (Manchester: Manchester University Press, 2007)

Wasson, Sara, 'Olalla's Legacy: Twentieth-Century Vampire Fiction and Genetic Previvorship', *Journal of Stevenson Studies*, 7 (2010), 55–81

Webster, Robert, *Methodism and the Miraculous: John Wesley's Idea of the Supernatural and the Identification of Methodists in the Eighteenth-Century* (Lexington, KY: Emeth Press, 2013)

Weinstock, Jeffrey Andrew, 'American Vampires', in Faflak and Haslam (eds), *American Gothic Culture*, 203–21

Weller, Shane, 'Decomposition: Georges Bataille and the Language of Necrophilia', in Anna Katharina Schaffner and Shane Weller, *Modernist Eroticisms: European Literature after Sexology* (Basingstoke: Palgrave Macmillan, 2012), 169–94

White, Luis, *Speaking with Vampires: Rumor and History in Colonial Africa* (Berkeley, Los Angeles and London: University of California Press, 2000)

Wicke, Jennifer, 'Vampiric Typewriting', *English Literary History*, 59 (1992), 467–93

Willis, Martin, 'Le Fanu's "Carmilla", Ireland, and Diseased Vision', in Ruston (ed.), *Literature and Science*, 111–30

Wilson, David, *Anglo-Saxon Paganism* (London: Routledge, 1992)

Wilson, Katharina M., 'The History of the Word "Vampire"', *Journal of the History of Ideas*, 46 (1985), 577–83

Winstanley, Michael J., *Ireland and the Land Question, 1800–1922* (London and New York: Methuen, 1984)

Winter, Alison, *Mesmerized: Powers of Mind in Victorian Britain* (Chicago, IL, and London: University of Chicago Press, 1998)

Winthrop-Young, Geoffrey, 'Undead Networks: Information Processing and Media Boundary Conflicts in *Dracula*', in Donald Bruce and Anthony Purdey (eds), *Literature and Science* (Atlanta, GA: Rodopi, 1994), 107–29

Wisker, Gina, 'Celebrating Difference and Community: The Vampire in African-American and Caribbean Women's Writing', in Tabish Khair and Johan Höglund (eds), *Transnational and Postcolonial Vampires: Dark Blood* (Basingstoke: Palgrave Macmillan, 2013), 46–66

Wolfgang, Marvin E., 'Pioneers in Criminology: Cesare Lombroso (1835–1900)', *Journal of Criminal Law, Criminology, and Police Science*, 52 (1961), 361–91

Woodard, Ben, *Slime Dynamics: Generation, Mutation, and the Creep of Life* (Winchester and Washington, DC: Zero Books, 2012)

Wright, Dudley, *Vampires and Vampirism* (London: William Rider and Son, 1914)

Wright, Dudley, *Vampires and Vampirism*, 2nd edn ([1914] London: William Rider and Son, 1924)

Wright, Edmond and Elizabeth Wright (eds), *The Žižek Reader* (Oxford and Malden, MA: Blackwell, 1999)

Young, Francis, *English Catholics and the Supernatural, 1553–1829* (Farnham: Ashgate, 2013)

Young, Mary de, *Encyclopedia of Asylum Therapeutics, 1750–1950s* (Jefferson, NC: McFarland & Co., 2015)

Zigarovich, Jolene, 'Courting Death: Necrophilia in Samuel Richardson's *Clarissa*', *Studies in the Novel*, 32 (2000), 112–28

Žižek, Slavoj, *For They Know Not What They Do: Enjoyment as a Political Factor* (London and New York: Verso, 1991)

Žižek, Slavoj, 'A Hair of the Dog that Bit You', in Edmond Wright and Elizabeth Wright (eds), *The Žižek Reader* (Oxford and Malden, MA: Blackwell, 1999), 268–82

INDEX